AN ANGLO-NORMAN READER

An Anglo-Norman Reader

Jane Bliss

OpenBook Publishers

ISBN Paperback: 978-1-78374-313-1
ISBN Hardback: 978-1-78374-314-8
ISBN Digital (PDF): 978-1-78374-315-5
ISBN Digital ebook (epub): 978-1-78374-316-2
ISBN Digital ebook (mobi): 978-1-78374-317-9
DOI: 10.11647/OBP.0110

Typeset in Junicode by Quentin Miller using XƎLaTeX and LyX.

Cover Design by Heidi Coburn.
Front cover image by Bill Black (2012): Wace, in Alderney Bayeux Tapestry Finale.
Back cover image by Danny Chapman (2017): Ormer Shells.
Cover images are licensed under a Creative Commons Attribution 4.0 International license (CC BY 4.0): https://creativecommons.org/licenses/by/4.0/

All paper used by Open Book Publishers is SFI (Sustainable Forestry Initiative), PEFC (Programme for the Endorsement of Forest Certification Schemes) and FSC® (Forest Stewardship Council®) certified.

Printed in the United Kingdom, United States, and Australia by Lightning Source for Open Book Publishers (Cambridge, UK).

Contents

Acknowledgements

Thanks are due to the following colleagues and friends:

Matthew Albanese, Laura Ashe, Katie Attwood, Ian Bass, Catherine Batt, Bill and Pauline Black, Marina Bowder, Glyn Burgess, Daron Burrows, Emma Cavell, Danny Chapman, Victoria Condie, Graham Edwards, Sarah Foot, Linda Gowans, Douglas Gray†, Huw Grange, Miranda Griffin, Richard Howard, David Howlett, Eliza Hoyer-Millar, Tony Hunt, Paul Hyams, Andy King, Carolyne Larrington, Jude Mackley, Quentin Miller, Ben Parsons, Stephen Pink, Jackie and Ed Pritchard, Gillian Rogers, Royston Raymond, Samantha Rayner, Kate Russell, Lynda Sayce, Ian Short, Ilona Soane-Sands, Eric Stanley, Justin Stover, Richard Trachsler, Judith Weiss. I am very grateful to the many anonymous readers of my book, who have submitted helpful and enthusiastic reports, and to the editors at Open Book.

In addition, my thanks are due yet again to Henrietta Leyser, who has always been so generous with ideas and advice for me; and to the librarians who have helped me to track untrackable material. Further, I am proud to honour the memory of another two remarkable women: Dominica Legge, and my old friend and colleague Elfrieda Dubois. Elfrieda often told me how she used to meet Legge in the Bibliothèque Nationale, who would hale her off for cups of coffee and amuse her endlessly with talk about Anglo-Norman 'because', said Elfrieda, 'nobody else would listen!' Lastly, I cannot sufficiently express my gratitude to Quentin for help and love and everything. This book is dedicated to them, and to the Oxford Anglo-Norman Reading Group.

Copyright Acknowledgements

I wish to thank the following people and publishers who have granted me permission to use their work. This book contains a large number of different texts, therefore my list must be set out as economically as possible. All the passages reproduced in this book are listed in my Bibliography in addition to being cited in footnotes, so it can easily be seen which passage is taken from which published work. Each publisher (or editor, in the case of previously-unpublished texts) is stated clearly in the principal citation of each text, normally in the introduction to it.

I am also very grateful to colleagues, and relevant institutions, for help and advice in my efforts to trace copyright-holders.

First, I thank the Anglo-Norman Text Society for their generous permission to use more than a dozen extracts, of varying length; each is identified in its place, as stated above.[1] I thank the British Library for permission to transcribe and use three pages, kindly provided by them, from three different manuscripts: the first introduces my second Part (An Anglo-Norman Miscellany), the second passage is appended to *A Medical Compendium*, and the third is appended to the *Credo* and *Pater Noster*.

Next, in alphabetical order, I would like to thank the following:

Alderney Bayeux Tapestry Finale

Emma Cavell, for the first of Maud Mortimer's Letters

Honoré Champion (Paris), for an extract from *Le Roman des Franceis*

Tony Hunt, for two substantial texts: the *Credo* and *Pater Noster*, and the *Sins* attributed to Robert Grosseteste

Livre de Poche (Paris), for an extract from *Le Roman de Thèbes*

PMLA, for permission to use the *Apprise de Nurture*, reprinted by permission of the Modern Language Association of America from *Anglo-Norman Books of Courtesy and Nurture*, *PMLA* 44 (1929), pp. 432–7

Royston Raymond, for the story printed in my Appendix

Selden Society, for permission to use part of the legal text *Placita Corone*

William Allen, for permission to use an extract from the *Roman de Fergus*

---

[1] Several of these are available to search (page by page) on the Anglo-Norman Hub.

Abbreviations

Short titles in notes, that can be found easily and alphabetically in the bibliography, are not listed here.

Alexander	*The Wars of Alexander*, ed. Duggan and Turville-Petre
AND	*Anglo-Norman Dictionary* (see http://www.anglo-norman.net/)
ANTS	Anglo-Norman Text Society; PTS = Plain Texts Series; OPS = Occasional Publications Series
AV	Bible (Authorized Version); *LV* = Bible (Latin Vulgate)
Bede	Bede, *History*, tr. Shirley-Price *et al.*
Cher Alme	*Texts of Anglo-Norman Piety*, ed. Hunt
Dean	Dean and Boulton, *Anglo-Norman Literature*
DMH	*Dictionary of Medieval Heroes*, Gerritsen & van Melle
Edouard	*La Vie d'Edouard*, Bliss
EETS	Early English Text Society; OS = Original Series; SS = Supplementary Series; ES = Extra Series
FRETS	French of England Translation Series
GL (Supp)	*Gilte Legende*, ed. Hamer and Russell (vol. 1 of 4, *Supplementary Lives*, 2000)
IPN	Index of Proper Names (or Index des Noms Propres)
JEGP	*Journal of English and Germanic Philology*
Larousse	*Dictionnaire de l'ancien français*, ed. Greimas
Legge	Legge, *Anglo-Norman Literature and its Background*
Liber	*Liber Eliensis*, tr. Fairweather
OCL	*The Oxford Concise Companion to Classical Literature*, ed. Howatson and Chivers
ODS	*Oxford Dictionary of Saints*, ed. Farmer
OED	*Oxford English Dictionary*
PL	*Patrologia Latina*
Receptaria	*Three Receptaria*, ed. Hunt
SGGK	*Sir Gawain and the Green Knight*
ZrP	*Zeitschrift für romanische Philologie*

Bible Books

Col.	Epistle to the Colossians
Cor.	Epistle to the Corinthians
Ecclus.	Ecclesiasticus (in *AV* Apocrypha)
Eph.	Epistle to the Ephesians
Ex.	Exodus
Ezek.	Ezekiel
Gal.	Epistle to the Galatians
Gen.	Genesis
Heb.	Epistle to the Hebrews
Jac.	Epistle of James
Jer.	Jeremiah
Joh.	Epistles of John
Jos.	Joshua
Matt.	Gospel of Matthew
Num.	Numbers
Pet.	Epistle of Peter
Prov.	Proverbs
Ps.	Psalm (numbering differs in *LV*)
Rev.	Revelation (Apocalypse in *LV*)
Rom.	Epistle to the Romans
Sam.	Samuel
Tim.	Epistle to Timothy

Introduction

This book is a new departure in Anthologies, a Reader with a difference. It presents a variety of Anglo-Norman pieces, some less well-known, specially chosen to cover a wide range of literature that would have appealed to a wide range of people who could read or at least understand French. It provides facing-page translations throughout, unlike many anthologies and readers. It presents passages, and a number of whole texts, in a variety of genres. The selections are arranged generically: the book is given a distinctive overall shape by its beginning with the writer Wace, born in the Channel Islands in the twelfth century,[1] through many named and unnamed writers and their work, through to another writer born in the Channel Islands in the nineteenth. Its aim is to help students at undergraduate and early post-graduate level, and general readers, to discover and enjoy some of the literature of the British Isles written in Insular French to amuse, instruct, entertain, or admonish medieval audiences.[2]

This volume cannot provide a full overview of all texts, literary and non-literary, used across several centuries in medieval Britain.[3] But it is intended to provide an engaging and thought-provoking introduction to some of the material available to medieval readers. *An Anglo-Norman Reader* offers a wealth of fascinating pieces, many not anthologized or translated anywhere else. There are little-known byways

---

[1] Almost all my selections appear in Dean's *Anglo-Norman Literature*. Dean includes Wace as Anglo-Norman, as do Legge and many other scholars from that day to this. Wace was writing at a time when both Normandy and Britain were parts of the same kingdom, the Anglo-Norman *regnum*, so that even apart from the Insular subject-matter of his work he may be considered Anglo-Norman.

[2] Some of the texts, not originally written in the British Isles, are known to have been read, copied (that is, rewritten), and used here. Some are deemed to be Anglo-Norman because of their subject-matter: written for, if not demonstrably in, this country. Dean (p. x) prefers 'such cultural evidence over narrowly linguistic criteria.' See also Burrows, 'Vers une nouvelle édition', pp. 14–15, for Anglo-Norman texts' circulation and reception. I have used Dean's catalogue as a template; of the few texts not in Dean, each will be explained in its place.

[3] See Butterfield, *The Familiar Enemy*: 'giving due weight to the practice of French in England … means more than merely acknowledging … French texts circulating in England; it means more than identifying a separate "Anglo-Norman" culture; it means grasping that "English" could be defined precisely as a form of French' (p. 99). Her book provides wide-ranging insights on language, *passim*.

         https://doi.org/10.11647/OBP.0110.01

of Arthurian legend, crime and punishment in real life; women's voices tell history, write letters, berate pagans; advice is offered on how to win friends and influence people, how to cure people's ailments and how to keep clear of the law; stories from the Bible are retold with commentary, together with guidance on prayer and confession. Authors range from the well-known to the lesser-known and anonymous, readers include clerical and lay, men and women, aristocratic and ordinary. My title is designed to focus on the importance of readership: its double meaning includes the word 'reader' used in modern times for a kind of anthology, and 'reader' as the person who enjoyed, used, read, and listened to the literature available to them in a medieval Anglo-Norman world. Needless to say, no single medieval reader can be envisaged as sole audience, any more than can any single modern reader of this book; I envisage a variety of people in either case.

The sudden wealth of literature produced in French, after the Norman Conquest in the eleventh century, has been variously explained: French became the dominant vernacular as the new 'English' settled in and began building their culture. A good proportion of literature produced during this time reflects an interest in history, but in fact the earliest literature of many genres in French was produced in this country.[4] Middle English as a literary language developed later. It is not my purpose to provide a history of the use of French in Britain, but this Introduction can at least explain the genesis of the present book. Students of Middle English and Old English have recourse to wide-ranging anthologies of the literature: *A Book of Middle English*; *Early Middle English Verse and Prose*; and *A Guide to Old English*;[5] there are likewise anthologies for students of medieval French.[6] But a course of Anglo-Norman literature, in Oxford recently, involved studying half a dozen long texts in their entirety during a single term; no Anthology or Reader was available. A Reader would have been a useful and enjoyable supplement, to provide an overview of a wider linguistic world closely entwined with that of English. Ruth Dean's call for more workers in the 'fair field' of Anglo-Norman is still an inspiration sixty years after its publication;[7] together with the sheer enjoyment of the 'fair world' of wider medieval studies, it inspires this book.

Those with some experience of medieval French will have no difficulty going directly to editions of the texts, many available from the Anglo-Norman Text Society. However, my experience as a reader and teacher has warned me that students unfamiliar with any kind of medieval French find the thought of Anglo-

---

[4] See, for example, Howlett, *Origins* (*passim*). Hans-Erich Keller, in *Medieval France, An Encyclopedia* (p. 969), explains the flourishing literature in this period as due to the interest of the Norman dynasty in the predecessors of the Anglo-Saxons.

[5] Burrow and Turville-Petre; ed. Bennett and Smithers; and Mitchell and Robinson.

[6] For example, *A Medieval French Reader*, ed. Aspland; and *Historical French Reader*, ed. Studer and Waters.

[7] 'A Fair Field needing Folk', *passim*.

Norman daunting.[8]   Hence this book. Anglo-Norman is the name by which this language has been commonly known. 'The French of England' has recently become popular as an alternative, but appears to ignore other parts of what is now the United Kingdom. 'Insular French' covers the whole of the British Isles, including the Channel Islands where my book begins and ends. The Introduction to *AND* gives this language the alternative name of Anglo-French. 'The French of Britain' might be a new and better name. However, for simplicity I prefer to remain in line with (for example) the Anglo-Norman Text Society, and use this term more frequently than any other. The exact range of what may be called 'Anglo-Norman' is a matter for some discussion which would be out of place in a book for comparative beginners.[9] The language was used throughout a kingdom that, until the early thirteenth century, included parts of what is now France. For example, historians and language scholars disagree about whether Wace, a writer born in the Channel Islands but writing in Continental France about British history, is really Anglo-Norman in its narrowest sense. I take a relatively wide view: I follow Dean's range, which includes Wace and other writers considered marginal. Merrilees argues that no simple definition of Anglo-Norman literature can be given, pointing out that writers (and readers, I would add) of medieval times would be unlikely to perceive any distinctions that modern writers might make in their definitions.[10] 'There is no more tiresome error in the history of thought than to try and sort our ancestors on to this or that side of a distinction which was not in their minds at all. You are asking a question to which no answer exists'.[11] I extend Dean's range here and there, with explanation of my reasons for doing so; any collection of this kind is bound to reflect personal preferences.

There has been an upsurge of interest in Anglo-Norman in recent decades, and it is no longer the Cinderella among medieval literatures that it used to be. No student of Anglo-Norman can be without one or more of the following key text-books: Pope, *From Latin to Modern French*; Legge, *Background*; and her *Cloisters*; Short, *Manual of Anglo-Norman*; Dean and Boulton, *Anglo-Norman Literature*.[12] Several important anthologies have recently been published, partly or entirely devoted to Anglo-Norman texts. Douglas Gray wished to do for Anglo-Norman and Anglo-Latin what Bennett and Smithers did for Middle English; the result was his wide-ranging anthology entitled *From the Norman Conquest to the Black Death*. His book attempts to illustrate the richness and variety of the

---

[8] However, some readers find it easier to understand than Continental Old or Middle French. For a comparison between the two forms, the Appendix to Short, *Manual of Anglo-Norman* (which also includes miscellaneous specimens from the 12th to the 15th century), is instructive.

[9] Fashions change, too: see Corrie, 'The Circulation of Literature', pp. 433–4 & 443 for what some scholars deemed to be Anglo-Norman in past years, in this 'outpost of the French-speaking world'.

[10] Introduction to Anglo-Norman Literature, in *Dictionary of the Middle Ages* (vol. 1, pp. 259–72).

[11] Lewis, 'Is Theology Poetry?', p. 160.

[12] See also Hunt, *Teaching*; and articles such as O'Donnell, 'Anglo-Norman Multiculturalism'; and Baswell *et al.*, 'Competing Archives, Competing Histories'. Further references are given below.

period's literary material as fully as possible, therefore his original plan to provide texts facing his translations had to be abandoned. *The Idea of the Vernacular*, an anthology of Middle English literary theory in the period 1280–1520, includes a small proportion of material from French or Anglo-Norman sources.[13] Carolyne Larrington mentions the women, of Barking and elsewhere, who wrote saints' lives in Anglo-Norman, although she cites only one of the former and does not print the passage in question.[14] Laura Ashe's collection for Penguin Classics includes some Anglo-Norman pieces, but none are facing-page translated and most are already anthologized elsewhere.[15] However, since 1990 a splendid volume of Anglo-Norman Lyrics has been available.[16]

Religious writing has been well served not least by Tony Hunt in his anthology of previously unedited texts with facing-page translations;[17] Maureen Boulton has published a selection of such texts, mostly on the Passion.[18] Four of the Anglo-Norman verse Saints' Lives are translated by Russell;[19] and a glance at the website of FRETS (publisher of Hunt's and Boulton's books, above) will show that more are on the way.[20] These volumes help to fill a perceived gap in such Anglo-Norman religious writing as is currently available. In Dean's catalogue, however, religious literature accounts for five of the fourteen headings; page-ranges show that just over half her book is filled by this group.[21] Merrilees points out that in the Anglo-Norman corpus more serious works outnumber the purely entertaining.[22] Much of this material is in fact very lively and entertaining indeed. It is important to remember that churchmen (including some women, for example nuns) wrote biblical, hagiographical, and homiletic works, to educate their ignorant flock and also to meet readers' enthusiastic demand for such literature. In fact many such enthusiastic 'readers' needed others to read to them, because they could not read for themselves; 'literature' is not only for the literate classes. Another anthology of interest has recently been published: *Vernacular Literary Theory*, ed. Wogan-Browne *et al*. This is a study book, dealing with prologues and other texts in which authors discuss their work; it is not a Reader in the sense that the present book is intended to be.

There is good reason, after taking into account the collections listed above, to include a number of broadly religious pieces in my collection. This is intended not

---

[13] ed. Wogan-Browne *et al*. There is nothing actually in French, but see pp. 389–90.

[14] *Women and Writing*, p. 224.

[15] *Early Fiction in England*.

[16] ed. Jeffrey and Levy.

[17] *Cher Alme*. This book is cited *passim* in the present work.

[18] *Piety and Persecution*, ed. and tr. Boulton.

[19] *Verse Saints' Lives*, tr. Russell.

[20] However, FRETS volumes, except for Occasional Publications such as *Cher Alme*, do not provide facing-page texts with translations.

[21] Her numbers 442–986 likewise account for more than half the book.

[22] Introduction to Anglo-Norman Literature, in *Dictionary of the Middle Ages* (vol. 1, p. 261).

only to reflect the range offered by Dean, but also to help counter any secularizing tendency especially among historians. The central importance of acknowledging the weight attached to religious thought in all periods, but above all in the Middle Ages, has recently been argued by Sarah Foot.[23] In making this selection of texts I consciously reflect a recent trend in historical and literary study: a 'religious turn', where writers argue for the importance of religion in understanding cultures and societies from different places and periods.[24]

Lecco's two books published in Italy, a History and an Anthology, together offer a range of literary texts with facing-page translations.[25] However, they are not widely available in this country,[26] and in any case are useful only for readers fluent in Italian.[27] The works Lecco chose to include are among the better-known Anglo-Norman texts; I range somewhat farther afield. With the intention of filling some of the gaps left by anthologists, I have chosen texts that may be less familiar, although I do not aim deliberately at the obscure. Certain key works have been extremely well served by editors, translators, teachers, critics, and commentators; they have been studied by historians and Arthurians, feminists, and Romanists who judge some of these classic texts to be part of the heritage of Continental French literature.[28] There is no need for me to include any of the *Lais* of Marie, or extracts from Wace's well-known *Roman de Brut*, to name two of the most obvious candidates. However, Wace's *Roman de Rou* is less well known; Lecco offers some hundred lines (8011–116), in which the famous Taillefer episode (in the Battle of Hastings) occurs. Scholars have mined the *Rou* for accounts of the Norman Conquest, but there is plenty more of this romance to choose from dealing with the legendary history of these islands. Another consideration, which would encourage any anthologist to branch out, is that Plain Texts from the Anglo-Norman Text Society are published without a glossary, so that reproducing passages from them with translations in this book could be useful for unpractised readers. Further explanation of my reasons for the present selection are set out later in this Introduction.

My extracts are arranged more or less generically, approximately as in Dean's Catalogue. This indispensable volume is the first port of call for anybody wishing

---

23 'Has Ecclesiastical History Lost the Plot?'.

24 See, for example, Chapman *et al.*, eds, *Seeing Things Their Way*.

25 *Storia della letteratura anglo-normanna (xii–xiv secolo)*; *Antologia del romanzo Anglo-Normanno*.

26 Burrows ('Review: *Storia della letteratura Anglo-Normanna (XII–XIV secolo)*, Margherita Lecco') judges the book would be more useful if it gave Dean's catalogue numbers (as I do in the pages that follow), so that its users could refer easily to basic bibliographical and other material including information about manuscripts.

27 See also *Lectures françaises de la fin du moyen âge*, Duval, although this collection (for readers of modern French) focuses on the most widely-read texts of a later period.

28 Readers (such as Aspland's, cited above) often contain pieces that are definitely or at least probably Anglo-Norman.

to discover Anglo-Norman Literature,[29] and so I have used it as a template. This in spite of the fact that my extracts may not by themselves represent the genre of the text as a whole (for example, I choose a historical passage from *Audree* and an extended descriptive passage from *Roman de Thèbes*). In the case of texts not in Dean (*Roman de Thèbes*, and *Roman d'Yder*, for example),[30] I have placed them where they would be had she included them; legal texts, however, are placed in the Miscellaneous section of my book which includes texts to do with social history. I cannot attempt to fill every heading of Dean's, nor to provide a number of texts in any way proportional to the number of texts in sections of her book.[31] I have branched out by including a few pieces that are arguably, if marginally, Anglo-Norman. These reflect the fact that some texts although written in Continental France were in fact widely read, copied, and used in Britain; others deal with Insular subject-matter, even if not written in this country. This stretches the definition of Insular French, but allows a generous range of riches to interest a medieval audience. The result could risk becoming a rag-bag of passages taken at random or at least according to fancy (as some medieval manuscripts quite clearly were); I have therefore grouped the pieces into three main Parts, based on Dean's broadest categories.[32] I have also attempted to make internal correspondences and connections. My inclusion of a few medical and legal pieces aims to provide interesting non-literary context for the various branches of literature represented. Then, passages in one genre have been chosen so as to reflect themes or stories that appear in another, for example: a passage about Edward the Confessor in the *Roman de Rou* balances an interpolation in the Nun of Barking's *Vie* which, although a miracle, is also a piece of legendary history; historical passages in *Audree* compare with 'historical' passages in my Chapter 1; the prologue to a life of Saint Clement is comparable to the self-introduction by the historian Wace and the epilogue to *Maniere*; Saint Katherine's story of the Creation is comparable to that found in texts such as Herman's *Creation*. Although I follow Dean, the selections are deliberately eclectic. Daron Burrows chooses a *florilegium* of texts for his translation class,[33] mixing forms and registers, tones and dialects, so as to give some idea of the wealth of different types offered by medieval French literature. He also points to the juxtaposition within manuscripts of courtly and comic, religious

---

[29] The list of texts used for compiling the *AND* may also be consulted, especially by those wishing to explore the vast range of non-literary texts that are also available.

[30] Tony Hunt made a good case that *Yder* ought to have been included ('Review: *Anglo-Norman Literature*, Ruth Dean and Maureen Boulton').

[31] Her headings are as follows: 1) Historiographical, 2) Lyric, 3) Romance, 4) Lais Fables Fabliaux & Dits, 5) Satirical Social & Moral, 6) Proverbs, 7) Grammar & Glosses, 8) Science & Technology, 9) Medicine; finally, Religious Literature includes the following: 10) Biblical, 11) Apocryphal, 12) Hagiography, 13) Homiletic, 14) Devotional.

[32] These are: 1) texts that are essentially Story, covering several kinds of secular narrative, 2) a Miscellaneous group of social and largely non-fiction texts, and 3) Religious texts.

[33] Hilary Term 2016. I thank him for allowing me to attend sessions.

and obscene; accepting such diversity is part of learning to grasp the alterity of medieval culture.

I begin with Wace's *Roman de Rou*; a memory of Wace's father talking about the Norman invasion forms a short epigraph. The Conquest conventionally marks the beginning of the Anglo-Norman period, although French was known and used in England before this time: Edward the Confessor was brought up in Normandy, and there were French speakers at his court, to give only one example. I continue with a passage about Edward, before moving on to other historical texts. After revisiting the Channel Islands briefly around the beginning of the Hundred Years War, and continuing with my parts 2 and 3, the book ends with an Alderney man's memory of his grandmother telling stories.[34] To this day the Channel Islands are subject to the Duke of Normandy and not to Queen Elizabeth II, although these titles refer to one and the same person. Literature (whatever its geography) looks forward to imagined futures, and backwards to a past that may never have existed ... or in which civilizations talked about themselves in other languages. Principally the latter are Old English, Greek (both classical and biblical), Hebrew (the Old Testament), and so on; Latin is ubiquitous in the medieval period, not least because of most people's wide knowledge of the Bible.[35] All such points of interest, as well as references to other literature, are signalled in the notes to each text.

---

[34] My Appendix contains one of the stories, with references to support what might be deemed an unexpected inclusion.

[35] This includes people who could not read the Bible for themselves, but who had a better knowledge of what was in it than many highly literate people of today.

Selection of Texts

> The literature of our England is practically illimitable ... But we make very
> little use of [it].[36]

Some explanation was given, earlier this Introduction, of what is not included in
this book and why; here is a further brief overview of reasons for including what I
have put into it. I do not wish to replicate what other anthologies have successfully
done; I have built my selections according to identifiable gaps among such material,
casting my net as widely as I could.

Dean introduces her Guide thus: '... to provide, in catalogue form, a listing of
extant Anglo-Norman texts and their manuscripts for students of medieval culture,
including those with particular interests in Anglo-Norman' (p. ix). The centre, as
it were, of Anglo-Norman literature has been well defined and is nowadays being
well explored (and debated) by scholars and students alike. Dean envisages the
Anglo-Norman 'canon', however this is defined or circumscribed, within its wider
culture; I have gathered texts which originate farther away from that centre, and
even on the boundaries, referring to literatures of a wider culture as well as creating
cross-references within my collection.[37]   I have chosen texts from this wider
culture, bearing in mind that any cross-section of medieval readers would have
been exposed to any number of texts of different kinds; but my choice of Dean as
an organizing principle is because Dean's catalogue is readily accessible in libraries,
shelved with other publications of ANTS. Legge's work is still extremely useful
as a general introduction to Anglo-Norman, and I cite her freely throughout.[38]
Because any criteria for the selection of texts was going to be problematic, I
have chosen according to what I thought twenty-first century readers would find
interesting and amusing. Anybody's choice is necessarily subjective, and even
the grouping of texts generically is a matter of personal judgement. This book
is a compendious yet necessarily limited tour of Anglo-Norman literature in its
broadest sense.[39] It includes works that are certainly Insular, and a few that are

---

[36] Kipling, 'The Uses of Reading', p. 83.

[37] Such references are confined to the best-known or most accessible editions, because I do not expect
my readers necessarily to be expert on (for example) Malory, Chaucer, or Geoffrey of Monmouth.
References to literatures of other periods, even up to the present time, are to strengthen and
deepen the web of themes and cross-references. They are intended to remind modern readers
that the medieval world is not a closed-off culture for specialists, but part of a universal tapestry
of literature and thought. Again, I do not provide masses of critical material on (for example)
T. E. Lawrence, Montesquieu, or Euripides.

[38] Legge includes Wace's work fully and repeatedly in her *Background* but does not say until the
Conclusion, rather apologetically, 'Wace, it is true, was not an Anglo-Norman writer ...'. But
she treats him as if he were, having remarked earlier in the same Conclusion 'In speaking of the
court of Henry II especially it is impossible to distinguish between what was written in England
and what was written in the continental provinces which made up the Angevin empire' (pp. 371
& 364).

[39] Scholars admit that definition of 'Anglo-Norman' literature is problematic (for example, MacBain
in *Medieval France, An Encyclopedia*, pp. 35–8).

arguably not; but these latter were unquestionably used, if not written, in Britain. It tries to include works that are less well known, avoiding those texts, especially the romances, that are already widely known and anthologized.[40] I have generally chosen pieces that have not been translated elsewhere, although some have been; the former are included either because I think they ought to be better known or, in the case of the latter, because the existing translations are relatively inaccesssible.[41] I have used Dean's catalogue as a template for arranging the pieces generically, and to give some idea of the proportion of fiction to what we would now call non-fiction (sermons and so on), because Dean is accessible and compendious; but I have included some pieces not in Dean. These find a place in my book either because the matter of the text is Insular (for example, a romance set in Britain) or, more contentiously, because the piece might not count as 'literature'.[42]

A book of this size cannot begin to offer a full overview of all possible uses of French in this country, but it ought to recognize if only briefly that French was not merely the literary language of the educated reading classes. Having said that, I must reiterate the fact that much religious literature was made for the uneducated classes: written and read by priests and other literate people, it was ultimately aimed at those illiterates who needed instruction, preferably of an entertaining sort so that they would pay attention to it. By literate, I here mean those who could read their own vernacular; some could also write it. Elsewhere 'literate' is more narrowly used to mean those who could read and write Latin. To reflect other uses of French across this period, I have added some legal texts, and some medical receipts, as a small reminder of social reality. They need not stand out as oddities in a book of this kind, because they can be grouped into a section that includes other utilitarian pieces such as letters. It should also be remembered that texts such as prayers, even lyric poems (generically very different from prayers, letters, and recipes), were also intended for use in the sense that people did not read them only for pleasure.[43] However, any attempt to group texts into 'for use' and 'for pleasure' would be much more problematic than grouping them according to genre, however roughly. Most of the texts chosen are from earlier rather than later times, during those centuries when Anglo-Norman was the dominant vernacular: in this earlier period literature was truly flourishing.

But there are a number of texts drawn from a somewhat later medieval period, so as to give as wide a spread as possible. The latest of all is from the twentieth

---

[40] For example, four of the best-known Anglo-Norman romances have recently appeared in translation: Thomas' *Romance of Horn*, the *Folie Tristan*, the *Lai d'Haveloc*, are in *The Birth of Romance*, tr. Weiss (revised reissue of a popular and valuable book); and *Gui de Warewic* from FRETS in 2008. See my brief overview of Anglo-Norman texts in other previously-existing anthologies, above.

[41] For example, if the translation is not into modern English. All such details are given at the head of the appropriate chapter or section, below.

[42] This is not the place to discuss a definition of literature, I note merely that Dean's book contains the word 'literature' in the title although many of the texts could be considered non-literary.

[43] See, in this context, *Poems Without Names*, Oliver.

century, from an island that is part of this country by historical accident.[44] The Channel Islands, called 'les Îles Anglo-Normandes' in French, are part of the British Isles and so it can be argued their French is likewise 'Anglo-Norman'; this alone warrants inclusion of their language in a wide-ranging anthology such as mine. The vanishing patois of Alderney is the closest, of all the islands' patois, to the French of Cap de la Hague, because it is geographically the closest of them all to the French coast. It has been used among fishermen of the two regions, not to mention smugglers and privateers, over generations. Further justification for including a story in modern patois is given in the Appendix, below.

In addition to this general Introduction, each selection is prefaced by a short introduction raising points of special interest that pertain to it; footnotes signal unusual words and phrases, and so forth. Readers wishing for further and more specialized information are advised to consult the editors' own introductions to each text, as well as standard textbooks such as Short's *Manual* and others mentioned above.

This book is intended to be a general introduction to a range of interesting texts, literature in its widest possible sense made for a wide range of audiences (such as I hope my own will be); it is not a full-scale introduction to the history or philology of Anglo-Norman.[45] My aim is two-fold: to encourage readers to look up the editions of any or all of the texts in this book and read them in full, and to encourage them to follow my references to other works in (or on) Anglo-Norman and beyond.

The next section of this introduction broadly groups some of the most notable points otherwise discussed, within my chapters, in footnotes. The final section, below, describes my treatment of the texts chosen.

---

[44] The islands remained with the English crown after the loss of Normandy in the early thirteenth century.

[45] For more on the history and philology of Anglo-Norman, see Ingham, ed., *Anglo-Norman*, and Ingham, *The Transmission of Anglo-Norman*; also Wogan-Browne *et al.*, eds, *French of England*; and Jefferson and Putter, eds, *Multilingualism in Medieval Britain*. In Lusignan, *La langue des rois au Moyen Âge*, chapter IV (pp. 155–217, 'Le français du roi en Angleterre') is especially interesting. The related topic of multilingualism cannot hope to be explored in this book; see preceding references, as well as (for example) Hsy, *Trading Tongues*. Interest in Anglo-Norman and its place in medieval Insular culture continues to flourish (for example, the recent journal Gautier and Pouzet, eds, *Langues d'Angleterre*; and *Anglo-français: philologie et linguistique*, ed. Floquet and Giannini). Further evidence that this literature is of interest beyond the British Isles is the publication of Lecco's two volumes: *Antologia del romanzo Anglo-Normanno*; *Storia della letteratura anglo-normanna (xii–xiv secolo)*. Readers are also directed to bibliographies in the works I have cited, in addition to those appended to this book.

Principal Themes and Topics

There are a number of broad themes or topics running through this book. Because they are common across medieval literature, an overview of the most notable is set out here. They include references to many famous figures (mostly fictional), ideas of the marvellous, the love (and otherwise) of women, the typical (often beautiful) settings for stories, and the significant objects that tend to occur across not only stories but also non-fictional texts. Although my passages are arranged generically into chapters, themes and topics are no respecters of genre, and they lead through and across the texts presented below.[46] A glance at the Table of Contents will easily locate titles within chapters of this book.

First, there are the great figures of medieval literature, such as King Arthur and his knights (including Tristan). The story of Arthur begins with the Latin book by Geoffrey of Monmouth (the *Historia Regum Britanniae*),[47] which was translated or rather adapted into French by Wace.[48] The present book begins with Wace's *Roman de Rou*, but it is not long before we find a mention of Arthur's world: a reference to Hengist and Horsa comes early in the second piece, the *Description of England*. This is the point in legendary history where Merlin the enchanter, our first Arthurian figure, appears.[49] It is not until the romance of *Fergus* that we find Arthur and his knights in the flesh, among the heroes; in *Yder* some of them are anti-heroes, especially Kay and Arthur himself. A version of some of Arthur's adventures is found in the *Roman des Franceis*, a satire aimed at the French, who are shown to have a completely wrong idea of what happened in those days: the author puts the record straight.

Tristan was originally the hero of stories and romances that developed independently of the Arthur legends,[50] but in later cycles (for example in Malory) he becomes a member of the Round Table.[51] In *Fergus*, Tristan is mentioned as the slayer of a dragon that was not as big as the one that will be slain by Fergus.[52] Thus Tristan appears by repute; such intertextual reference shows that stories about him were current and his name known to audiences, otherwise Guillaume (the author) would not have put him in. I have chosen Tristan pieces in which Arthur is never

---

[46] Citations from other literatures are intended as a reminder that many such themes and topics are universal.

[47] Numerous editions and translations of this important work are available; a good starting point is *The History of the Kings of Britain*, tr. Thorpe.

[48] *Wace's Brut*, ed. and tr. Weiss. Although Wace was writing in what is now Continental France, Dean and others class his work as Anglo-Norman. It was immensely popular; see Dean's number 2 for reasons to include both his chronicle histories (her number 3).

[49] Although Merlin does not appear in the *Description* itself, Arthur is invoked towards the end of it.

[50] See, first, Thomas d'Angleterre, *Tristan*, ed. Wind; and Béroul, *Tristan*, ed. Ewert.

[51] Malory, *Works*, ed. Vinaver.

[52] *The Romance of Fergus*, ed. Frescoln, vv. 4204–223, & p. 24 of the introduction (p. 139 in 'The Romance of Fergus', tr. Owen).

mentioned; Tristan is even more famous as a lover than as a knight. Among the great themes of romance is of course the interesting subject of love; knights and ladies meditate upon it, discuss it, suffer it.[53] However, there is only one mention of 'fin' amur', or what has come to be known as 'courtly love', in the romances I have included.[54] One other mention is in a rather surprising place: the *Proverbes of Sanson*, a commentary on the Old Testament Book of Proverbs. However, early medieval use of this term was first, exclusively, a matter of divine love and not human or fleshly love.[55]

The marvels of romance include unexpected meanings: 'merveille' can be something catastrophic! Some might be a matter of taste: a blood-stained head on your host's table, set before a lady, is not everybody's idea of a marvel.[56] This use of 'marvel' to mean horror or catastrophe is not uncommon in medieval literature,[57] and even in the literature of today: one of Stevenson's protagonists uses both this and 'ferly',[58] speaking a Scots dialect in the nineteenth century (the story is set in the eighteenth). Here, 'wonders' are the judgement of God, and 'ferlies' are frightful uncanny sea-devils.[59] Eric Stanley has pointed out, in a paper delivered to the Oxford Medieval Graduate Conference, that 'wundor' in Old English can likewise have a distinctly negative meaning; examples include a passage from *Beowulf*, in which 'wundordeað' means agonized death.[60]

Treatment of women, in both senses (by contemporary society, and by writers working within that society), is conflicting and often contentious. On the one hand, we are regaled with accounts of women's beauty and virtue; on the other, we are shown their wickedness and vice. Names of ladies famously loyal and loving, as in the *Donei des Amanz*, may be found in other texts labelled as wicked women who destroy their lovers. For example, Helen loved Paris enough to elope with him, but she caused his death; Dido loved and helped Aeneas, but she tried to turn him from his destiny. Ysolt is notoriously unfaithful to her royal husband, yet remains a romance heroine; other wives delude and cuckold their husbands in the fabliaux, and are held up as a mirror of bad behaviour. It is a medieval truism that Eve, the

---

[53] *Tristan Rossignol*, for example.

[54] See *Protheselaus*, below.

[55] This term, with others, is discussed in the Glossary to my *Edouard*.

[56] In *Protheselaus*. Other examples, in this book, are indexed.

[57] *La Vie d'Edouard*, ed. Södergård, vv. 396–7; and *Edouard*, p. 69 (and note 7).

[58] King Arthur habitually delayed the start of dinner until some 'ferly', or marvel, occurred. See, *inter al*, *SGGK*, ed. Burrow: v. 94, 'mervayl'. 'ferly' also occurs in the poem; and see glossary to *Sir Ferumbras*.

[59] Stevenson, 'The Merry Men', pp. 169–71 (introduction, pp. xii–iii for the dates). In Middle English, for example *Alexander*, 'wondirly' can mean 'terribly' (see glossary).

[60] 'The Wonder of It', 9th April 2016. He explains that it is a feature of Germanic, citing a parallel in Old Saxon, from *Heliand*; see his 'Beowulf's *Wundordeað*'.

first wicked woman, is balanced and redeemed by the Virgin Mary, the ultimate good woman.[61] A passage of typical anti-women satire is found in the *Apprise*, where a young man is warned about how to behave towards these tricksy creatures: they are two-faced, and will bitch about you behind your back,[62] but at the same time good behaviour towards them is necessary if you wish to be considered well-bred and good-mannered. Female audiences must have been very familiar with this tiresomely ambiguous situation. Christine de Pisan was well aware of the difficult position she was in as a writer, given contemporary attitudes; she cleverly used historical women as examples of good behaviour when attempting to get her point across in a letter to the queen. The ladies of romance must necessarily fall between two extremes, being neither Eve nor Mary, and some are more nuanced than such polarities might lead us to expect: the heroine of *Yder* is 'good' but quite feisty and independent;[63] the young lady in the *Protheselaus* story is 'bad' but entirely sympathetic.

A setting for poems and stories may often be a garden, with flowers and birds and beasts.[64] Dream-visions typically open with a scene of this kind; the *locus amoenus* topic is very common, not only in dream-vision poetry.[65] The rare beauty of fresh flowers and fruit, in a world without hothouses or refrigerators, can barely be imagined. However, objects found in a romantic garden can also appear in many other sorts of text. Flowers and fruit are identified as remedies for human ills (in medical treatises); an apple may be simply food (in *Des Grantz Geanz*), or an occasion of sin, in the story of the Fall.[66] A plant cures the hero Yder (we are not told what it is); a prayer is prescribed when gathering the herb Centaury, in the *Medical Compendium*.[67] Other foods are suggested by the sacrificed animals and trapped birds in the *Proverbes*. Birds are found not only in gardens but in Bestiaries (for example, the eagle's beak is crooked and so he cannot say the Pater Noster); a moulting hawk is a simile for an ill-mannered young man in the *Apprise*, a healthy one helps Tristan to catch food.[68] A beast fable does duty as a moral tale, towards

---

61 I have indexed Saint Mary in the same format as for indexing other saints. Anybody wishing to study the use of her name will thus be able to track different forms: as the Virgin, as Our Lady, or as ordinary invocation ('seinte Marie!'), and so on.

62 Men bitch about women likewise, in the Knight's book: see ed. Wright, and ed. Offord, chapters 118 & 113 respectively.

63 There is not space in this book to include a passage about her, as well as the adventure I have chosen about the hero; I am currently working on an article that examines all the women in the romance.

64 Birdsong alone (often described at length) would merit a substantial study.

65 See, for example, *Alexander*, vv. 4507–14, and note (which further refers us to Curtius, *European Literature*, tr. Trask, pp. 195–200).

66 There are several versions of, and references to, events from the Book of Genesis.

67 Oil of roses, we are told, is good for cooling all manner of hurts.

68 The princesses in *Des Grantz Geanz* have no dogs or falcons to help them; they must improvise.

the end of this book; real dogs appear in *La Maniere de Langage*, and a supernatural hound in the Alderney story.[69] The snake or serpent is familiar as the tempter in the story of the Fall.[70] A swallow appears frequently in medieval story, often as a metaphor: for example the swiftness of the wicked dwarf as he leaps to catch the fleeing Ysolt in *Tristan Rossignol*.[71] It is not inconceivable that 'arundel' refers to a famous horse: Bevis of Hampton's was named Swallow. The earliest Bevis romance may be from the late twelfth century,[72] and the *Donei* (in which *Rossignol* is found) may be thirteenth-century, because of its reference to *Amadas and Ydoine*. Swallow was also the name of Hereward's horse.[73] Even if the *Donei* author does not mention the famous Arthur in this passage, there is no reason to suppose s/he did not know other romances. There are two 'swallows' in *Fergus*: a horse, and one of the heroine's ladies.[74] The most romantic of birds is the nightingale, because of its song; Tristan knows how to imitate it, and John of Howden uses it as a metaphor for his work of devotion: 'as the nightingale makes one melody out of many notes, so this book makes a concordance out of diverse materials'.[75] Human musicians in the present book include the trumpeters of Jericho, and Tristan the harper; other instruments are heard, such as the 'rote'.[76] It is not entirely certain what the latter was; editors' notes and reference books yield inconclusive results.[77] The word was used for different instruments by writers across languages and centuries: it is a generic term, and different forms developed (all sources consulted give more than one definition). Therefore no single instrument can be definitely meant, in every case even in this book, when a 'rote' is mentioned.[78]

It is a fascinating habit of medieval literature, to repeat certain themes and ideas in completely different genres. The fact that a magical spring full of precious stones can appear in a romance, a dream-vision, and a parody of Utopia,[79] points to important thematic relationships among different genres. In a Middle English

---

[69] There are hounds of sin in the *Contes* by Nicole Bozon (my epigraph to the legal texts, below), as well as sheep and fox in the *Conte* near the end of this book.

[70] Modern versions of the Creation story include one, complete with serpent, by Kipling ('The Enemies to Each Other').

[71] The dwarf who helps Fergus is not wicked.

[72] See *DMH*; Dean dates the Anglo-Norman version, her number 153, to the first half of the thirteenth century.

[73] Gray, *Simple Forms*, p. 138, note 47.

[74] See IPN in that romance.

[75] *Rossignos*. These two titles, Rossignol and Rossignos, both mean 'nightingale'; the first is a Tristan story, and the other is a work of devotion.

[76] Themes or topics appearing in more than one text may be dealt with here to save much cross-referencing later.

[77] In, for example, *Chansons de Geste, extraits*, ed. and tr. Bossuat (note on p. 20), it is said to be a small Breton harp. The minstrels of epic may have accompanied themselves on a harp, but harp is contrasted with rote in one of the Tristan stories so it cannot have been the same instrument in that case.

[78] My thanks are due to colleagues, and to knowledgeable friends in the early music world.

[79] In the Kildare MS (full details of these are in *Fergus*, below).

treatise of instruction in good behaviour, written by a knight for his daughters, the 'mirrour of auncient stories' is held up as a rich source of moral precepts rather than as a place to find exciting adventures of love and chivalry.[80] Perhaps the contrast between homily and romance was not as great as we might think.

Certain objects or events, literal or metaphorical, turn up over and over again. Not all examples of food, fighting, animals, sins, and so forth can possibly be indexed fully. Feasting takes place in romances, but is also the subject of lessons in proper deportment. Heroes and villains ride horses and carry swords, sometimes special ones; a murderer's sword in a legal case is specifically described as being from Cologne. Among the multitudinous beasts, real or imaginary, dogs alone comprise a long list: Tristan has one as a pet and one for hunting, Albina and her sisters used to have hunting dogs, there are two 'real' dogs in *Maniere*, Cerberus greets Amphiarax in Hell, mastiffs guard a lady in *Protheselaus*, kindness to dogs and other creatures is recommended in the *Apprise*, a dog that has been kicked is one of Christine de Pisan's metaphors, dogs are carrion-eaters in *Joshua*, dogs are allegorical hounds of the Devil in Bozon, a dog is thought to be a werewolf in the Channel Islands. A similar list might be compiled for apples, for serpents, or for pieces of armour.

Medieval stories, like stories universally, often refer outside themselves to other historical or legendary figures. These may be inset mini-narratives, referring to an identifiable historical time or event, or simply an evocation that conjures up a picture or story not fully explained, adding authority to the main narrative. The medieval audience would recognize such references, and be reminded of the stories thus alluded to; they would have heard or read them elsewhere. Intertextual references below include mention of the Sibyl in Clemence's *Catherine*, of the Tristan legend in *Fergus*, and of Egypt and its wickedness in the *Proverbes*.[81] Classical references abound, as might be expected: ladies in the *Donei* include Dido and Helen, a Caesar finds Hippocrates' book of medicine, the mother of Alexander is invoked by Christine de Pisan. Greeks are represented by the heroes of Thebes, but Greece is also the birthplace of Albina and her sisters. Hippocrates himself, the supposed author of the *Compendium*, anachronistically appears to quote the later Galen. Medicine itself is not restricted to the textbook: romance knights and ladies, or wandering herbalists, are able to treat sickness or wounds.[82] A knight, really an angel in disguise, appears in a life of Saint Cuthbert to treat the holy man's troublesome gout.[83] Further, some divine attributes are explicitly claimed

---

[80] Chapter I in both ed. Wright, and ed. Offord.

[81] Morrissey, 'Lydgate's Dietary', points out that creative intertextuality can include referencing shared cultural commonplaces (p. 271). My attempt to provide cross-references throughout this book is a way of reflecting a kind of narrative enhancement that is not only medieval but also universal.

[82] Luckily for Yder, two of the latter came along just in time to save him from dying of poison; his own lady treated his wounds in an earlier episode.

[83] I have appended a short passage from this Life to extracts from the *Compendium*.

as medicine ('treacle', or antidote) against sin.[84]   As for the history narrated by medieval texts, it is not only in chronicles that we find it. Anglo-Saxon historical events (including a king who might be Alfred) are found in the *Description*, and in the life of Saint Audrey. A story of Augustine's companion Mellit is a flashback in the life of Edward, a pre-Conquest king; an Old English king is evoked in the *Roman des Franceis*; Vikings are remembered in a modern adventure story.

Part of the joy of reading the old romances, and sermons too, is when as well as marvels we find material things such as weights and measures now lost: pounds and ounces, leagues and rods, marks and pence. Proverbs may turn up sounding as modern as if we heard them in the street today, although many of the proverbs in the present book are those found in the Old Testament.[85]   Vices and other allegorical figures enter the scene looking like human, if stereotyped, characters; when these appear to act of their own free will, I capitalize them as Personifications. This is not unlike the way some descriptions of visual art seem to get up off the page and start having their own adventures.[86]   However, one of the most interesting things is the appearance of stories in different genres, being used for different purposes. A moral tale with analogues all over the medieval story-hoard appears in the romance *Protheselaus*, a beast fable appears in a moral tale, to give only two examples. The story of (for example) the Fall, which everybody would have known from childhood, is narrated and glossed in numerous different ways.

As will be seen, I offer a large number of genres in this book, sometimes presented cross-generically (as with the beast fable in a moral tale, and so on). But my only examples of the dream-vision setting are the openings of *Donei des Amanz*, and of *Rossignos*; there are no 'chansons de geste', or lyrics. This is merely because not everything can be covered in a single volume. However, a wide range of authorial manners can be seen: compare the way Wace introduces himself, with that of the author of *Clement*. Some authors name themselves, and the Marie who wrote *Audree* is one; others, such as the Nun of Barking, refuse to do so. Female authorship is represented in this book by three saints' lives, in addition to three letters written by women; the final story (Appendix) was transmitted to us by an identifiable 'raconteuse'. I have not attempted to focus especially on women's writing, merely to remind readers that more women may have been writers than is generally assumed. We have no way of knowing how many anonymous authors were women; it is possible some female writers preferred anonymity out of low self-esteem, or perhaps out of prudence. It has been remarked, however, that anonymity could allow a text to circulate free of the expectations that an attribution might generate.[87]   The Nun of Barking (whose self-esteem is anything

---

[84] *Rossignos.*

[85] These, with other headings touched on here, will be cross-referenced wherever possible and/or indexed.

[86] Pictures painted on the chariot in *Roman de Thèbes* and, perhaps more surprisingly, figures on the tapestry described in *Proverbes.*

[87] Morrissey, 'Lydgate's Dietary', note 28 on p. 275.

but low) tells us explicitly she wishes to remain anonymous, incidentally disclosing that she is female; there may well be other female-authored texts without such information, and we should not be too quick to assume that anonymous texts are male-authored.[88] Sometimes the manuscript page on which writers might be expected to explain (or name) themselves is missing; such pages are typically at the beginning or end, and get lost over the years. The passages in question may be opening dedications or concluding prayers; either may include information about the writer. Beginning with Wace's introduction, there follow a number of self-conscious comments or explanations by various writers in this book. These may be flattering remarks aimed at a (hoped-for) patron, prayers for the writers themselves, conciliatory addresses to an audience or indeed meditation upon who the audience may be.

Tricks of narration include addresses to the audience, which cannot always be taken at face value (as with expressions of modesty); sometimes these are calls for attention (as at the beginning of *Des Grantz Geanz*), and sometimes they are assurances of a story's truth. Some writers claim the wonders they are describing cannot be described, all the time describing as vividly as they know how. This topos is known as 'inexpressibility'. A not dissimilar claim, called *occupatio*, is when writers announce that because a story is too long they will shorten it; this is often a prelude to some considerable expansion. Another favourite topos is the claim that something is 'still there to this day' to prove the veracity of their account. This topos, very common in medieval narration, and persisting into modern times, has been studied by (for example) Andrew King and Jacqueline Simpson.[89] The opening scene of Charles Dickens' *Barnaby Rudge* contains an example of the 'still-there' topos exploited to good effect: a mounting-block, still to be seen outside the inn, is claimed as proof positive of the truth of a story about Queen Elizabeth I, whereupon 'the doubters never failed to be put down by a large majority.' It is not surprising to find self-conscious references to the language in which the text is being written: many of these texts mention how they have turned the book in question into 'romanz'[90] because that way more people will be able to read and understand it. It is particularly apt at the end of *La Maniere de Langage*, which is intended as a language guide. In Anglo-Norman texts, Latin breaks in frequently,

---

[88] A problem of 'authorship' is that some anonymous works, over time, become attributed to known writers. An example is Robert Grosseteste (the *Deadly Sins*), below: it is not certain whether he wrote this piece. Some critics are still attributing the Nun of Barking's work to Clemence, out of a desire to have a named author at any cost. 'Marie de France' is almost certainly a composite figure (see *inter al.* Trachsler, 'Review: Logan E. Whalen, ed., *A Companion to Marie de France*', esp. pp. 38–9). References to authors such as Augustine are very common in medieval texts of all kinds; however, when compiling *Cher Alme* we found that many of these were 'pseudo-Augustine'.

[89] King's *The Faerie Queene*; and Simpson's *British Dragons*. The story of Saint Barbara, in *GL* (Supp), contains several examples of objects 'still there'; they include the saint's thumb-prints, and the sheep she turned into grasshoppers (pp. 408–9 & 415).

[90] The word 'romanz' occurs frequently throughout this book, usually footnoted with comment.

and not only when the Bible is being cited directly.[91] Middle English also breaks
in: there is an English couplet (a proverb) in Bozon's *Conte*,[92] English names
can be learned from the *Description*, I have added a couple of prayers in Middle
English to the Anglo-Norman *Credo* and *Pater Noster* for comparison.[93] Prayers
also appear in places deemed to be appropriate: Pater Noster is to be said when
gathering a herb for medicine, and *De Profundis* is found in *Maniere*. Narration
itself is a chameleon: in the *Folie Tristan* a whole romance can be reconstructed
from the hero's own specular account of the lovers' past adventures. The story of
Mellit and the Fisherman is a flashback in the life of *Edouard* and has nothing really
to do with the main story: the Nun likes it, so she decides to include it! The story
of Audrey is prefaced by a version of English history lived by her predecessors;
stories of battling gods interfere (hardly too strong a word) with the account of
battles in long-ago Thebes.

Medieval audiences are quite frequently addressed as 'my lords', but it is widely
recognized that we cannot assume this address indicates an audience of (noble)
men. The word 'Seignurs' in such a context is more likely to mean 'Ladies and
Gentlemen', or simply a 'Hello, all!' to attract listeners' attention. I have indexed
references to 'audience' throughout the book, so readers can follow them up and
study them if they wish. The address to 'Seygnours', for example, in the story
of the *Roi et Jongleur* cannot be taken to mean an audience of lords; although we
can't be sure who they were, they were in all probability a mixed group of readers
and listeners.[94] A wandering minstrel in search of adventure is the very stuff of
romance; the writer is drawing the audience in.

Prayers were a routine part of everybody's everyday life in the Middle Ages.[95]
Bible knowledge included familiarity with the various orders of angels. It is to be
noted, however, that only Archangels have names. Nobody is visited by a Throne
or a Dominion; if an unnamed angel appears we must assume it is one of the
ordinary Angels unless (as with the angel who visits Mary) it is one whose name
is already too well known to need repeating. There are traditionally nine orders
of angels; there was a tenth, but this was the company that fell into Hell with
Lucifer.[96] Every writer (in any language) was able to cite Bible passages from
memory, although inaccuracies in wording were common and incidentally did not
matter very much. Sometimes writers tell us which Bible book they are citing;

---

[91] In a culture where three languages were being used for different purposes by different groups of
people, over several centuries, there is bound to be overlap and mixing. This book cannot claim
to be a study of, or guide to, medieval language use (some references are given above).

[92] See Gray, *Simple Forms*, p. 171, for a literary fascination with proverbs.

[93] Everybody was expected to know these, the simplest of all prayers. They appear in contexts that
suggest they were taught to all, including the common people (or knights in some cases) who
cannot read.

[94] The question is discussed in my introduction to that piece.

[95] For the increase in 'lay piety' during the thirteenth century, see *Cher Alme*, Introduction (which
includes further references).

[96] See *The Kildare Manuscript*, ed. Turville-Petre, 'Fall and Passion' and the note to v. 30 on p. 117.

more often a vague reference to 'The Evangelist', 'The Prophet', or 'Solomon' gives the reader an idea where to look: any medieval audience would know most of these references through repeated exposure in church, for example. Some classical authors were effectively 'Christianized', and cited as freely as if they were Fathers of the Church: Aristotle is a common example. Ovid's popular work was 'moralized' by being given Christian interpretation, and figures such as the Sibyl were deemed to be Christians 'avant la lettre'. It has often been noted that searching a database for citations from (for example) Aristotle is usually pointless: for one thing, the citation may not be from Aristotle at all, and in any case the wording may have been altered so much that keywords cannot be guessed reliably. It may be remarked that if the *Liber Eliensis* had not come down to us we might take Marie's statement at face value, that she is drawing from Bede in her *Audree*. Many writers used *florilegia*, collections of useful citations, and these even if they can be tracked down often contain incorrect information.[97] When the writer's intention was to explain and comment on the Scriptures, precise citation was less important than spiritual understanding and the good of readers' or hearers' souls. For example, Maurice de Sully makes a point of explaining, in his *Credo* and *Pater Noster* (below), that if we don't understand a prayer properly we may be doing more harm than good when we say it.

The increase in lay piety just mentioned was part and parcel of the growing importance of regular confession among all parishioners; this was administered by the parish priest, who needed guidance on how to ask the proper questions. Guides to Confession, lists of Vices and Virtues, and the like (often elegantly written and full of lively examples) began to abound. Not every priest could be relied upon to know Latin, so such guides were written in French and later in English. The various figures of Vices and Virtues became part of a daily language, and found their way into many genres of literature. An example is the discussion of Jealousy in the romance of *Yder*, and in *Tristan Rossignol*.[98] Other common figures, sometimes personifications, are Sloth and Covetousness. Sometimes the priest asks the penitent whether s/he has indulged in any form of black art, using enchantment or sorcery to attract a lover, or to peep into the future.[99] Such things were taken extremely seriously, and they turn up in lists of sins; they turn up in romances, unsurprisingly. *The Mirror of Justices*, a legal history book, gives an account of Sorcery in the chapter on 'Laesa Majestas'.[100]

The result of confession would normally be a penance, enjoined by the priest as part of the cleansing process. Penance could involve anything from the recital of a certain number of set prayers to a full-blown pilgrimage to some important shrine.

---

[97] The introductions to *Cher Alme*, and to my *Edouard*, contain further discussion of this problem.

[98] I have omitted it from *Yder*, because the extract is already very long, but included it in the *Rossignol* passage.

[99] Sorceresses act as the evil queen's butchers in the story of Fair Rosamond (in *The French Chronicle of London*); perhaps only sorceresses can safely handle diabolical creatures such as toads.

[100] ed. Whittaker, pp. 15–16.

Very serious sins might lead to excommunication, which means the sinner was barred from all sacraments of the Church. Visiting a saint's tomb or other sacred shrine, and praying there, might earn indulgence: pardon for a proportion of one's sins that could also result in a reduction of the time to be spent in Purgatory.[101] *Gilte Legende* contains a list of churches in Rome together with the period of remission, that is, so many days or years of pardon. One church is so holy that only God can number the indulgences pertaining to it: 'if men knewe the indulgence þat be graunted þer thaye wolde do moche evylle ...'.[102]   In the Knight of the Tower's book, sinful ladies even use pilgrimage as an excuse.[103]   The trope is not uncommon: 'Et ont entreprins d'aler au voyage pour ce qu'elles ne pevent pas bien faire a leurs guises en leurs maisons.'[104]

Pilgrimage is a useful trope in literature: a hero may disguise himself as a pilgrim (or minstrel, or leper) in order to remain unknown;[105] this happens in many romances. The garb is not merely a disguise for romance heroes: a divine messenger is sometimes encountered in the guise of a palmer or pilgrim.[106]   More prosaically, a pilgrimage is a useful reason for a journey, and is a way of getting a character from one place to another — or out of the way altogether, as in the fabliaux, below. The wicked lady in *Proverbes* also has a conveniently absent husband. 'Sometimes a pilgrimage seemed nothing but an excuse for a lively and pleasant holiday ...'.[107]   Further, pilgrimage as a metaphor for human life was a medieval commonplace.[108] The canonical hours, that is the daily routine of Holy Office, also became part of general vocabulary naturally occurring in narrative texts, as well as a way of structuring private devotion.[109] Mention of an 'hour', as a way of saying what time of day it is, is common across all kinds of literature: Amphiarax is swallowed up soon after the hour of None (in ancient Thebes), the hero says it's time for Vespers in *Yder*, Frollo sleeps until Tierce in the *Roman des Franceis*.

---

[101] The prayers of the living could reduce the time one's dear departed spent in Purgatory, too.

[102] *GL* (Supp); Pardon of All the Churches, p. 76, lines 54–6.

[103] ed. Offord, and ed. Wright, chapters 33 & 34 respectively.

[104] These ladies' excuse is that they can't get enough fun at home in their houses (Crow, ed., *Les Quinze Joyes de Mariage*), lines 46–8 in the 8th *Joye*; each 'joy' sarcastically represents misery for husbands.

[105] Pilgrims were supposed to dress frugally. Disguise was not uncommon in real history; see (for example) Weir, *Eleanor of Aquitaine*, pp. 66, 209, & 287.

[106] A well-known example is the appearance of St John in *Edouard* (the story, with full references, is ch. 25).

[107] van Loon, *The Story of Mankind*, p. 480.

[108] See *Alexander*, vv. 4775–6 and note.

[109] For example, the Meditation of the Hours, pp. 254–61, in *Cher Alme*.

Treatment of Texts

> Authors are only read properly when they are translated, or one can compare
> the original text with its translation, or compare different versions in more
> than one language.[110]

The quotation above, from Calvino's *Letters*, is a valuable thought to keep in
mind for a book such as this. I have chosen to present all the material facing
its translation, to aid comparison and study.[111] I have made some comparisons
among different versions, where it is possible to do so, although a book of this
size is not the place for a collection of parallel texts. The pointers I have included
(necessarily few but as representative as possible), to other texts and contexts, are
designed to allow readers to look further for themselves.

Although the book is intended as an aid to reading Insular French, I have erred
on the side of freedom, rather than rendering the originals word for word; I have
attempted to catch the flavour of the texts, which could sound rather wooden or
heavy if translated too literally. The facing-page format allows readers to look
across and follow the process closely.

Readers will notice that the style and spelling of the extracts themselves often
differ very substantially, from one text to another and sometimes even within
the text itself. Many of these traits are editorial and reflect differing editorial
conventions. However, copyright permission requires me to reproduce the edited
text as closely as possible; therefore I copy them as they appear on the page, altering
lightly where necessary for clarity or sense only, indicating where I have done so.
Many of these traits are scribal, others are authorial. The language also varied
across the centuries, developing and changing over time; and it is possible that
some variations are regional.[112] Editors sometimes correct or 'modernize' spelling;
the use of diacritics may vary from one editor to another. These are sometimes
to disambiguate,[113] or to adjust the number of syllables (especially in verse);[114]
an acute accent can be added in prose (where the syllable count does not matter)
to differentiate between 'apele' and apelé' (for example), where one means 'call'

---

[110] Italo Calvino, cited at the conclusion of Eliza Hoyer-Millar, '*Chaitivel*: A Lesson in 'Rapidità'
(Chapter 5 in Blacker and Taylor, eds, *Court and Cloister*, forthcoming).

[111] Some shorter introductory passages, beginning with the all-important Wace, are presented as
epigraphs.

[112] Some work is being undertaken on this latter question, notably by Jean-Pascal Pouzet, but so far
it seems Insular French cannot be localized as readily as Middle English (for which see *A linguistic
atlas of late medieval English*, McIntosh *et al.*, Aberdeen 1986).

[113] The word 'pais' can mean either 'country' (modern French 'pays') or 'peace' ('paix'). Editors may
distinguish the two by writing the former as 'païs'; however, the meaning is usually clear from the
context.

[114] Anglo-Norman verse was long thought to be 'incorrect', and some editors took a lot of trouble
to adjust the text to make (for example) a seven-syllable line into a 'correct' eight-syllable one.
However, differences of pronunciation between Insular and Continental French mean that some
words in Anglo-Norman are likely to have sounded longer (or shorter) than in 'correct' medieval
French. Masters' work, cited at the end of this paragraph, has much to say on the topic.

and the other 'called'. Not all editions distinguish between i and j,[115] or u and v;[116] some editors separate words not separated in the MS (or vice versa). Another practice that varies with editorial style is whether to show contractions by use of an apostrophe. These are some of the elements to be noticed, and it would be undesirable to try and standardize all the passages in this book even were I permitted to do so. There is no space here to discuss either scribal or editorial practices in greater detail, but a valuable article by Masters is a good starting point for those wishing to investigate the questions and controversies involved.[117]

All translations are mine.[118] I have consulted previously-published translations of some texts, but without copying them; I have taken advice from contributors (Emma Cavell, Tony Hunt, and Royston Raymond), but have not copied their own versions. I have not translated later Middle English, or non-medieval French; in all cases the passages are very short and easy to read.

As a general rule, I translate 'doublets' (pairs of words appearing to have the same meaning) as they stand, as faithfully as possible. We cannot be sure whether writers intended extra meaning to be conveyed by such apparent repetitions, so I prefer to respect them. Sometimes doublets are used to clarify meaning, in the case of francophone readers being unfamiliar with English or vice versa;[119] or, a pair of near-synonyms may also be used to create emphasis: somebody desiring 'freedom and liberty' may be described as desiring great freedom or absolute liberty.

Some translators normalize 'wandering tenses', where a narrative may switch from past to present and back apparently at random. Although reproducing tense-switches exactly can sometimes make for awkward prose in English, I prefer to follow them approximately, to give a flavour of what the original may have sounded like.[120] As with more modern narrative, tense-switching may add a feeling of immediacy and in fact pass unnoticed unless a reader is looking for it.

Finally there is the question of 'tu' and 'vous', where some writers waver between forms even within a single speech to the same person; 'thou' forms are so unfamiliar in modern English that I use them sparingly without, however, ruling them out altogether. I have indexed the most notable cases, but since each raises a different question or discussion they cannot all be covered in this Introduction. It is not easy to pin down any reason for this mixture of forms: Justin Stover tells me there was sometimes a departure from strict first and second person forms (that is, there was a 'royal we' for first person singular, and a 'polite' plural 'you' for second person

---

[115] For example, 'ie' may be corrected to read 'je', the first person pronoun.

[116] For example, 'ouert' is clearer (meaning 'open') if spelled 'overt'.

[117] 'Anglo-Norman in Context'.

[118] I am especially grateful to Judith Weiss for looking through my drafts. Remaining errors are of course my own.

[119] See, for example, *The Universal Chronicle of Ranulf Higden*, Taylor, p. 137.

[120] See the introduction to *Le Roman de Thèbes*, ed. and tr. Mora-Lebrun: 'nous nous sommes efforcée de conserver le mélange des temps ... car l'emploi du présent traduit sans doute une volonté d'actualisation qui ne devait pas être gommée' (p. 37). Sutherland, 'On the Use of Tenses in Old and Middle French', has more on this question.

singular) in Latin as early as the fourth century. The editor of *Thèbes* (below) says that a mixture of forms is typical of Anglo-Norman; Bossuat, that such a mixture is typical of chansons de geste.[121] It may quite simply be that writers did not perceive it as a problem; occasionally it can be seen that one form or the other has been used merely to fit the metre, though this does not 'explain' all cases.[122]

Formal presentation of the original texts tends to vary, as explained above. I have standardized details here and there, but retain different editors' styles in the main: folio numbering, lineation of prose, line-numbering of verse (sometimes in fours, sometimes in fives), initials in bold type, and so forth.

This book contains a large number of titles and references, therefore I have adopted the lightest punctuation that is consistent with clarity. Because of the numerous primary texts, line or verse numbers or page numbers and further reading, quotations and so on, I avoid italicization as far as possible. My general rule is to use italics for book titles; that is, editions of medieval texts selected and presented, and titles of other literature mentioned for comparison and illustration. I use conventional italics for words and passages in Latin, and for citations from the King James (*AV*) Bible. This may have the effect of making italics appear on a page facing plain type, or vice versa. Further, I use italics for Pater Noster only when it is the title of a text (for example, by Maurice de Sully, below), so as to distinguish it from the title of an everyday prayer (Our Father). Because of all this, I do not italicize French words and phrases: I use plain type for both 'chanson de geste' and 'epic', 'fabliau' and 'fable', and so on; most editors and critics use plain type for 'fabliau' and so on in the titles of their work. Any titles that are translated or interpolated (as in The Severed Head, from *Protheselaus* below) are likewise in plain type. I aim to make the main titles stand out, and to make my pages less cluttered and more friendly to the reader's eye. Further, I have indexed (for example) Protheselaus the hero in plain type, but the romance about that hero in italics: *Protheselaus*.

My notes, and introductions to each chapter, have two functions: first, for every text presented, editions with their notes and line-references are cited fully. Other footnotes identify sources of selected secondary material, critical scholarship and so on. More generally, certain suggestions for further reading within the range of medieval studies, as well as from literatures that are not medieval, are added for interest. These are not necessary for overall understanding and enjoyment of this book, and (as with online material) cannot be exhaustive. My Bibliography lists all Primary and Secondary texts cited in this book; many Primary and a few key Secondary texts are listed by title, because they are best cited by title. But I list nothing that I have not personally consulted. A search on the internet will yield

---

[121] *Chansons de Geste, extraits*, p. 31; and *Pseudo-Turpin Chronicle*, ed. Short, p. 21. Woledge, 'The Use of *Tu* and *Vous*', on this subject, is also cited below in my introduction to the *Apprise*.

[122] *Receptaria* is another text that mixes forms (here, in English prose): 'ye gost' (p. 167 & note); in *Shorter Treatises*, ed. Hunt, p. 167 at [125]. The 'sociological' difference between 'thou' and 'you' does not appear until after the Conquest (Hogg, ed., *The Cambridge History of the English Language*, ch. 3, p. 144).

other editions of my texts, a number of useful articles or references, and so on; some of the available material is signalled in my footnotes. Online references to my Primary texts, if available, are added to their Bibliography entries.

This book may be used on its own without the necessity of consulting any of the others cited. However, I would like to think that anybody could use it as a starting point for exploring Anglo-Norman literature, by looking up some of the texts excerpted here, or by following up topics of interest; they might wish to consult some of the Middle English texts I have cited; or enjoy revisiting some works in a wider field of literature, whether novels or other classics.

Story

Longue est la geste des Normanz
E a metre grieve en romanz.
Se l'on demande qui ço dist,
Qui ceste estoire en romanz fist,
Jo di e dirai que jo sui
Wace de l'isle de Gersui,
Qui est en mer vers occident,
Al fieu de Normendie apent.
En l'isle de Gersui fui nez,
A Chaem fui petiz portez,
Illoques fui a letres mis,
Pois fui longues en France apris;
Quant jo de France repairai
A Chaem longues conversai,
De romanz faire m'entremis,
Mult en escris e mult en fis.

'The tale of the Normans is a long one, and it's hard work to turn it into French. If anybody wants to know who says this, and who put this story into French, I say and I'll tell you that I am Wace from the island of Jersey,[1] which is in the sea away to the West; it belongs to Normandy. I was born in the isle of Jersey, and taken to Caen when I was small. There they set me to learn my letters; I spent a long time at my studies in France.[2] When I came back from France, I stayed in Caen for a long time. I set myself to making histories in French;[3] I wrote many, and I composed many, of these.' (vv. 5297–312)

---

[1] There is an ancient misreading which gives him a 'first' name, as if Wace were a family name. But Wace is his given name (cf. Gace, and other forms; one of the MSS spells him Vaicce), and if anything he would be identified outside his own place as 'Wace de Jersey'. See Wace, *The Roman de Rou*, ed. Holden, p xvi & note 11; *Wace's Brut*, ed. and tr. Weiss, p. xi & note.

[2] France (Île de France) was then a different country, distinct from Normandy; hence André de Coutances' xenophobic fury at the French (in *Roman des Franceis*, below).

[3] Wace also wrote saints' lives and other kinds of narrative.

© 2018 Jane Bliss, CC BY-NC 4.0   25   https://doi.org/10.11647/OBP.0110.02

The modern French word 'histoire' conveniently includes both History and Story,[4] whereas the English language distinguishes between them. In medieval literature it is usually a waste of time trying to decide which is which; here I simply group passages according to Dean's catalogue. Her sections are ordered generically, and my passages are taken from the following: (1) Historiographical, (3) Romance, (4) Lais Fables Fabliaux & Dits. However, it will be seen that there are plenty of stories in the later part of this book.[5]

For this book I begin, as I end, with a Channel Islander: Wace tells us he was born in Jersey. One of the earliest 'histories' in the vernacular was written by the father of Arthurian literature and thus of many romances and, later, novels. My book travels from Wace of Jersey back at last to Alderney, another Channel Island and also home to story-tellers.

Wace uses several terms for story and writing:

Geste means both Action (doings, exploits, adventures),[6] and Story (Wace is referring to the history of the Normans), although the terms may be interchangeable.[7]   Chansons de Geste is a widely-used term for epic poems,[8] which are conventionally distinguished from romances by their theme of a hero representing his culture and kin-group against a common enemy, typically Saracens.

Romanz means both Language (early, and often Insular, French) and Story (the word quickly became standard for narrative, often historical and often romantic).[9] Both Wace's chronicles are entitled *Roman* (*de Brut*, and *de Rou*). Wace says both 'romanz faire' and 'romanz escrivre' (above). He is both making and writing, not only history but also story, in French.[10]

Estoire, as has been pointed out, means both History and Story. The two words mean different things in modern English. Wace identifies himself as the one who has put the 'estoire' (fictional or not) into French.

Letres means, straightforwardly enough, 'letters': Wace learns to read and write when he learns his letters, and he continues his education later. However, he would

---

[4] See, for example, Legge p. 30.

[5] See Walters, 'Wace and the Genesis of Vernacular Authority', for the status of 'romanz' in Britain as closer to Latin and therefore preferable to Old English.

[6] 'gestes' (*gesta*) originally meant the acts; it is also used for tales that recount them.

[7] One of the other MSS has 'estoire' instead of 'geste' in v. 5297; we would suppose that one scribe's preference was to emphasize the 'doing', another's was for the 'telling' of events.

[8] The *Chanson de Roland* is the best-known example (a good translation is *The Song of Roland*, tr. Sayers; details of editions are in Sayers' introduction). A hundred years ago, in Arabia, 'the tribal poets would sing us their war narratives: long traditional forms with stock epithets, stock sentiments, stock incidents grafted afresh on the efforts of each generation' (Lawrence, *Seven Pillars of Wisdom*, p. 128); this is a fair definition of the genre.

[9] Romance heroes are less likely to be fighting Saracens than dragons; their adventures are more likely to involve ladies. 'romanz' first meant French, then story (the first romances were written in French). In v. 5311 above it refers to narrative.

[10] Burgess, the modern translator of this version (details given below), prefers as I do not to collapse the two verbs in v. 5312 into one. Wace seems to distinguish between 'escris' and 'fis' (unless he is merely filling up a line).

have become *literatus*, which meant lettered in Latin; you could not call yourself lettered if you could read only French. Nor did the skills of reading and writing go together automatically as part of medieval education: some people learned to read, at least in French (or English) but could not write except perhaps their name. Others might be 'literate' in a more modern sense in that they were familiar with a good range of literature, but (in a less modern sense) they enjoyed it by getting somebody to read to them.

Given the number of different terms for language and literature used by Wace in one short passage, it is not surprising he uses a double phrase for his method of composition in the last line.

History

Ne vos voil mie metre en letre,
Ne jo ne m'en voil entremetre,
Quels barons e quanz chevaliers,
Quanz vavasors, quanz soldeiers,
Out li dus en sa compaignie
Quant il out prest tot son navie;
Mais jo oï dire a mon pere
— Bien m'en sovient, mais vaslet ere —
Que set cenz nes, quatre meins, furent
Quant de Saint Valeri s'esmurent,
Que nes, que batels, que esqueis,
A porter armes e herneis;
E jo ai en escrit trové
— Ne sai dire s'est verité —
Que il i out trei mile nes,
Qui portoent veiles e tres.

'I don't want to write it all down for you — I don't even want to bother — which barons and how many knights, how many vassals and soldiers, the Duke had in his train when he had got his navy ready. But I heard my father say, I remember quite clearly though I was only a little chap,[1] that there were seven hundred ships less four when they set out from Saint Valery: various ships, boats, and hulks for transporting arms and equipment. And I have found it written, though I don't know whether it's true, that there were three thousand vessels with their masts and sails.' (vv. 6417–32)

The Anglo-Norman period conventionally begins with the Conquest of England by William Duke of Normandy. Themes in the present chapter, some of whose texts describe pre-Conquest events, include invasion (Hengist and Horsa), possession (Albina's arrival in the land one day to be called Britain), political building (Westminster Abbey, some of the main roads we know today) ... the stuff of history.

---

[1] If his father had been quite old at Wace's birth (some time between 1090 and 1110), this is just possible. Alternatively, because the word for grandfather would take up more space in the line (it does not appear as a variant in any copy), he may be using a shorter word and stretching the truth. A modern 'finale' of the Bayeux Tapestry, made recently as an Alderney community project, has placed the figure of Wace writing at his desk in one of its borders because of this connection between the Channel Islands and the Battle of Hastings (the image is reproduced on the cover of this book, and see http://www.alderneybayeuxtapestry.com/).

Wace's *Roman de Rou*[2]

Besides introductions to three versions of *Rou*,[3] see also *Wace's Brut*, ed. and tr. Weiss, for a sketch of Wace's life and work.[4] My extracts, two short (above) and one longer, are taken from the later Holden edition (Jersey, 2002). I have provided my own translation; that of Burgess may readily be consulted, as the text is facing-page.[5] My only reference to the Conquest is in the passage heading this chapter;[6] the *Rou* has been plundered for historical references to this event, and anthologies such as Lecco's contain passages from it.[7] I have chosen the author's identification of himself, together with what his father said about William's navy, before moving to another kind of story altogether. There are numerous passages in Wace's history which are interesting to compare with the Nun of Barking's Life of Edward the Confessor:[8] descriptions and actions of Edward, and of Godwin and Harold, for example. This passage has been chosen to match a passage in the Nun's life which complements it.[9]

---

[2] Dean 2.1. I am grateful to Glyn Burgess for advice about the presentation of passages from this important text.

[3] *Le Roman de Rou de Wace* (SATF, edition only); Wace, The *Roman de Rou* (Jersey, ed. & trans); Wace's *Roman de Rou* (Woodbridge, trans. only). Volumes I & 2 of Pluquet's 1827 edition are available at http://gallica.bnf.fr/ark:/12148/bpt6k65499509 and http://gallica.bnf.fr/ark:/12148/bpt6k65499435

[4] *Wace, the hagiographical works*, ed. Blacker *et al.*, General Introduction; and Hans-Erich Keller in *Medieval France, An Encyclopedia*, pp. 969–70; and *Wace: A Critical Biography*, Blacker, may all be consulted for details and context of this important writer.

[5] The text is from Holden's, as reprinted in this Jersey edition (without folio numbers). I omit editorial emphasis indicating corrections, because Holden's footnotes explaining them are not included in the Jersey reprinting (p. lii). I have added square brackets to words supplied by the editor, and conventional capital letters to the beginning of each line; I have made selected reference to variants printed in Holden's original edition.

[6] French in England did not begin in 1066: for one thing, because Edward the Confessor was brought up in Normandy, there were numerous French speakers at his court.

[7] Her *Storia* contains the celebrated Taillefer episode. Wace's *Brut* is well known and much anthologized, hence my choice of his other *Roman*.

[8] The Nun was writing probably soon after 1163, the date of her source, Aelred of Rievaulx' *Vita*. She and Wace are therefore roughly contemporary, although there is no evidence they knew each other's writings. Neither of these Edward hagiographers is mentioned in the introduction among Wace's sources for *Rou*. My extract from the life of Edward (below) gives further information on the Nun and her sources.

[9] There are several chapters in the Lives of Edward that describe why he founded Westminster. Lives include *La Vie d'Edouard*, ed. Södergård, translated in my *Edouard*; also 'Vita S. Edwardi Regis et Confessoris', Aelred of Rievaulx (in *PL*); and Aelred of Rievaulx, *The Historical Works*, ed. Dutton. Other Lives (references are supplied in the foregoing) may be consulted for different versions of this story.

Text

Li reis Ewart fu de bon aire,   5457
Ne volt a home nul tort faire,
Sainz orgoil e sainz conveitise[10]
Volt faire a toz dreite justise;   5460
Assez estora abeïes
De fieus e d'altres mananties,
E Westmostier meesmement,
Oez par quel entendement!
Par un besoig aveit voé   5465
— Ne sai sel fist por enfermté,
Ou por son regne recovrer,
Ou por poor qu'il out en mer —
Que por orer a Rome ireit,
De ses pechiez pardon querreit,   5470
A l'apostoile parlereit,
Penitance de lui prendreit.
A un terme que il proposa
Li reis son eire apareilla,
Li baron furent assenblé   5475
E li evesque e i abé;
Communement ont porparlé
E par conseil dit e loé
Qu'il nel lairront nïent aler,

Cel vo fait bien a trespasser.   5480
Ne porreit pas, a lor quider,
A grant travail longues durer;
Trop i a lonc pelerinage
Ker li reis est de grant aage,
S'a Rome vait, qu'il ne revienge,   5485
Que mort ou mal [la] le retienge;
Mult lor sereit mesavenu
S'il aveient le rei perdu.
A l'apostoile enveieront,
Del vo assoldre le feront;   5490
Bien en porra aveir quitance,
Si en face altre penitance.
A l'apostoile ont enveié,
Cil a le rei del vo laissié,
Mais enjoint li a e loé,   5495
Por aveir del vo quiteé,
C'une abeïe povre quere
Que seit fondee el non saint Pere;
Tant i doinst del soen, tant l'enort
E de ses rentes tant i tort,   5500
Que toz tens mais seit asazee
E el non saint Pere enoree.

---

[10] MS convertise.

Translation

King Edward was a gentle man, and never wanted to do harm to anybody. Without pride, and without envy, he wanted to give proper justice to everybody. He provided for many abbeys, with their fiefs and all maintenance; including Westminster. Listen to why this happened! In his need, he had made a vow — I don't know whether it was because of some illness, or because he wanted to recover his kingdom, or because he was afraid of sea-travel — that he would go to make his prayers at Rome, and ask pardon for his sins; he would talk to the Pope, and accept penance of him.[11] At a time when he decided it was right, he made preparations for his journey; the barons were gathered, and the bishops and abbots. They all spoke together, giving their advice and telling him that they would never let him go. He would have to give up his vow! They said that in their opinion he couldn't stand a long journey,[12] and the pilgrimage was too far for such an old king.[13] If he went to Rome, he might never come back; death or sickness might keep him there. And if they lost their king, terrible things would happen to them. They would send to the Pope and make him absolve Edward of his vow; he could easily be forgiven it if he carried out some other penance. So they sent to the Pope; and he let the king off his vow but commanded him by his advice, in return for freeing him from the vow, to seek out an impoverished abbey that was founded in the name of Saint Peter. He was to give it enough of his own goods, and honour it so much, and divert enough of his incoming rents to it, that it would have adequate provision for ever and the name of Saint Peter would be glorified.

---

[11] There is frequent confusion in medieval French between 'penitence' and 'penance' (penitence is contrition for sins committed; penance, the satisfaction enjoined by the priest after confession); one of the MSS reads 'Pentance'. The two may be distinguished by their context.

[12] 'travail' in Anglo-Norman usually means 'travel' (cf. modern French 'work').

[13] There is no suggestion in *Edouard* that he was old at the time of this incident (in ch. 10; his marriage happened not long before, in ch. 8). There, he wanted to fulfil his vow as soon as he possibly could.

Ewart reçut le mandement
De l'apostoile bonement.
Dejoste Londres, devers west,   5505
Si com encore i pert e est,
Out de saint Pere une abeïe,
Qui de viel tens ert apovrie;
En un islet esteit assise,
Zornee out non, joste Tamise.   5510
Zornee por ço l'apelon
Que d'espines i out foison,
E que l'eve alout environ.
Ee en engleis isle apelon,
Ee est isle, zorn est espine,   5515
Seit raim, seit arbre, seit racine;
Zornee ço est en engleis
Isle d'espines en franceis;
Westmostier fu pois apelez
Quant le mostier i fu fundez.   5520
Li reis Ewart [vit] Westmostier
Ou mult aveit a redrecier,
Vit le leu qui apovrisseit

E le mostier qui dechaeit;
Par conseil des clers e des lais,   5525
Od le boen tens qu'il out de pais,
Par grant cure e par grant entente,
De son aveir e de sa rente
A Westmostier bien estoré,
E tant i a del soen doné,   5530
Beles viles e boens maneirs,
Croiz e textes e boens aveirs,
Ja mais li leus n'avra chierté
S'il est deduit par lealté.
Mais quant chascun moine fait   5535
    borse
Li communs bien faut e reborse;
Moines qui quert obedience
De deniers velt aveir semence.
Li reis Westmostier estora,
Le lieu tint chier e mult l'ama;   5540
Emprés dona a saint Edmont
Tant donc li moine manant sunt.

Edward accepted the Pope's orders willingly. Just near to London, towards the west, where it is still and can be seen,[14] there used to be an abbey of Saint Peter, which had been poor for a very long time. It was situated on an islet, called Thorney, beside the Thames.[15] We call it Thorney because it is full of thorns and because the water goes around it! 'Ee' is what we call an isle, in English, so 'ee' is isle and 'zorn' is thorn — whether branch or tree or root. What is Thorn-ey in English, is 'Isle of Spines' in French. Afterwards it was called Westminster, when the great church was founded there. King Edward saw that Westminster had much that needed doing to it; he saw how the place was impoverished and the church was falling down. He consulted with his clerks and his laymen, and given the good time of peace that he now had, he rebuilt Westminster with his own money and rents, attentively, taking the greatest care. He gave much of his wealth to it, fine towns and manors, as well as crosses and books[16] and other rich goods. The place would never lack for anything again, if its affairs were managed faithfully. But when every monk makes himself a money-bag, ordinary people go short and so renege [on an agreement to contribute]. Any monk seeking a position of authority wants to have a good sprinkling of cash.[17] The king built Westminster, and he held the place dear, loving it fondly. In after days he gave a lot of money to Saint Edmund's, so that the monks there are thriving.[18]

---

[14] Medieval storytellers are fond of supplying pointers to something that is still there to be seen, as proof of their narratives' veracity.

[15] It is interesting that Wace says 'we call it ...' in the next lines, as if he felt himself to be English. There are difficulties with this name: the MS spelling is Zonee (corrected by Holden to Zornee throughout), and other copies call it Bornhee, Cornhee, Ahornie, and more. There may be underlying confusion with the English letter 'thorn' (th), or even with 'yogh' (gh, or sometimes z). Perhaps, if the word began with 'thorn' (Thonee, Thornee), scribes unfamiliar with English letters thought it was a yogh and transcribed it as zed (or one of the other letters in spellings given here). For a similar confusion, see Jeffrey, 'Authors, Anthologies', n. 33 on p. 270: Bozon's name was properly Bohun or something like it, but scribes took the yogh for a zed.

[16] 'textes' would have been Gospel books, perhaps richly bound.

[17] Holden notes at this point, in his earlier edition, 'obedience' must have a special meaning of 'authority' or 'control' (of a religious house). I have followed his suggestion.

[18] Other Lives describe Edward's vow and the Pope's absolution, and much is made of the founding of Westminster Abbey. But the Nun (for example) nowhere mentions St Edmund's.

Description of England[19]

This text is edited in *Anglo-Norman Anniversary Essays* (pp. 31–47); there is an Introduction to it in the same volume (pp. 11–30).[20] Such an important piece therefore takes up two of the volume's chapters. What could be a rather dry description is enlivened with authorial comments, making it very readable. The writer expects an audience to share the feelings of French-speaking English people against the wild Welsh, and to understand references to ancient (legendary) history in which figures such as Hengist and Corineus, Belin and Arthur, shape the land as we know it; it is possible, if the audience are Northerners, that they share the writer's preference for York over Canterbury as chief seat of archbishops.

The following introductory notes are taken from the aforementioned chapters in *Essays*, with page numbers marked 'LJ' and 'AB' (Lesley Johnson and Alexander Bell, respectively).[21]

The *Description* was probably composed soon after 1139, certainly before the end of the twelfth century. There are four extant texts; the base for this edition is in Durham Cathedral Library C. iv. 27. Describing a country inevitably involves charting its history. The contents and context of the manuscript reflect the complex relationship between twelfth-century Latin and vernacular traditions. The *Description* draws from Henry of Huntingdon's *Historia Anglorum* (c. 1129) but also some details from Geoffrey of Monmouth's *Historia* (c. 1138). It was used as part of the epilogue to Gaimar's *Estoire des Engleis*; elsewhere part of his prologue, and also as part of a larger descriptive survey (LJ pp. 11–13). Its format is drawn from Henry of Huntingdon, opening his history with 'a portrait of the island'; Henry follows Bede and Gildas, who use description not only as setting for their histories but also to signal some of the latter's themes (LJ pp. 17–18). However, the process by which the material was further transmitted to the vernacular is not entirely clear: it is possible there was an interim version of excerpted material,[22] because it seems to contain more contextual information than is found in Henry (LJ pp. 20–1). The *Description* amplifies the situation in Wales, mentions cultural distinctions on account of the Saxon conquest, the names of shires or counties; and stresses the narrator's superior knowledge. Details of Corineus, Belin, and perhaps the mention of Hengist's treachery, all suggest material drawn from Geoffrey, as in Gaimar (LJ pp. 22–3). Versions of history in Henry, as in William of

---

[19] Dean 4.

[20] 'Anglo-Norman *Description*'; and Johnson, 'Description: An Introduction'. The *Essays* are published by ANTS (OPS 2).

[21] 'The Shires and Hundreds of England' (pp. 145–6 in *An Old English Miscellany*, ed. Morris) is hardly comparable, but there are one or two spellings of note (below). The book's title is misleading: the language of the pieces is Middle English (the one cited here is second half of thirteenth century), not Old English. Comparable descriptions are often found in books of 'history': there is a passage in *La Vie seint Edmund le Rei*, ed. Russell, vv. 317–432, in which Vortigern and other such figures are mentioned. In *The Mirror of Justices*, see 'Of the Coming of the English' (pp. 6–8, in which Lincoln is spelt Nichole in the Anglo-Norman way).

[22] See also AB p. 31.

Malmesbury, are at odds with Geoffrey's view which notoriously draws on 'the old book' rather than on Bede and others. The *Description* provides yet another view of the transition to Saxon rule. Its schematic effect is comparable to the so-called 'platte' of England which precedes the *Brut* in London, BL, Royal 13. A. xxi;[23] and Johnson emphasizes its mnemonic quality (on pp. 27–8).

MS D, the base text for the edition, seems to accept Gaimar's authorship, but it cannot be by Gaimar. On further examination, the possibility of common authorship with the *Anglo-Norman Brut* is suggested; the author manages to use a remarkable number of characteristics common to the latter in only 260 lines.[24]

'The history of early British and English chorography has yet to be written'; it is a history that stretches back at least to Orosius, and (among later writers) Ranulf Higden's highly detailed outline must have a special place '... The Anglo-Norman *Description of England* has a modest place within this history' (LJ pp. 29–30).

A notable detail in this text is the spelling of the town Bath: Baðe (vv. 91 & 93). The Middle and Old English letter eth is unusual in French; it seems one of the copyists failed to understand it, writing Bae. Two manuscripts have Baðe, and a fourth has transliterated correctly: Bathe (IPN, AB p. 46). Evidently the name was taken over either from an English text or from a text containing the English spelling. Other names where eth might be expected include Sudsexe (v. 77), spelt as here with a d. The trilingual *Receptaria* contains the letter thorn in both French and Latin (as well, of course, as English); for example, I found one of each on the facing pages 116 & 117.

The king of Wessex mentioned, but not named, in the poem may perhaps have been meant as Athelstan (925–39). The tenth century was when the shires took shape (Brooke, *From Alfred to Henry III, 871–1272*, pp. 70–71), and England was not beginning to look like a whole country until some time after Alfred's day (pp. 49–52). Alfred is sometimes mentioned as a well-known king in medieval texts, in a vague sort of way.[25] However, apart from this king's power, his laws, and the making of the shires, there is scant evidence to show which king our writer means.

---

[23] See Dean 6 for a description of this 'circular diagram'.

[24] AB pp. 35–6, & 36–7.

[25] For shires, see *The Blackwell Encyclopedia of Anglo-Saxon England*; and *Dictionary of the Middle Ages*, ed. Strayer (the entry is in vol. 11). According to the latter (s.v. Shire, pp. 253–4) their origins were diverse. Emerging during the ninth century, they were organized by Alfred and his successors; evidence for their existence before this time is conjectural. Thanks are due to Henrietta Leyser for advice on this matter, and for introducing me to the *Description* (her *Beda* gives further context).

Text

[137a]
Sicum Hengist e li Seisun
Orent faite la traïsun
E furent saisi des citez,
Des chastels e des fermetez,   4
Les Bretuns unt dechacié,
Des lur le païs hebergié.
En .vii. departent le païs
E .vii. reis i unt asis;   8
As realmes nun ont doné,
A chascun sulunc lur volenté.
Kent apelent le premerain,
Icest tint Hengist en sa main;   12
Plenier esteit mult le païs,
Dous citez i ot de pris:
Cantuorbiri l'arcevesquéd
E Rouecestre l'evesquéd.   16
L'autre unt Sudsexe apeléd;
En Cicestre ert le real siéd.
Westsexe apelent le tierz,
U dedenz ad plusurs citez,   20
Kar Wiltune chief en esteit,
En demeine li reis l'aveit,
U ore est grant abeïe,
Nuneins l'unt en lur baillie;   24
E de Wincestre la citéd
U ore ad riche evesquiéd,
E l'evesque de Salesbire
Od la cité de Ambresbire.   28
Li quarz est Essexe apeléd
Qui gueres nen ad durét,
Kar povre ert a demesure,
Ne durad pur ço gueres d'ure.   32
Estengle est li quinz numé,

De dous cuntrees onuré:
La dedenz est Norfulke
[137b]
E la terre de Sufolke.   36
Cum nus recunte li legistres,
Des Mercïens fu fait li sistes;
Citez i ot asez plusurs,
Viles, chastels, riches burcs.   40
Cest realme riche esteit
E plusurs citez i aveit,
Kar i apendeit Dorkecestre
E Nicole e Leïrcestre.   44
Li setme mult riche esteit,
Kar Everwic i aveit
E trestut tresqu'en Cateneis;
Plus ot cist sul que les .vi. reis.   48
Cist ot suz sei Norhumberlant
E la terre de Cumberlant
E le cunté de Loeneis,
E d'Escoce ert cist reis.   52
A la parfin un rei poanz
Qui par armes fud mult vaillanz
Par force les .vi. reis cunquist,
A sun os lur onurs prist.   56
De Westsexe cist ert reis,
Es païs mist nuveles leis,
Par proesce tuz les cunquist
E a sei sujez les mist.   60
Sitost cum il le regne tint,
Sil departi en .xxxv.;
A chascun sun nun donat,
En engleis 'scire' l'apelat,   64
Mes nus ki romanz savum
D'autre maniere les numum:

Translation

As soon as Hengist and his Saxons had done their treason;[26] as soon as they had possessed themselves of cities, castles, and fortified places; and had chased out the Britons from the country, settling it with their own people; they divided the country into seven. They established seven kings, and they gave such names to each kingdom as suited them. They called the first one Kent, and Hengist himself took charge of it. The land was rich, and had two valuable cities in it: Canterbury the archbishopric, and Rochester the bishopric. The next one they called Sussex,[27] with a royal seat at Chichester. The third they called Wessex, and there are several cities in it. For Wilton was the principal one, which the king held personally; there is now a great abbey there, with nuns in charge of it. There is Winchester, now a powerful bishopric;[28] and the bishop of Salisbury, with the city of Amesbury. The fourth one is called Essex, but it didn't last long: because it was so poor it endured for a very short time. East Anglia is the name of the fifth, and it boasts two countries: in it is Norfolk and also the land of Suffolk.

As our learned source tells us,[29] the sixth was made up of the Mercians. It had many cities, towns, castles, and rich boroughs. The kingdom was rich with many cities, for Dorchester belonged to it, as well as Lincoln and Leicester.[30] The seventh was extremely powerful, for it had York and all the land as far as Caithness. Its king had more than all the other six. He was lord over Northumberland, the land of Cumberland, and the county of Lothian; and he was king of Scotland. In time, a strong king who was most valiant in arms conquered the other six kings in battle, and took their honours for himself.[31] This one was a king of Wessex, and he established new laws in the land. He conquered all of them by his prowess, and made them all subject to him. As soon as he had hold of the land, he divided it into thirty-five, giving each its name.

---

[26] Legends say Hengist and his people got hold of England by underhand means. 'The brutal Saxon invaders drove the Britons westward into Wales and compelled them to become Welsh; it is now considered doubtful whether this was a Good Thing' (*1066 and All That*, p. 13). Given the problem with Wales, below, the writer would seem to agree with Sellar and Yeatman.

[27] In any list, the word 'l'autre' means 'the second' (a third or fourth is never called 'l'autre'). See Ivanov and Kleyner, 'The Friday Legend', p. 192, for 'nihsta/oþer' meaning 'second' in early Middle English. The life of Audrey, below, contains an example of 'secunde' instead (in v. 157).

[28] 'riche' can mean powerful, as well as rich in money.

[29] 'legistres'; there is a variant 'registres' in another manuscript, mentioned by Johnson (p. 21). She remarks that the author does not name specific authorities.

[30] Lincoln is very commonly spelt 'Nic(h)ole' in Anglo-Norman texts (see *Edouard*, p. 129; and 'The Anglo-Norman "Hugo de Lincolnia"', ed. Dahood). The IPN (AB, p. 46) shows that all copyists have used this spelling; neither LJ nor AB comments on it. The description cited above, in *An Old English Miscellany*, spells it 'lyncholne'.

[31] 'onur' here refers to property (feudal domains; see *La Vie seint Edmund le Rei*, ed. Russell, glossary 'honur').

Ço que 'schire' ad nun en engleis
'Cunté' ad nun en franceis.   68
Par nun tuz les numerai,
Kar numer mult ben les sai.
Kent i est el premier chief:
[137c]
Iloches est l'arcevesquiét   72
En Dorobelle la cité
Que Cantorbire est apelé,
E si ad un evesquié
En Rouecestre la cité.   76
Sudsexe ad nun l'autre cuntree,
D'un evesquié est äurnee,
Cicestre est chief del cunté,
Iloc est l'evequal sié.   80
Le tierz cunté fud Surrie,
E le quart Hamtesire;
Iloc si est un evesquié
Dedenz Wincestre la cité.   84
Le quint apelent Berkesire,
E le siste Wiltesire,
U dedenz ad un evesquiéd,
En Salebire est le sied.   88
Le setme païs est Dorsete,
E puis le oitime Sumersete;
En Baðe est l'evesquié
Dunt en Welles fud ja le sié;   92
Ceste Baðe ot jadis autre nun,
Sicum dient li Seisun
Qui primes la herbergerent,
Achemannestrate l'apelerent.   96
Devenesire le nofme ad nun;
C'est un païs mult riche e bon.
Iloc ad riche evesquié,
En Essecestre en est le sié.   100
Le disme si est Cornuaille;

Cil sunt pruz en bataille;
Corinëus la herbergat,
Cil qui les jeanz enchaçat.   104
Essexe apele um le unzime,
E Middelsexe le duzime;
De Lundres i est l'evesquié
[137d]
Qui cité est d'antiquité.   108
Suffolke i est le trezime,
Norfolke le quatorzime;
Or est en Norwiz l'evesquié
Dunt en Tiedfort fu ja la sié.   112
De Cantebruge le cunté
Al quinzime est acunté.
De Ely i est l'evesquié,
En cest mareis siet la cité,   116
Cil qui la maint ad grant fuisun
Suventesfeiz de bon peissun
E volatille e veneisun;
Dedenz le mareis le prent l'um.   120
Le sezime est mult renumé,
De Nicole est icel cunté,
Riche en est mult l'evesquiez,
Kar la apendent .viii. cuntez: 124
Nicole e Norhamtune,
Herteford e Huntindone,
Leïrcestre e Bedeford,
Bukingehame, Oxeneforde.   128
Mult est riche l'evesquié,
Dous eves l'unt enviruné,
Humbre apelent la menur,
Tamise ad nun la greignur.   132
Le vint e quart est Gloucestre,
Le vint e .v. est Wirecestre;
De Wirecestre l'evesquié
Cel païs est mult onuré.   136

He called each 'shire' in English; but those of us who know French call them differently: what is 'shire' in English we call 'county' in French.[32] I shall name them all in order, because I know them all well.

Kent is the very first of them: the archbishopric is there in the city of Dorobelle,[33] which is called Canterbury. There is also a bishopric in the city of Rochester. Sussex is the name of the next region,[34] and it is adorned with a bishopric; Chichester is the county town, and the episcopal seat is there. The third county was Surrey, and the fourth Hampshire. Here there is a bishopric in the city of Winchester. The fifth is called Berkshire,[35] the sixth Wiltshire, where there is a bishopric whose seat is in Salisbury. The seventh region is Dorset, and then the eighth is Somerset. The bishopric is in Bath, whose seat was in Wells.[36] This Bath once had another name, as the Saxons tell who first settled it: they called it Akeman Street.[37] The ninth is Devonshire, and is a very fine rich county; it has a powerful bishopric whose seat is in Exeter.

The tenth is Cornwall, and these people are fierce in battle. Corineus settled it, the man who chased out all the giants.[38] The eleventh is called Essex, and Middlesex the twelfth. Its bishopric is of London, which has been a city since antiquity.[39] Suffolk is the thirteenth, and Norfolk the fourteenth; now the bishopric is in Norwich, that was once in Thetford. The county of Cambridge is counted as the fifteenth.

Here is the bishopric of Ely; the city sits in marsh that supplies it so well, with frequent good fish, and fowls and venison; they catch these in the marsh. The sixteenth is very famous, this being the county of Lincoln[shire].[40] It is a very powerful bishopric, for eight counties belong to it: Lincoln and Northampton, Hertford and Huntingdon, Leicester and Bedford, Buckingham and Oxford. So it is a very rich bishopric, and two rivers surround it: the lesser is called Humber, and the greater one is the Thames. The twenty-fourth is Gloucester, and the twenty-fifth is Worcester; the bishopric of Worcester is the pride of this county.

---

[32] 'romanz' meant French (sc. based on Roman), before it became used for 'romance' as story.

[33] See IPN: Dorobelle, a supposed name for Canterbury, does not appear in the Middle English list. But in *GL* (Supp) the name Dorroburnence is glossed as *Durovernum*, Canterbury's Latin name (p. 371, and note to line 105).

[34] Sussex is a county, but the writer calls it 'cuntree'; cf. 'païs' for the county of Dorset in v. 89.

[35] The verb is sometimes plural 'apelent', meaning 'they call it'; cf. 'apele um' (one calls it) in v. 105.

[36] There is still a bishop of Bath and Wells.

[37] The IPN notes confusion with a Roman road-name (Bath was called something like this at one time).

[38] Legend has it that when Brutus arrived in Britain it was inhabited only by giants. The invaders cleared them all out; see Wace's *Brut* (ed. and tr. Weiss), vv. 1063–168 (pp. 28–31). A separate legend was written as a prequel to the *Brut*, to explain how the giants got there in the first place (see *Des Grantz Geantz*, Dean 36–41; a version is presented below).

[39] Not many now remember being taught that London is the capital or county town of Middlesex.

[40] AB (pp. 32–3) notes this incorrect description of Lincolnshire. Many of the following names are written as if they were the towns and not the counties.

Le .xx. e .vi. est Hereford
Qui de l'evesquié est plus fort,
Kar mult en sunt reduté
Qui mainent dedenz la cité.   140
Le .xx. e .vii. Salopesire,
Le vint e uitme Cestresire;
[138a]
Dedenz Cestre la cité
Si a mult bel evesquié.   144
Warewic est vint e nof,
E Stafford .xxx., qui est aprof.
Derebi est trente e un
Od le païs tut envirun.   148
Notingehame le cunté
A trente dous est acunté.
Everwic est trente treis,
Chief est devers les Norreis;   152
Cité est d'antiquitét,
Iloc si est l'arcevesquét
D'Engleterre la meillur;
Iloc est, ben le savum.   156
La lungur est de Toteneis
Desci tresqu'en Cateneis,
Sifaitement le nus descrist
Belins qui mesurer le fist.   160
Le cunté de Norhumberlande
Est acunté a .xxx.iiii.,
E la si unt tut aturné
De Durelme l'evesqué.   164
La terre de Cumberlant
Od tute Westmerilant
Al derain unt tut acunté;
La ad nuvel evesqué.   168
Issi cum jo vus ai mustré,
En Engleterre est acunté
A sul dous arcevesquiez
E a dis e set evesquiez.   172
Asez i ad plusurs citez

U il n'i ad nul evesquiez,
Que Oxenefort que Leïrcestre,
Que Warewic que Gloecestre;   176
Plusurs en peusse numer,
Meis ne me quier tant travailler!
[138b]
Mais de Guales parlerai,
De cez de la vus dirai.   180
En Wales ot plusurs citez
Que mult par furent renumez
Cum Carwein e Karliun
E la cité de Snaudun,   184
E la si ot .v. evesquez
E un autre arcevesquez.
De cez n'i ad ore remés for treis;
De cez vus dirai les faiz.   188
A Saint David en est li uns
Qui jadis fud a Karliuns;
Ço fud jadis arcevesquié,
Ore si est povre evesquié.   192
L'autre est a Bangor recetez,
A Clamorgan si est li tierz.
Ne sunt en nule cité,
Par la guerre sunt deserté.   196
Mais neporquant ben savom
Que li evesques ot pallium
De Saint David, sil deraisnad;
Ben le savum, a Rome alat.   200
Ore n'i a cité remis,
Kar destruit est tut le païs,
Premierement par les Seisuns,
Puis par la guere des Bretuns;   204
De l'autre part puis que Franceis
Vencu orent les Engleis
E orent cunquis la terre
Par feu, par faim e par guerre.   208
L'eve passerent de Saverne,
As Waleis si murent guerre.

The twenty-sixth is Hereford, whose bishopric is very strong: those who live in the city are greatly respected for it. The twenty-seventh is Shropshire,[41] the twenty-eighth Cheshire. In the city of Chester there is a very fine bishopric. Warwick is twenty-nine, and Stafford the thirtieth comes after it. Derby is thirty-one, with the country all around it. The county of Nottingham is counted as the thirty-second. York is thirty-three, and its capital faces in the direction of Norway.[42] It has been a city since ancient times. Here is the best archbishopric in England; it is here, as we know.[43] The length of it is from Totnes all the way to Caithness. That is how Belin describes it, who had it measured.[44] The county of Northumberland is counted as the thirty-fourth, and the whole bishopric of Durham is established here. The region of Cumberland, with the whole of Westmorland, counts as the last, where there is a new bishopric. So, as I have told you, there are in England only two archbishoprics, and seventeen bishoprics. There are quite a lot of cities where they have no bishop, such as Oxford and Leicester, Warwick and Gloucester ... more than I can name, because I don't want to make so much work for myself!

But I'll tell you about Wales, and say what they are there. In Wales there are many cities that used to be very famous, such as Caerwent and Caerleon, and the city of Caer Saint.[45] There are five bishoprics, and another archbishopric. Of these, there are only three left, and I will tell you how it is. One of them is at St Davids, which used to be at Caerleon; this was once an archbishopric, and is now a poor bishopric.

The next has its abode at Bangor, and the third is at Llandaff. None of them is in a city, having been wasted by war. Nevertheless, we do know that the bishop had the *pallium* for Saint Davids, and defended it; we are well aware that he went to Rome.[46] Now there is no city remaining, for the whole country was destroyed: first, by war with the Saxons, and then by war with the British. Then again, it is because the French had conquered the English, and overcome the land with fire and famine and war. They passed over the river Severn and took the war into Wales.

---

[41] In the days before modern post-codes for addressing letters and so on, the proper abbreviation for the county of Shropshire was 'Salop.', another forgotten relic of old names for places. The Middle English list of shires and hundreds, cited above, spells it 'Slobschire'.

[42] 'Norreis' can mean either the Norse, or simply people of the North (see *AND*). Therefore it is not clear whether this is a city of Northerners or a city facing Norway. Likewise, 'chief' may mean it is the capital, or the top of it is near to Norway.

[43] This gesture of praise may 'imply that the status of the York archbishopric is superior to that of Canterbury' (see LJ pp. 21–2, and note 22 for this twelfth-century rivalry).

[44] Belin and his brother Brenne were kings of Britain; their story is found in Wace's *Brut*, and they reappear in the *Roman des Franceis* (below). Belin's name is immortalised in the place of his burial: Billingsgate (*Wace's Brut*, ed. and tr. Weiss, pp. 82–3). The dimensions of Yorkshire are wrong: see LJ p. 22.

[45] The old name is a form of 'Snowdon'.

[46] It was necessary to travel to Rome to receive this official (arch)bishop's mantle.

De la terre mult cunquistrent
E mult grieves leis i mistrent, 212
Kar les Galeis enchacerent,
Des lur la terre herbergerent
[138c]
E si i firent mult chastels
Qui mult par sunt e bons e bels. 216
Mais nepurquant suventesfeiz
Ben s'en vengerent les Waleis.
De noz Franceis mult unt ocis,
De noz chastels se sunt saisiz; 220
Apertement le vont disant,
Forment nus vont maneçant,
Qu'a la parfin tute l'avrunt,
Par Artur la recoverunt, 224
E cest païs tut ensement
Toldrunt a la romaine gent,
A la terre sun nun rendrunt
Bretaine la repelerunt. 228
De Wales ore nus tarrum,
Des chemins si parlerum
Qui furent fait en cest païs;
Faire les fist li reis Belins. 232
Li premerain vait dés orient
Desci que vient en occident;
Cist traverse le païs,

Ikenild ad nun li chemins. 236
L'autre sulunc les Seissuns
Erningestrate or l'apeluns;
Cel chemin est ben cuneud,
Del north vait dreit el suth. 240
Li tierz si est mult renumé,
Watlingestrate est apelé;
A Dovre comence cest chemin,
Dreit en Cestre si prent fin; 244
Del païs purprent la lungur.
Li quarz si est mult encumbrus;
Cest chemin est Fosse apelez,
Si vait par multes citez; 248
Cel cumence en Totenes
[138d]
E dure tresqu'en Kateneis;
.Viii. cenz liues i sunt cuntez.
Cest chemin est mult renumez. 252
Belins, ki faire les fist,
En grant franchise les mist:
Quikunques dechaciez esteit,
En cez chemins sa peis aveit. 256
Descrit vus avum les cuntez
Del païs e les evesquez,
E des chemins les .iiii. nuns.
Or aïtant le vus larruns. 260

They conquered much of the land, and put harsh laws in place: they chased out the Welsh and settled the land with their own people, and they made many castles — very powerful and fine. However, the Welsh frequently took vengeance! They killed many of our Frenchmen, and seized our castles. They go round saying openly, fiercely threatening us, that in the end they will have the whole lot back! They will recover it with the help of Arthur,[47] and they will take the entire country away from the French-speaking people.[48] They will give the country back its name, and call it Britain again. Now I shall leave off about Wales, and talk about the roads that were made in this country.

King Belin had them made. The first one goes from the East, whence it comes to the West. It crosses the country, and is called Icknield. The next, according to the Saxons, we now call Ermine Street; this road is very well known, and it goes straight from the North to the South. The third is very famous, and is called Watling Street; this one begins at Dover and goes all the way to Chester where it ends. So it crosses the whole length of the country. The fourth is called Fosse Way; it gets very clogged up, because it goes through many cities. It begins at Totnes and runs all the way to Caithness — a distance of eight hundred leagues![49] A very famous road. Belin, who had them made, endowed them with special privileges: anybody who is exiled will have the King's peace on these roads.[50]

I have described the counties of the land, with their bishoprics, and the four names of the roads. And there I must now leave you.

---

[47] Legend has it that King Arthur sleeps until he is needed by his people.

[48] 'la romaine gent'.

[49] A league is a varying measure, usually about three miles. Late Latin *leuga, leuca*, of Gaulish origin (*OED*).

[50] Nothing must stand in the way of exiled people finding their way out of the land as quickly as possible. In (for example) *The Mirror of Justices*, the passage on Sanctuary mentions how exiles and outlaws ought to be treated (pp. 33–5).

The French Chronicle of London[51]

Some excerpts from this chronicle,[52] headed 'Croniques de London, depuis l'an
44 Hen. III jusqu'à l'an 17 Edw. III' on its title-page, have been added to this book
out of the order chosen by Dean.[53] This is because the very 'romantic' *Des Grantz
Geanz* will make a suitable piece with which to end this chapter and lead into
the next. Not that the *Chronicle* is unromantic: in the first passage chosen, the
story of Fair Rosamond was clearly added for a readership far more interested in
romantic fiction, rivalling the most lurid of modern media scandals that involve the
Royal Family from that day to this, than in genuine lists of mayors and sheriffs.[54]
Further, many parts of the *Chronicle* are taken from one of the *Brut* texts that were
so well known in England.[55] One of the prophecies of Merlin was known and, after
a fashion, acted upon: in the year xi Edward I (1282–3) Llewellyn Prince of Wales
was taken in battle and beheaded. His head was placed on a lance, crowned with
a silver circlet. This was to fulfil or to ridicule the prediction of Merlin, who told
the prince that one day his head would parade through Cheapside adorned with
a silver coronet.[56] Some London chronicles were planned as *Brut* continuations;
it is probable this one originally began in the year 1189 when, as popular belief
would have it, the commune was first established and the first mayor elected. The
audience for this kind of chronicle, which so mixes annalistic history with tabloid
gossip, may be envisaged as the Londoners who idolize the King's favourite (perhaps
even copying her hair-style), who mistrust the 'foreigners' at court, who are familiar
with Merlin's prophecies (as if they were regularly copied among horoscopes on the
back page), who gather open-mouthed to watch the translation of a saint (perhaps
hoping to touch the holy casket), and grumble about salty beer at times of flood.

It should be noted at the outset that the *Chronicle* is arranged by regnal year,
counting from the day of the monarch's coronation (or accession). But the *Liber*
from which it takes some of its material, and which both its editor and its translator
consult for footnotes, is arranged by civic year, that is from one Michaelmas

---

[51] Dean 71.

[52] ed. Aungier, and see Legge pp. 302–3. It is edited from BL, Cotton Cleopatra A vi; the
handwriting of the MS indicates that it was compiled around the middle of the fourteenth century.
The text is available online, but I copied the following extracts from the printed book. As well as
being available online (see bibliography), a searchable version is available on the Anglo-Norman
Hub, together with some of the ANTS publications.

[53] A full translation of the *Chronicle* was made in 1863 (*Chronicles of the Mayors and Sheriffs*, tr.
Riley); it is less well known than the text itself, being mentioned in neither Legge nor Dean; I
have consulted but not copied it. However, Riley's volume also contains a translation of the *Liber
de Antiquis Legibus*, one of the sources for our chronicle, which is very useful for comparison.

[54] A comprehensive account of the Rosamond legend, including a reference to this *Chronicle*, may
be found in Weir, *Eleanor of Aquitaine*: see pp. 171, 175, 219, 225 (and index).

[55] Cox, 'The French Chronicle of London', analyses this Brut source (dated c. 1333) in the *Chronicle*
(esp. p. 206; the 'Brut' in question is here printed in plain type, not italic).

[56] *Chronicle* p. 18 and note (Riley p. 240).

(29th September) to the next; the date when the sheriffs were elected.[57] Therefore some dates do not appear to fit, if they have been copied or calculated wrongly: Edward's proclamation and Isabel's landing, in the second extract below, are both dated after the end of the regnal year but before Michaelmas, so they do in fact come into the year 1325–6.

Like many of the texts here presented, this *Chronicle* deserves to be better known.[58] I have chosen three passages as widely differing as possible:[59] the year containing the scandal of poor Rosamond,[60] a year in which the doings of another queen are interspersed with titbits of local gossip, and a year in which the Channel Islands are mentioned as part of the wars with the French. The Hundred Years War was proverbial in Guernsey into modern times, becoming a byword for a long-drawn-out legal case.[61]

As usual, I have copied the French text as exactly as possible with very minor modernization; I have added line numbers, and the editor's notes where they shed light on the events of the year in question. Folio numbers are not provided in the edition.

---

[57] Riley, p. xii.

[58] See, first, Prestwich, *Plantagenet England 1225–1360*, for the period covered by this chronicle. *Dictionary of the Middle Ages*, ed. Strayer, is very useful for specific items (entries are alphabetical, so any volume could be the one to consult). My thanks are due to Andy King for advice, especially on dating in the extracts below.

[59] Riley's translations of these passages are on his pp. 231–4, 260–2, & 272–5 respectively.

[60] As mentioned earlier, I have tried to choose passages cross-generically: this tale, inserted into a city annal, resembles the martyrdom of a female saint (cf. the folk-tale in *Protheselaus*; the *Chronicle's* editor considers the Rosamond story to be a folk-tale). The present version may be the earliest known (Riley's Introduction, p. xi); it is evidence of readers' appetite for such stories that they appear in such unlikely contexts. I make no attempt to examine the *Chronicle* as historiography.

[61] In Edwards, *Ebenezer Le Page*: a bitter complaint against doctors and lawyers (this sentiment is widespread) is followed by references to the capture of Guernsey by the French (p. 54).

Text

xlvii Henry III[62]

(p. 2) Thomas fitz Thomas, meir. Robert de Mounpelers et   7
Hubert de Suffolk, vicountes.[63]
En cele an comensa la guerre entre le roy et ses barouns pur les
purveaunces d'Oxenford. Adonk fu pris l'evesk de Hereford
par les barouns. Cele an fut la novele sale de Weimouster ars.
(p. 3) Cele an fut la reyne vileinement escriré et ledengé à le Pount
de Loundres, sicome ele voleit aler del Tour a Weymouster,
pur ce qe ele avoit fait occire une gentile damoysele, la plus
bele qe homme savoit, et luy mist sure qe ele estoit la concubine le roy. Par quey la reyne luy fist prendre et despoiller   5
tut nue, et luy fist seer entre deus grauntz fues en une chaumbre mult ferm clos, si qe la tresbele damoysele estoit mult es-
pountée, qar ele quidoit bien daver estre ars, si comenza graunt
deol demesner. Et endementers la roygne avoit fait faire une
baigne, si fist la bele damoisele leinz entrer, et meintenaunt fist   10
une mauveise vielle ferir la bele damoisele ove une launce en
ambe deus les bras, et si tost come le saunk hors sailist vint une
autre escomengée sorceresse, si porta deus horribles crapaudes
sure une troboille, si les mist sure les mameles au gentile damoisele, et taunttost seiserent les mameles et comenserent à leiter.   15
Et deus autres vielles tindrent ses braz estendues, qe la bele
damoisele ne poeit en l'eawe avaler, taunqe le saunk q'estoit
en son corps fust hors curru. Et totdis les ordes crapaudes
les mameles de la tresbele damoisele leterent, et la roygne riaunt
totdis le moka, et out graunt joye en queor, qe ele estoit ensy   20
vengée de Rosamonde. Et quaunt ele fu morte, si fist prendre
le corps et en une orde fossée enterer, et les crapaudes oveske
le corps. Mais quaunt le roy avoit entendu les noveles, coment
la roygne avoit faite de la tresbele damoisele q'il taunt ama et
taunt chiere avoit en queor, graunt deol demesna et graunt   25
(p. 4) lamentacion fist:

---

[62] This year is, according to Cheney, *A Handbook of Dates*, ed. Jones, 28th October 1262 to 27th October 1263. There is an online calculator for regnal years (http://people.albion.edu/imacinnes/calendar/Regnal_Years.html). The entry for this year is found on pp. 2–5 of the edition.

[63] The arms of each mayor and sheriff are described in the footnotes.

Translation

Henry III and Fair Rosamond

Thomas Fitz-Thomas, Mayor.

Robert de Mounpelers and Hubert de Suffolk, sheriffs.

In this year began the war between the king and his barons, because of the Provisions of Oxford.[64] Then the Bishop of Hereford was taken by the barons.[65]

In this year the new hall of Westminster was burned.[66]

In this year the queen was disgracefully provoked[67] and slandered at London Bridge, as she was making her way from the Tower to Westminster,[68] because she had had a gentle damsel murdered, the most beautiful any man had ever seen, and she accused her of being the king's concubine.[69] Therefore the queen had her taken and stripped, and put between two huge fires in a room that was locked fast; the lovely girl was terrified, thinking she was going to be burned, and began to cry pitifully. And then the queen had a bath prepared, and forced the lovely girl into it; now she makes a foul old woman strike the beautiful young woman with a lance, in both arms. As soon as the blood starts to burst forth, then comes another cursed witch, she is carrying two horrible toads on a shovel. She puts them on the gentle lady's breasts! Immediately, they seize the nipples and begin to milk her! Two other old hags hold her arms stretched out, so that the sweet lady can't sink in the water until all the blood in her body has run out. All the while the filthy toads are sucking at the lovely lady's breasts, and the queen laughs, mocking her the while. She is overjoyed to have got her revenge thus on Rosamond. When she was dead, she had the body taken and buried in a dirty ditch, and the toads with her.

But when the king heard the news, what the queen had done to the lovely girl that he so loved and cherished in his heart, he mourned and made great lamentation:

---

[64] These Provisions, extorted from Henry the Third by Simon de Montfort, led to a civil war (editor's note).

[65] Peter de Egeblaunch, or Egueblank, a Frenchman (the note remarks on the unpopularity of the French among the barons).

[66] The note says a Latin account of this event is recorded for 7th February 1262 (see also Riley pp. 54–5). However, Andy King has judged that this note incorrectly inserts '1262' into the Latin account: the fire was in February 1263.

[67] 'escrire' corresponds to no entry in *AND*; the nearest being 'escrire' (to write). But its meanings do not include 'libel', and therefore I take the verb to be 'escrier', to cry out upon, accuse, or provoke (Larousse). Riley says 'hoot'.

[68] The note dates this occurrence as 14th June, and describes the unpleasant things that were thrown at the queen (named Eleanor, as Henry II's queen was). She may have been unpopular only because of her 'foreign' relations (Brooke, *From Alfred to Henry III, 871–1272*, p. 227); Riley suggests their 'avarice' was to blame (note on his p. 232). Andy King tells me other sources date it as 13th July 1263 (see also Prestwich p. 112 for the attack).

[69] The note remarks that this story, abridged from some romance or legend, was erroneously supposed by the writer to refer to Henry III instead of Henry II. See Cox, pp. 201–2.

'Allas! dolent! qe fray pur la tresbele Rosa-
monde? qar unkes son pierre ne fust trovée de beaute, naturesse,
et cortesie.' Et quaunt lungement avoit fait tiele lamentacion,
il voleit savoir où le corps de la bele damoisele fust devenu.
Lors fist le roy prendre une des mauveises sorceresses, et la fist   5
mettre en graunt destresse, pur luy counter tot la verité come
avoyent fait de la gentile damoisele, et jurra par Dieu omnipotent qe si nul parole mentit qe ele avera auxint vile jugement
come homme purra ordeiner. Lors comenza la vielle à parler
et counter au roy tot la verité, coment la roigne avoit fait de la   10
tresbele corps au gentil damoysele, et où e en quele lieu l'en la
troveroit. Et endementiers la roygne fist prendre sus le corps
de la tresbele damoisele, et comaunda amener le corps à une
mesoun de religioun qe aad a noun Godestowe près de Oxenford
à deus luwes, et illoqes le corps Roseamond enterer pur colurer   15
ses mauveise faitz, si qe nully aparcevereit les ordes et trop
vileines faitz qe la roygne avoit fait, et de ele excuser de la
mort la tresgentile damoisele. Et lors le roy Henry comensa
de chivacher vers Wodestoke là où Rosamonde q'il taunt ama
en queor estoit si trecherousment murdriz par la roigne. Et   20
sicome le roy chivacha vers Wodestoke, si encountra le corps
mort de Rosamounde enclos fortement dedeinz une ciste bien
et fortement liée de fer. Et le roy meintenaunt demaunda quey
corps çeo estoit, et quele noun avoit le corps mort q'ils amenerent.
Lors luy respondirent qe çeo estoit le corps la tresbele Rosa-   25
mond. Et quaunt le roy Henry çeo oyist, si comaunda erraument de overir le cyste q'il purreit veer le corps qe si vilement
estoit martirée. Lors meintenaunt firent le comaundement le
roy, et luy mostrerent le corps Rosamond, qe estoit si hidouse-
ment mis à mort. Et quaunt le roy Henri vist tot la verité, pur   30
graunt dolur à tere paumist et lungement jeust en traunce avant
qe homme poeit avoir parler de luy. Et quaunt le roy reveilla
de son paumysoun, si dist et jurra à graunt serment, qe bien se
vengereit de la très orde felonie qe au gentile damoysele fu faite
(p. 5) par graunt envie. Lors comensa le roy à waymenter et graunt
deol à demener pur la tresbele Rosamounde, q'il taunt ama en
queor. 'Allas! dolente!' fist il, 'douce Rosamonde, unkes
ne fust ta pere, si douce ne si bele creature ne fust unkes trovée:

'Alas! ah, wretched! What can I do for fair Rosamond? Never was her like ever seen, for beauty and good nature and courtesy!' And when he had lamented in this way for a long time, he wanted to know what had become of the lovely lady's body.

Then the king had one of the wicked sorceresses taken up, and put to torture so that she would tell the whole truth of what they had done to the gentle lady, and he swore by God Almighty that if she lied by one single word she would be subjected to the vilest punishment that could be devised. Then the old hag began to speak, and told the king the whole truth: what the queen had done to the lovely lady's body, and where and in what place it might be found.

So the queen immediately had the body of the lovely lady fetched up, and ordered this body to be taken to a religious house named Godstow, some two leagues out of Oxford. There they were to bury Rosamond's body, to cover up her wicked deeds,[70] so that none would know the horrible and most shameful deeds that the queen had done, and to clear herself of the sweet lady's death.

Then King Henry rode forth to Woodstock, and he met the dead body of Rosamond sealed up in a strong casket well and truly bound with iron. Now the king asks what body this is, and the name of the dead body they are carrying. They reply that it is the body of fair Rosamond. When King Henry hears this, he immediately orders them to open the casket so that he can see the body of Rosamond who has been so shamefully martyred.[71] They obey the king's order right away, and show him the body of Rosamond who has been so cruelly put to death. When King Henry saw the full truth, he fell to the ground in agony; he lay unconscious for a long time before anybody could get a word out of him.[72] When he awoke from his swoon he spoke, and swore a great oath that he would avenge the disgraceful felony that was perpetrated because of great jealousy upon the gentle lady.[73] The the king began to lament and make great mourning for the fair Rosamond, whom he loved so deeply.

'Alas! ah, poor darling', he cried, 'sweet Rosamond, you had no peer, never was seen so gentle and lovely a creature!

---

[70] 'colour' is a word also found in *The Mirror of Justices*, meaning excuse or pretence, covering or 'colouring' something to look better (the glossary to *Sir Ferumbras*, ed. Herrtage, gives evidence of its use in Middle English). In this sentence 'her' deeds are of course the queen's.

[71] Parallels with a saint's life (and death) abound in this version of the story: a female saint is often stripped as well as beaten or tortured; the word 'martyr' makes the narrator's opinion clear.

[72] An example of a strong man fainting for grief, as happens in romance (it is a mark of strength, not of weakness).

[73] The story illustrates the evil resulting from the sin of jealousy (as elsewhere in medieval narrative); we are not told what punishment, if any, is meted out to the wicked queen.

ore douce dieux qe meint en trenite, del alme douce Rosamonde   5
en eyt mercy et luy pardoint touz ses meffaitz; verray Dieu
omnipotent, qe estes fyn et comensement, ne suffrez jà l'alme
en nul horrible peine estre perii, et luy doigne verray remissioun
de tous ses pecchez, pur ta graunt mercy.' Et quaunt çeo out
pryée, il comaunda meintenaunt de chivacher avant droit à   10
Godestowe ove la corps de la meschyne, et là fist faire son
sepulture en ceste religiouse mesoun de nonaynes, et illuques
ordeina tresze chapeleins à chaunter pur l'alme la dite Rosamonde taunqe le siecle dure. En ceste religious mesoun de Godestowe, vous die pur verité, gist la bele Rosamonde ensevely.   15
Verray dieux omnipotent de s'alme en eit mercy. Amen.

xix Edward II[74]

(p. 49) Hamon de Chikewelle, meir.
Gilbert de Mordone et Johan Cotoun, viscountes.
En le mesme temps fut cryé par le roy qe nul homme portoit
lettres de la reygne, ne de son fitz heir d'Engeltere, qe adonkes
furent en les parties de Fraunce, et si nul porteit lettre qe il   5
fut attaché, et celuy à qi la lettre irreit, et q'ils fussent amenez
devant le roy et son counseil. En cele temps la reyne usa
simple apparaille come dame de dolour qe avoit son seignour
perdue. Et pur langwis q'ele avoit pur maintener la pées, le
commune poeple mult la plenoit. En cele an, le dymeygne   10
prochein devant le conversioun seint Poul, un sire Roger Belers,
justice le roy et graunt seignour, fut occys près de Leycestre,
dont graunt clamour y fut, et mult des gentz enprisonez. En
cele temps fut sire Henry de Beaumond et autres grauntz de
poer attachez et enprisonez par le roy, pur çeo q'ils ne voleient   15
acorder de faire la volunté sire Hughe Despencer le fitz. Et
donk le roy par se[s] conseilers fit estover le tour de Loundres et
autres chastels de vitaille.

---

[74] Cheney's table (see heading of previous passage) gives this regnal year as 8th July 1325 to 7th July
1326. The passage is on pp. 49–51 of the edition.

Now sweet God abiding in Trinity have mercy on the soul of sweet Rosamond, and pardon her all her misdeeds. True God Almighty, thou that art the beginning and end of all things, never suffer the soul to perish in horrible torment, and grant her true remission of all her sins, by thy great mercy.'[75]

When he had made this prayer, he gave the order to ride straight to Godstow with the body of the maiden, and there had a sepulchre made in this holy house of nuns, and there established that thirteen chaplains should sing [Mass] for the soul of the said Rosamond as long as this world shall endure. I tell you truly that in this religious house of Godstow the body of Fair Rosamond lies buried. May the true God Almighty have mercy on her soul. Amen.[76]

Edward II and London Gossip

Hamo de Chigwell, Mayor.

Gilbert de Mordone and John Cotoun, Sheriffs.

At this time the king had it proclaimed that no man must carry letters for the queen, nor for her[77] son the heir of England, who were now in regions of France. If anybody carried letters, let him be taken up together with whomever the letter was directed to, and let them be brought before the king and his council. In those days the queen wore simple apparel, as a mourning lady who has lost her lord. Because of the suffering she endured for the keeping of the peace, the common people sorrowed greatly for her.[78]

In this year, on the Sunday next before the Conversion of Saint Paul,[79] one Sir Roger Belers, a king's justice and a great lord, was killed near Leicester.[80] This caused a great outcry, and many were imprisoned.

During this time, Sir Henry de Beaumond and other powerful lords were taken and imprisoned by the king, because they would not agree to do the will of Hugh Despenser the younger. So then the king, at his councillors' advice, had the Tower of London and other castles provisioned.

---

[75] The writer mixes 'tu' and 'vos' forms as though a distinction were not important.

[76] The familiar version of the story has the murder taking place at Woodstock, but in this version there is no mention of the maze into which Eleanor penetrates nor the choice of death she offers to the girl. However, to this day Rosamond is said to be buried at Godstow; the ruins of the nunnery stand near the river just outside modern Oxford (two leagues would have been measured from the city centre).

[77] 'son', her or his son. This difference between French and English grammar may be noted several times, below.

[78] See Prestwich, pp. 213–14. Here, as elsewhere in this chronicle, the importance of popular opinion is stressed.

[79] That is, the Sunday before 25th January (see *ODS*).

[80] Notes in the edition and in Riley give more detail of this incident.

Et sire Hughe Despencer le fitz fist
prendre touz les carpenters et masouns et fevres qe adonk
estoient en Loundres, et par tut entour, si fist faire sus touz   20
les turettes et kerneux en la tour, et à totes les portes illoqes,
barrer et bretaxer del plus grosse meryn qe par mi Engeltere
puet estre trovée, et fit faire magneles, springaldes, et autres
maners engins, à graunt costage, et rien ne luy valust, kar son
propos fust bestourné en autre manere, et tot çeo fu faite pur   25
doute de la venue d'estraunge en la companie la reigne. En
cele an, le surveille de la chaundelure à nuit, fut mis seint
Erkenwolde en sa novele fertre en l'eglise seint Poule. Lors
(p. 50) comaunda le roy qe sire William de Hermine, eveske de Norwiz,
doit estre tenu pur traitour, et le roy luy mist sure q'il fut enchesoun qe la reigne se tenist et son fitz en les parties de Fraunce.
Et le comune poeple pleinout mult le dit William Hermyn, pur
çeo qe il fut prodhomme, et mult avoit travailée pur mayntener   5
l'estat de la tere. Adonk fut le roy à Dovere, et messagers de
l'apostoile vindrent là à luy, et ils retournerent ove lour respounce prevément, qe comune parlaunce ne fust pur quey ils
vindrent ne quele respounce ils avoyent. En cele an fut graunt
secheresse de rivers et de fountaigne, issint qe il avoit graunt   10
defaute de ewe en plusours paiis. En cele temps, devant le
feste seint Johan, ardoit la vile de Roiston et partie de Wandles-
worth, l'abbeye de Croxtone pres de Leicestre, et autres
arsouns furent adonke en Engeltere. En cele temps, pur defaute de ewe douce, la mer surmonteit issint qe le ewe de Tamyse   15
fut salé, dont mult de gentz se pleinoient de la servoyse fut salé.
En cele temps, à le sein Barnabé, les Engleisse conquistrent la
tere de Gascoigne, qe le roy de Fraunce avoit chivauché, issint
qe plusours gentz furent occys, pur quey le roy fist cryer le
jour de seint Margarete qe nul Fraunceis deit marchaunder en   20
Engeltere, ne venir en ces parties, et contient en le dit cri qe la
reigne d'Engeltere ne doit estre apellé reigne.

And Hugh Despenser the younger had all the carpenters and masons and smiths gathered, who were then in London or all round about, and he had all the turrets and crenellations of the Tower done up; as for all the gates there, they were barred and reinforced with the strongest timber that could be got anywhere throughout England. And he had mangonels and catapults and all manner of other engines made, at great expense. But all this achieved nothing, for his plans went awry; all this was done for fear of the arrival of foreigners in the queen's company.

In this year, two days before Candlemas, Saint Erkenwald was put into his new tomb in the church of St Paul during the night.[81]

Then the king proclaimed that Sir William de Hermine, bishop of Norwich, was to be regarded as a traitor, and the king accused him of being the reason why the queen remained with her son in France.[82] The common people greatly mourned the said William Hermine, for he was a gentleman and had worked hard to maintain the good of the land.

Then the king was at Dover, where messengers came to him from the Pope; they went back again secretly with their reply, so that there would be no common talk about why they had come and what reply they had had.

In this year there was a great drought in the rivers and fountains, so that there was a severe lack of water in many areas.

During this time, before the feast of Saint John,[83] the town of Roiston burned, as did part of Wandsworth; also the abbey of Croxton near Leicester, and there were many other fires around England.[84]

During this time, for lack of fresh water the sea came up so far that the water of the Thames became salty, and because of this many people complained the beer was salty.

At the same time, at Saint Barnabas,[85] the English conquered the land of Gascony, that the King of France had overrun, so that many people were killed. Therefore, on Saint Margaret's Day,[86] the king made a proclamation that no Frenchman was allowed to market his wares in England, nor even to come over here. In the same proclamation he said that the Queen of England should not be called queen.

---

[81] Erkenwald was the founder of Barking Abbey, whose Nun wrote a life of Edward the Confessor in the twelfth century, and was also the subject of a medieval poem (see, for example, *St. Erkenwald*, ed. Morse). The date of this translation, 1st Feb. 1326, is recorded in Erkenwald's *ODS* entry; Riley says the ceremony took place at night so as not to attract crowds of people.

[82] This man, whose name is variously spelt in the notes, had been highly regarded by Edward; he 'privately assisted [Isabel] in her wicked contrivances against her husband'.

[83] 24th June.

[84] The notes say the Croxton fire was caused by a careless plumber (on 11th June); it is possible all these fires were exacerbated by drought. The last of the words for fire in this sentence is 'arsouns', which looks like modern 'arson'; it is unlikely in view of the weather that the fires were started deliberately, but Riley chooses the word 'conflagration' here.

[85] The same day as the Croxton fire.

[86] 20th July.

En cele temps
touz les Engleisse qe furent en Fraunce furent attachez en un
jour, qe fut graunt multitude de gentz. En cele temps le dit
sire Edward, heir d'Engeltere et dame Isabele sa miere, reygne   25
d'Engeltere, acrocherent à eux graunt poer de gentz, et graunt
(p. 51) navye, de venir en Engeltere ove multz des Henaud, et lors
comaunda le roy de assembler graunt navye d'avoir destourbé
le venue son fitz et la reyne et lour companie. Mès les mariners d'Engeltere ne furent pas en volunté à destourber lour
venue, pur le graunt errour q'ils avoyent vers sire Hughe le   5
Despencer, et pristrent lour conseil d'aler en Normondie, et la
ariverent, robberent, et ardoyent, à graunt destruction de la tere,
mès multz de nos gentz Engleisse furent illoqes occys. Et lors
le meskerdi devant le feste seint Michel, qe fut par lundi, la
reigne d'Engeltere et son fitz et le Mortimer, ove graunt com-   10
panie de grauntz seignours et gentz d'armes, ariverent à Herwiche
et Orewelle en Essex, pur destrure les enemys de la tere.

xiii Edward III[87]

(p. 71) Henry Darcy, meir.   10
William Pountfreit et Hughe Marberer, vicountes.
En cele an nostre joevene roy se apparila ove graunt poer
des Engleis et de Gales, si passa la mer à Orewelle en Essex,
et ariva sus en Flaundres, et ses gentz passerent avant en le
ysle de Cagent, et tuerent touz qe leinz porroyent estre trovez,   15
et si avoyent illoqes graunt avoir, et puisse ardoient sus tot
le dit isle. Et adonke nostre joevene roy prist son host, si s'en
ala en Braban, et demorra pur long temps à Andwerp, et tint
illoqes son parlement, et là furent jurez à luy tous ceux de
Flaundres, de Braban, de Henaud, et de Alemaygne à nostre   20
joevene roy, de vivere et morir ovesqe luy en sa querele vers le
roy de Fraunce. Auxint nostre joevene roy graunta d'estre
lour lige seignour, de vivere et morir ovesqe eux et lur defendre
et meintenir vers totes gentz de mounde pur touz jours.

---

[87] pp. 71–5 in the edition. Cheney's table gives 25th January 1339 to 24th January 1340 for this
regnal year.

At this time all the English who were in France were apprehended, all in one day; this was a huge number of people.

Then at this time the said Sir Edward, heir of England, and Lady Isabel his mother the Queen of England, gathered to themselves a great force of men and a great navy, to come to England with a large number of Hainaulters. So the king commanded a large navy to assemble, so as to hinder the arrival of his son and the queen with their company.[88] But the mariners of England were not so eager to prevent their arrival, because of their violent dislike[89] of Sir Hugh Despenser, and took the decision to go into Normandy; once arrived there, they pillaged and burned, causing great destruction in the land. But many of our English people were killed there.

And then on the Wednesday before the feast of Saint Michael, that was on a Monday, the Queen of England and her son, and Mortimer, with a large company of great lords and men-at-arms, arrived at Harwich and Orwell in Essex, to destroy the enemies of the land.[90]

Edward III and the Hundred Years War

Henry Darcy, Mayor.

William Pountfreit and Hugh Marberer, Sheriffs.

In this year, our young king prepared himself, with a great army of English and Welsh, and he crossed the sea from Orwell in Essex, and arrived to land in Flanders. His men went ahead into the Isle of Cadzand, and killed everybody they found there; there was much booty to be had there, and then they burned up the whole of the said island.[91] Then our young king gathered his host and went to Brabant; he stayed at Antwerp for a long time, and held his parliament there. All those of Flanders, of Brabant, of Hainault, and of Germany were sworn to him there, to live and die with him in his quarrel with the King of France. And so our young king promised to be their liege lord, to live and die with them, and to defend and keep them for ever against all the peoples of the world.

---

[88] 'son fitz'; the boy, still in his teens, was of course the son of them both. He will be called 'the young king' throughout the next episode below.

[89] 'errour' looks like 'mistake'; but is an attested spelling for 'irur' (anger).

[90] The note gives 24th September 1326 for this arrival, and that a large body of malcontents joined the queen in spite of the king's proclamation that all should resist her landing. For dating the end of Edward II and beginning of Edward III, see Prestwich p. 217 and note (this chronicle is one of the sources). Edward II was probably murdered; but, like other figures of ambiguous reputation, he was rumoured to have survived and ended his days as a holy hermit somewhere abroad. A similar story circulated about Harold after the Battle of Hastings (see *Edouard*, p. 136; and Doherty, *Isabella and the Strange Death of Edward II*). Czar Alexander is another such (a brief account is in Colegate, *A Pelican in the Wilderness*, pp. 35–6).

[91] Cadzand was taken in November 1337 (the note cites Froissart), the year before this entry begins. Riley says that as many prisoners as possible were taken (not killed). A sketch of Froissart's account is in his *Chronicles*, ed. and tr. Brereton, pp. 57–61. Therefore 'his men went ahead' must mean 'they had gone ahead'; the action precedes Edward's arrival in Flanders. See Prestwich pp. 310–11 & 345–6 for Walter Mauny's raid.

Et
quaunt ceste alyaunce fu fait par assent des avantditz teres, sire　　　　25
Edward nostre joevene roy prist son host, si se remua de Andwerp, et comensa de chivacher sure le roy de Fraunce dedeinz
sa tere, si ardoit par tot et conquist plus qe viii^{xx}. luwes de la
tere. Et lors estoit sertein jour assigné d'aver en bataile
parentre les deux rois. Et quaunt le houre avint qe la bataile　　　　30
doit aver esté feru, Phelip de Valoys le roy de Fraunce, le qeor
(p. 72) luy chaunga, et comensa à fremir quaunt il vit nos gentz tous
prest en chaumpz batailez sertein assys, si se retrait come chivaler desleaux, et dit come coward qe son qeor luy dona
d'estre desconfit en la bataille à ycele jour. Par quey il se
retrait ove son host vers Paris, à graunt hounte de luy pur touz　　　　5
jours, et à nostre roy d'Engeltere honour et victorie pur touz
jours. Et à cele houre Phelip de Valois perdit le noun d'estre
appellé le roy de Fraunce, et à sire Edward nostre roy fust
donée le noun d'estre apellé droiturel roy de Fraunce et d'Engeltere, et fust graunté de tot le chivalrie de cristienté. Et　　　　10
adonke nostre joevene roy, le duk de Braban, le counte de
Henaud, le counte de Julers, le counte de Gerle, et plusours autres grauntz de diverses teres, se retournerent chescun
vers son paiis. Mès avaunt qe le host se departist, les Ale-
mauns riflerent les Engleiss de çeo q'ils avoyent gaigné à cele　　　　15
alée, et occyrent plusours de nos gentz. Mès sire Edward nostre roy et le duk de Braban et autres grauntz firent la graunt
conteke sesser et peser, si qe touz furent acordez. Et adonkes
le roy ove son poeple revint à Andwerp en Braban, et la demorra longe temps ove graunt conseil de touz les grauntz qe　　　　20
estoyent jurez à luy. Et unqes en le mesme temps ne osast
Phelip de Valoys ove son orgeliouse bobaunce aprocher à nostre
(p. 73) joevene roy. Mès dit à touz qe entour luy erent, qe ly suffreit
giser en pées et despendre quaunt qe il avoit, e plus qe tot son
realme d'Engeltere ne poeit suffire, issint qe luy ferroit le plus
riche roy ou le plus poveres de tot le monde. Et adonkes
nostre joevene roy prist son congée del duke de Braban, et de　　　　5
touz les grauntz de là qe à luy furent jurez, de revenir en Engeltere pur ordeiner son estat de son realme, taunqe à sertein
houre q'ils porroyent mieutz estre avengée de Phelip le Valois,
roy de Fraunce. Adonqes revint nostre roy en Engeltere, et lessa
la reigne dame Phelipe illoqes en hostage,　　　　10

And when this alliance had been made with the assent of those aforesaid lands, our young King Edward gathered his host and moved out of Antwerp, and began to ride against the King of France in his territory; he burned all over the land, and conquered more than eightscore leagues of it.[92] Then a certain day was assigned for the battle to take place between the two kings. But when the hour of battle arrived Philip de Valois, King of France, had a change of heart. He began to tremble when he saw our men drawn up all ready in the battlefield, and he withdrew like an unworthy knight, saying in most cowardly fashion that he knew in his heart he would be discomfited in battle that day. Therefore he retreated with his host towards Paris, with the deepest shame to himself for ever, and for our King of England honour and victory for ever.

In this hour did Philip de Valois lose the name by which he was called King of France, and to Sir Edward our king was given the name by which he was called the rightful King of France and England, and it was granted by all the chivalry of Christendom.[93]

And then our young king, the Duke of Brabant, the Earl of Hainault, the Earl of Juliers, the Earl of Gueldres,[94] and many other great nobles of many lands, all returned each of them towards his own land.

But before the armies separated, the Germans rifled the English of what they had gained during the expedition, and killed a number of our men. But Sir Edward our king and the Duke of Brabant and other nobles put a stop to this mighty quarrelling, and restored peace, so that all were reconciled. Then the king, with his people, came back to Antwerp in Brabant. He stayed there for a long time, with a great council of all the nobles who were sworn to him.

Never in all this time did Philip de Valois in his arrogant pomposity dare to come near our young king. But he said to all those around him that he will let him stay in peace and spend whatever he has got, and yet more than his whole realm of England could afford him, this will make him either the richest king or the poorest in all the world.

Then our young king took his leave of the Duke of Brabant, and all the nobles of that region who were sworn to him, to return to England and order the state of his kingdom until such time that they would be able to take better revenge on Philip de Valois King of France.

So then our king came back to England, and left the lady queen Philippa there as hostage,

---

[92] Allowing for hyperbole, this ought to mean some five hundred miles.

[93] See note: this is when Edward first used the motto 'Dieu et mon droit'. He continued to use the title King of France until the Treaty of Bretigny in 1360.

[94] Notes in the edition (and in Riley) explain these personages.

et ses enfauntz en la
garde le duke de Braban, et autres grauntz assocyez à luy, et
demorra à Gaunt jeske le revenue de son seignour. Et en le
mesme temps furent pris monsieur William Mountagu, counte
de Salesbury, et monsieur Robert de Offorde, counte de Suffolk,
et amenez à Paris vilement. Et adonkes le roy de Fraunce à   15
eux dit, 'A! tretours, vous serrez pendus pur çeo qe vous ne
pussetz amender le damage qe vostre roy et vous avetz fait en
ma tere.' 'Sertis, sire,' dit monsieur William Mountagu,
'vous avez le tort et nostre roy le verité, et çeo voille jeo prover vers qi qe le countredirra, cum leal chivaler ferra en es-   20
traunge tere.' Et adonke dit la royne de Fraunce jurra q'ele
ne serra jammès lée ne joyouse, si ils ne soyent vilement mis
à mort. 'Sire,' dit le roy de Beame, 'çeo serreit mult graunt
damage et folie de occyre tels seingnours; kar si il avigne qe le
(p. 74) roy d'Engeltere entre autre foithe en vostre reaume de Fraunce
et preigne ascun pere de vostre reaume, uncore put un aler en
eschaunge pur un autre de nostre amis.' Et si ariva adonkes
nostre seignour le roy à Herwiz en Suffolke, et vint à Loundres
devant le qaremme pernaunt, et illoqes demorra, et tint son   5
general parlement à Weymouster de tous les grauntz de sa
tere. Et à cele parlement vindrent messagers d'Escoce pur
demaunder pés, mès nule ne lour fust graunté. Et en le mesme
temps Phelip de Valoys fist faire tote la navie qe homme savoit
ordeiner, des galeyes, spynagtz, grosses barges, et tous les grauntz   10
niefs d'Espaygne de Normondie, et par tot où eles pussent
estre trovez, de forbarrer la venue de nostre joevene roy ariere
en sa tere, et tot le realme d'Engletere avoir pris et occys. Et
en le mesme temps graunt mal et graunt destruccion sure Engeltere fesoit. Car à le houre la vile de Suthamton et Portes-   15
mouthe furent ars nutaundre, robbez, et enportez. Et le chastel de Gerneseye pris, et les gentz leinz occys, par tresoun del
conestable du dit chastel. Mais quaunt nostre joevene roy çeo
(p. 75) oyst, et aparceust la graunt felonye et compassement de son
enemy Phelip de Valoys, il comaunda en haste qe tote son navie
d'Engletere fust prest, et chescun bien apparaillé et vitaillé à
sertein jour assis.

with the children, in the keeping of the Duke of Brabant and other great men of his entourage, and [she] remained at Ghent awaiting the return of her lord.

At this time Monsieur William Mountagu, Earl of Salisbury, and Monsieur Robert de Offorde, Earl of Suffolk,[95] were captured and led in shame to Paris. Then the King of France said to them: 'Ah, you traitors! you shall be hanged, as you are not capable of making amends for the damage that you and your king have done to my land.'

'In truth, Sir,' said Monsieur William Mountagu, 'you are wrong and our king is right. This I wish to prove against any who shall contradict me, as any loyal knight should do in a foreign land.'[96]

The the Queen of France spoke, swearing she would never be happy or joyful unless they were shamefully put to death.

'Sire,' said the King of Bohemia, 'it would be the greatest injury and folly to kill such lords as these, for if it happened that the King of England should come again into your realm of France and capture any peer of your realm, one could still go in exchange for another from among our friends.'

And thus arrived our lord the king at Harwich in Suffolk, and came to London before the start of Lent, and he stayed there and held his general parliament at Westminster with all the nobles of his land. To this parliament came messengers from Scotland seeking peace, but none was granted to them.

At the same time Philip de Valois had the biggest navy assembled that any man could command, of galleys and pinnaces and great barges, and all the big ships from Spain to Normandy wherever they could be found. [This was] to prevent the arrival of our young king back into his land, and so that the whole kingdom of England should be taken and slain. And all the while he caused dreadful harm and wrought enormous destruction to England. This was when the towns of Southampton and Portsmouth were set ablaze by night, and pillaged and [the spoils] carried off. And the Castle of Guernsey was taken, with the people inside killed, through the treason of the Constable of the said castle.[97] But when our young king heard of this, and perceived the great wickedness and machinations of his enemy Philip de Valois, he hastily commanded his whole navy to make ready, each to be prepared and provisioned for a certain set day.

---

[95] 'monsieur'; since these are titled nobles they cannot properly be called 'mister' in English. See note (and in Riley): it seems it was the Earl of Suffolk's son, not the Earl himself, who was captured on this occasion.

[96] This speech echoes not only the common epic formula that 'pagans are wrong and christians are right', but also the romance theme of single combat, body to body, for settling affairs of honour.

[97] Probably Castle Cornet. The islands were held for some three years before being recaptured by the English (see note): they were ill provided to defend themselves against so formidable a force, but they (Guernsey and Jersey) resisted the French bravely. A Latin Memorandum (August 29, 1338) reads: ... *captum fuit Castrum Cornet cum Insula de Geners, Serk, et Aulneray, per Gallos.* That is, also Sark, and Alderney.

Des Grantz Geanz[98]

> Il n'a manqué à cette victorieuse nation que des historiens, pour célébrer la
> mémoire de ses merveilles.[99]

Wace's *Roman de Brut* was (and is) immensely popular: it translates Geoffrey
of Monmouth's *Historia Regum Britanniae*, very freely, into the vernacular, and
develops the story of King Arthur. The legend that Britain was founded by men
of Trojan descent (matched by similar legends in other European countries) was
believed by many, and London is frequently termed 'New Troy' in chronicles. But
how did the giants get there, whom Brutus and his companions overthrew when
they arrived? A prequel was composed, known as *Des Grantz Geanz*: the Albina
legend.[100] It is an interesting example of a medieval story almost exclusively about
women, and not very heroic ones at that.[101] It will be seen, from the closing
portion of the text presented here, that this version does not explain how the story
of the giants was transmitted to posterity (hence my epigraph): it omits the passage,
present in the other version published in Brereton's edition, where it is explained
that Gogmagog survived to tell his history to the newcomers.[102] The proliferation
of versions of this story may be surmised by looking at the number of entries in
Dean's catalogue;[103] unsurprisingly, it was often added as a prologue to versions of
the *Brut* chronicle — itself a version or versions of the story of Britain based on
Wace's narrative.[104] Although the heading of my chapter is History, there is much
that is 'romantic' about the story of the giants.[105] It has been noted that the Latin
title *De Origine Gigantum* makes the text appear more historical; the French title
suggests a fabulous narrative.[106] For the sources of the work, or at least the chief
themes, see Brereton's pp. xxxiii–v; analogues include the story of the Danaïds.[107]

---

[98] Dean 37 (and her 36 & 38–41). The text is from *Des Grantz Geanz*, ed. Brereton (Medium
Aevum Monographs).

[99] Montesquieu, *Lettre LXXXI* (p. 139, in *Lettres Persanes*, ed. Roger).

[100] Albina is supposed to have given Britain its old name, Albion. Brereton dates the work to the
mid-thirteenth century (p. xxxii). A Latin version of it was used as a 'prolegomenon' to Geoffrey's
work (Carley, 'A Glastonbury translator').

[101] See my footnote to 'beguines', below: this word can be problematic (it is unlikely the women
are being presented as saintly in any sense). Les Beguines in Alderney patois translates 'beacons';
although historians might surmise there was once a religious house there on the headland, it is
more likely wreckers were responsible for the beacons.

[102] Gog and Magog are separate giants in *Alexander* (v. 5613, and see note to this line for studies).

[103] See also '*Des grantz geanz* — a new text fragment', ed. Tyson.

[104] Marvin, 'John and Henry III in the Anglo-Norman Prose *Brut*', esp. 169–71, gives an overview
of the complexities of this work. It was written in Anglo-Norman and translated into other
languages, and even retranslated from Latin back into Anglo-Norman.

[105] Wace's history of the British is entitled *Roman*; it is impossible to make sharp distinction between
history and romance at this period (Carley and Crick, 'Constructing Albion's Past', pp. 44–5). The
narrator of this story calls it (mostly) a 'geste'; the word often used for epic poems, and means the
'doings' of heroes (or heroines).

[106] There is no double meaning in Latin that corresponds to 'grantz' meaning both large and also
great or distinguished (cf. English 'grand'), as Evans points out in her article cited below.

[107] See *The Romance of the Rose*, tr. Horgan, note to p. 297 (on p. 349); and *OCL*.

There are a number of romance motifs, such as the unhistorical king of Greece, the rudderless boat, the lack of names (except for one special name).[108] The demons' ability to father children on mortal women resembles the story of how Merlin was begotten.[109] In vv. 13–15 we are offered a pseudo-historical precision, which is tied to precisely nothing historical, not even to Biblical events. However, at the end of the story we are firmly grounded in chronicle history, perhaps because the *Brut* narrative is coming up. Legge mentions this text briefly in her *Background* (pp. 277–8), in context of Wace's *Brut* (there is no separate discussion of his *Rou*).[110]

The short account of the giants prefacing the *Boke of Brut* known as *Castleford's Chronicle* differs substantially and unsurprisingly from the version presented here.[111] In this 'Prolog Olbyon' the king (of Syria) and his wife are both named, and so are two of the giants; no daughter rebels against her sisters; the giants survive until the coming of Brutus so that the story can be passed on to the next possessors of the land. It can be seen how widespread this legend became. The narrator of the present version attempts to woo his audience by modestly claiming not to know everything. He does not know all the daughters' names, nor where the harbour was from which they were set adrift; he points to structures made by the giants that are still to be seen; he reminds us several times of his source, especially at the end. This attitude enhances the pretended veracity of the facts he does know and is offering for our enjoyment. The parallel version of this text explains that the Brut narrative was to be recited at feasts;[112] no doubt the writer envisaged such an audience, although the story could equally have been enjoyed 'en famille' or with a few friends.

The text presented here is taken from Brereton's edition; I give the shorter version because this one accompanies *Brut* in most MSS.[113] I follow the line numbers in the edition; breaks in the numbering show where the other manuscript, on Brereton's facing page, gives more detail.[114] As far as I know mine is the first translation of this version into modern English. For further editions, translations, and criticism see Evans, 'Gigantic Origins'; Johnson, 'Return to Albion'; and Carley and Crick, 'Constructing Albion's Past'.[115]

---

[108] History cannot be written without names (Bliss, *Naming and Namelessness*, p. 5 and note 11).

[109] For more on such demons, see Curley, 'Conjuring History'.

[110] See also Bernau, 'Beginning with Albina' (I have been unable to access this volume of *Exemplaria*, but the article is summarized in the ICLS bulletin *Encomia* for 2015; I thank Linda Gowans for an abstract of it).

[111] ed. Eckhardt, in vol. I (unfortunately a promised third volume, containing notes and glossary, has not appeared).

[112] See my footnote, near the end of the text.

[113] Oxford, Bodleian Library, Rawlinson D. 329; text in *Des Grantz Geanz*.

[114] See notes in the edition. The longer version (BL, Cotton Cleopatra D ix) has been translated, but the book (*The Origin of the Giants*, tr. Mackley) is self-published and not widely available.

[115] The articles by Carley & Crick, and Evans, were republished in Carley, ed., *Glastonbury Abbey and the Arthurian Tradition* (Woodbridge, 2001).

Text

[f.8] Ci poet home saver coment
Quant et de quele gent
Les grauntz geantz vindrent
Ke Engleterre primes tindrent,
Ke lors fust nomé Albion,   5
Et qe primes mist le noun.
Ore escotez peniblement,
Et l'em vous dirra brevement
Des geantz tote la some,
Come jeo l'oi d'un sage home.   10
Aprés le comencement   13
Du mound, trois mil et neef cent
Et .lxx. aunz,   15
En Grece estoit un roi puissauntz,
Ke taunt feust pruz, noeble et feer
Ke sur touz rois aveit poer.
Reigne aveit bele et gent
De qui engendra filles trent,   20
Forment beles, qe totes crurent;
Nories ensemble furent.
Piere et mere furent grauntz,
Auxi devendrent les enfauntz.
Lour nouns ne vous sei counter,   25
Onqes ne les oi nomer,
Fors cele q'estoit eigné,
Ke mult feust bele et haut levee;
Mult estoit bele meschine:
Cele fust nomé Albine.   30
Et qaunt totes furent d'age,
As grauntz rois de graunt parage
Totes lour feilles donerent,
Et as hautz rois marierent.
Chescune out roi et fust reigne,   35
Mes par lour orgoil demeine   36
Tost aprés assemblerent,   43
Et ensemble counseillerent   44
Ke a nuli, en nule guise,   47
Nul ne feust de les soumise;   48
Mais chescun de son baroun   51

Teigne en subjection.
Feilles furent au roi de pris   55
Ke a nulli feust souzmis;
Ne ne voleient eles estre,
Ne ne voleient aver mestre,
Ne estre souz nulli destresce;
Mes touz jours estre mestresce   60
De son seignur et de quant q'il
    out.
A chescune cest conseil plout.
Si lur seignurs a lur voleir [f.8v]
Ne se voleient obeier
A faire tote lur volenté   65
De qaunt q'il ount en poesté,
Entre eux issint assurerent
Et par lour foi affermerent
Ke toutz, chescun en un jour,
Occiereit mesmes soun seignur,   70
Privément entre ses bras,
Com melz quidereit aver solaz.
Un certein jour assignerent
A faire come purparlerent.
Touz ount en volenté   75
Fors qe soulement la puisnee;
Cele ne vout mesprendre rien
Vers soun seignur, q'ele aime bien.
Qant tut lur counseil ount finee,
En lour pais sount retournee.   80
Ceste chose purparlee
Riens ne plout au puisnee,
Ke son seignur ataunt aime
Come ele fait son corps demeine.
Ele ne voleit a nule foer   85
Damage ver de son seignur;
Mes kaunt furent au parlement,
Ne les osa countredire nent;
Car, si ele eust riens contredit,
Moerdré la eussent saunz respit.   90

Translation

This is where you can find how, when, and from what people came the great giants who were the first to hold England. It was then called Albion — who gave it that name? If you will take the trouble to listen carefully, I will briefly tell you the whole story of the giants, just as I heard it from a wise man.[116]

After the beginning of the world, three thousand nine hundred and seventy years,[117] there was a mighty king of Greece. He was most worthy, noble, and fierce, and had power over all other kings. He had a beautiful and graceful queen, on whom he engendered thirty daughters — very beautiful, as everybody said — and they were brought up all together. The father and the mother were big, and so the children grew big. I can't tell you what they were called because I never heard their names,[118] except for the eldest one, very fair, and highly-bred. She was a most beautiful maiden, and she was named Albina. When they were all old enough, [the parents] gave all their daughters to magnificent kings, and married them to these high kings. Each one of them had a king, and was a queen, but because of their own pride they later got together and took counsel among themselves, that nobody at all would subject them to anybody in any way, and each would hold her husband in subjection! They were daughters of a king so powerful that he was never subject to anybody. So, nor did they want to be subject to anybody, and nor did they want to have masters or be under any constraint. Each wanted to be absolute mistress of her husband and everything he possessed. This plan pleased all of them. If their husbands didn't want to obey their will in all things within their power, then they resolved among themselves, each pledging her faith, that they would all at once, all at the same time, kill their husbands! It was to be done privately in bed, where any man would expect to find the greatest pleasure. They agreed on a day to carry out what they had planned.

They were all of one mind, excepting only the youngest. She didn't want to hurt her husband because she loved him! When they had completely finished their discussion, they all went home. But this thing they had discussed didn't please the youngest one at all, because she loved her husband as if he were her own self. She really didn't want to see any harm come to him, but when they were all talking together she didn't dare to disagree with them. For, if she disagreed with them in any way, they would slaughter her mercilessly!

---

[116] Two extra lines in the other version give a brief account of this (unidentified) man's learning. Henceforth I do not give details of the other version unless they are of interest for the sense of the story.

[117] Some chronicles pause at such moments, to give a parallel date from Old Testament history; here there is none.

[118] This is a narrator's oblique way of saying s/he does not invent anything, not even names for the daughters.

Bien li avent ke lors se tent.
Pluis tost come poeit al ostel vint;
Kaunt vist son mari son doel crust;
Et qant son seignur aperceust
K'ele feseit murne semblaunt,   95
Il la demaunda maintenaunt
Pur quoi ele est taunt dolent.
Et la dame, qe mult ert gent,
As peez son seinur s'estendi
Et en ploraunt cria merci.   100
De son trespas merci cria
Et de la treson lui counta;
Coment ses soers, a graunt tort,
Lui feseient jurer sa mort,
Ke de ceo n'aveit talent.   105
Et son seignur hastivement
Tost la prist entre ses braz,
Et beise, et fist greignor solaz
Ke fait lui aveit onqes mes.
'Dame,' fet il, 'tenez en pes,   110
Et lessez passer la dolour.'
Et l'endemain, au point du jour,   112
Ne demora graunt pece,   117
Vers son seignur, roi de Grece,
Ambedeux lour voie tindrent.
Tant erreient qu'il vindrent;   120
Mult sount au roi bien venuz,
Et tut sicome feust avenuz [f.9]
De ses filles lui ount conté.
Et le roi feust tut espounté
De ceo qe sa fille li dist.   125
Brefs et lettres escrivre fist:
Ses filles maunda erraument
Ke a lui veignent hastivement,   128

a) Et trestouz lur barouns
b) Par ses brefs fist somons.
c) Ke bien font soun
        comaundement,
d) A lui veignent hastivement[119]
Et qaunt touz furent assemblez,
Le roi les ad aresonez   130
De la mortele treson
Ke chescun de son baron,
Par graunt malice, aveient purveu,
Dont dolour lour est acreu.
Les dames sount touz espountez   135
De ceo qe sount si accoupez
De la treson dount sount arettez,
Dont ja ne serront acquitez;
Mes chescun, a soun poer,
Se voet defendre par jurer.   140
Mes riens ne vaut le contredire,
Car les rois ount si graunt ire
Ke toutz les vount mettre a mort
Pur lur malice et lur tort.
Lour piere, qe out ire graunt,   145
Taunt s'en ala aresonaunt
Et taunt les ad aresonee
Ke riens ne pout estre celee
De ceo que purveu aveient
Kant a lour counseil esteient.   150
Par lour piere, qui fust queint,
La feust chescun atteint
De cele malice purpensee;
Fors soulement la puisnee,
Ke tut conta a son seignur,   155
Ke puis la tent a graunt honour.

---

[119] These four lines are not in the other version.

It was well she did so. She hurried home as fast as she could, and when she saw her husband her distress redoubled; when her husband saw her looking so terribly unhappy he immediately asked her why she was upset. The noble lady threw herself at her lord's feet and burst into tears, begging for mercy. She asked mercy for her sin, and told him all about the treacherous plot; how her wicked sisters had made her swear to kill him, and she didn't want to! Her husband immediately snatched her into his arms, kissing her, being more affectionate than ever before.

'Lady,' he said, 'calm yourself, and let this grief go from you.' The next morning, at break of day, he didn't delay long; they both made their way to his overlord, the king of Greece, travelling until they reached him. The king welcomed them warmly, but as soon as they arrived they told him about his daughters. The king was horrified to hear what his daughter said. He had letters and documents written; he hastily summoned his daughters to come to him at once. And he sent for their husbands by letter as well; they obeyed his call and came immediately. When everybody was gathered, the king explained to them the deadly treason that each one had maliciously plotted against her husband, for which they would suffer.[120]

The ladies were dismayed to hear themselves accused of the treason for which they were being blamed, and for which they would never be forgiven. Each one tried to defend herself as best she could, by swearing, but denial was useless. The kings were so angry they wanted to put them all to death for their malice and wickedness. Their father, who was furious, began to argue so well, and set out the whole case[121] so fully, that nothing could remain hidden of what they had decided to do at their meeting. By the father, who was a clever man, each one of them was proved to be guilty of planning malice;[122] all except the youngest, who had told her husband everything — he treasured her for ever after.

---

[120] 'dolour'; the other version has 'deshonur'.

[121] 'aresonee'; the other version has 'examiné'.

[122] 'malice aforethought'; this passage abounds in legal or legal-sounding terms.

Kaunt chescune fust atteinte
De cele dolourouse pleinte,
Totes furent a dolour pris
Par lur pere et lour mariz. 160
Doné lour feust par jugement 166
Pur ceo qe a si haute gent 173
Furent totes mariez,
Ne deivent estre dampnez, 175
Ne aver nule vile mort. 176
Mes menez furent a un port 186
— Ou ceo fust ne sei counter — 188
Bien d'illoques a la meer,[123] 187
Mes qe totes furent pris
Et puis en une nef mis, 190
Ke estoit fort et graunde, [f.9v]
Saunz governaile et viaunde.
Illoqes graunt doel y ount demené,
Mes nul n'aveit d'eux pité,
Pur lour graunt iniquité 195
Ke feust entre eux purparlé.
En la meer la neef botirent;
Les oundes la nef chacerent
En grant peril, ça et la;
De la terre les esloigna. 200
En graunt dolour sount ore mis
Ke exillez sont de lour pais,
Dount furent riches reignes —
Ore sount povres begeines.
Ne sevent queu part il devendrent, 205
Si mortz ou vifs eschaperount.
Cestes dames ount graunt
peine:
Aventure la neef meine,
Les graunts ventz par meer les
chacent,

Et les undes les manacent; 210
Mes rien taunt de mal lour fait
Come la feime que lour crest,
Car riens n'aveient a manger;
Mes pur perils de la meer
Pitousement weimenterent, 215
Et la feime oblierent.
De totes partz sount turmentez,
Morir voleient de bon grez.
Chescune graunt dolour tent,
Car en la meer leeve un vent 220
Ke la meer fist crestre et lever,
Et les grauntz undes reverser;
Tressailler fist la neef amont,
Et puis flater a pluis parfount;
Qe tant la torna enviroun 225
Qe les dames en palmeson
Les fist cheir, et si giser
Par trois jours et nuytz entier,
Ke riens ne se moverent,
Mes tut temps en trans sirent. 230
Endementers les apport
La tempeste qe fust fort,
Et les chace par graunt travaile
K'eles ne poeient trover rivaille.
  Kaunt cessé feust la tempeste 235
  — Come nous trovoms en la geste
  —
Le temps devent serri et swef,
Et taunt par ert chacé la neef
Ke a la terre esteit hurté
Ke Engleterre est ore nomé; 240
Mes en cel temps santz noun
  esteit,
Pur ceo qe nul home y maneit.

---

[123] Two lines reversed, compared to the other version.

When each one had been found guilty in this miserable case, they were all taken away by their father and husbands to suffer durance.[124] It was judged that because they were all married to such high kings they could not be condemned, or suffer a mean death. But they were taken to a harbour of the sea nearby — I never heard tell where it was, but they were all taken there. Then they were put into a boat, a big strong boat, but without a rudder and without any provisions on board. Then they had a terrible time, and nobody was in the least bit sorry for them because of the wicked thing they had planned among themselves. The boat was shoved out to sea, and the waves hurled them back and forth from one peril to another, driving them far from the land. Now they are suffering dreadfully, and exiled from their homes, where they were all great queens — now they are nothing but poor fools.[125] They have no idea where they will end up, nor whether they will escape with their lives. The ladies are in great distress, as Fortune drives their ship! The howling winds chase them, and the waves threaten them; but nothing is as bad as their growing hunger, because they have nothing to eat. Then the terrors of the sea make them cry out piteously and forget they are famished.

They were tormented on all sides, and wished only for death. Each of them suffered dreadfully, for a great wind sprang up across the sea, making the waters swell and rise up and the huge waves crash down. It made the boat shudder on the crests, and then dashed it down into the gulfs, and thrashed it around so that the ladies fell fainting; they lay as if lifeless for three whole days and nights, in a swoon for all that time. Then this great storm carried them along, sweeping them a great distance, far from any shore.[126] When the storm was over — as it says in the book — the weather turned sweet and mild. The boat had been driven so far that it had beached upon the shore of what is now called England! In those days it had no name, because nobody lived there.

---

[124] The other version makes it clear that they were thrown into prison, while it was decided what was best to do with them.

[125] 'begeines'; there are a number of spellings, and meanings, for 'beguine' (Larousse, s.v. begart). Evans considers that a lay community of women is being suggested ('Gigantic Origins', p. 206), perhaps to put the ladies in a better light, but it could be simply a rhyme-word. In *GL* (Supp), in a miracle of St Barbara, it seems the translators did not expect their readers to understand 'beguine', and so rendered *quedam beghina* as 'a symple poore womman' (p. 465, and note to line 3041 on p. 521).

[126] 'ne poeient trover rivaille'; the other version has 'pres sunt venuz a un rivail'.

Kaunt la mere retrete feust,
La neef a secche terre just.
Les dames tost esveillerent,   245
Et lur testes susleverent.   246
Ke de terre si pres furent [f.10]   248
Graunt joie touz eurent.   247
Tauntost de la neef issirent,
Ou treis semeines sojorn firent;   250
Mes cele soer qe feust eigné
Devant touz se est hasté
Tote primereine en saillant,
La terre prist tut en hastaunt.
Cele que feust nomé Albine   255
De la terre prist seisine,
Et les autres hors saillerent
De la neef, qe febles erent
Pur la dolour et le juner
Q'il aveient en la meer.   260
Chescune a terre se gist;
Et lur grant feime les reprist,
Ke tut feust oblié devaunt
Pur la tempeste que feust graunt.
Feime aveient a desmesure,   265
De autre riens n'aveient cure
Mes q'eles eussent a manger.
Ne le saveient ou trover,
Mes pur grant necessité
Des bones herbes ount mangé,   270
Dont grant plenté y troverent,
Et des frutz qe as arbres erent.
Glans, chesteines et alies
Susteneient bien lour vies,
Et des espines les bremeles,   275
Botons des haies et meles;
Peires, poumes y troverent,
Autre manger ne mangerent.
Totes sount en grant pensee,
Ne saveient ou sount arivé,   280
Ne coment ad a noun la terre.
Ou seit de pees, ou de guere,
La covent sojourn faire,

N'estut aillours autre quere.
    Kant revigorez estoient   285
De la dolour q'il aveient,
Amont alerent en la terre
Pur espier et enquere
Quele gent i enhabitoient
Et quele vie demenoient.   290
En la terre taunt alerent
Ke par mi tote la sercherent.
Rien ne troverent humaine
N'en boscage, n'en plaine,
N'en valaie, ne sur mount,   295
Qe hautes et bas illoqes sount.
Home ne femme ne troverent,
Dont grandement se
    esmerveillerent;
Ne nule rien ount aperceu
Ke onques home i feust venuz.   300
Mes beles forestz et boscage
Et meintes bestes sauvage
Il troverent a graunt fuson,
Et graunt plenté de veneson [f.10v]
Sur terre; et en rivers   305
Des pessons furent pleners.
Les champs furent et les prez
Delitablement florez,
E les oiseux, qe sunt sauvage,
Chauntent haut en lour boscage,   310
Ke les ad mis en graunt confort.
Mes qaunt virent qe par nule sort
Ne purront ja aver poer
De lour pais recoverer,
Mes biens saveient et certeins   315
    sount
Ke la terre qe trové ount
Onqes ne feust enhabité
Par nul home de mere nee
— Ceo ount trové tut apert
Ke tutdis ad esté desert —   320
Adonqe dist la soer eigné,
K'estoit Albine nomé:

When the tide had gone out, the boat lay on dry land! The ladies soon woke up and lifted their heads. They were all so happy to be near land! Soon they got out of the boat, where they had spent three weeks. But the sister who was the eldest hurried ahead of all the others; she jumped out first, and grabbed some earth quickly. She who was called Albina took possession of the land.[127] The others tumbled forth out of the boat, weak with the pain and fasting they had suffered on the voyage. Each one lay on the ground, and hunger attacked them anew, that they had forgotten about while the tempest was raging.

They were so mad with hunger they couldn't think about anything else except finding something to eat! They had no idea where to look, but in their dire need they ate sweet herbs, and there were plenty of those; and there was fruit on the trees. Acorns, chestnuts, and sorb-apples[128] kept them alive, and spiny bramble [fruit], berries on hedge-bushes,[129] and medlars. They found pears and apples, but there was nothing else for them to eat. They were all very puzzled, not knowing where they had fetched up, nor what the name of this land was. War or peace, they had to stay here because they couldn't go looking for anywhere else.

When they had recovered somewhat from their ordeal, they went up into the countryside to have a look round and explore; they wanted to know what people were here and what sort of life they led. They went all over the place, hunting about everywhere, but found no trace of humans. Not in the woods or on the plains, not in the valleys, or in the hills both high and low. They found neither man nor woman, and they were immensely surprised at this. Nor did they see any sign that anybody had ever been here. But they found splendid forests and woods, full of all manner of wild beasts, including plenty of game.[130] This was on land; the rivers, too, were full of fish.

The fields and meadows were deliciously flowery, and the wild birds sang loudly in their woodland, which gave them great pleasure. But when they realised there was absolutely no chance they would ever be able to get back to their own country, and they became certain without any doubt that the country they'd found had never been inhabited by any man born of woman,[131] as it was now obvious the place had always been empty of people, then the eldest sister who was named Albina said:

---

[127] Taking seisin (Evans has stressed its importance); the action is reminiscent of Duke William's action on landing at Hastings where, it is said, he stumbled. Jumping up with a handful of sand, he announced he had taken possession of England.

[128] The word could mean garlic, or (since it is plural) garlic-bulbs. Larousse gives 'worthless thing' as a second meaning for 'ail, aille' (the first meaning is garlic); *AND* (and Evans, 'Gigantic Origins') gives 'sorb-apple', and 'worthless thing' for 'alie'. Inversion from ail- to ali- is possible. The derivation is 'sorbe' from Latin *sorbus, sorbum*, whence a jump to 'alie' seems unlikely. Brereton's glossary gives 'beam-tree' (whitebeam or *pyrus aria*, related to sorbus); 'alis' is also found as tree, not garlic, in Larousse's *Dictionnaire étymologique et historique*. Garlic grows wild in Britain, so the women might have found some to eat.

[129] 'boutons'; buds, or berries (Brereton gives 'hips', wild-rose fruit).

[130] 'veneson'; the other version has 'oyseloun' (birds).

[131] This may be a reference to the monstrous children, engendered by no man, that are to come.

'Trestouz sumes exillez
De la terre ou fumes nez;
Touz savez la decert   325
Par ont nous vient la pert
Ke mes a nous n'ert restoré.
Tele est nostre destinee;
Mes fortune nous ad graunté
Ceste terre. Nostre avowé   330
Estre doi cheveteine,
Car jeo fu la primereine
K'en la terre prist seisine,
Al issir de la marine.
Si nule le voleit countredire   335
Rien qe touche la matire,
Maintenant le mostre a moi
Pur quoi estre nel doi.'
Communement le ount graunté
K'ele seit lour avowé.   340
Donqes dist dame Albine:
'La terre a nous toutz encline,
Dont ne savom le noun dire,
Ne si onqes i aveit sire.
Pur ceo de moi, qe su feffé,   345
Deit la terre estre nomé.
Albine est mon propre noun,
Donc serra appellé Albioun;
Par ount de nous en cest pais
Remembrance serra tutdis.   350
Ci nous covent tutdis manoir,
Ne avoms cure aliours aler,
La terre est plaine de touz biens,
Mes qe viaunde ne faut riens.'
Mult desirent aver viaunde   355
Tele come lur queor demande.
Bestes veient a graunt plenté,
Et oiseux, dount sount tempté;
Volenters i mangereient
Si entre mains les aveient. [f.11]   360

Et totes furent en graunt pensé
Coment puissent a volenté
Aver bestes ou oiselon,
Dount la vient graunt fuson.
Assez saveient de chacer   365
Qaunt aveient lige poer,
Et de bois et de rivere
Bien saveient la manere;
Mes lors n'aveient nule rien,
Ark ne sete, faucon ne chien,   370
Dount preissent oisel ne beste
Ke manger puissent a lour feste.
Queintes et enginouses erent,
Et estreitement purpenserent,
Dount, par graunt avisement,   375
Engins firent pluis de cent.
Des verges firent hardilloun
Dount ils perneient veneisoun;
Trappes feseient des friseux
Dont ils perneient les oiseux;   380
Divers engins sovent firent,
Et si cointement tindrent,
Dount les bestes deceurent
Et oiseux assez pristrent.
Qaunt eurent pris a volenté,   385
La veneison ount escorché;
Des caillous ount feu alumé,
Tut avent a plenté;
En quirs de bestes quistrent,
Et par breses rostirent   390
La veneson et les oiseux
Ke pris aveient, bons et beaux;
Dount mult leement se purent,
Eawe de fountaigne burent.
Tele vie sustindrent   395
Ke lour forces tut revindrent,
Et bien furent revigorez
Du mal qe einz aveient endurrez.

'Every one of us is an exile, from the land where we were born. You all realise the wrongful conduct which led to our loss, and it will never be restored to us. Such is our destiny! But Fortune has vouchsafed us this land! I ought to be the lord and mistress of it,[132] since I was the first to take possession of the land as I got out of the boat. If any of you wants to argue about anything to do with this, tell me now why I ought not to be your leader.'

They all agreed she should be their leader.

Then Lady Albina said: 'This whole country is ours, whose name we don't know; and we don't know whether it ever had a lord before. And so it ought to be named for me, because it is mine. Albina is my right name, so it shall be called Albion! By this we shall be remembered for ever in this land. We might as well stay here permanently; we've no desire to go anywhere else. The land is full of all good things, except that we haven't got any meat!'

They wanted so much to have meat; their souls craved it. They saw there were plenty of beasts, and birds too — so tempting! They would have been very happy to eat them, if they could get their hands on them. They all thought hard about how they could get as much meat and fowl as they wanted, since the creatures were flocking to the place.[133] They knew all about hunting, when they had the legal right to do so [at home], not only in the forest but also on the banks.[134] They knew just how to do it, but now they had nothing to do it with! No bows or arrows, no falcons or dogs, to get birds and beasts to make a banquet. But they were clever and inventive, and put their minds to thinking of something; at last, with a lot of ingenuity they made a good number of devices. Using branches, they made nooses to catch animals; they made traps out of wood to catch birds. They made lots of such things, and set them cunningly, to snare game and also to take fowl. When they had got as much as they wanted, they prepared the game and made a fire by striking pebbles together — there were plenty.[135] They cooked the meat wrapped in its skin; they roasted the game and fowl they had caught over the coals — delicious! They stuffed themselves, and then drank water from the stream. They went on like this so that all their strength came back to them, and they were completely restored after all the ills they had suffered.

---

132 'Nostre avowé'; it would make more sense to read 'Vostre' here.

133 However, 'vient' may be a mistake for 'veient' (they could see them in abundance).

134 'rivere' is usually translated as river[bank], but falconry may be successfully practised away from water, at (for example) the eaves or 'banks' of a wood. The ladies used to have falcons, but have none now.

135 The alternative line makes equally good sense: 'there was plenty of brushwood'.

Kant char et saunc perneient,
Gros et gras devenoient.   400
La chaline de nature
Les surmont a desmesure
Par desir de lecherie
De aver humaigne compaignie —
De ceo sont sovent temptez.   405
Ceo aperceurent li maufez   406
Ke tel poer aveient: 409
Humaine forme perneient,   410
Ovesqe ceo la nature;
Ove les femes firent mixture;
Kaunt en delit les troverent
En cel point les pargiserent,
Sovent enfauntz engendrerent,   415
Et tost aprés se esvanirent.
A les dames veignent issi;
Kaunt lour deliz les assailli
Mult pres estoient lui maufez [f.11v]
D'acomplir leur volentez   420
En la forme avandite.
Ne feust graunt ne petite
Ke enceint feust de un malfé;
En la furent engendrez
Enfauntz qe grauntz devindrent,   425
Et aprés la terre tindrent.
Touz lur deliz acomplirent;

Mes les dames riens ne virent
Ceux qe parjeu les aveieint,
Mes qe soulement senteient   430
Come feme deit home faire
Kant se entremettent de tiel
   affaire.
Et qaunt furent de greignure age,
Les enfauntz, par graunt outrage,
En lur meres engendrerent   435
Fiz et feilles qe grauntz erent.
Soers des freres conceurent
Fiz et feilles que mult crurent;
Grauntz geantz de corps furent,
Et graunt force en eux eurent.   440
Grauntz erent a desmesure
De corps et d'estature.[136]
A regarder hidous erent,   457
Car malfez les engendrerent.
Des deables furent engendrez,
Et les meres dont furent nez   460
Furent grantz et mult corsuz,
De forz genz furent venuz.
Par reson si deveient estre
Les enfauntz qui deivent nestre
De tele gent come cil erent   465
Ke les geantz engendrerent.

---

[136] There is a gap in the text at this point.

As they took on more flesh and blood, they grew large and fat! Then Nature's heat warmed them into feeling lecherous desire,[137] and they longed for male company. They were often tempted thus, and the evil spirits took note of it![138] These had the ability to take human form, together with human powers;[139] they could mate with women if they found them in a state of desire. At that moment they could lie with them, often making children, and vanish immediately afterwards. So they came to these women when they were feeling lustful; they were very ready to do their will in the form just described. Any woman large or small, who was pregnant by an evil spirit, in her were engendered children who would grow huge, and who afterwards would hold this land. They had all their desire, but the ladies saw nothing of those who had lain with them. They merely felt what a woman does with a man when they set about the business.[140] It is shameful to relate that the children, once they were grown to maturity, coupled with their mothers to have enormous sons and daughters. And sisters conceived their brothers' children,[141] who grew to be huge! They were great giants in body, with strength to match; they were massively big, both in body and in size.[142] They were hideous to look upon, for they were fathered by evil spirits and engendered by devils. The mothers, too, who bore them were big and very stout because of the huge race they came of. So it's not surprising the children were likewise [big and stout], born to such a race as this was, which engendered the giants.

---

[137] It was believed that women, being cold and moist by nature, had to be 'warmed up' for sex. Evans notes the importance for this passage of the Hippocratic-Galenic theory, that women produced seed as men do. See also Weiss, 'Swooning', pp. 130–34.

[138] Extra lines in the other version explain that these spirits are called 'incubi'. See *Merlin*, Robert de Boron, ed. Micha, for the seduction of Merlin's mother; Bliss, *Naming and Namelessness*, gives an account of that romance which includes explanation of the incubi (pp. 97–102 & 202–3).

[139] Compare the *Castleford* version: the Devil saw that the women desired man's company, and 'toke body of the ayre' (v. 209).

[140] It is unclear whether the second 'they' refers to the women or to the incubi (as Evans points out; this illustrates a typical difficulty of Anglo-Norman).

[141] In *Creation*, below, there is no suggestion that coupling with close relatives is incest.

[142] Omitted lines here describe the finding of these creatures' monstrously large bones.

Cele gent de faerie
Mult graundement se multiplie;
Par la terre se partirent
Et caves en terre firent;   470
Grantz mures entour firent lever
Et des fossez environer;
Sur montaignes herbergeient
Ou mult estre sure quideient.
En multz des lues uncore apperent   475
Les grauntz mures qe eux leverent,
Mes mult sont ore abessé
Par tempeste et par orree.
Cele gent la terre tindrent
Desqes les Brutons vindrent.   480
Ceo fust avaunt qe Dieu feust nee,
Come par acompte le ai trové,
Mil .c. aunz trent et sis,
De ceo seiez certein tutdis.
   Du temps qe les dames   485
    vindrent
Ke primes la terre tindrent,
Desqes les Brutons vindrent [f.12]
Et la terre a force conquirent,

Et le noun de Albion ousta,
Et puis Bretaigne la noma,   490
Si come le cronicle count
Deux et .lx. aunz amount;
Taunt de temps, ceo fait a crere,
Les geantz tindrent la terre.   494
   Di vous ai la verité   547
Come la geste nous ad counté,
Kaunt et coment cil vindrent
Ke Engleterre primes tindrent,   550
Et de queu noun esteit nomé,
Et de qi l'ert doné,
Et combien la terre tindrent,
Atant qe les Bretouns vindrent,
Et le primer noun ousterent,   555
Et Bretaigne la nomerent.
Tut est bon a remembrer,
Rien grevera de saver
Les estiles et les escriptures
Des auncienes aventures.   560
De Jesu Crist seit beneit
Ke en escripture les mettreit.
Amen.

This superhuman[143] race multiplied abundantly, and spread out all over the land. They made caves in the ground, and built great walls around them, encircling them with moats. And they made their homes on the mountains, where they believed themselves safe. In many places you can still see the great walls they made, although many have now been broken down by weather and storms. These people held the land until Brutus and his men came.[144] This was before God was born, as I have found in the account of these things: one thousand and one hundred years, plus thirty-six. You can be sure of that. From the time when the ladies arrived, who had the land first, until the time of Brutus who conquered the land by force and took away the name Albion, calling it Britain afterwards, as the chronicle says it was two-and-sixty years all told.[145] That is as long, believe me, as the giants held the land.[146]

I have told you the truth, just as the story tells us, about when and how they came, those people who first held England; and about what name it was given, and who gave it, and how long they held it before the Britons[147] came and took away the first name, calling it Britain. It is all good to remember, and it never hurts to know about the manners and writings of old adventures. May Jesus Christ bless all who put them into books! Amen.[148]

---

143 'de faerie'; modern English 'fairy' would be misleading. They are of supernatural and non-human origin (*AND* gives 'accursed race'; Evans prefers the nuance, in the Anglo-Norman, by which the giants are products of enchantment).

144 'les Brutons'; the word keeps the idea of Brutus, before the place-name is developed.

145 The editor rejects the reading 'cxx aunz' in this MS because too different from other versions. But sixty-two years is not very long for the race to have become so widespread. Other MSS have 260.

146 Intervening lines, in the other version, tell how the giants divided up the land and fought one another so much that only twenty-four were left to fight Brutus. He destroyed them all except Gogmagog, whom he spared: to be wondered at (he was twenty feet long), and to be asked for the story which has just now been told ... and how Brutus made sure the story would be remembered, by telling it at feasts. The arrival of Brutus and his conquest of the giants will be told in the *Brut*, so it is not necessary to relate it here.

147 Now spelt 'Bretouns', as in the other version.

148 The following thirteen lines of Latin prose, not in the other version, divide this from 'the Brute Chronicle'. It recapitulates the story briefly, adding that the third name of the land was Engistlond, after the Saxon Hengist.

Romance

> Back into storyland giants have fled ... [1]

The old hymn is about how knights were supposed to be virtuous as well as valiant. Medieval romances may (or not) have been 'escape literature', but nobody escaped from the habits of religion. Even outside the Grail romances, and the 'pious romances' in which the hero's adventures are in some sense a penance or pilgrimage, knights would hear Mass before setting off on their exploits. Grace would be said at meals; one was expected to confess one's sins regularly, [2] baptize foundlings, and reverence all in holy orders. Furthermore, knights were frequent visitors at monasteries; some retired into a religious life once their campaigning days were over. [3]

Having met some giants in the History chapter, we meet more of them in this chapter. The texts chosen include passages from lesser-known romances: the first is from 'antiquity', followed by one that takes themes and episodes from a wealth of sources and recounts a rambling series of adventures (included here because it has not been widely studied). The third romance is Arthurian, but not one of the best known; last comes a full-length story extracted from a Tristan romance. Tristan is not among the heroes of Arthurian romance at this date, [4] and Arthur does not appear in any of the Tristan pieces I have included. There are a number of 'ancestral' romances in Anglo-Norman, which give the history of an Insular hero; these may have been composed as part of the Norman settlers' process of adapting and adopting the history of their new country as the next generations after the Conquest settled into their new culture. [5] I have not included any of these because they are widely anthologized. Legge's *Background* gives a comprehensive account of them. [6]

---

[1] *Songs of Praise*, number 377.

[2] Certain kinds of warfare (especially against the Infidel) were considered to be godly, and therefore gained indulgence from the Church. See, for example, the context of Roland's confession in *Pseudo-Turpin Chronicle*, ed. Short (p. 63): the ritual was undertaken by all knights before battle.

[3] An example in *GL* (Supp), p. 196, is the story of Saint Theophilus. Interestingly, the first thing the monks do is try and teach the illiterate knight to say his Pater Noster. The historical Guillaume d'Orange, hero of a chanson de geste cycle, withdrew into monastic life and founded an abbey. Colegate, *A Pelican in the Wilderness*, includes a number of examples of retired soldiers across the centuries.

[4] There is a reference to Tristan in *Fergus* (at v. 4216), but he does not appear in person.

[5] 'The pride and curiosity of the Norman conquerors prompted them to inquire into the ancient history of Britain ...' (*Gibbon's Decline and Fall*, vol. 4, pp. 94–5). Gibbon's chapter XXXVIII continues with a vision of Europe as one great republic (p. 107), a poignant comment for our times.

[6] Legge, pp. 139–75.

Roman de Thèbes (Amphiarax)

Written probably around 1150, the romance has been deemed the earliest in French.[7] The editor considers it to be Anglo-Norman, judging that it is from Henry II's court.[8] I have chosen it because, according to Dean, French texts existing in Insular MSS may be regarded as Anglo-Norman if they are of sufficient (insular) interest.[9] It is clear this romance was known and read, even if not originally composed, in Britain. These two extracts (one introductory) give the story of Amphiarax, 'archbishop' of the Argive army (vv. 2119–49, & 5042–309 in Mora-Lebrun's edition). Some details about the romance, and of the MS in question, are taken from Mora-Lebrun's Introduction. The narrator delights in learned references, to names of the Liberal Arts, and to names such as Turpin and Godfrey from other stories. But this does not necessarily mean the audience was highly learned; the narrator delights in showing off, and some of the battle descriptions are pure Boys' Own stuff.[10]

The author does not leave us his (or her) name, nor any dedication, but there are indications s/he was part of Henry II's intellectual circle (pp. 6–7). Clues indicating an audience both warlike and educated include the sword of Tydeus and a motif on Eteocles' shield; above all, the editor judges that the strife between Oedipus' sons recalls strife among William the Conqueror's successors (p. 7). *Thèbes* was the first of three 'romans antiques'; next came *Eneas*, c. 1156–60; last was *Troie*, c. 1165 (p. 8); here, Statius' *Thebaïd* is transported to an Anglo-Norman milieu (p. 9).

The base MS for this edition belongs to the tradition of the 'rédaction courte' (p. 10). Mora-Lebrun discusses *inter al.* some 'souvenirs' of the First Crusade (pp. 16–17): for example, the mention of Godfrey de Bouillon in comparison with Amphiarax (vv. 5184–5 and note). There is also a comparison (pp. 21–2), drawn from the *Chanson de Roland*, with Turpin (vv. 5186–9); but the writer distances himself from chansons de geste (pp. 26–7). Notable passages of *ekphrasis* (pp. 29–30) include the description of Amphiarax's chariot.[11] This description becomes more and more vivid as the pictures come alive, as if it were cinema, with passages of direct speech, rivalling and somehow reflecting the real action taking place in the war of Thebes. Notes to Mora-Lebrun's edition and translation offer information

---

[7] *Le Roman de Thèbes*, ed. and tr. Mora-Lebrun, published by Livre de Poche (Paris). Kelly, *Medieval French Romance*, gives 1150–55; Gaunt, *Retelling the Tale*, gives 1160. Both scholars list a few earlier romances and a number of earlier chansons.

[8] The MS is mentioned in Dean (her number 706r, see below), but not *Thèbes* itself.

[9] Her Introduction sets out the criteria she and Boulton use. The romance is not in her catalogue, although the manuscript (S) Mora-Lebrun uses for her edition and translation is mentioned in her index (see 706r). This, also used by Studer and Waters (*Historical French Reader*), is London, BL, Add. 34114 (ex-Spalding).

[10] Petit, *Aux origines du roman*, contains a valuable range of (previously published, and collected) articles on this romance.

[11] Ekphrasis is the representation of an artwork, of any kind, in a literary work. This example illustrates the meaning 'to speak out' with extraordinary force, because the figures really do 'speak out': they shout and fight.

about the writer's debt to Ovid, and other matters of interest. A startling passage in Euripides' *The Phoenician Women* (which cannot be a source for the romance) reminds us how vivid such pictures could be, whether in contemporary life or in literature: Antigone watches, from a roof-top in Thebes, the arrival of the enemy warriors led by her brother. Noticing one of them, she exclaims 'How prideful, how hateful to see! Like an earth-born giant hurling flame *in a picture* ...' (my emphasis).[12] Compare the passage at vv. 5062–85, below. The latter part of the passage is unique to this manuscript, being inspired not only by the *Thebaïd* but also by Aeneas' descent into the nether world in Virgil's *Aeneid*.[13] A translation of *Thèbes* into English was made by John Smartt Coley,[14] but not of our MS S; he translates the version in Constans' first volume.[15]

The *Roman de Troie* may be read in comparison.[16] The edition cited here gives approximately half the romance, using the Anglo-Norman copy as its base text. It contains magnificent set-pieces, for example: description of the Chambre des Beautés, and the tomb of Hector. But the images, although vividly detailed, do not come alive and speak on the page as the figures do on the chariot of Amphiarax. An American MA thesis, available online,[17] studies this romance and Chrétien's *Erec et Enide* (see especially her chapter 2). Extracts from the story of Amphiarax, with translation, are given in an appendix. But the version cited in this thesis gives no dialogue to the painted figures (the author's bibliography lists her sources).

MS S is of relatively recent date (late fourteenth century) but appears to follow closely an earlier (twelfth-century) French MS from the West or North-West. It has rare interpolation from a 'purement français' MS of intervening date (pp. 33–4). Mora-Lebrun attributes this to the fact that the copyist is English and, not knowing French very well, copies very carefully. The language is Anglo-Norman (p. 34; examples of typical forms are given at p. 35). Further, she considers that a mixture of 'tu' and 'vous' in speech is typical of Anglo-Norman (p. 37).

I have copied the text from the edition, slightly modifying only certain of the punctuation to conform to English usage; the arrangement into paragraphs is editorial, and folio numbers are not marked. Page numbers refer to the edition, which gives translation into modern French.

---

[12] *Euripides: Three Tragedies*, ed. Greene and Lattimore, p. 77. Amphiarax (Amphiaraus) is among the figures watched by Antigone.

[13] See note to v. 5240 in the edition.

[14] New York, Garland, 1986.

[15] *Le Roman de Thèbes*; the verses special to MS S, which include the most vivid passages of my extract below, are printed in an appendix to Constans' vol. II. Constans vol. I (only) is available online.

[16] *Le Roman de Troie, Extraits*, ed. and tr. Baumgartner and Vielliard.

[17] Mayrhofer, 'From Ekphrasis to Fetishism'. The author takes for granted that not only *Thèbes*, but also the works of Chrétien, and even of Wace, are written 'in the Anglo-Norman tradition' and of course for an Anglo-Norman audience.

Text

Amphiarax Introduced[18]

Amphyarax manda li reis,   2119
un archevesque molt corteis.
Cil estoit maistre de lour lei,
del ciel saveit tout le secrei,
...[19]
et reviller fait hommes morz;
des oiseals entent le latin:
soz ciel n'aveit meillor devin.   2125
Li reis lui prie qu'il li die
come iert del host, ne li ceilt mie.
Amphiarax forment sospire,
enbroncha sei, ne li volt dire;
mais li reis forment le conjure   2130
qu'il li di veir del augure.
    'Sire,' fait-il, 'jel vous dirrai,
de rien ne vous en menterai.
Ceste gent que vous veiez,
si vous a Thebes les menez,   2135
si je onques rien de augurie soi,
molt en retornera cea poi.
Car tu perdras Capaneüs,
Polynicés et Tydeüs;
Ypomedon cil y morra   2140
et Parthonopex si ferra;
et des autres y morra tant,
ne puisse dire par nul semblant.
Et g'i morrai, si tu me menez,
ne viverai mie deux semaignes;   2145
et ja nus homme m'ocira,
mais la terre me sorbira;
sorbira mei et mon cheval,
jusqu'en parfounde abisme aval.'

Doom of Amphiarax[20]

D'Amphiarax dirre vous dei,   5042
come se contint a cel tornei.
En un curre ert Amphiarax,
qui fu fait outre Seint Thomas;   5045
Vulcans le fist par grant porpens
et a lui faire myst grant tens.
Par estudie, par grant cunseil,
i myst la lune et soleil,
et tregieta le firmament   5050
par art et par enchantement.
Noef esperes par ordre y myst,
en la maior les signes fist;
es autres set, que sont menors,
fist les planetes et les cours.   5055
La noefme assist en mie le monde:
ceo est la terre et miere parfonde;
en terre peinst hommes et bestes,
en mer peissons, venz et
    tempestes.
Qui de fisique sot entendre   5060
es peintures poet molt aprendre.
Li jaiant sont en l'autre pan,
tout plain d'orgoil et de boban:
les diex volent desheriter
et par force del ciel jetter.   5065
A poier sius ont fait eschale;
onc homme qui vive ne vit tale,
car un mont ont sur autre mys,
— plus de sept en y ont assis —
et montent sius pur les diex   5070
    prendre,
si de eux ne se poent defendre.

---

[18] pp. 168–71.

[19] A break of (at least) one line is presumed here, indicated by dots. There is no rhyme-word for 'morz', so something must have got lost.

[20] pp. 340–57.

Translation

The king sent for Amphiarax, a noble archbishop. This man was an expert on all their laws; he knew all the secrets of Heaven, and how to revive the dead. He understood the language of birds;[21] there was no better sorcerer in all the world.

The king asked him to tell him everything about the army, and not to conceal anything from him. Amphiarax sighed deeply, hanging his head: he had no desire to tell. But the king commanded him sternly to tell the truth revealed in the oracles.

'My lord,' he said, 'I'll tell you, and I'll tell you no lies. These people you see here, if you lead them to Thebes — if I ever understood anything about the oracles — hardly any of them will come back here afterwards. For you will lose Capaneus, Polynices, and Tydeus. Ipomedon will die there, and Parthonope will too. And so many others will die that I cannot begin to say. I shall die too, if you take me there; I shan't live two weeks. No man will ever kill me, but the earth will swallow me up. It will swallow up me and my horse, down into the deep abyss below.'

Doom of Amphiarax

I must tell you about Amphiarax, and how he fared in this battle. Amphiarax was in a chariot which was made far away beyond the Indies.[22] Vulcan built it after careful planning, and it took him a long time to make. Having studied hard, and thought long, he decorated it with the moon and sun; he conjured up the firmament by his art and his magic.[23] He placed nine spheres in order there, with the signs of the Zodiac in the greatest of them. In the next seven, smaller ones, he made the planets and their courses. He put the ninth in the middle of the universe: this is the Earth and the deep sea. He painted men and beasts in the earth, and in the sea he painted fish and winds and tempests. If you understand natural philosophy, you can learn a great deal from such pictures.

The giants, all full of pride and boasting, were pictured on the other panel. They want to usurp the gods, and throw them out of Heaven! To climb up there they made a ladder. No man had ever seen anything like it, for they piled one mountain onto another (seven altogether), and up they went, to get at the gods — unless they were able to defend themselves against this attack.

---

[21] It is very common for the song of birds to be called their 'latin'. The idea of any strange language being thought of as Latin is reflected in the word for 'translator' or 'interpreter': 'latimier' (and the still-current proper name Latimer).

[22] St Thomas was said to have evangelized India (note to v. 5045). Vulcan was the blacksmith of the gods.

[23] The word 'tregieta' (see 'tregetee' below, v. 5162) has a number of different spellings; meanings include casting in metal or making by magic (*AND*).

Jupiter est de l'autre part,
une foieldre tient et un dart;
Mars et Pallas y sount aprés,
cil dui sustienent tout le fés.   5075
Tout liu autre [qui]²⁴ el ciel
     regnent
isnelment lor armes pernent;
cel d'els n'i ad qui quierge essoine,
tout se combatent par le trone.
Fort se combatent li jaiant,   5080
maces de plom font faire ardant;
gietent as diex iriement,
car cil y claiment chasement;
gietent brandons et ardanz çoches,
et rouges flambes par lour   5085
     bouches,
car vers les diex ount plus grant ire
que je ne puisse penser ne dire.
Tanz pesanz pierres lour enveient
que la menor ne portereient
sés boefs ne dis, treze ne quinze: 5090
quant qu'aconseut froisse et
     demince.
Contre les dex forment s'iraissent
por le trone, qu'il ne lor laissent.
Li dieu trestout ensius se traient,
car li jaiant pas nes manaient.   5095
Conseil pernent tout ensemble;
li plius hardis de poour tremble,
car il n'ont pas escus de chesne,
espiés de fer, hanstes [de] fresne,
glaives ne lances ne espees,   5100
maces de fer ne granz plomees,
fors solement danz Jupiter,
qui tint un dart agu de fer.

Mars fu dejoste lui a destre,
la proz Pallas fu a senestre;   5105
cil dui vailent en la bataille
plus que toute l'autre raschaille
et que les autres diex salvages
qui habitent en ces boscages.
Phebus y fu, molt bons archers   5110
qui fu vaillanz, hardis et fiers;
cil tint son arc tenduement,
cels esguarde molt fierment,
atant une saiete encolche.
Al jaiant vait prendre une roche;   5115
Phebus li dist par grant contraire:
'Ja savras come je sai bien traire!'
E cil respont par grant orgoil:
'Je te deffi, car mal je voil;
je ne redot tei ne tes darz,   5120
car fils es Jupiter bastarz;
il t'engendra en la putain
qui ot de toi le ventre plain.
Par patremoine le ciel claimes,
mes compaignons ne moy nen   5125
     aimez.'
Li jaianz finist sa parole;
Phebus destent et li darz vole:
si le ferist parmi la longe
que n'i ot puis par lui chalonge;
aprés lui dist: 'Poi a duré,   5130
ce m'est avis, vostre fierté.'
Mars et Pallas forment s'airassent,
darz esmoluz corre lor laissent;
foildres gettent cil autre dé,
fort defendent lour majesté;   5135
morz les oscient rubatant:
n'en puet nul ester en estant.

---

²⁴ 'qui' absent from MS, supplied from Constans' edition (see note).

On the other side we find Jupiter, holding a thunderbolt and a lance; then came Mars and Pallas next, holding the defence between them.[25] All the other gods who reigned in heaven hurried to take arms, and not one of them sought an excuse: they were all in the battle for the throne.[26] The giants fought furiously, heating red-hot their leaden maces. Then they hurl them angrily at the gods, because these want to hold onto their own domain! They throw firebrands and burning branches, and shoot red flames from their mouths! They are so frenzied against the gods I can't even imagine how to tell you.[27]

They lobbed such heavy stones; the least of them couldn't be carried by six or ten oxen — no, not even by thirteen or fifteen! Even the smallest would smash into tiny pieces anything it hit. They were utterly enraged against the gods, for the domain they wouldn't give up to them.[28] The gods all withdraw, because the giants are relentless, and they hold a council together. The bravest of them is trembling with fear, because they have no oaken shields, no iron lances with shafts of ash, no blades or pikes or swords, no iron maces or great leaden clubs. Only Lord Jupiter grasps a sharp iron dart. Mars was beside him on his right, and gallant Pallas on his left. These two were more worthy in battle than all the rest of the mob, including all the other wild gods living in these woods.

Phoebus was there, a champion archer who was brave and hardy and proud, holding his drawn bow. He casts a fierce eye at the giants, and fits an arrow to the string. To the giant who is about to pick up a rock Phoebus cries angrily 'Now you'll see I'm a good shot!'

That one shouts back arrogantly 'I defy you! I wish you ill! I'm not scared of you or your darts — you're a bastard of Jupiter's, by the trollop whose belly was filled with you! You want the heavens as your birthright, and you hate both me and my companions!'

As the giant finished speaking, Phoebus loosed and the arrow flew. It struck him right through his spine,[29] so he could never challenge ever again! Then he cried 'I don't think that pride of yours lasted very long!'[30]

Mars and Pallas were whipped to fury, and let fly against them with sharpened darts. The other gods dashed forth thunderbolts, strongly defending their royal status. They felled them all dead; not one was left who could stand up.

---

[25] The goddess Pallas Athene was known as a fierce warrior.

[26] Note to v. 5079 remarks (*inter al.*) on the improbable dialogue that follows.

[27] Nevertheless, the writer continues with vivid description.

[28] 'trone' is translated as 'heaven' by Mora-Lebrun. Literally 'throne', it seems to have a flexible meaning (victory, dominion, as well as the royal place being fought for).

[29] 'longe' means back or spine, but it could be an alternative spelling of 'lange' (tongue; *Larousse*, and *AND*). If the latter, such a wound would explain why the giant could make no challenge.

[30] Phoebus calls the giant 'thou' in his first speech; he says 'you' here; he may be meaning 'the pride of you all'.

Jupiter molt s'en esleesce,
cil qui il fiert pas ne se dresce;
si en fiert un par la pectrine,   5140
ne li ot puis mestier mecine.
Ne vous en quier faire longe plait:
tous les monz asseeir refait.

 El curre fu ceste peinture,
Vulcans l'entailla par grant cure.   5145
Et a pierres et a esmals
fu faitz darriere li frontals,
et enlevees les sept ars:
Gramaire y est peinte oue ses pars.
Dialetique oue argumenz,   5150
Rethorique oue jugemenz;
l'abaque tint Arimetique,
par la gamme chante Musique:
peint y est diatesseron,
dyapenté, dyapason;   5155
une verge ot Geometrie,
un autre en ot Astronomie:
l'une en terre mette sa mesure,
l'autre es esteilles ad sa cure.

 El curre ot molt sotil entaille: 5160
bien fu ovré, onc n'i ot faille.
Un ymage i ot tregetee
qui vait cornant a la mené,
une autre qui tout tens frestele,
plius douce que rote ne vïele.   5165
L'ovre del curre oue la matiere
vaut bien Thebes oue tout
  l'empere,
car li pan sont d'or fin trifoire

et li timon de blanc yvoire;
les roes sount de crisopase,   5170
colour ount de fu qui embrase.
Le curre traient quatre azeivre;
l'esclos ne poet homme aperceivre
en sablon ne en terre mole,
car plius tost vont qu'oiseals qui   5175
  vole.

 Amphiarax point et s'eslaisse
la ou vit le meillor presse.
Trait l'espié que fu forbie,
del bien ferir pas ne s'oublie;
por doner grantz coups maintenant   5180
sont tout liu autre aprenant.
Molt trencha bien le jour s'espé,
a ceux dedenz fu molt privé:
onc l'espé al duc Godefrei
ne mist les Turs en tiel effrei,   5185
ne taunz gentz coups ne fist
  Torpins
en Espaigne sur Sarazins
come fist l'archevesque le jour
sur ceux de Thebes en l'estour.
Molt fu appareilliés d'armes,   5190
des meillors que l'en fait a Parmes;
al col ot un escu vermeil
que molt reluist countre soleil;
bocles d'or i ot plius de set,
n'i ad cele ou dis mars n'en eit;   5195
sis haubers fu forz et legiers
et plus luisanz que argent mers:
qui l'ad vestue ne dote plaie.

Jupiter was full of battle-joy: whomever he hit never rose again, and any he pierced through the heart had no more need of doctors.

To make a long story short, they put all the mountains back where they had come from.

This story was painted on the chariot, engraved by Vulcan with the greatest care. The inside of the front panel was made with precious stones and enamel-work; with the Seven Arts in relief.[31] Grammar is shown there with all her parts; Dialectic with arguments, Rhetoric with judgement. Arithmetic holds an abacus, and Music sings her scales; they are all painted there: the fourth, the fifth, and the octave. Geometry is holding a rod, and Astronomy has another.[32] One of them uses her measure for the earth, and the other does the same for the stars.

There was so much subtle carving all over the chariot; it was so beautifully made there was not one flaw in it. He had contrived an image, of one who went blowing his horn to summon the hounds. Another whistled continuously on a flute, more sweetly than any rote or viol.[33] The decorative art on this chariot, and the quality of the materials, were worth more than Thebes and all its empire put together. For the walls of the chariot were of encrusted gold filigree, and the shafts were of white ivory. The wheels were of chrysoprase, the colour of flaming fire.[34] Four zebras drew the chariot! Nobody could ever see their hoofprints, even in sand or soft earth, for they went more swiftly than the bird that flies.[35]

Amphiarax spurs forward, charging where he can see the best of the mêlée. He draws his well-burnished sword: he won't forget to strike well! All the others can take lessons from him when it comes to dealing great blows! That sword chopped magnificently all day, making itself well known to those besieged inside. Never did Duke Godfrey's sword strike such terror into the Turks, and nor did Turpin deal such knightly blows upon the Saracens in Spain, as the archbishop did that day upon the Thebans in battle.[36] He was brilliantly equipped with armour, the best that was ever made in Parma: at his neck was a bright red shield that glowed in the sunshine; there were at least seven buckles upon it, not one of them less than ten marks.[37] His hauberk, strong and light, shone brighter than pure silver; whoever wears this hauberk need fear no wound.

---

[31] See note to v. 5148 for personification of the Arts.

[32] Geometry and Astronomy are shown to be strict teachers, as well as scholars of space. A rod is an instrument of correction, and also a measure of both length and area (*OED*, rod, 2a and 2b). The note to v. 5156 explains that (French) 'verge' has a similar semantic range: a tangible stick, and a term of measurement.

[33] See Introduction, above, for the rote; the vïele may be a viol, or a vielle (similar to a hurdy-gurdy). Here too the picture takes on a voice.

[34] *OED* says chrysoprase is green, but it is a rhyme-word so the writer may simply have chosen a suitably exotic gem-stone.

[35] This description is drawn from Ovid's *Metamorphoses* (note to v. 5175).

[36] References are to Godfrey de Bouillon (leader of the First Crusade), and Archbishop Turpin's participation in the battle of Roncesvalles (told in the *Chanson de Roland*).

[37] A mark was an eight-ounce measure of gold or silver (see note to this line).

A entresigne ot un daumaie,
et soz son healme un veloset   5200
de sei blaunche bien toset.
Li soleilz lust cler come en mai,
el curre d'or fierent li rai:
reflambist en sius la montaigne
et de desouz tote la plaigne.   5205
Del curre et de ses guarnemenz
s'esbahissent tout cil dedenz;
cil dedenz s'esbahissent tout,
li plius hardiz avant li fuit,
car quident que seit asquuns deux 5210
qui se combate por les Grex.
     Amphiarax sot bien par sort
qu'a ycel jour receivra mort;
par augure sot li guerriers
que ceo esteit sis jors darriers.   5215
Puis que certeinement le sot,
emploia le come il mielz poet;
de ceux dedenz fait grant martire,
ne veil ne joefne n'en revire.
Quant qu'il en trove en sa veie   5220
en enfern avant sei enveie.
Grant perte y refont cil dehors
de lor chevals et de lour cors,
mais a nïent le tenissant
si il lui sol ne perdissant.   5225
Molt en furent desconseillé:
de ce se sont molt esmerveillé
que il morit en tiel maniere,
que sa mort fust horrible et fiere.
Car al vespre, soentre none,   5230
la terre crosle et li ciels tone
et, si come Dex l'ot destiné
et cil l'ot dit et deviné,

terre le sorbit sanz enjan,
si come Abiron et Datan.   5235
     Cil qui cele merveille virent
s'espo[e]nterent et foïrent;
molt foïrent a grant desrei,
car chescuns ot poor de sei.
En enfer chiet Amphiarax,   5240
ou li chaitif sount et li las;
en enfer chiete, l'espé trete
dont il ot grant ocise faite.
Mais la veie fu molt hidouse,
de forz trespas et tenebrose: 5245
a la porte trove un portier
qui le comencie a abaier,
tant laidement come il plus poet,
oue treis testes que li fels ot.
Par sa porte estuet touz passer   5250
cels qui illoec deivent entrer;
Amphiarax par cel pertus
avant passa, non par autre us.
Idonc entra en un sentier
ou oït almes traveillier;   5255
puis passe avant, a une planche,
l'eve Acheron, que n'est pas
        blanche:
cest Acheron, que molt s'enbrive,
laide est et grant et loing la rive,
et de serpenz mordantz fu pleine.   5260
Cel passa a quelque peine,
cil et toute sa compaignie
qu'enfern sorbit en la champaigne.
A un flueve revint aprés
qui d'Acheron estoit molt prés;   5265
bestes y ot de mil maniers,
qui lor font molt horrible chers.

He was distinguished by a dalmatic robe,[38] and wore a fine veil of close-napped white silk under his helmet. The sun was as bright as May, throwing its rays upon the golden chariot; the splendour flashed to the mountains above and all over the plain beneath. Everybody inside the city marvelled at the chariot with its adornment, and the boldest fled before it: they thought it must be some god, who had come to fight for the Greeks!

Amphiarax knew, through his own divination, he was certain to meet his death that day. The great warrior had learned from the auguries that the day would be his last. Because he knew this for certain, he used it to the full as best he could! He made enormous slaughter among the besieged, and neither old nor young survived it. Whomever he found in his path, he drove them to Hell ahead of himself. The besiegers suffered huge losses, of horses and men; but they would have made nothing of that if only they could save him alone from being lost. They were in despair, and what filled them with horror was that he died so: his death was savage and frightful. For in the evening, soon after the ninth hour,[39] the earth shuddered and the skies thundered. And, as if God had decreed it and as he himself had spoken and foretold, the earth swallowed him up ... no word of a lie! Just like Abiram and Dathan![40]

Everybody who saw this awful thing was terrified,[41] and fled; they fled in great disarray, for each was terrified for himself. Amphiarax fell down into Hell, where all the wretched and miserable are. He fell down into Hell, holding the drawn sword with which he had done so much slaughter. But the way down was ghastly, a shadowy and dreadful passage. At the gate he encountered a porter, which began to bark at him as horribly as it could with its three heads,[42] the brute! Through this gate all must pass who have to go into that place. Amphiarax went through this gate, as there was no other way in. Then he followed a path, where he could hear souls groaning in travail. Then he went on to where there is a plank to cross the water of Acheron, so black. This is Acheron, a rushing river: ugly, huge, whose banks are so far apart; it is full of biting snakes. He passed it with difficulty, he and all his company whom Hell had swallowed in the battle. Then he came to a river that was quite close to Acheron. It was full of a thousand kinds of creatures, that glared hideously at them.

---

[38] This ecclesiastical garment was originally of Dalmatian wool.

[39] The canonical hour of None (the ninth hour of the day, about three o'clock) was the hour of Christ's death on the Cross (editor's note to this line); 'vespre' here means late afternoon or evening, not the hour of Vespers.

[40] Num. 16:23–33.

[41] 'merveille' in its bad sense: disaster, calamity, terrible event.

[42] The three-headed dog was called Cerberus.

Notoniers en fut Acheron,
il et sis compaigns Acharon;
ent[r]e els deux out un nacele,   5270
oue quel passent la gent meisele.
Cochiton ot non ycil fluvies,
fiers estoit plius que nuls deluvies;
cist est ardant a toutes leis
assez plus que nuls fous grezeis;   5275
molt sont chaitis qui ainz
        remaignent,
molt sospirent fort et se plaignent.
    Amphiarax ceste eve passe,
et des autres oue lui grant masse;
mais Amphiarax vait premiers,   5280
qui fut noveals gonfanoers.
A un trespas vint molt pudnés,
ou mil dragons movent lour becs;
neir fut et grant et molt horrible.
Une eve i ot qui fait molt grant   5285
        rible;
plius est trenchanz que nuls
        rasours,
plus tost cort que ne vole ostours:

Styx l'apelent tout li autor,
et li petit et li graignor.
Sur cele n'ot planche ne pont,   5290
ne nul rien qui mot li sont.
Thesiphoné illoec se baigne
et ses crins de serpenz aplaigne;
come lou ule et crie et brait,
et vers Amphiarax se trait.   5295
Amphiarax fort s'effroït
quant le Sathan venir oït,
car pleine fu de marrement
et dist lui molt iriement:
'Mar entras cea ens a cheval,   5300
molt y avras pullent ostal.'
Amphiarax oue grant poor
s'en passa outre et [oue] dolour;[43]
atant parvint davant le rei,
trestouz armez de son conrei.   5305
Pluto li reis oue son trident
d'Amphiarax prist vengement:
des puis qu'Amphiarax fu morz,
n'en poet il puis garder en sorz.

---

[43] 'oue' missing from the MS, supplied by the editor.

The ferryman here was Acheron, with his companion Charon.[44] The pair of them had a skiff, which served for all those wretches to pass over. This river is called Cocytus, and is fiercer than any deluge. It blazes all over its surface, worse than any Greek fire.[45] So terribly tortured are those in there, and they sigh and groan piteously.

Amphiarax passes across this water, together with a great mass of others. But Amphiarax goes first, as a new standard-bearer. He came to a filthy passageway where a thousand dragons wriggled their snouts; it was huge, black, and horrible. There was another river, flowing fiercely, which was sharper than any razor and swifter than any goshawk in flight. All the authors, great and small, call it the Styx. Over this one is neither plank nor bridge, nor is there any living thing to speak to him. Tisiphone is bathing there,[46] and smoothing her serpent locks. She howls like a wolf, screaming and shouting, and draws close to Amphiarax.

Amphiarax is terrified when he hears this devil coming, for she is filled with viciousness and says angrily to him 'Curse you for coming in here on your horse! You'll get nasty smelly lodging!'

Fearfully, painfully, Amphiarax passes her by. At length, still armed in all his war-gear, he comes before the king; this king, Pluto, takes vengeance on Amphiarax with his trident.

Now Amphiarax is dead, and he can no longer gaze into the future.

---

[44] The poet has made two ferrymen out of one (note to this line).

[45] Greek fire, unquenchable, was a legendary and deadly weapon; it is not known how it was made.

[46] Tisiphone is one of the Furies (variously named and described by classical authors); *OCL*, s.v. Furies.

Protheselaus

The Severed Head[47]

The long and rambling romance of *Protheselaus* (Dean 163) contains some hidden treasures, and I include one in this book in order to help it become better known. Further, to remind readers that Anglo-Norman is a French of other parts of Britain and not just of England, its author represents Wales. Critics have not been kind to *Protheselaus*;[48] I would like to do something to redeem it. Hue de Rotelande's first romance, *Ipomedon*, also composed at the end of the twelfth century, was vastly more popular.[49] Because much of the *Protheselaus* material is drawn from 'romans d'antiquité', and other themes are from folk-tale, Arthurian romance, and so on, I have placed the present excerpt between *Thèbes* and *Yder* so as to keep an approximate generic grouping. Neither of those romances is in Dean; although *Thèbes* arguably does not count as Anglo-Norman, it is important to realise it was read, if not composed, here. Hue borrows some names from *Thèbes*, therefore he must have known it (or a version of it), and assumed his readers knew it too. He may have taken names from Statius, but either situation is possible. This is further evidence that texts written in Continental France were known and read and copied in Anglo-Norman Britain.

The passage I have chosen is found elsewhere as a folk-tale, 'Le conte du mari trompé'; sixteen versions have been recorded and examined.[50] Hue's version, according to Holden, is only a faint echo of the original tale: the theme is of a wicked wife helped out of her predicament by the intervention of a stranger (here, the hero Protheselaus).[51] The present version predates, but is unlikely to be a source for, the version in *Gesta*.[52] Lecoy says Gower's version, which goes back ultimately to Paul the Deacon (eighth century), is 'un autre thème' (p. 479, note 1); he judges this tale of Hue's to be the earliest known example. He does not suggest Hue invented it, but that he was telling and adapting only part of an existing tale (unknown before this date, p. 504). I have been unable to trace the motif, either of this or of the Gower version, in Thompson, *Motif-Index*.

An interesting early lexical item, in this very passage, is the use of two words 'guage' and 'plege' occurring together in a situation of dispute and its resolution (vv. 4970–86). It has been remarked that twelfth-century appearances of 'gage'

---

[47] vv. 4800–5002.

[48] Hue de Rotelande, ed. Holden, p. 3; the Introduction is in vol. III (ANTS 47–9). But see Weiss, 'A reappraisal of *Protheselaus*', for an appreciative study of the romance.

[49] See Legge, pp. 85–96, for both Hue's romances.

[50] Lecoy, 'Un épisode du *Protheselaus* et le conte du mari trompé'. The version in *Gesta Romanorum* (ed. and tr. Swan and Hooper), is number 56; the Middle English collection of the same name (ed. Herrtage, p. 519) does not contain it. It also appears in Gower's *Confessio Amantis* (ed. Macaulay; but see Lecoy).

[51] See Introduction, pp. 5–10 (on Sources).

[52] See also Gowans, 'Sir Uallabh O Còrn: A Hebridean Tale of Sir Gawain'.

clearly predate its legal specialization, it and 'plege' are already associated in the *Leis Willelme* (before 1189).[53] *Protheselaus* followed hard on the heels of *Ipomedon*, which was probably composed in the 1180s (Dean 162); this puts it very close in time to the *Leis*.

The episode is in Holden's vol. I (notes pp. 52–3 in vol. III); the events that took place before the beginning of this extract are explained in conversation. The base manuscript is Holden's A (Paris, Bibliothèque Nationale, fr. 2169, see p. 10 of the Introduction),[54] which is incomplete.[55]

---

[53] Hyams, 'Thinking Law', pp. 184–5 and note 41.

[54] Dean dates this MS to the first third of the thirteenth century.

[55] The end of the poem is missing in the base MS, but this does not signify for the passage chosen here.

Text

[38c] Li Blois s'est asis al manger.
Protheselaüs od lui set,
Merveilles ora, ainz qu'il liet.
Ey vus un vassal fort e grant!
De vers la cambre vent portant   4804
Une chaiere grant de ivoire
Uvree de fin or a triffoire;
En la chaere un oreiller
A fin or broisdé bon e cher;   4808
De fin or i ot meint boton
Ovré de l'ovre Salomon.
Cil qui la chaere porta [38d]
Devant le Bloi asise l'a;   4812
Protheselaüs, que ço vit,
S'esmerveille, mes mot n'en dit.
Wastels, walfres e simenels
E vins e mes pleners e bels,   4816
Cum al Bloi memes la maniere,
Aset l'em devant la chaere;
N'i set dame ne chevaler,
Si y venent lé mes plener.   4820
Protheselaüs en pes set,
Il verra el, ainz qu'il se let.
Vers la cusine en un effrei
Dous palteners a grant desrei   4824
Menent une meschine avant
A mult grant hunte demenant.
Ben semblot franche dammeisele,
Mult esteit alingné e bele,   4828
Mult ot en li bele figure,
Mais mult ot povre vesteüre
E mult esteit a grant mesaise;
Chemise ot neire e malveise,   4832

Unes pels ot mult enfumees
De gros mutuns e mult usees.
Cil paltener, que mult sunt grant,
La butent, ferent de vergant,   4836
Laidissent d'estrange guise;
Enmi cel aire l'unt assise,
Tut par sei a un escamel,
N'i ot dubler ne laid ne bel,   4840
Mult s'est asise murnement.
A mes li vent priveement [39a]
Une teste tute sanglente;
Quant la vit la pucele gente,   4844
De joie li mua color,
Un poi suzrist par grant dulçur.
Li Blois Chevaler l'esgarda,
Ire ot, mes mot ne parla.   4848
Protheselaüs l'aparçut,
Mervaille s'en que c'estre dut;
Pur la pucele alques se dolt
Mais un mot parler ne volt.   4852
Neir pain d'orge devant li mistrent
E mes mult fiebles i asistrent;
N'i aveit guaires de moré.
Saillent cil paltener devé;   4856
Par les tresces sus l'aracent,
Arere od lur verganz la chacent.
Protheselaüs tel dol a
Unques puis ne but ne manga;   4860
E li Blois en ot tel pité
N'ad guaires beü ne mangé;
Ben veit que Protheselaüs
Est tant dolent qu'il ne pot plus.   4864

Translation

The Blond Knight sat down to dinner, and Protheselaus sat with him. He will hear something amazing before he gets up again! Here comes a great strong knight, who arrives in the chamber carrying a big ivory chair worked with fine gold inlay; in the chair is a pillow richly and beautifully worked with gold thread, and ornamented with golden buttons made in Solomon's style.[56] He who was carrying the chair set it down in front of the Blond Knight; Protheselaus, who saw this, was astonished but said not a word.[57] Several kinds of cake were served,[58] together with delicious meats and wines a-plenty, placed before the chair as well as before the Knight. There was not a lady or gentleman at the table for whom the dishes did not arrive in abundance. Protheselaus sat there quietly — he will see something else before he gets up! Then there is a rumpus from the kitchen, and a couple of rogues come violently dragging forth a young girl. It is a shameful business; the girl looks like a noble damsel, fair and elegant. She has a lovely face but wretched clothes, and seems in a very unhappy state; her chemise is filthy and ragged, and her smoky old furs are of coarse and worn-out sheepskin. These huge scoundrels push her, beating her with sticks and insulting her outlandishly. They seat her in the middle of the place all by herself on a stool. No tablecloth for her, neither fine nor fair; she sat down miserably.

A special dish arrived for her: a head, all bloody! When the gentle damsel saw it, her colour rose for joy and she gave a sweet little smile. The Blond Knight was watching, angrily, but he said never a word. Protheselaus saw it, and wondered what on earth it could be all about. He was rather upset for the girl, but he didn't want to say anything. They put black rye bread before her, and gave her very inadequate fare; there wasn't much spiced wine for her! Then the rough chaps sprang forward, grabbing her up by her hair and chasing her back with their sticks.

Protheselaus was so distressed he couldn't eat or drink any more, and the Knight had such pity for him[59] he had hardly eaten or drunk anything. He could see that Protheselaus was so sorrowful he couldn't bear it.

---

[56] This, together with the inlay work of the chair, matches descriptions found in Romances of Antiquity (Holden's note), and elsewhere. For example, *Le Roman de Troie, Extraits*, Benoît de Sainte-Maure (pp. 96–7, v. 1818 and note); another in Marie de France, *Lais*, ed. Ewert (*Guigemar*, v. 172 and note on p. 166).

[57] The scene is reminiscent of where, in the Grail story, Perceval witnesses marvels but fails to ask the timely and relevant question.

[58] Holden's glossary does not specify; they appear to be: cakes (wastels = gâteaux), waffles or wafers (walfres), and simnel-cake (made with fine flour). In *Receptaria*, 'wastel' is glossed as 'bread of the finest flour', and 'simnel' as 'bread of light flour' (p. 124).

[59] 'en', unclear; this could in fact be pity for her.

'Bels sire,' fait il, 'qu'avez vus?
Mult vus vei murne e anguissus.
Dites, sire, que vus avez!
Del tut ferrai voz volentez.'   4868
Protheselaüs li dit: 'Sire,
Or vus dirrai dunt ai cest' ire,
Quel qu'a ben u mal me turt:
Merveilles vei en ceste curt.'   4872
Li Bloi dit: 'Sire chevaler, [39b]
Ne vus devez pas merveiller.
Le veir del tut vus conuistrai
E l'ovre vus descoverai: 4876
Vus veïstes la dameisele,
Jo vi l'ure que mult fu bele;
Certes, el m'esteit si amie
Que plus l'amoie que ma vie;   4880
A mult grant onur la tenee,
Devant mei servir la fesee
Sor ceste chaere doree,
Tant cum mon cors fu onuree.   4884
Ces dous guainnuns que pendu
      sunt,
Que veïstes al chef del punt,
Deüssent ma cambre guaiter
Que n'i entrast cel chevaler   4888
Ki vus enterrastes al gué;
N'en firent pru, sin fu gabbé,
E jo pur ço d'els m'en vengai,
Cum veïstes, pendu les ai.   4892
Les dols qui pendent armez
Furent sor tuz de mei privez,
De m'onur durent guarde prendre;
Nel firent, pur ço sis fis pendre.   4896
Cil chevaler qui sul i pent
Ot tut a sun cummandement

E mei e trestute ma terre,
Ne lassa pas ma honte a quere;   4900
A tot son poër me honi
E jo l'aperceu, sil pendi.
Sacez que ceste dammeisele
A cel' ure esteit gente e bele, [39c]   4904
Mais par cunseil fol que d'eus ot
Cel vassal, dunt vus di, amot.
Defendue li oi ma terre,
Mais ne volt fors ma hunte quere;   4908
Mais qu'il guaitai al païs,
A li cumbati, si l'occis.
Chescun jor de la semaine e feste
Devant li faz mettre la teste;   4912
Mais ele en fait joie grant
E j'en sui vif desvé par tant.
Ja n'avra al quor tel dolur,
Si tost cum el la veit le jor,   4916
De joie li estait si ben
De la dolor n'i est ren;
C'est la ren dunt plus su marri,
Kar s'el vosist crier merci,   4920
De ren si haitez ne serreie,
Al premier mot li pardoree.'
Protheselaüs dit: 'Bels sire,
Nel tenez a curuz ne a ire;   4924
Donez mei de parler congé
A li, kar j'en ai grant pité.'
Li Bloi dit: 'Sire chevalers,
Parlez! Mult le voil volenters.   4928
Se poez son quer aturner
Que sulement me voille amer,
Grez e merci vus renderee,
Tot le forfait li pardurroie.'   4932

'Good sir,' he said, 'What's the matter? I can see you're very anxious and unhappy. Tell me what's wrong, friend! I'll do whatever you want.' Protheselaus said 'Friend, I will tell you what's distressing me, whatever happens for good or ill: I have seen something awful in this court!'

The Blond Knight said 'Sir knight, don't be astonished. I shall make the whole truth known to you, and show you the whole affair. You saw that damsel: I saw her when she was so beautiful. Yes, it's true she was my sweetheart, so much that I loved her more than my life. I held her in the highest honour, and had her served before me on that golden chair, as if I were honouring my own self.[60] Those two mastiffs you saw hanging by the end of the drawbridge? They were supposed to guard my chamber so that knight should not enter: that knight whom you buried at the ford.[61] The devil they did! I was tricked, and so I took my revenge and hanged them, as you saw. Those poor wretches hanged in their armour were among my special men. They were supposed to guard my honour and they didn't, so I had them hanged.[62] The knight hanging there alone was one who had everything he wanted, of me and of all my territory; but he never ceased his efforts to shame me, and humiliated me every way he could. I discovered it, and hanged him. Let me tell you the damsel was then so graceful and lovely, but because of foolish things he heard from them about her he — that knight I told you about — loved her. I forbade him my lands, but he wanted nothing but to shame me. However, even though he kept a close watch about the place,[63] I fought him. And I killed him. Every day, weekday or feast-day, I have his head put in front of her. But she is so delighted with it, it maddens me! No matter how much pain she feels in her heart, as soon as she sees it that day she is so joyful that grief doesn't matter to her. That's what distresses me more than anything; if she would only beg forgiveness it would be the happiest moment of my life. I would forgive her at the first word.'

Protheselaus said 'Good sir, please don't be angry or offended: give me permission to speak to her, because I feel so sorry for her.'

The Knight said 'Speak, sir knight! I would very much like you to do so. If you can turn her heart, just so she will love me, I'll render you most grateful thanks, and I'll forgive her all her punishment.'[64]

---

[60] 'cum mon cors': this expression usually means 'myself'.

[61] At vv. 4575–85, & 4615–20 (the episode begins at v. 4534).

[62] 'sis' is 'si les' (not six); the narrative earlier specifies two of them (v. 4769). The hero and his companions saw them, the dogs, and the single hanged man, on their way in.

[63] Holden say this line is defective, and suggests a reading from another MS.

[64] This not uncommon formula means he will forgive her everything for which he is punishing her.

Protheselaüs est levez,
Desqu'a la meschine est alez;
Cum el le vit, sus se dresça,
Curteisement le salua. [39d]   4936
Protheselaüs s'est asis,
La pucele regarde al vis;
Sa grant belté mult li agree,
Mais feblement fu atournee.   4940
Il la mist tost a raison.
'Bele, jo vus requer un don.
Unc mais de mes oilz ne vus vi,
Certes, jo vus erc bon ami;   4944
M'amur vus ert a tot dis preste
Se faire volez ma requeste.'
La meschine respont sanz ire:
'Sire, ne saverez ren dire   4948
Que jo ne face volenters,
Kar mult semblez franc chevalers.'
'Dameisele, vostre merci!
J'ai mult parlé a vostre ami;   4952
De vus se pleint mult durement,
Mais c'est son major marrement
Quant vus vers lui forfait avez,
Que merci ne li demandez.   4956
Dameisele, tant ai enquis,
De ses paroles tant apris:
Se vus merci li demandez,
Tut ferra quant que vus vodrez.'   4960
La dameisele lui respont:
'Sire, si Deus onur me dunt,
J'en ai esté si treshuntuse,
De mon mesfait si vergonduse,   4964
De honte parler ne pooie,
Ne ne puis, mais que morir deie.'
'Avoi, bele, ne seez fole!

Jo musterai vostre parole; [40a]   4968
Mar ferez for agenuler,
Guage ofrez, lassez mei parler!'
Fait la meschine: 'Vez me preste.
Vostre voler, vostre requeste   4972
Ferai jo, sire, n'en sai plus.'
Dunc leve Protheselaüs,
Fait la pucele od li venir,
Eissent de cambrë, a l'eisir   4976
Li Blois les ad aparceüz,
De grant joie est tut esperduz;
La dameisele ne s'ublie,
A ses pez chet tut espasmie,   4980
Son guage tent, mes n'en dit ren;
Protheselaüs le dit ben:
'Sire, pur Deu, sire, merci!
Tut son mesfait pardonez li   4984
Par tel covant cum vus dirrai:
Jo meme plege en serrai
Qu'a tuz les jorz mais de sa vie
Vus ert leale e bone amie.'   4988
Li Blois regarda la meschine
K'il ama de grant amur fine;
Veit la plurer mult tendrement,
De li ad grant pité forment;   4992
Des oilz plure par grant tendrur,
Kar mult l'ama de grant amur.
Conseil ne demanda a nulli,
Il l'ot tut prest ensemble od li;   4996
La meschine par la main prent,
Si l'en leva mult bonement;
Son maltalent li pardona,
Plus de dous cent feiz la baisa. [40b] 5000
Par la sale sunt haité tuit,
Grant joie i ad e grant deduit.

Protheselaus got up and went across to the damsel. When she saw him, she arose and greeted him courteously. Protheselaus sat and looked into the girl's face. Her great beauty pleased him, even though she was poorly arrayed. He began to speak straight away: 'My fair one, I would ask for a favour. I have never set eyes on you before, but I will certainly be a good friend to you. My love will always be at your service if you will agree to my request.' The damsel was not offended, and replied 'My lord, there is nothing you could say that I would not do gladly for you, because you seem to be a noble knight.'

'Thank you, dear lady! I have spoken freely to your friend, and he complains bitterly about you. But the worst thing for him is that you have done him wrong and you will not ask his forgiveness. Lady, I have asked many questions, and I have learned from his words: if you ask his forgiveness he would do anything for you!'

The damsel replied to him 'My lord, God give me grace, I have been so very ashamed, and so cast down by my own fault, I cannot speak for shame. I couldn't if I should die for it!'

'Oh come, lovely, don't be a fool! I will tell him your words. All you have to do is kneel down, and offer a token;[65] let me do the talking!'

The damsel said 'I am ready. I will do what you want, and grant your request, sir; I don't know what else to do.'

Then Protheselaus got up, making the girl come with him. They went out of the chamber, and as they went out the Blond Knight saw them. He was quite mad with joy, and the girl didn't lose any time — she fell fainting at his feet. She held out the token, but didn't speak. Protheselaus said it beautifully:

'My lord! For God's sake have mercy, my lord! Forgive her all her misdeeds, on such a condition that I shall tell you: I myself shall be guarantee for her, that for all the days of her life she will be a good and faithful lover to you.'

The Knight looked at the lady, whom he loved with great and true love.[66] He saw how she wept bitterly, and was filled with pity for her; his eyes wept with tenderness, for he loved her very dearly. He didn't need to ask anybody's advice, because he had his decision ready: he took the lady by the hand. Raising her up, he forgave her all her transgressions;[67] he kissed her a thousand times. Everybody present in the hall was pleased, and there was great happiness and rejoicing.

---

[65] Holden suggests the 'gage' may have been a glove or similar token of submission.

[66] 'amur fine' is an example of the much-discussed term sometimes translated as 'courtly love'. It is often used to contrast the true love of God with mere earthly love (for example, in *La Vie d'Edouard*, ed. Södergård); here it underlines the genuine nature of the knight's feelings.

[67] See note to v. 4932: 'pardoner son maltalent' appears to mean *he* forgave *her* his [own] bad feelings; he forgives her [the thing that causes] his bad feelings. In *Folie Tristan*, below (v. 893), we cannot reasonably translate 'he forgave us for his anger.' A similarly elliptical expression obtains in Middle English: to pardon can mean to put aside or cease to harbour one's own 'euylle wylle' (see *The Book of the Knight of the Tower*, ed. Offord, heading to chapter 102 and note). See also Audiau, *Les Troubadours et l'Angleterre*, note 1 on p. 55: the lover says 'Je vous demande pardon de vos torts'.

Le Roman de Fergus

This romance is best known for its Scottish setting, another reminder that Anglo-Norman is not to be thought of as the French of England only.[68] It is dated between 1200 and 1233 by Frescoln, and simply 'thirteenth century' by Dean. Frescoln edits the Chantilly version (MS Musée Condé 472) with some corrections from the Paris version (BN f. fr. 1553). Unfortunately only these two Continental MSS survive. It is by Guillaume le Clerc, who names himself at the end of the work.[69]

Owen points out that its literary merit has been overshadowed by the geographical considerations that have interested so many readers,[70] therefore I have picked out from it an adventure that could have taken place anywhere.[71] In his account of this romance,[72] Owen remarks that Guillaume has abandoned a typically vague Arthurian geography for a setting designed to draw a Scottish audience into the action. In this, the earliest extant Scottish literary fiction, he invites his public to pursue debate on the place of women in society.

The episode chosen here nicely encapsulates much of the plot, because the dwarf tells some of what has happened and much of what is going to happen.[73] *Fergus* takes its place after *Protheselaus* in Dean's ordering, conveniently moving us towards Arthur's court and other Matter of Britain in this chapter.[74]

Fergus predictably encounters dragons and giants, including a fearful giantess; in the present episode he meets a dwarf whose helpful advice contrasts with the unpleasant behaviour of dwarfs in the two Tristan stories, below. The episode has something in common with dream-visions: the atmosphere is magical, and the beautiful spring has precious stones for pebbles. A famous description of a spring filled with precious stones is the setting for *Pearl*.[75] Another is in a parody of such

---

[68] Dean 167, and Legge's brief account (her pp. 161–2); see also Owen, 'The Craft of *Fergus*'. My text is taken from *The Romance of Fergus*, ed. Frescoln (published by William Allen), with some notes from '*The Romance of Fergus*', tr. Owen.

[69] Douglas Gray's anthology includes two passages, translation only, from *Fergus* (*Norman Conquest*, ed. Gray, pp. 251–7). His passages leapfrog mine presented here, happening before and after the incident.

[70] Including the surmise that it was written on this side of the Channel (Frescoln's Introduction deals with this and other matters).

[71] The passage is vv. 3655–916 in the edition (Owen's translation pp. 133–6). Frescoln points to parallels with *Le Chevalier au Lion* (his p. 25).

[72] Burgess and Pratt, eds, *The Arthur of the French*, pp. 426–9.

[73] Another specular narrative is retold by Tristan, below.

[74] Jean Bodel divided the matter of romance into 'generic' areas: romances of antiquity, and the Charlemagne material that includes many chansons de geste; then, anything to do with Arthur and his knights was deemed to be 'of Brittany' (see the opening of *La Chanson des Saisnes*, ed. Brasseur). The 'ancestral' romances (Legge classifies *Fergus* among these, although it probably does not belong there) have been dubbed 'Matter of England' by more recent scholars.

[75] In [Gawain] *Sir Gawain and The Green Knight, Pearl, and Sir Orfeo*, ed. Tolkien.

romantic excess: 'The Land of Cockaygne' (see its Introduction for analogues).[76] In line with Chrétien de Troyes,[77] whose work Guillaume clearly knew well, there is much to be said for calling it the romance of The Knight with the Splendid Shield (... chevalier au biel escu); this is what Guillaume calls it at the end of the text.[78] The audience's discovery of the hero's name, or his discovery of his own name, is an important theme of many romances.[79] Our hero first appears at v. 355 but is not named until vv. 736–9;[80] further, the narrator does not use the name until Fergus himself has announced it. Unsurprisingly (to those who are familiar with the stock traits of Arthurian knights), Kay is his usual ill-mannered self: he angers the hero by his mocking words, and Gawain is furious on his behalf. In this romance Arthur is polite to the newcomer; in *Yder*, below, we shall see that Arthur behaves as badly as Kay does.

---

[76] *The Kildare Manuscript*, ed. Turville-Petre, pp. 3–9, at vv. 83–94.

[77] Neither *Le Chevalier de la Charrete* nor *Le Chevalier au Lion* gives away the hero's name in the title, although they are often called *Lancelot* and *Yvain* by modern readers. *Perceval*'s subtitle, *Le Conte du Graal*, conceals the hero's name (as in the story); this title *Perceval* obscures Gawain's place as its other hero. Chrétien clearly thought a dramatic placing, of the revelation of heroes' names, to be of crucial significance.

[78] Frescoln's Introduction, p. 1.

[79] See my *Naming and Namelessness*, *passim*.

[80] Owen's translation, note on p. 174.

Text

[f.111e] En tel dolor et en tel cure 3655
Et en tele mesaventure
Fu Fergus un an trestot plain,
Que onques n'i manga de pain
De car cuite car ne l'avoit.
Mais quant li grant fains l'argüoit, 3660
Si chaçoit tant que il prendroit
Dain u cervreul dont le mangoit
Comme ciens la car tote crue.
Maigre avoit le ciere et velue 3664
Por ço qu'il n'ert res ne tondus;
Et li blïaus dont fu vestus
Estoit ronpus et descirés.
L'aubers li bat as nus costés 3668
Qu'il ot grailles et amagris.
Tos est alés et desnorris,
Et ses chevals tot autretel,
Qu'il ot eü mal ostel. 3672
Un an ot ja passé et plus.
Par le bois chevaucho[i]t Fergus,
Le plus bel et le mius follu
Que onques nus hom ot veü 3676
Puis que Dius le premier forma.
En cel bois une fontainne a
Qui sordoit devers orïant;
N'a plus biele, mien ensïant, 3680
Desi que la u Dius fu nés.
Et tels pooirs li fu donnés
Que nule autre fontainne n'a
Que ja nus hom tant [ne] serra 3684
Malades ne mesa[a]issiés,
S'il en boit, qui ne soit haitiés.
Fergus s'en vint a la fontainne,
Qui molt estoit et clere et sainne, 3688
Non pas por ço qu'il le quesist;
Mais Fortune la le tramist
Que des mals le voloit saner
Qu'ele li ot fait endurer. 3692
Lonc tans li ot esté contraire;
Or li est doce et deboinaire.
Fortune le veult ellever

Si haut com le porra monter. 3696
Fergus esgarde l'iaue biele
Qui sort sor molt haute graviele,
Qui ert de pieres presiouses,
Molt gentes et molt vertüousses 3700
Et bieles de mainte maniere;
El mont n'a presiouse piere
[f.111f] Qui ne fust sor la fonteniele.
Sor la rive ot une capiele 3704
Faite del tans anchïenor.
Uns nains le garde nuit et jor
Qui devinoit tot sans mentir
Ço qui estoit a avenir 3708
A cels qui illuec trespasoient
Et de la fontainne bevoient.
Mais s'aucuns illuec trespassast,
Si n'en beüst ne ne goistast 3712
De la fontenele corant,
Ne li desist ne tant ne quant;
Ja tant nel seüst araisnier.
Fergus voit l'iaue formoier 3716
Et aler arie[re] et avant.
Por sa biauté l'en prist talant
Qu'il en beüst un petitet;
Del destrier pié a terre met 3720
Et vint a l'iaue, si en but
A la main tant com il lui plut.
Maintenant qu'il en ot gosté,
Tot son corage et son pens[é] 3724
Et sa force et son hardiment
Li revint el cors eranment;
Or fu bials et liés et joians
Et plus legiers et plus tornans 3728
Que ne soit uns esmerillons
Et fu plus fiers que uns lions.
Totë a oblïee sa cure.
Ains s'afice forment et jure 3732
Qu'il n'a el monde chevalier,
S'or se voloit vers lui drecier,
Que grant estor ne li rendist.

Translation

In such pain and such care, in such evil fortune, Fergus had now spent a whole year. He never ate bread, nor cooked meat, for he had none. But when fierce hunger tormented him, he went hunting until he had caught a buck or a stag, and ate its flesh all raw like a dog. His face was haggard and hairy, for he was neither shaved nor barbered, and the shirt he was wearing was ragged and torn. His hauberk rattled against his bare ribs, that were so thin and skinny. He was completely haggard and starved, and so was his horse, for he had enjoyed pretty bad lodgings. This had been going on for a year or more.

Through the forest rode Fergus, the loveliest and the leafiest that ever human eye had seen since God created the very first one. In this forest there was a fountain, gushing out towards the East. There is none more beautiful, I'd say, between here and the place where God was born. It was endowed with a power that no other fountain had: never was there any man so ill or suffering who would not, if he drank from it, be cured. Fergus came towards the fountain, that was so clear and clean, but not because he was looking for it. Fortune sent him there, wanting to heal him of his hurts, that she had made him suffer for so long. She has been against him for so long, but now she is sweet and mild to him. Fortune wants to raise him up as high as he can possibly be lifted.[81] Fergus looks at the beautiful water gushing out onto a high bank of gravel; this was all of precious stones, that were kindly and virtuous,[82] all of them lovely in their different ways. There was no precious gem in the whole world that could not be found at that little spring.

On the bank stood a small chapel, built in ancient times. Night and day it is guarded by a dwarf who can tell everything, no lie, about what the future holds for those who pass by there and drink of that spring. But if one passes who drinks not, nor even tastes of that flowing fountain, he won't say a thing however much that one tries to persuade him.

Fergus sees the water swirling back and forth; it is so lovely that he is seized with desire to drink just a sip. He alights from his horse and goes to the water, then he drinks some from his hand, as much as he wants. But now he has drunk, all his heart and thought, all his force and hardihood, immediately return to his body! Now he is handsome and happy and joyful, and he is lighter and swifter than a merlin, fiercer than a lion. He has forgotten all his troubles! Rather, he asserts himself proudly, swearing that there is no knight in the world he would not take on and give a good drubbing to, should he stand up against him.

---

[81] The reference is to Fortune's wheel, on which lucky individuals are raised to the top when she spins it; the unlucky ones who had been at the top are thus dashed to the bottom.

[82] Stones had medicinal powers (lists of these were called Lapidaries); for example, the amethyst is supposed to prevent intoxication (*OED*).

Atant fors de la capiele ist   3736
Li nains. Si l'a reconneü
Et dist: 'Vasal, bien aies tu,
Li fuis au vilain de Pelande!
Joie et baudors et honors grande   3740
T'est aprestee, bien le di.
Je te connois mius que tu mi
Et bien sai que tu vas querant
Galïene o le cors vaillant,   3744
A cui t'escondesis t'amor;
Mainte painne, mainte dolor
Et mainte plue et maint oré
Aras soufert et enduré,   3748
Et mainte cop t'este[v]ra avoir
Ançois que le puisse[s] ravoir.
Mais ce saces, par moi saras
La maniere par coi l'aras: 3752
Se tu es tant preus et tant sages
Et s'en toi est tels vaselages
[f.112a] Qu'a Dunottre vuelles aler
Por le blanc escu conquester,   3756
Que garde la vi[e]lle moussue,
Encor poras avoir ta drue.
Se ne vius enprendre cest fais
Por li ne t'en travelle mais.'   3760
Quant Fergus ot que li nains dist
Molt durement s'en esjoïst;
Il cuide et croit en sa pensee
Que li nains est cose faee.   3764
Se li plaist molt a escouter
Ço que li nains li veut conter
Que il ravra encor s'amie;

Qui li donnast tote Pavie,   3768
Nel fesist on pas plus joiant.
Mais savoir veut comfaitement
Il le porra mius recouvrer,
Et le liu u le puist trover.   3772
Et dist au nain 'Cose petite,
Foi que tu dois Sainte Esperite,
Quant tu le dis et je t'en croi
Que mius me connois que je toi   3776
Et par mon non m'as apielé,
Se il te vient en volenté,
Ensaigne moi sans demorer
Le liu u le porrai trover;   3780
Car nule rien tant ne desir.
Se Damesdius par son plaisir
Me voloit avuec lui posser
Et tos mes mesfais pardonner   3784
Que je onques vers lui mespris;
Se Galïene o le clers vis
Fust en infer en tenebror,
S'iroïe je; por soie amor   3788
Lairoie paradiss la sus
Por venir avuec li ça jus
Soufrir mal et painne et torm[en]t
Dusques au grant forjugement.   3792
Ensigniés le moi, bien ferés;
Puis que vos mon consel savés
Et que autre chose ne quier
Bien le me devés ensignier,   3796
Et je serrai vos hom tenans
Trestos les jors qu'ere vivans.'

Then, out from the chapel came the dwarf! He recognized him, saying 'Noble youth, may the good be with thee, villein of Pelande's son![83]   Much joy and gladness, and great honours, are in waiting for you, I can tell you that! I know you better than you know me,[84] and I know you're in search of the shapely Galiene, to whom you refused your love.[85] You will have suffered much pain and endured much suffering, many a rain and many a tempest, and you will have to undergo hard knocks, before you can possess her again! But pay attention, for it is from me that you shall learn how to get her back. If you are wise and bold enough, with sufficient bravery to be prepared to go to Dunottre,[86] to achieve the White Shield, that is guarded by the hairy old hag, then you'll be able to win your sweetheart. But if you don't want to undertake this task then there'll be no point your undertaking any further travails for her.'

When Fergus heard what the dwarf had to say, he was absolutely delighted! He believed, and thought to himself, that the dwarf was a fairy creature.[87] So he was pleased to listen to what the dwarf wanted to tell him, how he was going to get his sweetheart back; he couldn't be more joyful if you had given him the whole of Pavia! But he wanted to know exactly how he could best go about recovering her, and the place where he would find her. He said to the dwarf: 'Little man, by the faith you owe to the Holy Ghost,[88] when you tell me, and I believe you, that you know me better than I know you, and you've called me by my name, if it's your will then tell me quickly the place where I can find her! She is the one I desire more than any other![89] If it pleased the Lord God to wish to place me with him, and forgive all the wickedness that I had ever sinned against him, and if the bright-faced Galiene was in the shadows of Hell, then I would go there too. For her love I would leave Paradise there above, to come down there below with her, to suffer ills and pain and torment until the great Day of Judgement.[90] Teach me all about it, you'll do well to do so. Since you know what's in my heart, and that there is nothing else I seek, you are bound to tell me; and I will be your liege man all the days that I live.'

---

[83] The dwarf begins speaking in the second person singular; Fergus replies in kind but later they both shift to the 'vos' form. Frescoln (note to v. 3738) remarks that the author occasionally intermixes singular and plural forms.

[84] So far, the dwarf has identified him, and named his lady, but has not named him Fergus.

[85] She fell in love with him (vv. 1495–2044), but he refused her advances saying he had to go and meet a Black Knight (Frescoln's Analyse, p. 18; Owen's translation, pp. 108–14).

[86] Dunottar Castle, Kinkardineshire (editor's note to v. 3755).

[87] Contrast this wise and benevolent dwarf, and the affectionate tone of this conversation, with the nasty creature in the Tristan stories, below.

[88] It is possible Fergus is taking a precaution here: if the creature is a demon then the Name of God will frighten it away.

[89] 'rien' (thing) is less derogatory than it sounds, and is often used for a person as well as for an object. The line could also mean 'there is nothing I desire more'.

[90] This is blasphemy: it was considered sinful even to pray for souls in Hell, let alone make a vow like this (only souls in Purgatory could be helped by prayer). Owen considers this passage an example of Guillaume's humorous attitude to the exaggerated love-language of chivalric romance.

Li nains li respont: 'Chevalier,
Tres bien vos saro[i]e avoier 3800
De ço que vos me requerés.
Mais ce saciés, pas ne l'arés
Si souavet que vos cuidiés;
Ançois en ert escus perciés, 3804
Et ce est en peril de mort,
Que vos puissiés avoir confort
[f.112b] Ne joie ne envoisseüre
De celi u metés vo cure. 3808
Saciés de voir, il n'i a tor:
Il couvient acater bon jor
A celui qui le veut avoir.
Et vos l'a[ca]terés por voir, 3812
Ains que l'aiés, molt cierement,
Et si n'ert pas d'or ne d'argent.
Mais ce saciés dou cors demainne.
Ja sanc ne jeterés de vainne 3816
Por plaie que ja recevés:
Seürement vos combatés
Se vos pöés venir en leu.
Molt vos este[v]ra estre preu, 3820
Se jamais avoir le volés.
Par proëche le conquerés;
Car por loier ne por doner
Ne pöés a li recovrer, 3824
Par hardement ne par vertu
Se vos n'avés le bel escu
Qu'en la tor de Dunostre pent;
Ja nel raverés autrement 3828
Par cose que je vos en die.'
Quant cil ot qu'il ne rara mie
S'amie se cel escu n'a
Lors dist au nain que il l'ara 3832
Se ja nus hom le doit avoir;
Mais il veut encore savoir
Le vertu que cil escus a
Et en quel liu le trovera. 3836
Li nains li dist tot a estrous:
'Li escus est si vertuous
Que cil qui l'avra en baillie
Ja par armes ne perdra vie 3840

Ne n'iert abatus de ceval
Por nul homme vivant carnal.
Encor a il autre nature
Que ja la nuis n'iert si oscure 3844
Qu'il n'ait clarté entor la tor,
Atant par nuit comme par jor,
U li escus est en repos.
Saciés que de trestoute l'os 3848
D'Engleterre estoit asanblee
S'eüssent vostre mort juree,
Mais tant d'avantage eüssiés
Que dedens cele tor fuissiés 3852
Si eüssiés levé le pont;
N'ariés garde de tot le mont
Perueuc qu'eussiés a manger.
Cele tors siet sor un rocier, 3856
Se li bat la mers environ.
Par une porte i entre l'on,
[f.112c] Car il n'i a que une entree;
Mais cele est forment encombree: 3860
C'une vielle — que maufés
[l']arde! —
La porte et la tornele garde
Si que nus n'i ose aprocier.
Ele tient une fauç d'acier 3864
Qui a pié et demi de lé;
Sous ciel n'a homme si armé
Ne chevalier, tant hardis soit,
Se la vielle a cop l'ataignoit 3868
Que le ne trençast par le bu.
Ço est la garde de l'escu.
Se tu le veus avoir sans faille,
De vos deus serra la bataille, 3872
Et molt le troveras pesant;
N'enduras tele en ton vivant,
Ne mais n'eüs si grant paor
Com tu ara[s] a icel jor 3876
Que la bataille ert de vos deus.
Sacés que ce n'iert mie jeus
De quintainne ne de tornoi;
La vi[e]lle est de molt grant 3880
bueffoi.

The dwarf replies: 'Sir Knight, I know very well how to guide you in what you ask of me. But understand this: you shan't get her as easily as you think. Before that, there will be shields pierced, and that in peril of death, before you can enjoy the comfort, the joy and pleasure, of her you care so much about. This is the truth, there's nothing else for it: one must pay at length for what one wants. And you shall well and truly pay before you get her, that's quite clear, and not by gold or silver either: you shall pay by means of your own body. But you shall not shed the blood of your veins from any wound you receive; you'll fight safely if you can come to the right place. You will have to demonstrate great prowess, if ever you want to get her. You'll win her by prowess, for you can't win her by any money either paid or given, nor even by strength and force,[91] unless you have got the splendid shield that hangs in the Tower of Dunottre. Not otherwise shall you have her, whatever I may say to you!'

When he heard he would never get his sweetheart without getting the shield, then he said to the dwarf that he would win it if any man could! But he still wants to know about the virtue of this shield, and in what place he might find it. The dwarf told him right away:

'The shield is so powerful that whoever has it in his possession can never lose his life in armed combat, nor can he ever be knocked off his horse by any mortal man alive. What's more, it has another property: no night can ever be so dark that there is not light around the tower, as bright by night as by day, where the shield is lodged. Believe me, if the whole host of the English were gathered, having sworn your death, you would have such an advantage if you were inside that tower and had raised the drawbridge, you could care nothing for the lot of them providing you had enough to eat. The tower is established upon a rock, and the sea beats all around it. You go in by one gate, for there is only one entrance, but this is most formidably blockaded! Both gate and turret are guarded by an old hag, may the Devil burn her! such a one that none dares approach it. She wields a steel scythe, a foot and a half wide. There's no man under Heaven so well armed, nor any horse however powerful it is, that wouldn't be sliced through the body if that old lady got in a blow at him. That is the guardian of the shield! If you are determined to have it, the battle will be between the two of you, and thou shalt find it tremendously hard.[92] You'll never endure anything like it again in your life, nor such great fear as you'll feel that day when the battle is between the two of you. I promise it will be no game of quintain or tourney:[93] the old lady is absolutely ferocious.

---

[91] 'vertu' can mean strength, or 'virtue' (see Mark 5:30 & Luke 6:19).

[92] The dwarf has again switched back to 'tu' (the editor suggests no reason).

[93] Quintain is a kind of target-practice, and tourneys are mock-battles.

Ains que departe la bataille
Aras bel escu sans faille.
Or fai do mius que tu poras;
Car autre noviele n'oras 3884
Par moi de t'amie la gente.'
Atant en la capiele en entre.
Fergus le siut deriere au dos;
Mais a l'encontre li est clos 3888
Uns huis de fer tot de son gre.
Molt i a feru et hurté.
Au nain dist qu'il li laist entrer;
Car encor veut a lui parler. 3892
Molt est dolans qu'il est repus;
Et quant voit qu'il n'en fera plus,
Si est sor son ceval montés,
Qui au pont estoit aregnés. 3896
Fergus cevauce le boschage;[94]
Tot son pensé et son corage
A torné a chevalerie.

Et nequedent pas ne s'oublie 3900
S'amie la gente, la sage;
Amors un poi le rasouage,
Et saciés bien qu'il aime asés.
Or est ses travaus atenprés 3904
Por ce qu'il set qu'ele n'est morte.
Bonne esperance le conforte,
Et li nains qui dit li avoit
Que par l'escu recoverroit 3908
Cele ke tant ot desiree.
Cevauçant vait par la contree;
[f.112c] Molt chevauça par ses
　　　　jornees
Et trespassa maintes contree[s] 3912
Et se herberga en maint liu.
Mais ce ne me sanbleroit preu
Se ci vos avoie aconté
Tos les lius u [l']ont ostelé. 3916

---

[94] After a blank line in the edited text, this line begins with a large capital.

As soon as the battle is over, you'll get the shield without fail. So, do the best you can, for you'll get no more advice from me about your lovely friend.'

With that, he went off into the chapel. Fergus was close behind him, but when he got there a great iron door had shut of its own accord against him. He knocked and beat hard at it, calling the dwarf to let him in because he wanted to go on talking to him. He is devastated at this response, and when he sees he'll get no further then he goes to mount his horse, that has been tied up at the bridge.

Fergus rides away through the woods. All his thought and all his heart is now turned towards chivalry. Nevertheless, he doesn't forget his lover, so sweet and wise.[95] Love comforts him somewhat, and you can be sure he is loving enough! His troubles are lightened because he knows she is not dead. Sweet hope comforts him, and the dwarf who has told him that by the shield he will recover her whom he so desires.

He goes riding through the land. He rode all day every day, traversing many regions, and sheltering in many places. But I don't think there'd be much point if I told you all the places that gave him lodging.[96]

---

[95] The editor notes that Fergus has now achieved the proper balance between love and chivalry.

[96] Needless to say, things turn out as the dwarf has foretold, and Fergus wins both shield and lady.

Le Roman du reis Yder[97]

Although this romance is not among the best known, and we lack the beginning of the only extant manuscript copy, it is a splendid adventure story.[98] Reviews of Adams' version (now superseded by Lemaire's) welcomed it as a valuable text and translation of a neglected romance. It was omitted from Dean's catalogue, but Tony Hunt believes it should have been included.[99] Because the episode with the bear, and the rather disturbing story of the hero kicking a lady, are comparatively well known even if only by reputation, I have chosen the exciting story of Yder's fight with the giants and what happened afterwards because of Kay's treachery.[100] The adventure begins with Arthur's journey to the giants' lair, accompanied by Kay, Gawain, Yvain, and Yder; they are to kill the giants, and win the knife Yder's beloved has demanded in return for her hand in marriage. Kay is, as always, bitterly jealous of any knight who is better than he is (that is, every other knight he ever meets); Arthur is bitterly jealous of Yder because Guinevere has said she admires him.

The passage chosen is vv. 5415–923, omitting the author's digression about the evils of jealousy because I wanted to keep the impetus of the story going. The battle is real, in the story-world, unlike the battle between gods and giants in *Thèbes*, that is a pictorial accompaniment to war between nations. It is skilfully told, keeping readers in suspense; the author resists the temptation to say 'Ah, but you will see he isn't dead!' It will be noticed that Yder's friends swoon onto his body, which modern readers might find a little excessive. It is surprising that critics of medieval literature even today retain a tendency to think that men swooning, or weeping, feminizes them. On the contrary, such behaviour is appropriate manly homage to the greatness of the object of their grief (or other strong emotion).[101] Weiss discusses the topic in 'Swooning', and so does Mills as recently as 2014 ('Male Weeping').

My text below is copied from Lemaire's edition; I preserve the spelling and punctuation, altering only spacing of the latter to ordinary English usage. I have also altered the quotation marks, because English readers may find the French convention less easy to read (for example, keeping track of which person is

---

97 I have consulted both editions: ed. and tr. Lemaire; and ed. and tr. Adams. The text is copied from Lemaire; Adams' notes and introduction contain useful material.

98 See Archibald, 'Variations', for criticism of Arthur and other comments pertinent to *Yder*; I am preparing an article on the role of women in this text and its mockery of dishonourable behaviour (Bliss, 'Honour, Humour, and Women in the Romance of *Yder*').

99 'Review: *Anglo-Norman Literature*, Ruth Dean and Maureen Boulton', and his 'Review: *The Romance of Yder*, Alison Adams'.

100 For an explanation of Kay's conventionally dreadful behaviour, see my note on the foal suckled by an ass in Bozon's *Conte*, below.

101 This is parodied in *Roman des Franceis* (below), when Frollo faints before a battle: he boasts that it is because of his great strength. A real-life albeit fictionalized king swoons for grief after the death of his mistress (in *The French Chronicle of London*). See for example *Le Roman de Troie, passim*, for heroes swooning.

speaking). The text, with facing-page translation into modern French, is found on Lemaire's pp. 340–69; those wishing to consult Adams' version, see her pp. 198–213.[102] Paragraphs in the text follow the edition, although I have added extra paragraph divisions in my translation.

---

[102] As usual, I have consulted but not copied her translation (facing-page into modern English).

Text

[f.43va] ... E tant ont le chemin tenu 5415
Que a la forte maison sunt venu
Ou li dui giant repairoent
Qui le païs entor gastoent.
De fors virent monz de os de
    bestes
Qu'il manjöent; mult i ot testes 5420
Sor pels aguz, qui d'omes furent.
Al baile de fors s'aresturent;
Chefs i ot bien plus de treis cenz.
'Keis,' dist li reis, 'vos irrés enz; 5424
Il vos i covient sol monter,
Lor estre nos vendréz conter.
Keis, si vos en avéz bosoing,
Nos ne vos serrom pas trop loing.' 5428
Tarjant, grosçant, s'en torne Keis,
Car il i vait mult sor son peis
N'en deit avoir ne los ne gré.
A cheval vint desqu'al degré, 5432
Del chief a regardé ariere;
Freior le prist de grant maniere
Quant il n'i vit entor sei home:
Mels volsist estre dela Rome. 5436
Il veit la cort laide e soltive;
Sor le degré out une eschive,
Large la vit com un portal,
La s'ensbusche tot a cheval 5440
Si qu'il onques n'i descendi.
Al rei Artur qui l'atendi
Fu avis qu'il demorolt mult.
Il ont pris longement escolt 5444
N'i ont oi noise ne temuire.
Ne quiert més que Yder i muire.
...

[f.44ra] 'Seignors,' ço dist li reis 5479
    Arturs,

'Jo ne sui pas tresbien seürs
De Kei, qu'il seit pas retenuz;
Bien peüst estre revenuz,
S'il eüst de soi pöesté.'
Gagain dist: 'Mult a demoré; 5484
Quant pechie a qu'il part de ci,
Més nos n'avons laienz oï,
Pus que ço fu, ne cri ne noise;
E c'il vos plaist que jo i voise, 5488
Jo irrai volentiers en prés lui.'
'Jo voil un altre envoyer cui:
Sire Yder en ai jo esleu.'
Yder en ad grant joie eü 5492
Quant il l'entent, si l'en mercie.
Il entre en la cort enhermie;
Al degré descent del destrier;
Quant il ne troeve o atachier 5496
N'il n'a esquier ne garçon,
La reigne passe ultre l'arçon:
Lors n'a garde qu'il puis se moeve.
Il vient sus el palais, si troeve 5500
Coste a coste les dous jaians;
Sinquante piéz ot li mains grans
De longor, o cinquante o plus.
Lor dos eurent torné vers l'us. 5504
D'un grant senglier sunt andui
    keu:
Li uns torne l'espei al feu,
Qui fu fait d'un gros bleteron,
E li autre trait le carbon 5508
Al porc que sis compains tornoie.
Od le peil fu e od la seeie. [f.44rb]
De lor espei lever se grevassent
Dui fort home, s'il le levassent. 5512

Translation

And they kept going until they arrived at the fortified house where the two giants lived, who ravaged the country all around. Outside they saw heaps of bones, from animals the giants had been eating, and there were a lot of heads stuck on sharpened stakes — these were the heads of men! At the bailey outside they stopped; there were more than three hundred heads.

'Kay', said the king, 'you go in! It's best if you go up there alone, then you can come back and tell us about them. Kay, if you need us we shan't be far away.'

Grumbling and dragging his feet, Kay goes. He goes very much against his will; and he won't be getting much praise or thanks for it. He approached the steps, on his horse; he turned his head and looked behind him. He could see nobody about, and overwhelming terror seized him. He wished he was as far away as the other side of Rome.

He saw a courtyard, ugly and deserted; he saw a corner[103] on the stairs that was as wide as a doorway, so he crept into it, horse and all. He never got down from there!

King Arthur, waiting for him, thought he was taking his time. He and the others listened out, for a long while, but could hear no noise or fearful sound.[104] Arthur no longer wanted Yder to die in there.

. . .[105]

'My lords,' says King Arthur, 'I don't feel at all easy about Kay. Perhaps he's got held up? He ought to be back by now, if he's in a fit state.'

Gawain says 'He's been a long time. Since he left here a while ago, we haven't heard a sound from in there. Nothing at all, not a cry and not a whisper. If you'll please let me, I'll happily go in after him.'

'I want to send somebody else in there; I have chosen Sir Yder.'

Yder was delighted to hear this, and thanked him. He went into the wasted courtyard, and got off his warhorse by the steps. Not finding anywhere to tether him — there was no groom or boy — he threw the rein over the saddle; after that he didn't expect him to go anywhere.

He went up into the palace. There were the two giants, side by side! The smaller of them was fifty foot long; fifty, or even more! Their backs were turned to the door; they had a large wild boar, and they were both being the cook. One was turning the spit in the fire, which was made from an enormous branch; the other was pulling the hot coals up round the pig as his companion turned it. It had its skin on, and its hair. As for their spit, two strong men would have had a job to lift it.

---

[103] 'eschive'; Adams gives 'hiding-place' (her note suggests a kind of fortification). Lemaire gives 'fortification de bois'. Either could be correct; since 'eschiver' can mean 'to turn aside', I have rendered it as 'corner' (sc. where one turns).

[104] 'temuire'; its meaning has been debated (notes in both Adams and Lemaire for v. 5445). I compromise: fearful can mean either frightening or frightened.

[105] Here I have omitted a passage on the subject of Jealousy.

Sil qui le feu apparailot
Veit Yder qui s'esmerveilot
De la grandor dont il estoient
E de la grossor qu'il avoient.　　　　　5516
Yder les escrie e cil saut,
Son tisonier a lievé haut:
A Yder en fera haschie.
Reisnablement en fust chargie　　　　　5520
Une charette a un cheval.
De halt l'en gete un cop aval:
L'escu li ad par tot fendu
Que Yder li out avant tendu　　　　　5524
Si com il vit le cop venir;
Ne l'i volt pas a ferm tenir,
Car tost le peüst afoler;
L'escu li fait del col voler.　　　　　5528
Bien veit Yder, se cil recoevre,
Que a cort terme il aura malovre.
Yder le requiert come proz
Nel poet grever fors par desoz:　　　　5532
De l'espee qu'il ot traite
Li ad une grant plaie faite
D'un pié desoz le braël;
Il le ferist plus haut son voel.　　　　5536
Li jaiant brait qui le cop cent,
Abaissiéz s'eist irreement.
Si come il le volt enbrasier,
Le fiert Yder del brant d'acier:　　　　5540
Del col li a sevré l'espaule.
Li reis ot le fruis en la haule [f.44va]
De l'aversiers qui chaüz est.
Gagains e Ywains furent prest　　　　　5544
D'aler i, ce li reis volsist;
Més n'ireient pas, ço lor dist.
Yder vait le jaiant overt,
Dedens le veit a descovert,　　　　　5548
La plaie esgarde, si li bote
Desciqu'al poign l'espee tote.
A peine avint al cuer le more,

Li autre jaiant li cort sore.　　　　　5552
Yder s'estut e cil li vient:
Morz est Yder se cil le tient.
Un cop a vers Yder rüé
Dont il le dut avoir grevé,　　　　　5556
Més un las qui desus pendi
Toli le cop quil deffendi,
Més ne fu pas si deffenduz
Q'il ne chaïst tot estenduz.　　　　　5560
Li jaianz le volt prendre a mains,
Yder resalt en piéz tot sains;
Corage ot fier e bone espee,
Ire li a force doblee:　　　　　　　5564
Halt gete por lui damagier,
Més ço le trait a l'esragier
Qu'il nel damage a geter halt;
Li cops est vains o del tot falt.　　　　5568
Veirs est que l'aïr n'a il pas,
Que cil qui par mesure est bas
Ne veit coment grever le pusse;
Il li gete un cop a la cuisse,　　　　　5572
E il trait son cop e si l'a plié
Qu'il li a la cuisse trenchié.
[f.44vb]
Sil le volt prendre, si s'abaisse;
Yder le veit, vers li s'eslaisse:　　　　5576
Al relever l'a si ferru
Qu'il li part le chief del beu.
Il se desarme demaneis,
Ses armes pent desor un deis　　　　　5580
Que sist sor piliers el costé
De la sale; si en a osté
Un riche cotel qu'il i vit:
Ço fu cel dont s'amie ot dist.　　　　　5584
Ains qu'il l'en porte aura ennui.
Quant Yder l'ot mis en estui,
Al feu s'est assis en un banc;
Od les breses estert le sanc　　　　　5588
De s'espee qu'il out mult chiere.

The giant tending the fire saw Yder, who was watching in amazement at the size of them and their thickness! He shouted to them, and this one leaped at him, raising his poker high in the air. He's going to make mincemeat of him — it would have been more sensible to load a horse-drawn cart with that thing! He smashed it down in a blow that split the shield; Yder had just swung it forward as he saw the blow coming. He didn't want to hold it tightly, because the giant could crush it instantly — he had already sent it flying from his neck. Yder can see that if the giant gets another blow ready then he will quickly be in frightful trouble. So he attacks him like a gallant warrior. It's impossible to get at him except from below, so quickly drawing his sword he swipes him a dreadful gash below the belt, about a foot long; he'd have stabbed higher up if he could. The giant howled as he felt the wound, and grabbed downwards in fury as if he wanted to embrace Yder. So he stabs again with his steel sword, and slashes the shoulder off from his neck.

The king hears the racket going on in the hall, as the enemy crashes to the ground. Gawain and Yvain were all ready to rush in, if the king wished it. But no, he says they are not to go. Yder sees that the giant has a wound wide open, all his insides showing. He considers the wound for a moment, then stabs his sword into the giant right up to the hilt. No sooner had its blade reached the heart, than the other giant rushed at him.

Yder stands his ground as he comes at him. He is dead if he gets hold of him! The blow he hurled at Yder would have caused quite an injury, had it not been for a rope hanging just up there which deflected the blow and so saved his life. But not enough to block it altogether: Yder measured his length on the floor. The giant was trying to grab hold of him when Yder jumped to his feet safe and sound. His courage was high and his sword was good; fury gave him the strength of two men! He struck high up, to wound him, but the blow only infuriated him: if he can't wound him by striking high, his stroke is in vain or fails altogether. It is vain because he hasn't the stature he needs: he is so much shorter that he can't see how to injure the giant. He makes a thrust at his thigh, stabbing and twisting so that he cuts it right off. The giant tries to get at him by bending down; seeing this, Yder goes for him, and chops off his head from his body as he tries to stand up again!

Yder took his armour off straight away, and hung it on a pillared daïs at one side of the hall. He picked up a fine knife he saw there — this is the knife his lady spoke of! But before he can take it to her he will face further troubles. When he'd put it in its sheath, he sat down on a bench by the fire. He cleaned the blood off his well-beloved sword, using the embers.

Quant il l'ot mise el foere ariere,
El banc la coche delés sei;
Iloec atent Yder le rei.   5592
Li reis e cil qui od li furent
Onc por la noise ne s'esmurent,
E Keis, qui dedenz ot sauté;
Oï oerent e escoté   5596
Les cris des jaians e les braiz
Qu'ils geterent e granz e laiz,
E l'espee qui resonout
Des cops quë Yder lor donot.   5600
La noeise öent remise tote;
Li reis lor dit qu'il set sanz dote
Que la bataille fu finee,
Sor cui que cort la destinee.   5604
Gagains, que molt fu angoissos,
Ad dist al rei: 'Que ferom nos?
    [f.45ra]
Trop l'aurom fait vilainement;
Oï avons apertement   5608
Qu'il i out lasus fier champ tenu.
Jo criem qu'il seit mesavenu
As noz, quant nuls d'els ne
    repaire.'
'E quei porrom,' dist li reis, 'faire?'   5612
Ywains respont: 'Laïnz irrons
Por delivrer noz compainons,
Si li dui jaiant lé ont pris,
O venger les, s'il sunt occis.'   5616
El baille sunt entré tuit trei.
Keis ot esté en grant effrei:
La noise out oï el palais;
E quant il out qu'il est a pais,   5620
Son chief met hors. Li reis le veit,
Vers l'eschive vait a lui droit
E si dui compaignon ovoec.
Li reis enquiert qu'il fait illoec.   5624
Keis li a respondu en bas:
'Poör ai grant, jo n'en ment pas,
Muscié me sui en ceste eschive.
Il n'est home qui en terre vive   5628

N'esteüst de poör trembler,
S'il estoveit assembler
Od ces monstrez sanz grant efforz;
E jo vos di que cil est morz   5632
Qui vos i aviéz tramis:
Ceürement m'en aramis.'
'Hee, Deus!' dist Gagain, 'quel
    damage!
Deu! tant mar fu son vassalage!   5636
Ho! sire Ywains, malement vait;
Vilanie li avoms fait. [f.45rb]
Poi a duré la compaignie
Que fu entre nos treis plevie!'   5640
Li reis respont: 'Gagains, bials
    niés,
S'il i ad mal, il fust mult pis
S'ore i fuissiéz ovec lui.'
'Ja ne sont li jaiant que dui,'   5644
Dist Ywains, 'e nos sumes quatre;
Tot sols s'ala od els combatre:
Veirs est qu'il fist trop grant
    enprise.
S'ore n'i alons, de coardise   5648
Ne nos porrons jamés deffendre,
Quant uns sols tant osa
    enprendre.'
'Ja Deus ne voille,' dist li reis,
'Tant com jo aie od moi vos treis,   5652
Que coardise i ait pensee!
Puis ne me soit vie tensee
Que li miens coers la pensera!
Gart chascons com il le fra,   5656
Car jo descent tot premerains!'
Od le rei descendi Gagains,
Ywains descent, Keis fu a pié;
Les degrés puient tuit rengié,   5660
Sor lor chefs ont mis lor escuz,
Es poinz tienent les branz tot nuz.
El palais veenent tot errant,
Al feu troevent Yder sëant;   5664
Desarméz iert e tot seürs.

Then he returned it to its scabbard and put it down beside him. So Yder sits there, waiting for the king.

The king, and the others who were with him, didn't stir a finger for all the noise that was going on; Kay likewise, who had hopped into cover. They heard, and listened to the howling and loud ugly yelling of the giants, and the sword that clanged with blows as Yder dealt them. Then the noise ceased! The king told them he was quite sure the battle was now over, whoever had met his fate there.

Gawain, desperately anxious, said to the king 'What are we to do? We'll have behaved villainously, since we heard, clear as anything, that he was holding the field like a hero up there. I'm afraid harm has come to our men, since neither has come back yet.'

'But what could we do?' said the king.

Yvain answers 'Let's go in there to rescue our companions, if those two giants have captured them. Or avenge them, if they've been killed!'

So they all three went into the fortress. Kay had been scared stiff; he could hear the noise in the palace. When he heard that it had all gone quiet, he put his head out. The king saw him, and went straight to the hiding-place with his two companions. He asked what he was doing there!

Kay replied in a low voice 'I was so frightened! I can't tell a lie! So I hid myself in this corner. No living man could have faced that without shaking with fear, having to tackle those monsters without considerable reinforcements. I tell you he's dead, that man you sent in, I swear it!'

'Ah, God!' said Gawain, 'What a loss! God, what a waste of such valour![106] Oh, Sir Yvain, it has turned out dreadfully; we have done the most awful thing to him. That pact we made among the three of us, it hasn't lasted long!'

The king said 'Gawain, my dear nephew, if he has come to harm only think how much worse it would be if you'd gone in with him just now.'

'But there were only two giants,' said Yvain, 'and there are four of us! He went to fight them all alone; it's true that it was an enormous undertaking. If we don't go in now, we'll never be able to hold up against a charge of cowardice, since one alone dared to take on so much!'

'God forbid,' said the king, 'that anybody should think cowardice of me, when I've got you three with me! Let my life no longer be protected, if such a thought ever entered my heart! You others, be careful what you do — I'll be the first to dismount.'

The king and Gawain got off their horses, Yvain dismounted, Kay got down onto his feet; one by one they went up the steps. They had put their helmets on, and held their naked swords in their hands.

They went straight into the palace hall, and found Yder sitting there disarmed and looking pleased with himself.

---

[106] 'tant mar fu ...'; this epic formula expresses regret (for example, *La Vie seint Edmund le Rei*, ed. Russell, v. 896 and note: 'destined from birth for this tragic end'; and see Larousse, 'marer' I).

Grant freior ot li reis Arturs
E li altre qui od li furent
Des monstrez qui el palais jeurent. 5668
Yder s'est encontr'els levéz;
Li reis quide qu'il seit grevéz [f.45va]
E Keis, més il fust mort lor voil,
Tost en eüssent fait le doel.   5672
De son estre li demanderent
Li dui qui fëelment l'amerent,
Ço furent Ywains e Gagains.
Yder respont qu'il est tot sains.   5676
Il se desarment de maneis,
Lor armes metent sor le deis;
El palais mainent grant lëesce.
'Or n'i ait lius,' dist Keis, 'peresce: 5680
Nos avons l'ostel a delivre,
Sachons s'il ad point de vivre.
Il n'i a qui en face deffens.'
Yder respont: 'Bien est, e tens!   5684
Vespre est: li soleil se resconse;
Jo en recoil bien vostre semonse.
Véz moi od vos apparaillié.'
Il ont un us destoreillié,   5688
En une chambre sont entré;
Gastials i troevent a plenté,
Vins freis e clers e granz pastéz,
E dé chapons e dé lardez,   5692
Tant que riche hostel ont eü.
Cele nuit ont illoec jeü.
Le feu firent grant e paleis;
Al rei Artur fu uns liz fais.   5696
Il dormi, li altre veillerent:

Por freior des jaians gaiterent;
Il les voldrent tramer fors,
Més tant furent pesanz les cors   5700
Qu'il nes peürent remüer.
L'om peüst un somier tüer [f.45vb]
A chargier le d'un sol des chiefs.
Lors i avint trop grant meschiefs.   5704
Tant se furent al feu deduit,
Mienuit fu e plus, çoe cuit:
A Yder prist une grant sei,
'Que i ferai, Keis?' dit cil. 'De   5708
        quei?'
'Seif ai trop grant.' 'Si bevéz donc!'
'Dont la porreie esteindre donc?'
'La fontaine vos en guarra;
Jo vos en dorrai.' 'Ore i parra'   5712
Dist cil, qui le pensé ne seet
De Kei, qui mortelment le het.
Sor une grant table de sap
Vit Keis adenté un hanap   5716
De blanc marre; Keis vait, sil
        prent,
Les desgréz del palais descent.
Jus de la cort vint soz un arbre;
Desoz out un perom de marbre   5720
E deléz sort une fontaine
Dont l'eve estoit e clere e saine;
Un hanap de boce estoit dedenz,
De cele peurent beivre genz.   5724
Més un autre fontaine i aveit
De l'altre part, qui Keis saveit,

King Arthur, and the others with him, were horrified at the sight of those monsters lying on the floor of the hall. Yder got up to meet them. The king thought he would be wounded; so did Kay. But, if he had been as dead as they wanted him, they would quickly have expressed grief. The two who loved him faithfully, that's Yvain and Gawain, asked him how he was. Yder said he was perfectly all right. Then they all took off their armour, and piled the pieces on the daïs. Now everybody in the palace can rejoice!

'No time to hang about,' said Kay, 'We've got the hostelry to ourselves! Let's see if there's anything to eat — nobody's going to stop us!'

Yder replies 'Good idea, and about time too! It's about the hour for Vespers,[107] and the sun's going down. I accept your suggestion; shall I come with you? I'm ready!'

They unlocked a door and went into another room, where they found all sorts of cakes; there was fine cool wine, and great pies; capons and roasts with bacon; so much, that it was a splendid lodging they had! That night they stayed in the place.

They banked the fire up high in the hall, and made a bed for Arthur. He slept, but the others kept watch for fear of the giants. They wanted to drag them outside, but the bodies were so heavy they couldn't budge them. You'd kill a pack-horse if you loaded it with even one of those heads!

Then disaster struck.

They were having such a good time round the fire that it was midnight or later, I think, when Yder was seized with a raging thirst.

'Kay, what am I going to do?'

'What?'

'I'm so thirsty!'

'Have a drink, go on!'

'What will really quench it, then?'

'The fountain will do it for you — I'll get you some.'

'We'll see', says he, never guessing what was in Kay's mind, who hated him so. On the big pine table Kay saw an upturned goblet of pale maple-wood.[108] He went over and took it, then went down the stairs outside the hall. At the end of the courtyard he stepped beneath a tree, where there was a block of marble. Beside it a fountain flowed out, whose water was clean and sweet; there was a goblet in it,[109] so that people could drink from this. But there was another fountain on the other side [of the courtyard],[110] which Kay knew about.

---

[107] 'vespre' means both 'evening' and the canonical Hour of evening prayer.

[108] 'marre' is unattested according to Lemaire's note. The mazer was commonly made of maple-wood, so I follow Adams' translation.

[109] Both translators say this was a cup, or vase, of wood; Lemaire's note says 'boce' as a form of 'wood' is not in the dictionaries. It could perhaps be a form of 'bocel', also meaning vase? However, wood seems a likely material for this sort of vessel.

[110] Its position is clarified, below.

Car il l'avoit de cels apris
Qui s'en fuirent de cel païs,   5728
Car veirs estoit qu'il n'en beüst
Nuls qui la mort n'en eüst.
De fort entosche ert entoschee:
Tote en ert l'herbe entor sechee,   5732
E grieve i estoit l'avenue
Por ço qu'ele estoit deffendue.

[f.46ra]

Més se Keis poet, en soi prendra
Engin, com il i avendra: 5736
Il nel larreit por nule chose.
De pels le fontaine fu enclose,
Més Keis fu fels a grant mervele:
Od s'espëe colpe la reille   5740
Ou les chevilles tindrent sus,
As pïels se prent, s'abat jus
Une joëe tote entiere;
Le hanap emple e vait ariere.   5744
El poing met le beivre mortel
A Yder qui ne coveiteit el
E mult li avoit ennoié.
Il a tot le hanap voidié;   5748
L'entosche li corrumpt les veines,
Sempres furent del venim plaines.
Li venims fu de male part:
Li cors li frist dedenz e art.   5752
Colchier se vait, mult est grevéz:
De la char li est sus levéz
Li cuiers que del venim li emple;
Li cols li est prés a la temple,   5756
Nis ne li est el vis remés
Semblant qu'il onques eüst nés
N'a sor li leus ou pous li bate.
Qu'en feroie longe barate?   5760
Ne li remaint, c'en est la some,
Nëis seemblant de forme d'ome.
Li reis s'eveille a l'enjorner;
Il a somons Keis d'atorner   5764

Qu'il se peüsse metre el repaire.
'Sire,' dist Keis, 'bien est a faire:

[f.46rb]

Nos avons ci asséz esté.'
Li chevals furent apresté;   5768
Li reis, Gagains, Ywains e Keis
Se sunt armé devant le deis.
'Ore fait,' dist Keis, 'a merveillier
Ke Yder ne se puet esveiler.'   5772
'Jo l'esveillerai,' dist Gagains.
Li traïtres, qui fu certains
Qu'il ert el some de la mort,
A respondu: 'Ore a il tort: 5776
Li reis l'atent, hastéz le nos,
Quë ore est il trop demoros.'
Gagains vint la o Yder jut,
Més ne sot dire que ço fut: 5780
Ne mie fut, més que ço iert,
Mult fu altres qu'il lores ne piert.
Gagains le veit deffiguré,
Mult se claime maleüré;   5784
'Mar vit', ço dist, 'la söe mort!'
Çom piz debat, ses poinz detort,
Mult plaint la pröesce de lui.
'Yder,' dist il, 'mar vos conui: 5788
Jameis ceste siecle n'amerai,
Trop est mavois. Deus, que ferai?
Las! jo ne puis remaindre ici
E coment larrai mon ami?'   5792
Li reis estoit jus en la cort;
Al doel qu'il out que hon fait
     acort!
'A il més si bien non?' dist il.
Gagains respont: 'Certes, oïl: 5796
Nos laissom ci trop grant treü.'
Quant li reis a Yder veü,
Seignié c'est, pus c'est trait ariere;

[f.46va]

Esbahi est de grant maniere.   5800

He'd heard of it from some people who were fleeing this land.[111] It's true, nobody drank from it who did not die! It was poisoned with such strong poison that all the grass around it was scorched; the way to it was perilous, because it was forbidden. But if he can, Kay is hatching a plot in his heart come what may; he won't abandon this for anything! The fountain is surrounded with stakes, but Kay is incredibly cunning. He cuts through the support of these stakes with his sword, and swipes out a whole row of them. He fills the cup and returns, putting it in Yder's hand. He wanted nothing better, having been tormented fiercely by his thirst. He has drunk the whole cupful!

The poison seeps into his veins, which are rapidly filled with poison. It is a fearful poison, making him shudder and burn inside. He goes to lie down, in awful pain. His flesh is all puffed out because full of poison, and his neck is swollen up to his temples. There's no trace of where his nose used to be on his face, and nowhere on his whole body is there any point where his pulse beats. How much more must I tell you? All I can say is, there is nothing left of him that looks like a man.

The king woke up when it was morning. He called for Kay, asking him to get everything together to begin their journey home.

'That's a good thing, Sir,' said Kay, 'we've been here quite long enough.'

The horses were got ready; the king, Gawain, Yvain, and Kay armed themselves in front of the daïs.

'Now that's funny,' said Kay, 'Yder can't seem to wake up.'

'I'll wake him,' said Gawain.

The traitor, who was certain he was in his death-throes, replied 'He's causing trouble now. Hurry him up — the king is waiting! What a time to be lingering in bed!'

Gawain went to where Yder was lying, but he couldn't tell what it was there. He couldn't tell what it was, except that Yder was there; he usually looked so different from what was now revealed. Gawain saw him deformed!

He lamented his evil fortune, crying 'How wretched is this death!' He beat his own breast, wringing his hands; he lamented Yder's prowess. 'Yder,' he said, 'wretched is this day that I recognize you! I shall never joy in this world again — it is so wicked. Oh God, what am I to do? Alas, I can't stay here, but how can I abandon my friend?'

The king was below, in the courtyard. May all acquiesce in the grief he felt! 'Is something not well with him?' he asked.

'Indeed, yes,' said Gawain. 'We are leaving here the great price we've paid.'

When the king saw Yder, he crossed himself and drew back, horrified.

---

[111] This suggestive detail implies that Kay has been associating with criminals, now exiled. They may have been using the very roads on which safe-conduct for such people was guaranteed (in *Description*, above).

Mult plore Ywains; Keis lor a dit:
'Seignors, dit il, si Deus me aït,
Sire Yder a fait grant efforz
De ces dous jaians qu'il a morz: 5804
Forz e fiers ierent e engrés,
Més ne poeit pas vivre aprés.
Venim portöent, mors en est:
Mult entent poi qui ne voit cest.   5808
Tant l'a ja le venim sopris
Que ne li piert ou il out vis:
Le cuir en voi plain e nerci.
Ore priom Deu qu'Il ait merci   5812
E del cors e de l'alme ambore!
Nel poöm més de plus socore;
Més tant poöm ci demorer
Que nos aurom plus a plorer.   5816
Ore vos en ai dit ma purté:
N'en i ai nule seürté,
Anceis me doel, e por le rei
E por vos dous, e plus por moi;   5820
Jo ne vos en quier ja mentir:
A tart en iert le repentir
Quant l'en iert sopris de la mort.'
'Keis, dist li reis, n'avéz pas tort.'   5824
Le cors a seignié, si s'en part;
Il prie Deu que l'alme en gart
Des mals e des peines d'enfer.
Gagain se priesme al cors Yder,   5828
Son piz bat e destoert ses mains.
'Yder, mar vos vi', dist Gagains.
Ywains acort qui forment plore;
[f.46vb]
Andui se sunt pasmé desure.   5832

Li reis les en a trait a peine,
Més tant a fait qu'il les amaigne;
Monter les fait, od li s'en vont,
Més mult est grant le doel qu'il   5836
   font.
N'out erré li reis si poi non
Quant venu sunt a la maison
Dui chevalier qui furent frere:
Un rei d'Yrlande oerent a pere.   5840
Cil rei fu apelés Alvréz
E li ainsnéz fiz Miröéz;
Li altre appelent Kamelin,
Beals chevaliers fu de grant fin;   5844
Chevaliers furent mult avable,
E per de la ronde Table.
Cinc anz aveit en l'esté,
Qu'il n'avoient a cort esté,   5848
Si fu en l'entree dë yver.
Sus el paleis troevent Yder,
De l'autre part troevent gisanz
Coste a coste lé dous gianz.   5852
Freior ont grant quant il les veient:
N'est merveille s'il s'en effroient,
Grant e laid sunt a desmesure.
Onc Deus ne fist la crëature   5856
Qui sens eüst, tant fust hardie,
S'il les eüst veüz en vie,
Que hisdor n'en eüst trop grande.
Li ainéz fiz au rei de Irlaunde   5860
C'est del cors Yder merveillié,
Car si mal est apparaillié
Qu'il n'a menbre que de home
   pere.

Yvain was in tears.

'My lords,' said Kay, 'as God is my help, Yder made a supreme effort when he took on these giants he has killed. They were strong and fierce, ferocious. But he couldn't survive them. They were poisonous, and he died of it; you'd be a fool not to realise that. The poison attacked him so quickly that you can no longer see where his face was. Look how the skin is swollen and black! Let us beseech God to have mercy on him, body and soul! There's nothing more we can do for him, but let's stay long enough to finish mourning him. I've told you the truth as I see it, though I can't be absolutely certain of it. But I am sorry for it, for the king and for you two — most of all for myself. I'm not lying to you! It would be too late to repent of that when Death takes a man by surprise.'

'You are quite right, Kay', said the king. He made the sign of the cross over the body, and went away. He was praying that God would guard Yder's soul from the pains and torments of Hell.

Gawain approached Yder's body, beating his breast and wringing his hands. 'Oh Yder,' he cried, 'I met you only for your misfortune!'

Ywain ran forward, weeping unrestrainedly; both of them fell senseless on the corpse. The king had some trouble getting them off him, but managed to drag them away. He made them get on their horses, and they went off with him. But they were lamenting bitterly.

The king had not gone far before two knights, brothers, arrived at the fortified house. Their father was a king of Ireland, named Alfred; the elder son was Miroet, and the younger was called Kamelin, an extremely handsome knight. They were very able knights, and peers of the Round Table. But it was five years that summer since they had been to court, and now it was the beginning of winter.

Up in the hall they find Yder. At the other end they find the two giants, lying side by side. They viewed them with horror; it isn't surprising they were horrified, because the giants were so enormous and unbelievably hideous. God never made any sensible creature, however bold, who could have seen them alive without being terrified out of his wits.

The elder son of the Irish king marvelled at the body of Yder, which was in such a state it looked nothing like a man in any part.

[f.47ra]

Miröéz apele i son frere.   5864
'Il n'a, dit il, gaire de tens
Que cist iert vifs, si com jo pens.'
Kamelins dist: 'Quidéz vos donc
Que ço seit home? Mielz semble   5868
    un tronc:
Il n'a boche ne il n'a vis.'
Miröéz ot bien son avis:
Sa main met a sa mamele,
As temples taste e soz l'aissele,   5872
Le cuer i sent qui se combat
Od le venim, feblement bat;
Il n'a més vers la mort defense,
Si Deus hastivement n'en pense.   5876
'Il vit, dist il a Kamelin,
Més mult par est prés de la fin;
Mult a males gardez eü,
Bien sai qu'il a venim beü.   5880
Més jo l'en quit mult bien curer;
Car venims ne porreit durer,
Ja ne saureit estre si pesmes,
Vers rien de l'isle dont nos emes.   5884
De Deu a don de tel maniere,
E joen ai ci en m'almoniere
Une racine que jo pris
Quant nos partimes del païs,   5888
Se il en eüse, garis est.'
'Veéz moi, dist Kamelin, tot prest,
Si m'aïde valeir vos poet.'
Miröéz dist: 'Ewe m'estoet,   5892
Ou jo peusse l'erbe quasser;

Il n'en porreit le col passer,
Se n'iert par acune licor.'
[f.47rb]
'Franz home, dist il, car vos i cor!'   5896
Lors a mostré a Kamelin
En la salë un blanc bacin
Que sor un deis fu adentéz;
E cil le prent, mult s'est hastéz.   5900
Il est corruz a la fontaine,
Cele qu'il troeve plus procaine,
Que jus al pee del degré sort;
La male estoit loin en la cort.   5904
Il peusse e vient a Miröet.
Miröéz trait son kenivet,
En l'iaue ret de la racine,
Desor le cor Yder s'acline,   5908
Le chief li lieve, bien l'avise,
Des lievres trove la devise;
Od le cotel oevre les dens,
L'ewe li fait coler dedenz.   5912
Li venims sent la medicine,
Par la boche ist a grant ravine.
Andui le lievent sor le deis.
Le venim voide de maneis   5916
Ne poet durer; li kuirs s'asiet
Si com li venims defiet.
Tot a recovré son semblant
E sain se sent plus que devant.   5920
Li boivres l'ad resanicié
Qu'il le venim ad desnicié.
Yder se dresce sor les piéz …   5923

Miroet calls his brother.

'It's not long since this was alive, I'd say.'

Kamelin said 'Do you really think this is a man? It looks more like a tree-trunk! It hasn't got a mouth, or even a face!'

Miroet heard his opinion, but he put his hand on its chest. Then he felt the temples, and under the armpit. He can feel a heart, struggling with the poison, that beats feebly — it can't hold out against death any longer, unless God will take thought for him very quickly.

'He's alive!' says he to Kamelin, 'but he's almost at death's door. He has been very ill-used, and I'm sure he's drunk poison. I think I can cure him, because poison can't resist — unless it's the very deadliest — something of the island's where we come from. God gave it such virtue, and I've got some in my scrip: a root I gathered when we left home. If he can take it, he is saved!'

'I'm ready to help,' said Kamelin, 'if there's anything useful I can do.'

Miroet said 'I need water, so I can crush the herb in it. It won't go down his throat unless it's in some liquid.'

'Good man!' he says, 'I'll run for it!'

Then he showed Kamelin a white vessel, upside-down on a table in the hall. He took it and rushed off, running to the fountain. He went to the nearest one, which sprang up just by the foot of the steps; the bad one was away down the courtyard. He dipped, and came back to Miroet. Miroet takes his knife and slivers some of the root in water, then he bends over Yder's body. Raising the head, he peers at it and finds the trace of the lips. Opening the teeth with his knife, he pours the water in.[112]

The poison feels the medicine, and rushes out through the mouth! Both raise him up on the daïs. The poison purges, it can't resist. The skin returns to normal as the poison loses hold. He now looks like himself! He feels better than he ever did; the drink that chased out the poison filled him with new health!

Yder got to his feet ...'[113]

---

[112] *Receptaria*, p. 23 (number 167), gives the following remedy in Latin: 'Chop up betony very finely, let him drink it and the poison will be forced out' (my translation). Betony was not found exclusively in Ireland, however, and the book contains a number of other remedies for poisoning.

[113] After a line-break, the first line of the next paragraph is the beginning of Yder's next adventures.

The Anglo-Norman *Folie Tristan*

There are two texts known as the *Folie Tristan*: this one (known as d'Oxford), and one of Berne; Dean's 159 and 160.[114] Because the former is published as an ANTS Plain Text (PTS 10), it is not furnished with a glossary; therefore a partial translation may be useful, though other translations are available.[115] I follow Short's text; sections, separated by a blank line, begin with a letter in bold type.

Tristan was originally independent of the developing stories about Arthur and his knights, but in later romance cycles this hero joins the Round Table. There are a few parallels, not least that both legends end in tragedy: Tristan and Ysolt die while still sundered by marriage and by society. Arthur is fatally wounded by Mordred, and rumours of his survival and future return are not generally believed.[116] Common themes include, notably, a hero in love with a king's wife; and an episode involving tell-tale blood in the lady's bed is found in both cases.[117]

As so often with medieval heroes, collectors and compilers of this legend borrowed from classical literature. There is a parallel with the hero Philoctetes:[118] during the expedition to Troy, he was bitten by a serpent and the wound would not heal; the stench of it caused the Greeks to abandon him (cf. Tristan's wound, dealt by a 'serpent' that is a dragon, and his exile). During his exile on the island of Lemnos he supported himself with a bow and arrows that never missed their mark (cf. Tristan's 'arc ki ne falt'). Some of these details were noted by Gertrude Schoepperle, who spotted the resemblance between our heroes in the matter of the wound and exile. But she does not remark that the bow used by the Greek during his exile resembles the one Tristan had.[119] Details differ from one version of the legend to another: here Tristan's unhealed wound is dealt by the Morholt, and the bow is not mentioned.

One of the beauties of the present text is the way the story is re-narrated by the hero in disguise. This meta-narrative, or story within story, provides a specular

---

[114] [Tristan] *The Anglo-Norman* Folie Tristan *(d'Oxford)*, ed. Short; and [Tristan] *La Folie Tristan de Berne*, ed. Hœpffner.

[115] *The Birth of Romance*, tr. Weiss, pp. 139–53, introduced on pp. 12–20; translation only (snippets of text are provided in an appendix). There is a translation into modern French, with the original text in small print at the bottom of the page (*Tristan et Yseut*, ed. Marchello-Nizia *et al.*, pp. 217–43; notes on pp. 1325–42), but this is not an easy book to use. However, it provides cross-references among all versions, tracing themes and motifs, so it is recommended for anybody wishing to study the legend further (see also Legge, pp. 121–8).

[116] For the Welsh hope of his return, see towards the end of *Description*, above.

[117] *DMH* contains useful summaries of both legends and their development, with principal characters. See (*inter al.*) Paradisi, 'Les premiers romans tristaniens', for discussion of the *Folies* and other Tristan texts.

[118] *OCL*, p. 418, q.v.

[119] *Tristan and Isolt: a study*. There is an online version; the reference is in vol. 2. Part of this work was presented as her thesis in 1909; it was expanded into a second edition in 1960, with bibliography and critical essay by R. S. Loomis.

version which shows us how a medieval author wanted the story to be retold and remembered. Three extracts represent this specular narrative.

Tristan has been away from his beloved queen for too long, and resolves to visit her. He changes clothes with a fisherman, and shaves his head (189–209).[120] He also dyes his skin with a special herb, and changes his voice (212–24); nobody could recognize him now! When he arrives at the court of King Mark and Queen Ysolt, even the text disguises him by suppressing his name: he is 'li fol' and not 'Tristan' (226ff). He begins to play the fool, telling Mark he will swap Ysolt for his own lovely sister (282–894), and describes the magic place where he will take her. He explains that he loves her, and that his name is Trantris (317–18). Mark does not react to this, and Ysolt pretends not to understand.

---

[120] The tonsure is in the shape of a cross. This was threatened as punishment for Yder, if he failed the test of King Ivenant's wife (v. 231 and notes, in both editions of *Yder*: Adams says it is the mark of a criminal, and Lemaire that it is the mark of an adulterer).

Text

Part One

[14d] Puis dit aprés: 'Raïne Ysolt,
Trantris sui ki amer vus solt.   328
Membrez vus dait quant fui
    nauvrez —
maint hom le saveit assez —
quant me combati al Morhout
ki vostre trëu aver volt: 332
a tel höur me cumbati
ke je le ocis, pas nel ni.
Malement i fu je navrés,
kar li bran en fu envenimés: 336
l'os de la hanche me entamat,
e li fors veninz eschauffat,
en le os s'erst, nercir le fist
e tel dolur puis i assist   340
ki ne pout mire guarir,
si quidai ben murir.
En mer me mis, la voil murir,
tant par m'enüat le languir.   344
Li venz levat turment' grant
e chaçat ma nef en Irlant.
Al païs me estot ariver
ke jo deveie plus duter,   348
kar je avei' ocis le Morholt —
vostre uncle fu, raïne Ysolt —
pur ço dutai mult le païs;
mais jo fu naufrez e chitifs.   352
Od ma harpe me delitoie; —
je n'oi confort ki tant amoie —
[15a] ben tost en oïst parler
ke mult savoie ben harper;   356
je fu sempres a curt mandez,
tut issi cum ere navrez;
la raïne la me guari
de ma plaie, süe merci.   360
Bons lais de harpe vus apris,

lais bretuns de nostre païs.
Menbrer vus dait, dame raïne,
cum je guarri par la meschine.   364
Iloc me numai je Trantris;
Ne sui je ço? Ke vus est vis?'   366
[15b] dunc dit aprés sifaitement: 415
'Raïne dame, del serpent   416
menbrer vus dait ke je le ocis
quant jo vinc en vostre païs.
La teste la severai del cors,
la lange trenchai e pris hors;   420
dedenz ma chauce le botai,
e del venim si eschaufai
ben quidai estre morz en fin:
paumés me jeu lez le chemin.   424
Vostre mere e vus me vistes
e de la mort me guaristes;
par grant meschine e par engin
me garistes del venim.   428
...
Del bain vus menbre u enz jo sis?
Iloc me avïez pres ocis:
merveile grant volïez faire
quant alastes me espeie traire;   432
e quant vus le avïez sachee, [15c]
si la trovastes oschee,
dunc pensastes — e ço a dreit —
ke Morholt ocis en esteit;   436
tost purpensastes grant engin
si defermastes vostre escrin:
la pece dedenz truvastes
ke del teste al Morholt ostastes;   440
la pece junsistes al brant:
cele se joinst demaintenant;
mult par fustes granment osee
quant enz el bain od ma espee   444
me voiles sempres ocire!
Mult par est femme de grant ire!

Translation

Part One

Then he said 'Queen Ysolt, I am Trantris who used to love you. You must remember, when I was wounded — there were many who knew about it — when I fought the Morholt, who wanted to take tribute from you. It was my good fortune to kill him when I attacked him, I can't deny that. But I was badly wounded because the blade was poisoned. He injured my hip-joint, and the strong venom heated up; it got into the bone and rotted it black. There was such pain, and no doctor could heal me; I thought I was going to die. I set out to sea, thinking to die there, I was so enervated by suffering. Then the wind got up and became a storm, chasing my ship to Ireland. I was going to arrive in the land where I most dreaded to be, for I had killed the Morholt. He was your uncle, Queen Ysolt, and so I was very afraid of the place. But I was wounded, and I was wretched. I took up my harp so as to have some delight, but there was no pleasure in what I loved so much. But by and by the word went round that I knew how to play well. Immediately I was summoned to the court, all wounded as I was; the queen cured me, for which I bless her.[121] I taught you good harp-tunes, Breton lays from our country. Don't you remember, my lady queen, how I was healed by the medicine? Then, my name was Trantris — am I not he? What do you think?'

Then he said this: 'Lady queen, don't you remember the dragon I killed when I came to your country? I cut its head off its body, then I cut the tongue and pulled it out. This I stuffed into my hose, but the poison so burned me that I thought it would kill me. I lay fainting beside the way. You and your mother saw me, and saved me from death: with powerful medicine and skill you healed me from the poison.

'Do you remember the bath I was sitting in? You nearly killed me in it! You wanted to do me a great mischief,[122] when you went to draw my sword.[123] When you'd pulled it out you saw that it was notched. You realised, quite rightly, that the Morholt was killed with it. You had a bright idea, and you unlocked your little box. Inside you found the piece you'd taken out of the Morholt's head. You joined it to the blade, and it fitted perfectly. You were greatly daring, when you suddenly wanted to kill me in the bath with my own sword — women are such angry creatures!

---

[121] The queen was Ysolt's mother, also called Ysolt.

[122] A 'merveile' is not always 'marvellous'.

[123] The sense must be that she drew the sword out of curiosity, and wanted to kill Tristan only after realising it had killed her uncle.

La raïne en vint al cri
kar ele vus aveit ben oï;   448
ben savez ke je me acordai
kar suvent merci vus crïai.
E je vus deveie defendre
vers celui ki vus voleit prendre: 452
vus nel prendrïez en nul fuur,
kar il vus ert encuntre quor.
Ysolt, jo vus en defendi —
n'est vair iço ke vus di?'   456
...
[15c] 'N'est pas vair, einz est
        mensunge!
Mais vus recuntez vostre sunge:
anuit fustes ivre al cucher,
e le ivreze vus fist sunger.'   460
'Vers est: de itel baivre sui ivre
dunt je ne quid estre delivre!
...
Ne menbre vus quant vostre pere
me baillat vus, e vostre mere?   464
En la nef nus mistrent en mer:
al rai ici vus dui mener.
Quant en haute mer nus meïmes,
ben vus dirrai quai nus feïmes: 468
li jur fu beus e fesait chaut,
e nus fumes ben en haut;
pur la chalur ëustes sei —
ne vus menbre, fille de rai? —   472
de un hanap bumes andui:
vus en bëustes, e je en bui.
Ivrë ai esté tut tens puis,
mais mal' ivreze mult i truis!'   476

...
Part Two
[17b]
Tristran respunt: 'Raïne Ysolt,   713
je sui Tristran ke amer vus solt.
...
Ne vus menbre del seneschal?
Vers le rei nus teneit mal: 716
mis conpainz fu en un ostel, —
fumes junes[124] par üel —
par une nuit, quant me issi,
il levat sus si me siwi;   720
il out negez, si me trazat:
al paliz vint, utre passat,
en vostre chambre nus enguatat
e l'endemain nus encusat.   724
Ço fu li premer ki al rei
nus encusat, sicum je crei.
...
Del naim vus redait ben menbrer
ke vus solïez tant duter.   728
Il ne amad pas mun deduit,
entur nus fu e jur e nuit:
mis i fu nus aguaiter
e servit de mult fol mester.   732
Senez fumes a une faiz:
cum amans ki sunt destraiz
purpensent de mainte veidise,
de engin, de art, de cuintise,   736
cum il purunt entreassembler,
parler, envaiser e jüer,
si feïmes nus: senez fumes
en vostre chambrë u sumes.   740

---

[124] Var. 'jeümes'.

The queen came, hearing you cry out. You know I admitted it, for I repeatedly begged for mercy. And more: I was to defend you against somebody who wanted to take you, and you wouldn't have him at any price because you found him repellent.[125] Ysolt, I saved you from him — isn't it true what I'm saying?'

'It's not true! It's a lie! You're telling us your dream; you were drunk at bedtime last night, and the drunkenness gave you dreams!'

'Yes, it's true, I am drunk from that drink, and I don't think I shall ever be sober.[126]

'Don't you remember when your father and your mother entrusted you to me? They put us to sea in a boat, and I was to bring you to this king here. When we were well out to sea, I'll tell you what we did. It was a beautiful day and very hot, so we were on the high seas; you felt thirsty because of the heat. Don't you remember, king's daughter? We drank from the same cup: you drank, and I drank. I have been drunk ever since then, but I find it a very unhappy drunkenness!'

[The fool continues by telling Mark about how he manages in the wilderness, and how he plays the harp (491–532). Mark decides to go out, and Ysolt goes to her room lamenting. Brengain the maid, who knows the whole affair, thinks it is indeed Tristan! Ysolt sends her to talk to him (600ff). He reminds her about more things in the story (626–59), and convinces her. She brings him back to Ysolt, who still insists she can see no resemblance to her lover.]

Part Two

Tristan says: 'Queen Ysolt, I am Tristan, who has loved you so much.

'Don't you remember the seneschal? He embroiled us with the king. We were companions in the same lodging, and shared a bed.[127] One night, when I went out, he got up and followed me; it had snowed so he could track me. He came to the fence and passed beyond; he waited for us in your chamber, and next day he denounced us. I think he was the first to accuse us to the king.

'But you must remember the dwarf? You were very suspicious of him! He didn't approve of my pleasures, and he was at our heels day and night. He had been set to watch us, and he used the maddest methods. One day we had been bled.[128] We were distracted as lovers are, always thinking of ways and means, of tricks and artful devices, how to get together so as to talk, to play, and to enjoy. So it was with us, and there we were after blood-letting in your chamber.

---

[125] This was the man who pretended to have killed the dragon.

[126] The drink was a love-potion, poured for the couple by mistake; it was intended for Mark and Ysolt on their wedding night.

[127] MS 'junes' would mean 'we fasted together', which makes little sense here. For the better 'jumes', there is a note to this line on p. 28 of the edition; and note *a* (for p. 236) on p. 1339 of the Marchello-Nizia volume.

[128] This was a routine health procedure in the Middle Ages, and even into more recent times.

Mais li fol naims de pute orine
entre noz liz pudrat farine
ke par tant quidat saver
le amur de nus, si ço fust veir;   744
mais je de ço m'en averti: [17c]
a vostre lit joinz peez sailli;
al sailer le braz me crevat
e vostre lit ensenglantat;   748
arere saili ensement
e le men lit refis sanglant.

...

Li reis Marke i survint atant
e vostre lit truvat sanglant;   752
al men en vint eneslepas
e si truvat sanglant mes dras.
Raïne, pur vostre amité
fu de la curt lores chascé.   756
Ne menbre vus, ma bele amie,
de un' petit' drüerie
kë une faiz vus envaiai,
un chenet ke vus purchaçai?   760
E ço fu le Petitcru
ke vus tant cher avez ëu.
E suvenir vus dait ben,
amie Ysolt, de un' ren: 764

...

Quant cil de Irland' a la curt vint,
li reis onurrat, cher le tint:
harpëur fu, harper saveit;
ben savïez ke cil esteit.   768
Li reis vus dunat al harpeur,
cil vus amenat par baldur
tresque a sa nef e dut entrer;
en bois fu si le oï cunter: 772
une rote pris, vinc aprés
sur mun destrer le grant elez.
Cunquis' vus out par harper,
e je vus cunquis par roter.   776
Raïne, suvenir vus dait
quant li rais congïé me aveit
e jë ere mult anguisus,
amie, de parler od 'us   780
e quis engin, vinc el vergez

u suvent eimes enveisez;
desus un pin en le umbre sis,
de mun cnivet les cospels fis [17d]   784
k'erent enseignes entre nus
quant me plaiseit venir a vus.
Une funteine iloc surdeit
ki delez la chambre curreit;   788
en ewe jetai les cospels,
aval les porta li rusels:
quant veïez la dolëure
si savïez ben a dreiture   792
ke jo vendreie la nuit
pur envaiser par mun deduit.

...

Li neims sempres s'en aperceut,
al rei Marke cunter le curut;   796
li rais vint la nuit el gardin
e si est munté el pin;
jo vinc aprés, ke mot ne soi,
mais sicum je oi esté un poi,   800
si aperceu le umbre le roi
ke seét el pin ultre moi;
de l'autre part venistes vus;
certes, je ere dunc pöerus   804
kar je dutoie, sachez,
ke vus trop vus hastisez,
mais Deus nel volt, süe merci:
le umbre veïstes ke je vi   808
si vus en traisistes arere,
e vus mustrai ma praiere
ke vus al rai me acordissez,
si vus fare le püussez,   812
u il mes guages aquitast
e del regne aler me lessast.
Pur tant fumes lores sauvez,
e al rei Marke fu acordez.   816

...

Isolt, menbre vus de la lai
ke feïtes, bele, pur mai?
Quant vus eisistes de la nef,
entre mes bras vus tinc süef; —   820
je me ere ben desguisee,
cum vus me avïez mandé:

But this maniac dwarf, the son of a bitch, he sprinkled flour between our beds so anybody could see the evidence that we were lovers, if it was true. But I realised it was there, and lifting my feet I jumped into your bed.[129] The jump broke the wound in my arm and I bled all over your bed; when I jumped back, I bloodied my own!

'King Mark came in immediately and found your bed bloodied. He came to mine straight away, and saw my bloody sheets. For your love, my queen, I was driven away from the court. Don't you remember, my sweetheart, a little love-token I sent you once? I bought you a dog, and that was Petitcru, whom you are so fond of. And you must remember, darling Ysolt, something else:

'When the Irishman came to court the king made much of him and held him dear. He was a harper, and played well; you know who I'm talking about. The king gave you to the harper, who took you joyfully all the way to his boat; he was about to go on board. I was in the forest when I heard of this; I snatched an instrument and came after you full tilt on my war-horse. He got you by playing the harp; I got you by playing the fiddle![130] You must remember, my queen, when the king sent me away and I was so anxious, my friend, for a chance to talk to you. I made a plan, and came to the orchard where we often used to pass delightful hours. I sat under the shade of a pine tree, and made little slips with my penknife, which were the messages between us when I wanted to come to you. A fountain sprang up there, which flowed close to your chamber. I tossed the slips into the water and the stream bore them away. When you saw these chippings, you knew for certain I'd come that night to take pleasure with you.

'The dwarf spotted this right away, and ran to tell King Mark. The king came that night into the garden, and got up into the pine-tree. Then I came along, knowing nothing of this, but when I'd been there a little while I noticed the shadow of the king sitting in the pine above me. You came from the other direction; I can tell you, I was terrified. You see, I thought you were in too much of a hurry. But God was with us this time, mercifully: you saw the shadow that I could see, and you drew back. I showed you my prayer,[131] that I wanted you to make peace between me and the king, if you could; or that he should free me of my obligations and let me leave the kingdom. That is how we were saved, and I was reconciled with King Mark.

'Ysolt, do you remember the oath you made for me, my lovely? When you were coming ashore from the boat, I held you sweetly in my arms. I was in deep disguise, as you'd advised.

---

[129] 'joinz peez' (feet joined); this common phrase distinguishes the standing jump from the leap with one leg leading.

[130] 'rote'; see my Introduction (there is also a rote in the Amphiarax story; see 'musicians' in my index). In some cases it would have been an early violin-type instrument (crwth).

[131] Mark is intended to think their meeting was only for Tristan to beg for a reconciliation; they know he can hear what they say.

le chef tenei' mult enbrunc — [18a]
ben sai quai me deïstes dunc: 824
ke od vus me laissasse chair; —
Ysolt amie, n'est ço vair? —
süef a la terre chaïstes
e voz quissettes me auveristes,   828
e m'i laissai chaïr dedenz,
e ço virent tuz les genz.
Par tant fustes, ce je le entent,
Ysolt, guari' al jugement   832
del serment e de la lai
ke feïstes en la curt le rai.'
...
'Mais jo vi ja, bele, cel jur   857
ke vus me amastes par amur:
quant rei Marke nus out conjeiét
e de sa curt nus out chascez,   860
as mains ensemble nus preïmes
e hors de la sale en eissimes; [18b]
al forest puis en alames
e mult bel liu i truvames: 864
en une roche fu cavee,
devant ert estraite le entree;
dedenz fu voltisse e ben faite,
tant bele cum se fust purtraite;   868
le entailëure de la pere
esteit bele de grant manere;
en ce volte conversames
tant cum en bois nus surjurnames.   872
Hudein, mun chen ke tant oi cher,
iloc le afaitai senz crïer:
od mun chen, od mun ostëur
nus pessoie chascun jur.   876
Reïne dame, ben savez
cum nus aprés fumes trovez:
li reis meïmes nus trovat,

e li naim ke l'i menat;   880
mais Deus aveit uvré pur nus,
quant truvat le espee entre nus
e nus rejumes de loins;
li reis prist le gaunt de sun poing   884
e sur la face le vus mist
tant süef ke un mot ne dit,
kar il vit un rai de soleil
ke out hallé e fait vermeil;   888
li reis s'en est alez atant
si nus laissat dormant;
puis ne out nul' suspezïun
ke entre nus öust si ben nun: 892
sun maltalent nus pardonat
e sempres pur nus envoiat.
...
'Isolt, menbrer vus dait ben
dunt vus donai Huden, mun chen;   896
ke en avez fet? Mustrez le mai!'
...

Part Three

[18d]
'Remenbre vus cum al vergez
u ensemble fumes cuchez   944
li rais survint si nus trovat
e tost arere returnat?
Si pensa grant felunnie:
occire vus volt par envie;   948
mais Deus nel volt, süe merci,
kar je sempres m'en averti.
Bele, dunc vus estot departir,
kar li rais nus volt hunir.   952
Lores me donastes vostre anel
de or esmeré ben fait e bel,
e je le reçui si m'en alai
e al vair Deu vus cumandai.'   956

I had my head bent right down; I remember what you said to me then: that I must let you fall with me. Ysolt, darling, isn't that right? You fell gently to the ground, opening your legs to me, and I let myself fall between them. Everybody saw that. You were acquitted in the judgement, Ysolt, by the oath you swore in the king's court.'[132]

'But then I knew days when you truly loved me, darling. When King Mark accused us and drove us from his court, we took each other's hands and went out of the hall. We went into the forest, and we found a wonderful place: there was a cave in a rock, with a narrow entrance in front, and inside it was well-shaped and beautifully vaulted, as if it had been made on purpose. The carving of the stone was fine and grand. We lived in this hall as long as we stayed in the woods. Hudenc, my beloved dog, I trained [to hunt] without barking; with my dog and my hawk I fed us every day.

'Lady queen, you remember how we were found, later? The king himself found us, and the dwarf who had led him there. But God was working for us, because he found the sword between us, and we were lying far apart. The king took the glove from his fist and put it over your face, gently and without a word, because he saw that a sunbeam was burning and reddening you. Then the king went away, leaving us asleep, having no suspicion there was anything but innocence between us. He forgave us, forgetting his anger,[133] and soon had us sent for.

'Ysolt, have you forgotten that I gave you Hudenc, my dog? What have you done with him? Show him to me!'[134]

Part Three

'Do you remember how, in the orchard, where we were lying together, the king arrived and found us? He went away directly. He planned a terrible thing, wanting to kill you in his jealous rage. But God didn't wish it, praise him! Luckily I realised in time. We had to be separated, my lovely, for the king longed to shame us. Then you gave me your ring, of fine gold well worked and beautiful; I took it, and I went away, commending you to the true God.'

[My extract ends with the lovers' parting, to chime with the tragic end of the story in almost all the many versions. The ending of this *Folie* is a happy one: although Ysolt is terribly distressed when she sees the ring, thinking the fool must have taken it from her dead lover, Tristan at last changes his voice back to normal and her remaining doubts dissolve. They go off to bed together.]

---

[132] 'lai' often means a lay or song, but here it is clearly another kind of narrative: she says 'That is the only man apart from my husband who has ever lain between my legs'. Tristan was disguised as a leper.

[133] Compare the use of this expression in *Protheselaus*, v. 4999 (above), and my note.

[134] When Brengain fetches the dog, he recognizes his master joyfully.

Short Stories

There is always some difficulty about 'short stories' and how to define them, except simply by length. Dean's category includes Lais, Fables, Fabliaux, and Dits; from the sublime through the ridiculous to the comparatively ordinary. There are a number of short stories in this book, that are not in this chapter: notably the folk-tale in *Protheselaus* (Romance), the miracle of Saint Mellit (Hagiography), and the animal story in Bozon's *Conte* (Homiletic). The adventure story in the Appendix is a fine example of the kind of tale that is handed down orally (it would have been enjoyed and no doubt capped in local pubs): it was not written down until this century. Gray's *Simple Forms* contains much useful commentary on short forms, although naturally he concentrates on what may be termed popular culture. The present chapter bridges a generic gap between romance on one side and satire (in the next chapter) on the other.

Tristan Rossignol[1]

Here is another Tristan story, included because the poem in which it appears is published as a Plain Text (PTS 17) without glossary. Like the *Folie*, too, it is edited and translated in *Tristan et Yseut*, ed. Marchello-Nizia *et al.* but, as previously noted, this useful volume is not very convenient to read and handle.[2] The episode is unknown elsewhere among Tristan stories, and pairs conveniently with the *Folie* above (crossing Dean's sections, from Romance into Fable and the like).[3] The passage is reproduced in full, including the digression upon the evils of jealousy.[4] It would be tempting to expand the theme of birdsong by adding the Lai of *Laüstic* (which is about a nightingale), but this is already very well known and much anthologized; instead, I offer a passage from the devotional piece *Rossignos* (entitled The Nightingale) elsewhere in this volume.

Garden scenes are of the greatest importance in medieval literature. Such settings often preface lyrics, romances, and dream-visions. A garden is a liminal space in which meetings and other key narrative events take place, between the enclosed space of the house and the sometimes dangerous spaces of open country or forest. In the Middle Ages, the interior of houses cannot always have been very comfortable, even for rich people: they were dark with inadequate windows, smelly unless over-ventilated and thus cold, furnished (except for the richest) with hard chairs and benches. In the rare moments of a beautiful English or northern French summer, the sounds and scents of a garden must have been enchanting, and soft grass provided somewhere delicious to sit or recline. Here, the scene is a garden where a lover is asking his lady to prove her love for him, invoking heroines of romance (Dido, Ydoine, Helen, and Ysolt);[5] Tristan is discovered in the same garden (as in the previous story), outside Ysolt's chamber as before.

The text below is taken from the ANTS edition, and I have consulted the other edition for comparison and notes. The story is part of a conversation, but I have removed opening and closing quotation marks so as not to interfere with speeches within the story; I retain only those necessary for the lady's remarks at the end.

---

[1] In *Le Donei des Amanz* (ed. Holden, vv. 453–683), see Dean 180; and an overview in Trotter, 'Review: *Donei des Amanz*, ed. Holden'.

[2] Text and translation pp. 967–73, commentary and notes pp. 1566–9. See, again, *DMH* for a concise account of the legend.

[3] See Legge, pp. 128–32 (and 333–4 for the *Donei* as debate poetry).

[4] In the romance of *Yder*, jealousy is a narrative theme. Not only is Kay's jealousy (of everybody) treated at length, but also Arthur's jealousy of his wife leads to the adventure that nearly kills the hero, because she regards him with (innocent) favour.

[5] Dido of Carthage appears in Virgil's *Aeneid*, and the even more famous Helen of Troy is from Homer's *Iliad* (originally in Latin and Greek respectively, but retold in many languages over the centuries). Ydoine belongs to an Anglo-Norman romance, *Amadas et Ydoine* (Dean 161).

Text

[20a] **Oi**, bele, poi vus sovent
E relement en memorie tent
Quele chose Ysoud fit pur
　　Tristrant,
Quant ne l'aveit veu d'un an,　　456
E il repeira de Bretaine
Sanz compaignun e sanz
　　compaigne.
Entur la nuit, en un gardin,
A une funtaine suz un pin,　　460
Suz l'arbre Tristan seeit
E aventures i atendeit.
Humaine language deguisa,
Cum cil que l'aprist de peça:　　464
Il cuntrefit le russinol,
La papingai, le oriol
E les oiseals de la gaudine.
Ysoude escote, la reine,　　468
Ou gisout juste le rei Mark,
Mes ele ne sout de quele part;
De cele voiz ne sout en fin
Si fu el parc ou el gardin,　　472
Mes par cel chant ben entendi
Ke pres d'eluec ot sun ami.
De grant engin esteit Tristrans:
Apris l'aveit en tendres anz,　　476
Chascun oisel sout contrefere
Ki en forest vent ou repeire.
Tristrans feseit tel melodie [20b]
Od grant dousur, ben loinz oie,　　480
N'est quer enteimes de murdrisur
Ke de cel chant n'eust tendrur.
Ore est Ysoud en grant anguise
E pru n'entent que fere pusse,　　484
Kar leinz sunt .x. chevalers
Ki unc ne servent d'autre mesters
Fors de guaiter la bele Ysoud;
N'istrat pas fors quant ele volt.　　488
Defors oit sun ami cher,
Cil sunt dedenz pur lui guaiter,

E li fel neims que mult plus doute
Ke trestut ceus de l'autre rute.　　492
Entre ses bras le rei la tent,
Tristran dehors e chante e gient
Cum russinol que prent congé
En fin d'esté, od grant pité.　　496
Ysoud en ad dolur e ire,
Plure des oilz, del quer suspire
E si ad dit mult belement,
Tut suspirant, sanz overir dent:　　500
'Ja nen ai jo fors une vie,
Mes cele est dreit par mi partie:
L'autre part ai, e Tristran l'une;
Nostre vie est dreit' commune.　　504
Mes cele part ki est la fors
Ai plus chere que le men cors;
Poi preisereie ceste de ça
Si cele part perist de la.　　508
Jo ai si le cors, il ad le quer,
Perir nel lerrai a nul fuer.
La vois jo, quei que m'en avenge,
Ki que fole ou sage me tenge,　　512
Reseive jo ou mort ou pleie.
Or seit tut en la Deu maneie!'
Mult belement des braz le rei
Se deslaça tut en cecrei;　　516
Tote nue fors sa chemise
Del lit le rei Ysoud s'est mise. [20c]
En un mantel forré de gris
Alee se est, covert le vis,　　520
E par les chevalers trespasce
Dunt ad leinz une grande masse.
E si les trova tuz endormiz,
Asquans en l'eire, asquanz en liz,　　524
Cum aventure adunc esteit,
Ke mult belement aveneit,
Kar il esteient custumer
Tut autrement la nuit veiller:　　528
Quant cinc reposent en dormant,
Li autre cinc furent veillant,

Translation

Ah, my lovely, you are too forgetful; you hardly seem to remember the things Ysolt did for Tristan. She had not seen him for a year, and he came back from Brittany with no companion, either man or lady. About night-time, in a garden by the fountain under a pine tree, Tristan sat under the tree and waited to see what would happen.[6] He disguised his human voice, something he had long ago learned to do, and imitated the nightingale. He imitated the parrot, the oriole, and all the birds in the garden.

Ysolt the queen heard him, as she lay beside King Mark. But she couldn't tell which direction this voice was coming from, whether it was in the park or in the garden. But by the sound of the song she knew very well that her lover was near.[7] Tristan was very clever, and had learned at a tender age to counterfeit every bird that comes into the forest or lives in it. Tristan made such melody, very sweetly, and carrying far; no heart, not even that of a murderer, could hear this song without feeling tenderness.

Now Ysolt is in great distress, really not knowing what she can do. For in here there are ten knights who have no other task than to guard beautiful Ysolt. She can't go out when she wants to! Outside she can hear her beloved friend, but these men are inside to guard her. And so is the horrible dwarf, whom she fears more than all the others.[8]

The king was holding her in his arms, and outside Tristan sang and sobbed like the nightingale when it takes its leave, piteously, at summer's end. Ysolt was miserable and angry, her eyes weeping and her heart sighing. Then she said very quietly, in a breath between her teeth, 'I have only one life! But it is torn exactly in half! I've got the other half, but Tristan has the one half, so our life is exactly shared! But that half out there is dearer to me than my own body; if that one died there I would hardly care about this one. I've got the body, but he's got the heart. I won't let him die, not for anything! I'm going out there, whatever happens to me, whether I'll be treated as mad or sane, even if I'm wounded or killed! Let it be in the hands of God!'[9]

Adroitly and secretly she unwound herself from within the arms of the king. All naked except for her chemise, Ysolt slipped from the king's bed. In her fur-lined cloak, out she went with her face hidden, and passed through the mass of knights who were there. She found them all asleep, some just where they were and some in bed. It was a stroke of luck it happened thus, for usually they kept watch in quite a different way: when five of them rested in sleep, the other five stayed awake.

---

[6] The episode where Mark hid in this very tree, to catch the lovers, is described in the *Folie* (above).

[7] In the *Folie*, Tristan's disguised voice is the last barrier to her recognizing him.

[8] There is a malevolent dwarf in the previous Tristan piece, who leads Mark to the sleeping lovers.

[9] In this text, as in the foregoing, God certainly seems to be on the side of the lovers.

Asquans as us, asquans ad
    fenestres
Pur despier defors les estres   532
Dunt il furent mult curius,
Kar dure vie unt li gelus.
Ire, tençun ont chescun jor,
La nuit suspeciun e por.   536
Tresben veium que lui dolent
Turmenté sunt assez greffment.
Si tel dolur, pur verité,
Suffrirent cil pur l'amur Dé,   540
Gelus que unt lor quer frarin
Serreient dunc martir en fin.

...

Ki me demande de ço non
E si en vult oir raisun,   544
Purquei seit cil nomee gelus
Ke pur sa femme est envius
E si la guarde estreitement
De home estrange e de parent,   548
La dreite reisun si orrez
Purquei gelus est apellez:
Gelus est nomee de gelee
Ke l'ewe moille tent fermee.   552
Ben aparceit k'i met sa cure
Qu'ele est gelee en sa nature.
Tost pora sa nature entendre
Ke alques velt de garde prendre: 556
Gelé est freide e si est dure
E mult estreit' a demesure. [20d]
Ewe corante si ferm lie
Ke ne se put remuer mie,   560
Coure de li ne departir
Plus ke dame de chambre issir
Ke gelus tent en sa baillie
E garde en prent par gelusie.   564
Gelee terre mole endure,
Cum cailloy eschet e dure,
E tant l'estreint par sun geler
Ke buef ne la put reverser;   568
Dure e freide est asprement.
E li geluz est ensement:

Par sa feme est refreidiz,
Durs est a granz e a petiz,   572
A sa femme nomeement,
Kar il la guaite estreitement.
Enteins que lui fait un reguard,
Le gelus tut se deive e art;   576
Ne put fere a sa feme ren
Ne il ne suffre que autre i ait ben,
Joie ne ben ne nul deduit,
Estreit la garde e jor e nuit   580
E mult espie sun afaire,
Trop li est durs e de mal eire.
Pur ço qu'il est durs e freiz
E tent sa feme en grant destreiz,   584
En fermine la garde e prent,
Cum gellee l'ewe tent,
Par tel reisun tut a estrus
De gellé est nomé gelus.   588

...

Ma dame Ysoud fu ensement
Guaité mult estreitement,
Mes cele nuit, quant fu levé,
Par mi les guaiturs est alee.   592
Belement vint ci que a l'us,
E quant la barre trait sus,
Li anelez un poi sona,
E li culvers neim s'eveilla.   596
Esgarde de totes parz
Cum fel culvert de males ars. [21a]
A ço que Ysoud le us deferma,
Li neims s'escrie: 'E ki est la?'   600
La reine s'en ist tut bel,
E cil saut sus cum arundel
E s'afuble de sun mantelet,
Corant aprés Ysoud se met.   604
Par cel braz destre le saka:
'Avoi! dame,' fet il, 'esta!
A quel ure de chambre issez?
Mar i portastes unc les pez,   608
E, par mun chef, ne poi ne grant
De leuté ne voi semblant.'

Some at the doors, some at the windows, they spied on who was going around outside, and they were very curious to know about them. For the life of a jealous man is a miserable one.

These men suffer anger and quarrels by day, and at night they suffer suspicion and fear. We can see clearly that these wretches undergo terrible torments. Such torments, really, that if these miserable-hearted men suffered them for the love of God they would be counted among the martyrs!

If you want to know about the name of this thing, and an explanation of it — why the man who is so avaricious about his wife, and guards her closely from strangers and even family, is called jealous — then you shall hear the true reason why it is called Jealousy. Jealous is named from 'gel', or frost, that grips liquid water so fiercely.[10] You can see why if you pay attention, that it is frozen by nature. You can easily understand its nature, if you take the trouble to look at it. Frost is frigid, and also hard; it has an incredible grip. It binds running water so firmly it can't move at all, it can't flow away or escape, any more than the lady can escape the room where her jealous husband holds her in his power and has her guarded so jealously. Frost hardens soft earth, making it ruinous and hard as a stone. It holds the earth so stiff that no ox can turn it [with a plough]. It is painfully hard and cold, just like the jealous man. He is cold because of his wife; he is harsh to everybody great and small, especially to his wife, for he guards her tightly. If she even looks at him, he goes mad and burns with fury. He's no use to her, but he can't bear anybody else to have anything to do with her; no joy, no good, no pleasure. He guards her jealously day and night, and spies on everything she does. He is terribly harsh and bad-tempered with her. Because he is hard and cold, and holds his wife in such misery, he holds and keeps her locked up in a fortress, as frost holds water. This is certainly why, because of the frost, the jealous man is called jealous.

My lady Ysolt was like this, guarded just as closely. But that night, when she got up, she went right past the watchers! She had got safely as far as the door, but when she lifted the bar the ring chimed, just a little. The horrible dwarf woke up! He looked all around, beastly artful creature that he was! As Ysolt undid the door, the dwarf yelled 'Halloo! Who's there?'

Ysolt managed to get out, and he darted forward like a swallow. Flinging on his cloak, he began to run after Ysolt. He grabbed her right arm.

'Oho, my lady!' he cried, 'Stop right there! What time do you call this, to be coming out of your room? Curse your footsteps, wherever you're going! I'll swear by my own head I can see no shred of loyalty in what you're doing!'

---

[10] Medieval literature is full of bad derivations; some really outrageous ones are found in the *Roman des Franceis*, below.

Ysoud en ad al quer irrur,
La palme leve par vigur   612
E pus tele buffe a le neim dona
Ke quatre denz li eslocha,
E si dit od murne chere:
'Soudé aiez de chamberere!'   616
Li naim trebuche sur un banc,
La gule aveit plein' de sanc;
Gust le crapouz e crie en halt,
Il chet e leve e pus tressaut.   620
Tel noise e brai e cri leva
Ke li rei Mark s'en esveilla,
Si demande quel noisse i ait.
'Sire,' fait il, 'malement vait: 624
La reine m'ad si tué
E de son poin tut endenté
Ke ele issi tut a larun,
Sanz compaignie ou compaignon.   628
Tantost cum jo la vi issir,
Si la voleie jo tenir;
Del poin me feri a tel ire
Ke quatre denz me sunt a dire.'   632
Li reis respunt e si li dit:
'Tais tei, wicard, que Deu te ait!
Quant dame Ysoud est si hardie,
Ben sai n'ad ren de folie.   636
Tu as que fous vers li mespris;
Tristran n'est pas en cest pais; [21b]
Cele en est mult plus iré
Quant tu a tort l'as chalengé.   640
Les la dame, s'ele ad mester,
Par cel gardin esbaneier!
Ceo peise mei ke plusurs feiz
Trop l'avum tenu' en destreiz.'   644
Ysoud surrist e vet avant,
Le chef coverte e enveisant,
E vet tut dreit a sun ami.
Tristran saut tost encuntre lui,   648

Entrelacent mult ferm les braz,
Cum il fussent cosu de laz.
Beissent estreit e entre'acolent,[11]
Ovrent assez e poi parolent;   652
Meinent lur joie e lur deduit
Mut grant pece de cele nuit,
Meinent lor joie e lur amurs
Malgré le neim e les guaiturs.   656
Ysoud mustra ben par cel fait,
Ke deit a essemple estre treit,
K'amie n'est fine ne pure
Ke ne se met en aventure   660
E en perilus hardement
Si ele aime del tut lealment.
...
'Sertes, amis, veir avez dit;
Ore m'escutez un petit.   664
Ysoud fit ben qui tant ama
Tristran, qui tant ne fausa.
Tristran pur li fit grant atie,
Plus que ore freit pur s'amie: 668
Rere se fit, dreit cum fol,
Barbe, gernuns, chef e col,
E bricun se feseit clamer,
Ewe de bro sur sei geter;   672
Apertement dunt il mustra
Ke pas en gaberes nen ama.
Vostre semblant pus ben noter,
Le quer dedenz nent aviser.   676
Meinte fez quer e semblant
En dous veies vunt descordant,
                    [21c]
Kar li alquant gettent suspir,
Dolent, pleinent cum al morir,   680
Vunt sovent amunt e aval,
E al quer n'unt point de mal,
Kar il nen eiment fors a gas.'

---

[11] The editor notes a single-line initial; they usually take up two lines (Introduction, p. 1).

Ysolt was mad with fury. She raised her hand forcefully, and struck the dwarf such a buffet that four of his teeth were knocked out. She growled 'That's the punishment for a chambermaid!'

The dwarf sank down on a bench, his mouth full of blood. As the filthy toad tasted it he screamed aloud.[12] He fainted, and rose, and then jumped up. He made so much noise and cry, and raised such a racket, that King Mark woke up asking what the fuss was all about. 'Sire,' he said, 'all is not well! The queen has injured me so badly, and has knocked my teeth out, because she was creeping about like a thief all on her own without a soul for company. As I saw her going out, I went to catch hold of her. She bashed me so furiously with her fist that I'm now four teeth short!'

The king replied, saying 'God help you, knave, shut up! If Lady Ysolt is so bold [as to hit you] I am quite sure she is not doing anything stupid. It's stupid of you to be so suspicious. Tristan is not in the country. No wonder she was angry that you were accusing her falsely! Leave her be, if the lady wants to enjoy being in this garden! I feel bad that we have several times been too strict about keeping her in.'[13]

Ysolt smiles, and goes forth happily, with her head covered. She goes straight to her lover. Tristan jumps forward to meet her, and they wind their arms round each other so closely it looks as if they are bound together with laces. They kissed closely, and embraced each other. They hardly spoke, but there was much to do. They enjoyed their pleasure joyfully for much of that night; they enjoyed their love joyfully in spite of the dwarf and the guardians. Ysolt fully demonstrated, by her actions, that she must be taken as an example: no lover is so fine and so pure if she won't put herself at risk, or bravely into danger, if she loves fully and faithfully.[14]

'Certainly, my friend, you've spoken the truth. Now listen to me for a while. Ysolt did well, who loved Tristan so much; he had never betrayed her. Tristan went to great trouble for her; more than any man would now do for his love. He had himself shaved just like a fool, beard and whiskers, head and neck, and made himself out to be an utter loony. He allowed kitchen-slops to be thrown over him.[15] So he demonstrated that he was not fooling as a lover. It's quite easy to see what your expression says, but it's harder to see what's in your heart, and the two things can be very different. There are some men who heave out sighs, moaning, complaining as if on the point of death, wandering up and down. But their heart is not suffering in the least, for their love is nothing but foolery.'[16]

---

[12] The other edition corrects 'gust' to 'gient'; he groaned and shouted out.

[13] For a jealous husband, Mark is not so very unreasonable: he is easily appeased (and fooled).

[14] Now the tale is over, the lady speaks.

[15] This detail is not in any other version of the Tristan legend.

[16] The lady goes on to relate how Aeneas treated poor Dido.

Two Fabliaux

No anthology would be complete without one or more of these naughty stories.[17] Much has been written about their genre, and who their audience might have been (the edition gives a brief and useful outline in the introduction); it is clear they were popular.[18] It is now generally accepted that fabliaux do not represent a genre especially enjoyed by the lower (or emerging bourgeois) classses, in contrast with the upper classes who enjoyed romances: any reader might enjoy either or both, as is more or less the case today. Fabliaux may have been copied and retold as moral or cautionary tales, as here, or just for fun (or both). The moral of these two stories would be: Beware of Women's Deceitfulness! The pious and even affectionate husband is fooled; the lover gets away with it, but he plays a rather passive role. In both these stories, the trickster is the wife's mother: the wife seems to have no ideas of her own. It is interesting that Dean has contrived to catalogue these as both Fabliaux and Proverbs.[19] They fit this book, insofar as they fit at all, after the Tristan stories (which have characteristics of the 'lai', and are also full of a woman's cleverness in deceiving her husband). Together with the humorous Dit, below, they make a link into the next section which begins with the irreverent and anti-heroic work of André de Coutances; they would be more out of place if I inserted them immediately after the (apparently) serious *Apprise de Nurture*. There is not room, in a single volume, to present any more of the stories collected in Dean's fourth section.

The two I have chosen are pp. 10–11 in Short and Pearcy; both are edited from MS. Oxford Bodleian Digby 86.[20]

---

[17] These are from *Eighteen Fabliaux*, ed. Short and Pearcy (PTS 14).

[18] See also the entry by Norris J. Lacy, in *Medieval France, An Encyclopedia*, pp. 332–4. *Selected Fabliaux*, ed. Levy and Pickford, although it does not include Anglo-Norman examples, contains a good introduction to this difficult genre. The introduction to *Roi et Jongleur*, below, gives further references.

[19] These items are not listed separately in Dean. The ANTS volume is mentioned (and incorrectly numbered 16) in the introduction to her section on Fabliaux, on p. 107, and there is a cross-reference to her number 263 which is under the heading Proverbs.

[20] Previously edited by Hilka & Söderhjelm, 1922. Digby 86 and Harley 2253 are the best-known mixed 'miscellanies' (this word ought not to imply any randomness in the selection and ordering of texts).

Text

De l'engin de femme: del velous[21]

[83a] Uns hom — dist il — out en
    corage
Que aler vout en pelrenage:
Aler vout requere seint Pere.
Sa femme baila a sa mere   4
Que la gardast e enseingnast
Quë entretaunt ne folëast.
La femme un sen amy avoit
A qui deduire se soiloit; [83b]   8
Mander le sout privëement,
Manger e beivere od ly sovent.
La mere ben le consentoit
E od eus mangoit e bevoit.   12
Cum assemblerent en un jour,
Eistes vus a l'us le sengniur!
Hurta a l'us e apela
E seus dedens mout efrëa.   16
Primes mucerent le lecheour
Pus overerent au seignour.
Ly sires estoit mout lasé

Car mout avoit le jour erré;   20
Son lit comanda apariler
Car talent out de reposer.
La dame fu tot esbaïe
Que consiler ne se sout mie;   24
E la mere se purpensa
Cumfaitement le enginera;
Sa file apele si li dist,
Quant si esbaïe la vist: 28
'Pur le amour Deu le glorïous,
Ou est devenu le velous
Que tu feïs apariler?
Moustrez lui, einz qu'il aut cocher! 32
Ja deïs tu qu'il le verroit
Sitost cum a mesoun vendroit.'
La viele corust aporter
Le velous cum pur lui monstrer: 36
L'une dé corneres leva
E le autre a sa file baila.
Taunt le ount par devaunt lui
    tendu
Que li lecheres est issu.   40

---

[21] Number 6 [Disciplina Clericalis], vv. 1123–62.

Translation

Pulling the Wool Over his Eyes

He told us about a man who decided that he wanted to go on a pilgrimage, to visit Saint Peter.[22] He entrusted his wife to her mother, to look after her and to make sure she didn't get up to anything foolish while he was away. The wife had a friend of her own, with whom she liked to enjoy herself. She would often send for him on the quiet, to come and eat and drink with her. The mother was quite happy about this, and would eat and drink with them.

As they were together one day, suddenly here was the husband on the threshold! He banged on the door, calling out, frightening those indoors like anything! First, they had to hide the lecher. Then they opened to the husband. His lordship was very tired, having been travelling all day. So he ordered his bed to be made, as he was longing to rest. The lady was worried to distraction, not knowing what on earth to do. But the mother had an idea how the man could be tricked. She called her daughter, seeing what a state she was in, saying 'For the love of God in Glory, what's become of that coverlet you were working on? Show him, before he goes to bed! You said he was to see it just as soon as he came home!'

The old woman ran to fetch the coverlet, as if to show it to him. She lifted up one of the corners, passing another to her daughter. They managed to stretch it out in front of his eyes so that the lecher was able to escape!

---

[22] This means a pilgrimage to Rome, to St Peter's tomb; 'requere' can mean to pray, to seek, but (in this context) usually to visit. The narrator is quoting from a book he has read or heard.

De l'espee: autre engin de femme[23]

[83c] De un autre hom oÿ counter
Que en oresons voloit aler,
E sa mulier, qu'il out mout chere,
Baila en la garde sa mere. 4
Icete un juvencel ama
E a sa mere le moustra.
La mere pas ne li vëa,
Mais bonement li ottrïa. 8
Un jour le juvencel manderent
E un beu digner apresterent:
Deduient soi privëement;
Od bon vin cler e o piment; 12
E autre esbaignement i out:
Cil qui en parti ben le sout!
Atant vint a l'us le seignur,
Hurta a l'us; cil ount pöour: 16
Trestout lor esbanniement
Est ja torné a marement!
N'i out liu ou celui botasent,
Ou si en haste le mussasent. 20
La viele pas ne se obblïa:
Derere l'us le valet mussa.
Baila lui une nuwe espee.
La veile n'ert pas esgarree, 24
Einz dist li qu'il mot ne sonast
Si li sires l'areisonast,
Mes qu'il feït itel semblant [83d]

Cum c'il ëust pöour mout grant. 28
Pus ala l'us defermer
E lessa soen seignur entrer.
Sitost cum entra le seignur,
Regarda, vist le lechëour; 32
Demanda li: 'Ki est ceo la?'
E cil nul mot ne li sona,
Mes estut cum homme esbaÿ.
Le prodom tout le sen perdy. 36
Donc dist la veile au seignur:
'Sire, merci pur Deu amour!
Deus hommes vindrent hui corant
E cetu devant eus chasçaunt: 40
Tout le voileient destrencher.
Nous le lessames cienz entrer;
Par tant li rendimes la vie,
Car autrement ne l'ëust mie. 44
Quant il vus oï a cel us,
Esfrëé fu si saila sus;
Grant pöour out, ceo me est vis,
Que feusez de ses enemis.' 48
E le prodom se fist mout lee,
Quida que ele deit verité
E dit: 'La Dampnedeu merci,
Que vus le avez de mort garry!' 52
Pus li dit qu'il venist avant:
Mar ëust pöour tant ne quant.
Ensemble burent e mangerent,
E annuit aler le lesserent. 56

23 Number 7 [Disciplina Clericalis], vv. 1271–83.

Another example of Women's Trickery

I heard the story of another man, who wanted to go away to pray.[24] His wife, whom he held very dear, he left in the care of her mother. This wife was in love with a young man, and introduced him to her mother. Mother didn't forbid it in the least, but graciously gave her permission. One day they invited the young man, and prepared a splendid dinner; they had a lovely time just the three of them, with wines both clear and spicy. There were other enjoyments, too — if you were of the party, you'd know!

Suddenly the husband comes to the door, and knocks at it — they are terrified. All their fun has turned into trouble! There was nowhere they could put this man or conceal him quickly. But the old lady kept her nerve, and hid him behind the door. She handed him a naked sword. No, the old dear hadn't lost her wits. She told him not to breathe a word if the husband spoke to him, but to make believe by his look that he was in great fear. Then she went to unlock the door and let his lordship in. As soon as the husband got inside, he looked and saw the lecher! He asked him:

'Who is this here?' and he answered him not a word, just stood there as if paralyzed with fright. The good man was baffled.

The old lady said to the husband: 'Sir, be merciful for God's sake! Two men came tearing along, just today, with this man in front of them — they were chasing him. They wanted to hack him to bits! We let him come in here, and so saved his life. He wouldn't have one, if it weren't for us! When he heard you at this door he was scared, so he jumped forward. He was frightened because, I suppose, he thought you were one of his enemies.'

The good man was very pleased, believing she spoke the truth, and said: 'God be praised, you have saved him from death!'

Then he told him to come out, and not to be fearful any more. They ate and drank together, and when night came they let him go.

---

[24] To go and make his prayers, at some shrine (cf. the pilgrimage, above).

Le Roi d'Angleterre et le Jongleur d'Ely

Cy comence le flabel du Jongleur d'Ely et de monseigneur le roy d'Engleterre,
lequel jongleur dona conseil au roi pur sei amender e son Estat garder.[25]

This text is found in and reproduced from 'Le Roi d'Angleterre et le Jongleur
d'Ely', ed. de Montaiglon and Raynaud (*Recueil*),[26] with reference to [Harley
2253] *Facsimile*, ed. Ker;[27] see Dean number 195.[28] Some passages are translated
in Bloch, *Scandal*. Bloch (p. 130) refers to the 'inscription' on the MS page, that
is clearly not in the facsimile — nor is the equally mysterious preface.

For a discussion of the fabliaux genre, see my introduction to the pair of
short anti-feminist tales, above; and *Le Jongleur*, tr. Noomen (avertissement, and
introduction).[29] However, this ambiguous story of the King and the Juggler is
a different kind of fabliau altogether, being homiletic as well as humorous:[30] the
Juggler gives advice about life, the universe, and everything in a disconcertingly
cock-eyed sort of way.[31] Not only is the genre a matter of differing opinions, so
also is the audience: to Nolan, the dialogue recalls fourteenth-century upper-class
conversation and thus indicates the target audience; to Fein's team, the intriguing
miscellany in which it is contained (Booklet 6 of the MS) suggests an audience
of young men, to mention only two possibilities.[32] The poem is full of double
meanings, mostly deliberate on the Juggler's part. It will be seen that some can be
rendered into English ('draw' a cart, or a bow), others need explanation for those
who know no French ('sain' meaning healthy, or holy), and a number that are more
or less incomprehensible except that they are obviously mischievous.

---

[25] This is the 'inscription' that does *not* appear at the top of the manuscript page (see below). It is
copied here to indicate that the text contains good advice as well as good jokes.

[26] The volume is available online.

[27] In 'La riote du monde', ed. Ulrich, the text of *Riote*, on which this piece is closely based, is edited
with it. I refer *passim* to [Harley 2253] *The Complete Harley 2253 Manuscript*, ed. and tr. Fein
et al., in which this piece is edited and translated together with the rest of the MS's contents.
Harley 2253, and Digby 86, are the best-known mixed 'miscellanies'.

[28] Dean calls it a Fabliau, but lists it among Dits (a sub-section) thus indicating its difference from
other fabliaux; she says nothing about what kind of stories they are. For the Dit as genre, see *inter
al.* Spearing, *Medieval Autographies*, pp. 53–64.

[29] Noomen gives useful information about fabliaux, minstrels or jugglers, and 'dits'; his text is not
a new edition (his p. 86). See also the following: Cobby, *The Old French Fabliaux*; Butterfield,
'English, French and Anglo-French'; Nolan, 'Anthologizing Ribaldry'.

[30] Among diverse generic titles offered by scholars, Butterfield includes 'pastourelle': the poem opens
with a scene reminiscent of such encounters between two socially different persons (*The Familiar
Enemy*, pp. 92–5). A search for adventure, a green meadow, and (instead of a knight and a
shepherdess) a minstrel meets a king.

[31] A more recent collection of fabliaux omits this piece (*Nouveau recueil*, ed. Noomen and van den
Boogaard), judging it not to be a true fabliau. However, it does conform to one classic definition:
'un conte à rire en vers' (cited *inter al.* in *Eighteen Fabliaux*, ed. Short and Pearcy, p. 2).

[32] See Reichl, 'Debate Verse', p. 231, for the poem as a debate; also Revard, 'French Fabliau
manuscripts', for the arrangement of texts in the MS.

Cobby's bibliography provides a much fuller list of works, both primary and secondary, than can be included here; Butterfield's article cites both Ulrich's edition and Nolan's article (neither in Cobby's main list).[33] The modern edition, with facing-page translation into English, in [Harley 2253] *The Complete Harley 2253 Manuscript*, may not be easy to find.[34] I offer my own translation here, based on the faulty but 'standard' edition because it is well known and a digitized copy is available (I make reference to other editions, and to the MS itself).

There is no trace, in the MS, of the first twenty lines printed in the edited text. Although they show a correct folio number, editors have copied this preface from elsewhere. It also appears in Michel's edition cited above; for Palgrave's, see below. The manuscript shows, and Dean's incipit confirms, that the text begins where I have begun it. On further investigation, I found that the first edition of 1818, by Palgrave, contains both the title cited by Bloch and the preface interpolated by de Montaiglon and Raynaud — both spurious.[35] This first edition contains no apparatus whatsoever, except for a few dagger-marks against certain words (with no note attached). A rare book, the Bodleian copy is one of only twenty-five printed; a note on the flyleaf says Palgrave later destroyed most of them. It was given to Francis Douce the antiquary, by 'his friends, the Editors'. It thus arrived in the Bodleian along with the rest of Douce's collection after his death in 1834. Palgrave's contains no more and no fewer errors than other editions, as far as I can judge from my own readings. Palgrave's additions are not in the MS, but early editions print them (Bloch prints the title too, likewise without consulting the MS). Nolan points out that the invented heading and preface to Palgrave's edition are so convincing that subsequent editors copied and even corrected the lines.[36] Butterfield refers to a history of rewriting, that began with the 'Roi and Jongleur' as a version of *La Riote de monde* (Dean 195.1) and continued into the nineteenth century (Palgrave's, and thereafter including Bloch in the twentieth).[37]

The edition (in the *Recueil*) gives no line numbers, so I have added them; I have also modernized the punctuation and format slightly to make for easier reading.[38] However, I make no attempt to provide a new edition, nor to correct more than very lightly from the MS;[39] I consulted the facsimile when readings looked odd or

---

[33] See also Busby, '*Esprit gaulois* for the English'; other essays in the volume are of interest too.

[34] Lockhart, 'The King and the Minstrel', gives a delightful verse rendering: very freely translated, with omissions. His mention of a 'recent' Roxburghe Club edition is erroneous (see also *La Riote, le Roi*, ed. Michel, Preface): I examined a large number of Roxburghe volumes in case the poem had been tucked into one without being listed in the title. Lockhart's confusion may have arisen because many Roxburghe volumes were published by the same firm as published the Palgrave edition, at around the same date.

[35] Palgrave, ed., *Cy ensuyt une chanson*; our text is at pp. xi–xxx.

[36] 'Anthologizing Ribaldry', in Fein, ed., p. 292 and note 9.

[37] 'English, French and Anglo-French', p. 255.

[38] I have allowed the Juggler's final speech to continue to the end of the poem (as in the edition), so his voice merges with that of the narrator.

[39] This would produce a hybrid text, which is generally undesirable.

difficult. Other editions show different readings in all sorts of places, some better and some worse than this one; I footnote the most interesting of them. I have translated very freely, hoping to catch the tone without archaizing.[40] One or two words remain puzzling,[41] but the context allows one to guess.

---

[40] For those who read modern French, Noomen's translation may help with difficult passages: it is generally closer than mine. I have noted where our opinions differ (as with the Fein translation into English).

[41] These are not in Larousse, or *AND*; this piece is not among those currently listed for the latter's compilation.

Text

Seygnours, escotez un petit,
Si orrez un trés bon desduit
De un menestrel que passa la terre
Pur merveille e aventure quere.   4
Si vint de sà Londres, en un pree
Encountra le Roy e sa meisnée;
Entour son col porta sun tabour
Depeynt de or e riche atour.   8
Le roi demaund par amour:[42]
'Ou qy este vus, sire Joglour?'
E il respount sauntz pour:
'Sire, je su ou mon seignour.'   12
'Quy est toun seignour?' fet le
      Roy.
'Le baroun ma dame, par ma foy.'
'Quy est ta dame par amour?'
'Sire, la femme mon seignour.'   16
'Coment estes vus apellee?'
'Sire, come cely qe m'ad levee.'
'Cesti qe te leva quel noun aveit?'
'Itel come je, sire, tot dreit.'   20
'Où vas-tu?' 'Je vois de là.'
'Dont vien tu?' 'Je vienk de sà.'
'Dont estez vus? ditez saunz gyle.'
'Sire, je su de nostre vile.'   24
'Où est vostre vile, daunz Jogler?'
'Sire, entour le moster.'

'Où est le moster, bel amy?'
'Sire, en la vile de Ely.'   28
'Où est Ely qy siet?'
'Sire, sur l'ewe estiet.'
'Quei est le eve apelé, par amours?'
'L'em ne l'apele pas, eynz vint tous   32
      jours
Volonters par son eyndegré,
Que ja n'estovera estre apelée.'
'Tot ce savoi je bien avaunt.'
'Don qe demandez com enfant?   36
A quei fere me demaundez
Chose que vus meismes bien
      savez?'[43]
'Si m'aïd Dieus,' fet le Roy,
'Uncore plus vus demaundroy: 40
Vendras tu ton roncyn à moy?'
'Sire, plus volenters que ne le
      dorroy.'
'Pur combien le vendras tu?'
'Pur taunt com il serra vendu.'   44
'E pur combien le vendras?'
'Pur taunt come tu me dorras.'
'E pur combien le averoi?'
'Pur taunt comme je recevroy.'   48
'Est il jevene?' 'Oïl, assez;
Yl n'avoit unqe la barbe reez.'

---

42 Palgrave punctuates the speech to begin at 'Par amour', a reasonable alternative meaning (more or less) 'if you please'.

43 The edition prints 'sa vez'.

Translation

Hello everybody! Have a listen to this! You're going to hear a good one, about a minstrel who went wandering through the land in quest of wonders and adventure.

He was coming here from London, and in a meadow he met the king with all his court. He was wearing his drum round his neck, painted with gold and bright colours.

The King asked him politely 'Who do you belong to, mister Juggler?' He replied fearlessly 'I belong to my boss, sir.'

'Who is your boss,' asks the King. 'Well, he's the husband of my lady.'[44] 'But who is your lady, then?' 'She's the wife of my boss, sir.'

'What's your name?' 'It's the same as his, who christened me.'[45] 'So, what's his name, who christened you? 'Just exactly the same as mine, of course, sir.'

'Where are you going?' 'I'm going thataway.' 'Where are you coming from?' 'From thereabouts.'

'Where are you from? Tell me straight!' 'Sir, I'm from our town.'

'Where is your town, mister Juggler?' 'It sits around the church, sir.'

'Where is the church, my dear friend?' 'It's in the town of Ely, sir.'[46]

'Where is Ely to be found?' 'Sir, it sits upon the water.'

'And how do you call that water, if you please?'

'You don't call it, it comes every day quite happily of its own accord; it never needs to be called.'[47]

'I already knew all that!' 'So why do you keep asking these childish questions, if you already know the answers?'[48]

'God help us,' says the King, 'I want to ask you something else: would you sell me your nag?'

'Gladly, sir, and more willingly than I would give it to you.' 'How much would you sell it me for?'

'For as much as the sale price.' 'And how much would that be?'

'As much as you'll give me.' 'So how much shall I have it for?'

'As much as I shall have for it.'

'Is he young?' 'Oh yes, quite young. He's never shaved off a beard!'

---

[44] 'baroun' can mean simply baron, but a woman's husband is often called 'son baroun'.

[45] Some children were named after a godparent, or after the priest who baptized them. Legend has it that Gawain was baptized by a priest of that name. 'lever' in this context is more likely to mean 'lifted from the font' than 'raised'; children are usually 'norri' by the adults who bring them up (*Audree*, v. 152; *Des Grantz Geanz*, v. 22; and cf. *Eight Deadly Sins*, v. 70: 'levee acun dé funz').

[46] This is the first answer that gives any information whatsoever.

[47] The tides, of course. The French say 'How are you called?' when asking your name. This is a nuanced way of asking what people say when they want to attract your attention.

[48] Switching between polite and familiar forms happens here and there. Some changes may be for the metre, or simply accidental. But it is clear the minstrel is getting confident about what he can say to the king, and the king is beginning to respect the minstrel's superior wit. Some address forms are untranslateable; I approximate.

'Vet il bien, par amours?'
'Oïl, pis de nuit qe de jours.'   52
'Mange il bien, ce savez dire?'
'Oïl, certes, bel douz sire;
Yl mangereit plus un jour d'aveyne
Que vus ne frez pas tote la   56
    symeyne.'
'Beit il bien, si Dieu vus gard?'
'Oïl, sire, par seint Leonard;
De ewe à une foiz plus bevera
Que vus ne frez taunt come la   60
    symeyne durra.'
'Court il bien e isnelement?"
'Ce demaundez tot pur nient:
Je ne sai taunt poindre en la rywe
Qe la teste n'est devaunt la cowe.'   64
'Ami, ne siet il point trere?'
'Je ne vus menterei, a quei feyre?
D'arc ne d'arblastre ne siet il rien;
Je ne le vi unqe trere puis qu'il   68
    fust mien.'
'Passe il bien le pas?'
'Oïl, ce n'est mie gas;
Vus ne troverez en nulle route
Buef ne vache que il doute.'   72

'Emble il bien, come vus est avis?'
'Yl ne fust unqe de larcyn pris;
Tant com ou moi ad esté
Ne fut mès de larcyn prové.'   76
'Amis, si Dieu vus espleit,
Je demaund si il porte dreit.'
Feit le Jogler 'Si Deu me eyt,
Qy en son lit coché serreit   80
Plus suef avereit repos
Qe si yl fust mounté soun dors.'
'Ces paroles,' dit le Roy, 'sunt
    neynz; [108r]
Or me dirrez si il est seinz.'   84
'Seinz n'est il mie, ce sachez bien;
Car si il fust seinz ne fust pas
    mien,
Les noirs moynes le m'eussent
    toleyt
Pur mettre en fertre, come s(')en   88
    serreit,[49]
Auxi come autres seintz cors sunt,
Par tot le universe mount
Pur pardon receyvre e penance fere
A tote gent de la terre.'   92

---

[49] Noomen's reading makes more sense: the MS contains no apostrophes. My guess is that 'fertre' in this line is a better reading than Palgrave's 'sercre'.

'Does he go well, I'd like to know?' 'Yes, but not so well by night as by day.'[50]
'Can you tell me if he eats well?' 'Oh yes, certainly, my dear man. He'll eat more oats in one day than you will eat in a whole week!'
'Does he drink well, God help you?' 'Yes, sir, by my saints,[51] he'll drink more in one go than you could the whole week long!'
'Does he run easily and swiftly?' 'There's no point your asking, because I can't gallop down the road fast enough for his head not to be going in front of his tail.'[52]
'My good man, has he been taught to draw?'[53] 'What would be the good of that? I kid you not, he knows nothing of the longbow or the crossbow either. I've never seen him draw ever since he's been mine.'
'Can he pace well when pacing?' 'Oh yes, you won't find any bull or cow, not on any of the roads, that he needs to fear in that regard. I'm not joking!'[54]
'Can he steal along at a soft amble?'[55] 'Well, he's never been caught stealing all the time he's been with me, so he's never been proved a thief.'
'My friend, may God bless you, I want to know whether he is nice to ride.' The Juggler says 'May God bless me, whoever is tucked up in his bed will have softer sleep than if they were mounted on his back.'[56]
'Your words are rubbish,' said the King. 'Now tell me if he is sound.'[57] 'Oh he's no saint, I can tell you that. If he were holy he wouldn't be mine. Those black monks would have taken him to put in a box, that would be sensible, just like other holy bodies everywhere, so as to get pardon and do penance, for all the people in the land.'[58]

---

[50] This is a play on 'vet': the king means 'go', but is understood by the trickster as meaning 'voit': does he see well? *AND* gives 'vet' as a form of 'aler' but not of 'voir'; Noomen translates 'vet' as 'see', thus losing the double meaning. *Riote* has, at this point (p. 280), 'Voit il bien?' This increases the likelihood that 'vet' is being understood to mean 'see'.

[51] Saints' names are often, though not always, chosen for the rhyme. The Juggler's speech is so quirky that I hesitate to copy the names as they stand. The Fein version claims St Leonard was the patron saint of horses (but see *ODS*: the saint is said merely to have ridden a donkey around lands donated to him).

[52] The Juggler is pretending to understand 'isnelement' to mean something else.

[53] The king wants to know whether he can draw a cart.

[54] Here the pretended confusion may be with a verb such as 'pestre', to feed: the horse fears no competition from other animals in the field. Noomen thinks the Juggler is deliberately confusing 'route' (one meaning of this is 'crowd') with 'troupe' (sc. of animals), and that the king is asking whether the horse can walk steadily past difficult places.

[55] To amble is a nice steady foot-pace; the Juggler pretends that 'embler' means 'steal': is he a good thief? But the king is certainly referring to the horse's gait (see Noomen's note on pp. 92–3).

[56] Noomen reads 'confortable comme monture'. The word 'son' is naturally ambiguous: it could mean one's own bed, or the horse's! The word for the horse's back is written 'dors' (cf. 'dorsal'), which is also a form of the word 'sleep'. The rhyme would be better with 'repos/dos', so another word-play is clearly meant.

[57] 'sain' means healthy, 'saint' means holy.

[58] Black monks were Benedictines.

'Seinte Marie!' fet le Roy,
'Comment parles tu a moy?
Je dis sauntz de gales e sorenz
E d'autres mals e tormentz.' 96
Fet le Jogler al Roy:
'Yl ne se pleynt unque a moy
De maladie qu'il out en sey,
 Ne à autre myr, par ma fey.' 100
'Bels amis, ad il bons piés?'
'Je ne mangay unque, ce sachez,'
Ensi le Joglour respount;
'Pur ce ne say je si bons sunt.' 104
'Qe vus est, daun rybaut?
Sunt ils durs, si Dieus vus saut?'
'Durs sunt il verroiement,
 Come je quide à mon escient; 108
Yl usereit plus fers un meis
Que je ne feisse mettre en treis.'
'Est il hardy e fort?'
'Oïl, il ne doute point la mort; 112
S'il fust en grange soulement,
Yl ne dotereit verreiement,
Ne ja n'avereit il poour
Ne de nuit ne de jour.' 116
'Dites moi s'il a lange bone.'
'Entre si e Leons sur Rone
N'ad nulle meilour, come je quyt;
Car unque mensonge ne dit, 120
Ne si bien noun de son reysyn[59]
Ne dirreit pur cent marcz d'or fyn,
Mès qu'il ly voleit apertement fere
Mavesté de chescune matere 124
Ou larcyn par le pays,
Ou homicide, qe valt pys;
Sire Roy, ce sachez,
Par ly ne serrez acusez.' 128
Fet le Roi: 'Je ne prise pas vos dys.'
'Ne je les vos, que vaillent pys.

Je di bourde pur fere gent ryre,
Et je vus en countray, bel douz 132
 syre.'
'Responez à droit, daunz Joglours;
De quele terre estez vus?'
'Sire, estez vus tywlers ou potters
Qe si folement demaundez? 136
Purquoi demander de quele tere?
Volez vus de moi potz fere?'
'E qe diable avez vus,
Que si responez à rebours? 140
Tel ribaud ne oy je unqe mès.
Diez de quel manere tu es?'
'Je vus dirroi, par seint Pere,
Volenters de ma manere: 144
Nous sumes compaignons
 plusours,
E de tiele manere sumes nous
Que nus mangerons plus volenters
Là où nous sumez priez, 148
E plus volenters e plus tost,
Qe là où nous payons nostre escot;
E bevoms plus volenters en seaunt
Qe nus ne fesons en esteaunt, 152
E, après manger que devant,
Pleyn hanap gros e grant;
E, si vodroms assez aver,
Mès nus ne avoms cure de travyler, 156
E purroms molt bien deporter
D'aler matyn à mostier;
E ce est le nostre us
De gysyr longement en nos lys 160
E à nonne sus lever
E puis aler à manger;
Si n'avoms cure de pleder,
Car il n'apent à nostre mester; 164
E nus vodroms estre tot dis,
Si nus pussoms, en gyws e rys;

---

[59] Palgrave reads 'veysyn', as I do; the v is clear, and it makes more sense.

'Oh Saint Mary!' says the King. 'How can you talk to me like this? I mean, without galls or sores,[60] or any other aches and pains.'

The Juggler says to the King 'He has never complained to me, of any malady he might have got. Nor has he complained to any other doctor, I can assure you.'

'My dear chap, has he got good feet?' 'Well, I've never eaten one, you know,' said the Juggler, 'so I don't know if they're good or not.'

'What's the matter with you? Are they hard,[61] for God's sake?'

'Oh yes, they're hard all right, as I know to my cost: he uses more iron in a month than I put on him in three.'

'Is he brave and strong?' 'Well, he's not in the least afraid of death. Just as long as he's in the barn, he'd certainly never be frightened, and he'd fear nothing all night and all day.'

'Tell me if he has a good tongue.' 'There's no better between here and Lyon on the Rhone, I'm sure. He never tells lies, and nor would he say anything but good about his neighbour, not for a hundred golden marks! Unless he needed to get something bad out into the open, such as thieving locally, or manslaughter which is even worse. My lord King, you can be quite sure he'll never accuse you of anything.'[62]

The King says 'I don't think much of what you say!' 'Same to you — but yours are a lot worse! I joke to amuse people, and then I met you, my dear sir!'

'Tell me straight, mister Juggler: what is your land?'[63]

'My lord, are you a tiler or a potter? What kind of an idiot question is that? Why are you asking about earth? Do you want to make pots of me?'

'What the devil is wrong with you, that you always answer widdershins? I've never heard such foolery! Tell me what thou art!'[64]

'I'll tell you willingly ... in my own way, for Pete's sake. We are a band of companions, and our own way is to eat more willingly where we are invited. More willingly, and more quickly, than where we have to pay our score. We drink more willingly sitting down than standing up. Also, rather after eating than before, with a big fat goblet full up. Also, we like having possessions, but we don't like having to work. We can easily dispense with going to church of a morning.

'It is our custom, to lie in our beds all morning and get up at None;[65] then we'll go and eat. We don't care for lawsuits — they are nothing to do with our profession.[66] We like playing and joking all the time, if we can.

---

60 'sorentz' is not in *AND*. Noomen gives 'suro', a tumour that afflicts horses' legs.

61 Noomen reads this to mean 'do they get tired easily?'

62 This malicious dig suggests that others might find something bad to say about the king.

63 'terre' also means earth.

64 The king says 'tu', but the trickster prefers to answer in the plural 'we'.

65 The canonical hour of Nones was the ninth hour of the day, therefore long after 'noon' or midday (see, for example, *Cher Alme*, note 23 on p. 259); Noomen translates 'midi'.

66 'pleder' also means to beseech, plead (*AND* does not give the added meaning 'beg', as do Fein's team).

E si vodroms aprompter e prendre
[108v]
E à nostre poer malement rendre;   168
Nus n'avoms cure d'aver,
For que nus eyoms assez à manger;
Plus despondroms à ung digner
Qu'en un mois pourroms gayner;   172
E uncore volum plus,
Quar orgoil est nostre us,
E à beles dames acoynter,
Ce apent à nostre mester.   176
Or savez une partie
Coment amenons nostre vie;
Plus ne puis par vilynye
Counter de nostre rybaudie.   180
Sire Roi, or me diez
Si nostre vie est bone assez.'
Le Roy respoygnant ly dit:
'Certes, je preise molt petit   184
Vostre vie ou vostre manere,
Quar ele ne valt mie une piere.
Pur ce que vus vivez en folie,
Daheit qe preyse vo vie!'⁶⁷   188
'Sire roi,' feit le Jogler,
'Quei val sen ou saver?
Ataunt valt vivre en folye
Come en sen ou corteysie.   192
Et tot vus mostroi par ensample
Qu'est si large e si aunple
E si pleyn de resoun,
Que um ne dira si bien noun.   196
Si vus estez simple et sage houm,
Vus estez tenuz pour feloun;
Si vus parlez sovent e volenters,
Vus estez tenuz un janglers;   200
Si vus eiez riant semblaunt,

Vus estez tenuz pur enfaunt;
Si vus riez en veyn,
Vus estez tenuz pur vileyn;   204
Si vus estes riche chivaler
E ne volez point tourneyer,
Donqe dirra sacun houme
Vus ne valez pas un purry poume;   208
Si vus estes hardy e pruytz,
E hantez places de desduytz:
"Cesti cheitif ne siet nul bien;
Taunt despent qu'il n'a rien."   212
Si vus estes houme puissaunt
E serez riche e manaunt,
Dount dirra hom meyntenaunt:
"De par le deable! où ad il taunt?"   216
S'il est povre e n'ad dount vyvre:
"Cest cheitif tot ditz est yvre."
Si il vent sa tere pur ly ayder:
"Quel diable ly vodera terre doner?   220
Yl siet despendre e nient gaigner",
Chescun ly velt cheytyf clamer.
S'il achate terres par la vile,
Si lur estoit autrement dire: 224
"Avey veu de cel mesel
Come il resemble le boterel
Qe unque de terre ne fust pleyn?
Ensi est il de cel vileyn."   228
Si vus estes jeovene bachiler
E n'avez terre à gaygner
E en compagnie volez aler
E la taverne haunter,   232
Vus troverez meint qe dirrat:
"Où trovera il ce qu'il ad?
Unque ne fist gayne à dreit
Ce qu'il mangue et ce qu'il beit."   236

---

⁶⁷ MS Daþeheit (see Fein edition). Editors have had trouble with the word: Palgrave prints 'Dathcheit', adding one of his mysterious dagger-marks; Noomen prints 'Dapcheit'.

'We like borrowing and taking things, and we take care to be slow about returning them.[68] But we don't care about getting goods, just so long as we get enough to eat. We'll spend more on one dinner than we could earn in a month! We want more still; we are so arrogant, and that is our way ... as well as wanting to get to know lovely ladies, which also goes with the job.

'Now you know a bit about how we spend our lives. It would be wicked of me to tell you any more of our foolery. Now, my lord King, tell me if you think we have a good life!'

The King's reply was like this: 'Well, really, I don't think much of your life and your ways. Not worth a pebble, in my opinion, since you live in such foolery; be damned to anybody who praises your life!'

'My lord King,' says the Juggler, 'What's the point of wit or wisdom? It's just as good to live in foolery as it is to live sensibly and courteously. Now I'm going to give you a f'r instance,[69] which is so big and wide, so very sensible, that nobody could find fault with it:

'If you're a simple wise man, you'll be taken for a criminal.

'If you're a cheerful and willing talker, you'll be called a blabber-mouth.

'If you've got a laughing face, you'll be treated like a child.

'If you laugh for no reason, you'll be taken for a boor.

'If you're a rich knight and don't want to play at tournaments, then everybody will say you're not worth a rotten apple.

'If you're strong and brave, and go about in places of entertainment, they'll say "This waster doesn't know anything, he spends so much he's got nothing."

'If you're a powerful chap, well-to-do and well-off, now everybody will say "Where the hell does he get all that!"

'But if he's a poor man without any livelihood, "That loser is pissed all the time."

'If anybody sells some land so as to help himself out, "Who the hell would want to give him land? He can spend, but he can't earn a penny." Everybody will call him a wretch.

'If he buys some land near the town, they'll think of something else to say: "Have you seen that sickie, who's like the proverbial bushel that's never full of earth?[70] That's him, miserable sod."

'If you're a young fellow with no property to get income from, and you want to go out socializing in the pub, you'll find plenty who say "Where's he going to find what he's got? He never did a decent hand's turn for what he eats and drinks."

---

[68] This catalogue of bad behaviour has moments that resemble the 'sermon' delivered to the French in *Roman des Franceis*, below.

[69] See Noomen's note for *exempla*.

[70] 'boterel' is not in *AND*; Noomen translates 'crapaud' (Larousse: bote III, crapaud; boterel would thus be a little toad). Fein's team read 'bocerel' and translate 'little goat' (as in 'bouc'). The consonant looks more like t than c in the MS, but neither animal fits the context; I have guessed a meaning, and invented a proverb to match.

Si vus alez poi en compagnie
E taverne ne hauntez mye:
"Cesti est escars, avers et cheytif,
C'est damage qu'il est vyf.   240
Yl ne despendi unque dener,
S'il ne fust dolent al departer:
De son gayn Dieu li doint pert,
Yl n'out unqe la bourse overt."   244
Si vus estes vesti quoyntement,
Donqe dirrount la gent:
"Avez veu de cel pautener,
Com il est orguillous e fier?   248
Ataunt usse je de or real [109r]
Com il se tient valer fient de
    cheval!
Il n'i averoit si riche houme, par
    Dé,
En Londres la riche cité."   252
Si vostre cote seit large e lée,
Si derra ascun de soun grée:
"Ce n'est mie cote de esté."
Donqe dirra le premer: 256
"Assez est bone, lessez ester;
Il resemble un mavois bover."
Si vostre teste soit despyné⁷¹
E soit haut estauncé:⁷²   260
"C'est un moygne eschapé."
Si vostre teste seit plané,
E vos cheveus crestre lessé,
Yl serra meintenant dit: 264
"C'est la manere de ypocrit."
Si vostre coyfe seit blanche e bele:
"S'amie est une damoysele,
Qe ly vodra plus coyfes trover   268
Qe ly rybaud pust decyrer."

Si ele est neyre, a desresoun:
"Yl est un fevre, par seint Symoun!
Veiez come est teint de   272
    charboun."⁷³
Si vus estes cointement chaucé
E avez bons soudlers al pié,
Si serra ascun par delee
Que vus avera al dey mostree,   276
E à soun compaignoun est torné:
"Ce n'est mie tot(,) pur Dé,⁷⁴
De estre si estroit chaucé."
Dirra l'autre: "A noun Dé,   280
C'est par orgoil e fierté
Que li est al cuer entree."
Si vus estes largement chaucé,
E avez botes feutré   284
Et de une pane envolupé,
Donqe dirra ascun de gree:
"Beneit soit le moigne de Dee
Qe ces veyle botes par charité   288
Ad à cesti cheytyf doné."
E si vus les femmes amez,
E ou eux sovent parler
E lowés ou honorez,   292
Ou sovent revysitez,
Ou, si vus mostrez par semblaunt
Qe à eux estes bien vuyellaunt,
Donque dirra ascun pautener: 296
"Veiez cesti mavois holer,
Come il siet son mester
De son affere bien mostrer."
Si vus ne les volez regarder   300
Ne volenters ou eux parler,
Si averount mensounge trové
Que vus estes descoillé!

---

71 The edition shows a dotted line after v. 259, signalling an omission. There is no gap in the
    manuscript, but there lacks one line of the running rhyme in this passage: an odd number of lines
    rhyme 'er', 'ée', and the like.

72 Palgrave prints 'estamite' with a dagger-mark; the present reading is I think preferable.

73 There is a dotted line here (as after v. 259); no doubt because there are only three lines rhyming
    'oun'.

74 Noomen prints this line without a comma (as does Palgrave), which makes more sense.

'If you don't get out much, and never to the pub, "He's stingy! He's mean and miserly! Pity they let that one live! He never spent a farthing without grudging where it went. God can take away everything he's got, the rotter who never opens his purse."

'If you are nicely dressed, then people will say "Have you seen this rogue? Isn't he just so arrogant and proud? I wish I had as much royal gold as that pile of horseshit he thinks himself worth!"[75] By God, you wouldn't find a man as rich as that in all the rich city of London."

'If your coat is large and wide, somebody will think it hilarious to say "That's never a summer coat!" Then the other will say "Ah, leave it. It's good enough for a lousy ox-driver like that."

'If your head has been well de-bristled,[76] and shaved up to the top, "Ooh! There goes an escaped monk!"

'If your head is sleeked, and your hair let grow long, it will now be said "That's how a hypocrite wears his hair."

'If you've got fine white headgear, "His lady-friend is the sort who'll find him more head-dresses than he could ever wear to shreds, the fool!"

'But if it's black, would you believe, "He's a blacksmith, saints alive! Look how stained with coal he is!"

'If you are neatly shod, with good shoes on your feet, there are instead those who will point the finger at you, and turn to their friend, "It can't be all for the sake of God, to have such narrow shoes!" Then the other will say "For God's sake, it's because his heart is soaked in pride and arrogance."[77]

'But if you're generously shod with felted boots, wrapped in a cloth, it will amuse them to say "Ah, bless the holy monk who gave these old boots for charity, to this poor fool."

'And if you like women, and you like talking to them, and you praise and respect them; if you often go and see them, or show by your manner that you care about them, then there is always a bad-mouth to say "Look at that lousy whoremonger! Doesn't he just show by his manner what he gets up to, and how it suits him!"

'But if you don't like looking at them, or prefer not to talk to them [the women], they [the gossips] will soon find out a truth about you,[78] that you haven't got any balls!

---

[75] Noomen judges that the royal gold must refer to a gold penny (1257–70) which could date the text. But it is hardly likely that a joking reference of this kind, to a heap of gold as against a heap of manure, would be anything but figurative.

[76] Nooman reads this as unkempt (that is, de-peigné); Fein's team translate 'spiked'. If it is shaved (next line), however, it will not be bristly.

[77] This may be a reference to the fashionable pointy shoes of the middle and later Middle Ages.

[78] That is, 'a truth' meaning a lie (mensounge).

Auxi di je par delà,   304
Come l'ensaunple gist par desà,
Si ascune dame bele
Ou bien norrie damoysele
Par sa nateresse e bounté   308
De nulli seit privée,
Ou si ele tant ne quant
Fasse à nully bel semblaunt,
Ou si ele vueille juer: 312
Cele est femme de mester
E de pute manere
E à gayner trop legere.
Si ele soit auqa hontouse[79]   316
E de juer dangerouse:
"Veiez come ele se tient souche!
Burre ne destorreit en sa bouche."
Coment qe ele ameyne sa vie,   320
Rybaudz en dirront villeynie.
Si volenters alez à mostier,
E à Dieu volez prier
De vos pechiés remissioun   324
E de fere satisfaccioun,
Si dirra ascun qe vus regard:
"Ja de vos prieres n'ey je part,
Qar vus n'estes qe un papelart;   328
Vos prieres serrount oys tart."
E si vus alez par le moster[80]
E ne volez point entrer,
Donqe dirra vostre veysyn: 332

"Cesti ne vaut plus qe un mastyn;
Si Dieu me doint de son bien,
Cesti ne vaut plus que un
    chien."[81]
Si vus volenters volez juner [109v]   336
Pur vos pechiés amender,
Dount dirra li maloré:
"Où à deables ad il esté?
Yl ad soun pere ou mere tué,   340
Ou ascun de soun parentee,
Ou femme, file ou enfaunt,
Pour ce qu'il june taunt."
Si vus sovent ne junez,   344
Donqe dirrount malorez:
"Cesti mavais chien recreant
Ne puet juner taunt ne quant,
Le bon vendredy ahorree   348
Prendreit il bien charité
Trestot par soun eyndegré
Ja de prestre ne querreit congé."
Si je su mesgre: "Bels douz cher,   352
Mort est de faim; il n'a qe
    manger."
E, si je su gros e gras,
Si me dirra ascun en cas:
"Dieu! come cesti dorreit graunt   356
    flaut
En une longayne, s'il cheit de
    haut!"

---

[79] MS 'auqe'.
[80] MS mostrer; Noomen corrects to 'mostier'.
[81] MS 'valt … qe'.

'Now I'm going to put an example on the other side, to put beside what I've said on this side.[82] If any lovely lady, or well-stacked lassie, in the kindness of her heart has ado with somebody privately, or if she shows favour to anybody in any way, or if she's in a playful mood; why, then that makes her a whore, and just like a pro she can be got too lightly. But if she is a bit prudish, and backward in her games,[83] then "Look at her shooting a line! Butter wouldn't melt in her mouth!"[84] However she goes on, somebody will put a bad interpretation on it.

'If you go to church willingly, and pray to God for remission of your sins, and to do penance,[85] anybody who sees you will say "I'm not having anything to do with your prayers, you're nothing but a pope-holy. Your prayers won't be answered yesterday!"

'But if you're walking past the church and don't feel like going in, then your good neighbour will say "That one's no better than a cur. God give me strength, he's only fit for a dog's blessing!"

'If you decide to fast, so as to atone for your sins, the bad-mouth will say "Where the hell has he been? Has he killed his father or mother, or some relation? Or perhaps a woman, or girl or child, to make him fast like this?"

'But if you don't often fast, then the bad-mouths will go "This dirty unbelieving dog! He can't restrain himself in the least! On blessed Holy Friday he'd help himself to charity,[86] all off his own bat, never asking the priest's permission!"

'If I'm thin, "Oh my dear chap, he's dying of hunger, he's got nothing to eat!" But if I'm nice and fat, there's somebody who says "Good Lord, he'd make one hell of a splash, if he fell down into a jakes!"[87]

---

[82] Notably, the Juggler makes the point that life is unfair in just this way for women, too; Dove remarks on this ('Evading Textual Intimacy', n. 50 on p. 344). The frequent change of person (if you, if one, if I ...) indicates that the lessons are universal; it would be perverse to try and disentangle each 'person' to sketch the different experiences of author and audience.

[83] Bel Semblaunt may be a conflation of two personifications: Faux Semblaunt and Bel Accueil. These, and Danger, are personified in (for example) the *Roman de la Rose*. One welcomes the lover, the other holds him at arm's length. Note the modern proverb (Noomen explains that the lady is a 'sainte nitouche').

[84] Noomen reads this line as I do, although he points out that 'de(s)tordre' is not attested to mean 'melt' in the dictionairies. But the *AND* meanings are close enough, to have been used in a wider sense.

[85] 'satisfaction' is when the sinner makes reparation, generally as instructed by the priest, for the sins they have confessed.

[86] Noomen takes this to mean charity in the form of food handouts. However, 'charité' is used for the (pretended) handout of boots, above.

[87] The text says 'from a great height'; some privies were very deep. Fein's team read 'cheit' to mean 'shit', but in *Riote* the verb is 'chaoit' (p. 285); this makes it slightly more likely that in this text it means 'to fall'.

Si j'ay long nees asque croku,
Tost dirrount: "C'est un bercu."[88]
Si j'ay court nees tot en desus,   360
Um dirrat: 'C'est un camus."
Si j'ay la barbe long pendaunt:
"Est cesti chevre ou pelrynaunt?"
E si je n'ay barbe: "Par seint   364
     Michel!
Cesti n'est mie matle, mès
     femmel."
E si je su long e graunt,
Je serroi apelé geaunt;
E si petitz sei d'estat,   368
Serroi apelé naym et mat.
Dieu! come le siecle est maloré,
Que nul puet vivre sanz estre
     blamé!
Plus y avereit à counter,   372
E assez plus à demaunder;
Mès je ne vueil estudier
Si vus ne volez del vostre doner;
Car ensi va de tote rienz   376
E des malz et des bienz;
Car nulle rien ne purroi fere
Qe um ne trovera le countrere.'
Donqe dit le Roi: 'Verroiement   380

Vus dites voir, à mien ascient.
Quei me saverez vus counsiler?
Coment me puis countener
Et sauntz blame me garder,   384
Que um me vueille mesparler?'
Respound le Joglour al Roy:
'Sire, moun counsail vus dirroy:
Si vus vostre estat veillez bien   388
     garder,
Ne devreez trop encrueler,
Ne trop estre simple vers ta gent;
Mès vus portez meenement;
Car vos meymes savez bien   392
Qe nul trop valt rien:
Qy par mesure tote ryen fra
Ja prudhome ne l'y blamera,
Par mesure meenement   396
Come est escrit apertement,
E le latim est ensi:[89]
Medium tenuere beati.
Qy ceste trufle velt entendre,   400
Auke de sen purra aprendre;
Car um puet oyr sovent
Un fol parler sagement.
Sage est qe parle sagement,   404
Fols com parle folement.'

---

[88] Palgrave prints 'bestu', Noomen 'bescu'; neither is any better (see note in my translation).
[89] MS 'latyn'.

'If I've got a long nose that's a bit crooked, they'll all say "Look at old bottle-nose!"[90] If I've got a short little nose up there, they say "Snubby face!"

'If I've got a long hangy beard, "Is that a goat, or is it a pilgrim!" And if I've got no beard, "For the love of Mike, that looks more like a woman than a man!"

'If I'm tall and broad, I'll be called a giant; but if I'm small of stature then I'll be called a useless dwarf.[91]

'Ye gods, what a mad mad world![92] Nobody can live without being calumniated! There's a lot more to tell, and even more questions to ask, but I want to stop scholarizing unless you want to give me something of yours. So it goes, everything, good and bad: there's nothing anybody can do that somebody won't go finding fault with.'

Then the King said 'You speak the truth as far as I can tell. What would you advise me to do? How can I conduct myself, and protect myself from blame, so that nobody speaks ill of me?'

The Juggler answers the King 'Sir, I'll give you my advice: if you want to keep your good status, you must not be over-cruel, nor be over-gentle with your people.[93] Behave with moderation, because you yourself know that excess can never be virtue.[94] Whoever does all things in moderation will never be blamed by any honest man. Moderation, moderately, as is clearly written; here is the Latin: Blessed are they that keep the middle path.

'Whoever listens to this trifling tale may learn something wise, for we often hear a fool speaking wisely. Wise is he who speaks wisely, and whoever speaks foolishly is a fool.'

---

[90] MS 'bostu', or similar (it looks more like 'os' than 'es'). *AND* gives 'a person with a bulbous nose' as a meaning for 'bossu', which is very likely the intended word. Noomen translates 'beçu' (not in dictionaries) without explanation; Fein's team give 'bescu', tr. beaked. In Michel's edition, there is a fragment of *Riote* printed after this piece: at the same point in this fragment the word is 'botchus', perhaps meaning 'bossu'. This means one redactor at least understood it as this and not as 'bercu' or similar.

[91] 'mat' has a number of meanings, also in Middle English (glossary to *Sir Ferumbras*, ed. Herrtage).

[92] *Riote*, p. 285: 'Tel est la riote del monde', hence the title of the companion piece. *AND* gives a variety of meanings: noisy, discordant, contentious, nonsense, and revel!

[93] 'simple' does not mean foolish here; it has positive meanings of openness, guilelessness, honesty (both Noomen and Fein's team translate 'familiar'). Edward the Confessor was said to be 'simple' in this way. The context of this passage indicates that an opposite to cruelty is meant.

[94] Edward's virtues included moderation, which tops almost all the lists in the Nun's life of him (in *Edouard, passim*).

An Anglo-Norman Miscellany

The next few chapters represent some of Dean's sections 5 (Satirical, Social, and Moral), 7 (Grammar and Glosses), and 9 (Medicine); they cannot be lumped into a single genre or even group of genres. The closest would be to describe it as a collection of moral or social pieces, mostly non-fiction (although the satirical poem below is clearly as fictional as any romance). My title here is adapted from the EETS volume, *An Old English Miscellany*, ed. Morris, whose contents are almost as varied as in this section of the present book.[1]

Before presenting the main chapters, I add here a pair of very short poems from the Kildare Manuscript.[2] Interesting because alliterative,[3] they are two of only three Anglo-Norman texts in this MS.[4] Like the romance of *Fergus* (for Scotland), they are evidence that the French of England was also the French of other countries in the British Isles.[5] These short meditations are listed by Dean among Proverbs (her number 271); they cannot easily be classified.[6] The verses are written on the MS page as if prose; I have copied them thus, but my translation shows them as (blank) verse.

---

[1] As is the case with Dean's catalogue, the collection (actually in Middle and not Old English) represents, in little, a larger proportion of religious pieces compared with others. Those others include a Bestiary, a Description of the Shires, and Proverbs of Alfred.

[2] I have transcribed them from a scan sent me by the British Library, of BL MS Harley 913, f. 15v (they are edited in *The Kildare Manuscript*, ed. Turville-Petre, pp. 21–2, which I have consulted but not copied).

[3] They do not conform to conventional patterns of medieval English alliterative verse, but may be influenced by it.

[4] A third is The Walling of New Ross, more substantial, and comparatively well known.

[5] Hue de Rotelande represents Wales.

[6] They could be listed among Lyrics; it is noted in my introduction to the Fabliaux, above, that Dean's categories can sometimes (unsurprisingly) be fluid.

     https://doi.org/10.11647/OBP.0110.03

Text

[15v] **(1)**

Folie fet qe en force sa fie, fortune fet
force failire. Fiaux funt fort folie,
fere en fauelons flatire. Fere force
fest fiaux fuir, faux fiers fount feble
fameler. Fausyne fest feble fremir,
feie ferme fra fausyn fundre.

(2) 'Proverbia comitis desmonie'

Soule su simple e saunz solas, seignury
me somount soiorner; Si suppris sei
de moune solas, sages se deit soul solacer.
Soule ne solai soiorner, ne solein estre
de petit solas; Souereyn se est de se solacer, qe se[7] seut soule e saunz solas.

---

[7] This word has been inserted above the line. Letters in italic type denote the expansion of abbreviated forms.

Translation

(1)

He is foolish who puts his faith in force,
for Fortune makes force fail.
Falsehoods make folly strong,
and make men to be flattered by fair speaking.
Fierce force makes deceivers flee,
false forces make the feeble man famish.
Deceit makes the feeble man tremble,
but firm faith will make falsehood to founder.

(2) 'The earl of Desmond's proverb'[8]

I am solitary, single, and without solace.
My rank obliges me to remain;
if I were surprised by my comfort,
it were wisdom to bring comfort to oneself alone.
I am not accustomed to staying alone,
nor to being alone with small comfort;
it is most important to bring comfort to oneself,
whoever knows himself solitary and without solace.

---

[8] The first earl, d. 1356, may have been the author of one or both poems; if so, this one refers to his imprisonment in 1331 (p. 21, & Introduction p. xxxv, of the edition).

Satirical, Social, and Moral

Le Roman des Franceis, by André de Coutances[1]

[129va] Il ont dit que riens n'a valu,
Et donc a Arflet n'a chalu
Que boté fu par Chapalu
Li reis Artur en la palu.
Et que le chat l'ocist de guerre,
Puis passa outre en Engleterre [129vb]
Et ne fu pas lenz de conquerre,
Ainz porta corone en la terre,
Et fu sire de la contree.
Ou ont itel fable trovee?
Mençonge est, Dex le set, provee,
Onc greignor ne fu encontree.

'They [the French] say that not one of them [the English] is worth anything,
and that King Arflet[2] didn't care about King Arthur being heaved into a bog
by the Cat Palug.[3] Next, that the cat killed him in battle, and then came
into England; he was not slow to conquer this, and soon wore a crown in the
land and was lord of the realm. Where did they find such a tarradiddle? It's
a downright lie, God knows; never was there heard the like!' (vv. 21–32)

Following some 'Arthurian' romances above, I begin the present chapter with a
satire on Arthurian material. For this humorous and 'indelicate' *roman*, I have
used Holden's text (and its glossary); Crouch's version was useful to consult, but I
have not used his translation. Both editions use five-line numbering across four-
line monorhymed stanzas.

A recent translation from Middle Dutch, of a parodic sermon on 'Saint
Nobody',[4] has recently been brought to my attention. It is a sixteenth-century
piece which illustrates the very popular genre of mock sermons; the translators
remark that few examples are extant in English and fewer still have been translated.
The tone and the exaggerated language, if not the content, of these scurrilous
and irreverent pieces (the sermon, and the *roman* here excerpted) is very similar.
The mindset of the audience must have been comparable, even if occasions for

---

[1] Dean 220.1. The *Roman* or *Romanz des Franceis* is also known as the *Arflet*. Written before 1204
and probably in the second half of the twelfth century, it survives in one insular MS (London, BL,
Add. 10289, dated mid-thirteenth century). See 'Le Roman des Franceis', ed. Holden (Honoré
Champion, Paris); and 'Roman des Franceis', ed. and tr. Crouch (my text is from the former).

[2] This imaginary figure may be intended as Alfred (in Holden's opinion), or Aldfrith (in Crouch's),
a forefather of the narrator.

[3] A legendary Welsh beast that Arthur is said to have fought (and beaten). See, for example,
Bromwich, 'Celtic Elements'.

[4] Parsons and Jongenelen, 'Saint Nobody'. The figure of Saint Nobody first appears in the thirteenth
century (their p. 96); see also Owst, *Literature and Pulpit*, pp. 63–4.

performance differed. Broadly, the sermon pillories the church and the *roman* pillories the French. Examples may be gleaned from a glance through the published translations; most notable is probably Frollo's advice to the French about how to behave, listing pleasant habits such as cowardice, bad faith, dishonour, and cruelty (see below). The sermon advises drunkenness, incontinence, gluttony, and the like. Elsewhere in the *roman*, the French are said to be blasphemous; even the English do not go unscathed, being characterized as 'bon viveurs' and excessive drinkers.

The historian is a man 'who had found the hurly-burly of present-day lunacy to be less well done than the savage decency of ages long overpowered, and overpowered because they had not been wicked enough to conquer the wickedness that time had brought to accost them.' T. H. White's bitter comment fits as well into this chapter as into my previous section entitled Story (whose historians do not, on the whole, display such cynicism).[5] Rather than reproduce the long and disgraceful account of Frenchmen's eating habits, I have chosen to offer André's take on King Arthur's battle with King Frollo, thus linking this chapter with the chronicle history of Arthur that is prefaced in *Des Grantz Geanz* (above). As a Norman, André is no friend of the French:[6] he is very scornful of what they say about English history.

---

[5] White, *The Goshawk*, pp. 112–13.

[6] Normandy was not then part of what is now France.

Text

[129vb] Trop ont dit d'Artur grant
    enfance,
Quer Artu fu de tel puissance
Que Franceis conquist o sa lance,
Mau eritage mist en France.   40
-
Bien savon que Bien et Belin,
Maximïen et Costentin
Furent a Franceis mal veisin
Et France orent, ce est la fin.
-
D'Engleterre furent tuit rei,   45
Chescun conquist France endreit
    sei.
Chescun en plessa le bofei,
Le gorgeïr et le desrei.
-
Au rei Artur le deraain,
De celui sommes nos certain,   50
Voudrent fere plet, mes en vain,
    [130ra]
Quer il les out bien soz sa main.
-
Quant de lor orguil s'averti
Maugré eus toz les converti
Et le païs acuverti;   55
Dites si ce est veir parti!
-
James n'iert jor que il n'i pere;
Douce esteit France, or est amere;
Mout ourent en Artur dur pere,
Sa sorvenue mout compere.   60
-
Mout fu Artur proz et corteis;
Quant out conquis Chartres et
    Bleis
Et Orliens et tot Estampeis,

A Paris vint o ses Engleis.
-
La vile asist, n'en dotez mie,   65
Mout out bone chevalerie
Et bien estruite et bien garnie,
Si a fierement asallie.
-
Engleis fierement assalirent,
Franceis merdement defendirent,   70
Au premier assaut se rendirent
Et hontosement s'en partirent.
-
A cel partir fu apelee
Paris, ci n'a nule celee,
Qui primes fu Termes nommee   75
Et mout ert de grant renommee.
-
Frolles ert apelé le reis
Qu'Artur conquist o ses Engleis,
Et de Frolles sont dit Franceis,
Qui primes ourent non [G]alleis.[7]   80
-
Frolles, qui de France fu sire, [130rb]
Ne sout que faire ne que dire,
Grant mautalent out et grant ire,
Franceis manda a un concire.
-
Li baron l'ont a ce amis,   85
Qui ses messages a tramis
A Artur, si li a pramis
Qu'encor porroient estre amis,
-
Se de sa terre s'en issist
Que a mout grant tort saisseïst,   90
Et s'il ne la guerpisseïst
De batalle le aasteïst,

---

[7] MS 'Bailleis'; Holden considers this a mistranscription.

Translation

They've talked infantile nonsense about Arthur, for Arthur was so mighty that he conquered the French with his lance and left France a painful inheritance. We know quite well that Belin and Brenne, Maximian and Constantine, were all bad neighbours for France.[8] Because they took it, and that's all there is to say! They were all kings of England, and each one conquered France for himself; each one curbed the arrogance, the boasts and the pride, of the French. As for the last of them, King Arthur, we're sure about him; they wanted to negotiate in vain, for he had them well under his fist. When he realised their arrogance, he converted them all in spite of themselves and enslaved the whole country. Ask them whether that's not so far off the truth! There will never be a day when he isn't famous there, in France that used to be sweet but is now bitter. He was a tough father to them, and his arrival was expensive! Arthur was extremely worthy and courteous; when he had vanquished Chartres and Blois, and Orleans and the whole land of Etampes, then he and his English came to Paris. He besieged the city, never doubt that; he had wonderful cavalry, well-trained and well-equipped, and fiercely attacked. The English attacked fiercely, and the French defended themselves like poltroons, giving up at the first assault and shamefully slinking away. Because of this 'de-par-ture',[9] 'Par-is' was named — there's no getting away from it — before, it was called Thermes[10] and was highly renowned.

Frollo was the name of the king whom Arthur conquered with his Englishmen. It's from Fr-ollo that the Fr-ench are so called, who were previously known as the Gauls.[11] Frollo, who was lord of France, had no idea what to do or what to say. He was bad-tempered and very angry, and summoned the French to a meeting. The barons persuaded him to this: he sent messengers to Arthur and promised him they could stay friends if he would get out of his land, that he had grabbed so wrongfully. If he wouldn't leave, then he challenged him to battle!

---

[8] These British kings made legendary conquests in France (the IPN in *Wace's Brut*, ed. and tr. Weiss, enables readers to find the story of each). The following is a burlesque version of Arthur's conquest, as narrated in *Brut* and other chronicles.

[9] Another exaggeratedly false derivation is coming up shortly, for the French.

[10] The Roman baths can still be seen in Paris.

[11] A more creditable, and credible, derivation for the name 'French' is found in *Pseudo-Turpin Chronicle*, ed. Short, p. 69 (and notes, including mention of the author's knowledge of legal terminology): all who paid their dues willingly were considered 'frank e quytes'.

Par eus dous, que plus n'i eüst,
Eissi le voleit, ce seüst;
Cous rendist qui cous receüst   95
Et plus feïst qui plus peüst.
-

Artur respondi: 'Dex i valle!
Defendré mei, s'est qui m'asalle;
A Paris, en l'isle, sanz falle,
Seit a demein ceste batalle.'   100
-

De ça et de la sunt certain
De la batalle a l'endemain;
Qui veintra tot eit en sa main,
Les bois, les viles et le plain.
-

Frolles durement menaça,   105
De jurer ne s'apereça,
Dex tot par membres depeça
Que Artur mal s'i aproça.
-

Artur, qui n'out pas cuer de glace,
Preisa mout petit sa menace,   110
Mieuz l'amast a tenir en place
   [130va]
Que voer Dieu en mi la face.
-

Artur, qui out grant desierrer,
Se fist matin apareillier,
Lui et Labagu, son destrier,   115
Et se fist en l'isle nagier.
-

Frolles jusqu'a tierce dormi
Et lors, quant il se desdormi,
Endeseetes s'estormi,
Com se l'eüssent point formi.   120
-

Franceis, qui moroient d'ennui,
Li distrent: 'Leverez vos hui?'
Il dist 'Aol!' et de nullui
N'ont Franceis aol, fors de lui.
-

Tot en gesant, sanz sei drecier,   125

Se fist Frolles apareiller;
D'ilonc sunt Franceis costumier
Que en gesant se font chaucier.
-

Ainz que Frolles se fust armez
S'est tierce fiee pasmez;   130
Lors fu des Franceis mout
      blasmez,
Mes il lor dist: 'Ne vos tamez!
-

Ce me vient de grant hardement,
Mort est Artur veraement.'
Lors les prist toz par serement   135
Qu'il tendront son
      commandement.
-

'Comment', dist il, 'que il
      m'avienge,
De mes bones mors vos sovienge;
Mar i avra cil qui Diu crienge,
Ne leauté a homme tienge.   140
-

Cruel seiez a desmesure, [130vb]
Avel, fei mentie, perjure;
El vostre garder metez cure,
De l'autrui prenez a dreiture!
-

Artur vos voudra del suen tendre;   145
Prenez le sanz guerredon rendre!
Ainz vos lessiez ardeir ou pendre
Que le vostre veiez despendre.
-

De dez seiez boens joeors
Et de Deu bons perjureors,   150
En autri cort richeeors,
Poi fesanz et boens vanteors.
-

Acreez si ne rendez rien,
Haez ceus qui vos ferunt bien,
Plus ordement vivez que chien   155
Et seiez tuit armeneisien!'

Just the two of them, nobody else; I can tell you, that's what he wanted. They would render all blows received with interest, and each would do the best he could! 'God be my strength!' cried Arthur in reply. 'I shall defend myself, whoever attacks me! On the island in Paris let it be,[12] tomorrow without fail, a battle!'

On both sides they are certain about this battle next day: winner would take all, woods and cities and plains. Frollo threatened ferociously, and never gave over blaspheming. He swore by all God's members in turn that Arthur will come off worst if he approaches him. Arthur was no faint-heart,[13] and thought nothing of the threats; he preferred to keep still rather than shout in God's face. Arthur, who was longing for the off, got himself readied in the morning: him and Labagu his war-horse. Then he had himself taken across the water to the island.[14]

Frollo slept in until mid-morning,[15] and then, when he awoke, he suddenly jumped as if ants had bitten him. The French, who were dying of boredom, shouted 'Are you getting up today?' He cried 'Aol!' None of the French had this cry from anybody, except from him.[16] Lying down, and without raising himself, he had himself arrayed. Ever since then the French are in the habit of getting their nether garments on while still in bed.[17] Before getting his armour on, Frollo fainted three times. The French didn't think much of him for this, but he said to them 'Don't worry about that! It's because of my great strength ... Arthur is a dead man!' Then he read them all a sermon, commanding them to keep to it:

'Whatever happens to me,' he said, 'remember my good morals. Woe betide him who fears God, and keep faith with no man! Be outrageously cruel, avaricious, disloyal, and dishonest. Look after your own business carefully, and help yourself rightfully to other people's goods. Arthur will offer you some of his, but take them without giving anything in return! Let yourselves be burned or hanged rather than spend anything of your own. Be good dice-players, and good God-deniers; swank about in other people's houses by doing as little as possible and boasting as much as possible. Take stuff on credit and pay nothing back, hate those who do you good, live like disgusting dogs, and all of you behave like absolute sods!'[18]

---

[12] The battle is said to have taken place on the Île de la Cité, in the middle of the river.

[13] Lit. heart of ice.

[14] 'nagier'; a boat-trip (they did not swim across).

[15] Tierce is one of the canonical Hours of the day (Prime is around dawn, and Sext is midday); see *Cher Alme*, esp. p. 11 & note 46.

[16] 'Aol' is a puzzle: Holden thinks it might refer to the stereotypical French love of garlic (referred to later). However, Crouch believes it refers to the exclamation 'AOL' (AOI) found between stanzas of the *Chanson de Roland* and that it therefore mocks the unchivalric behaviour of the French in this story.

[17] This strange detail is illustrated, perhaps, in *Durmart le Galois*, ed. Stengel (early thirteenth century). The hero reclines on a rich silken cloth to be armed: '... il a ses chauces lacies Tot par loisir et en seant' (he has his leggings laced up while he sits at ease, vv. 10113–28).

[18] Holden thinks this unusual word probably meant 'homosexual' or something considered in those days to be similarly insulting, given the context.

Frolles en Frances mist ces leis,
Bien le retindrent li Franceis,
Et encor i out il sordeis,
Mes je n'en diré or ampleis.   160
-
Quant armé fu a quelque paine
Son mestre chambellenc aceine.
'Va tost,' dist il, 'et si te paine
Que aie pullente aleine.'
-
Cil conut bien sa volenté,   165
Que d'allie s'ert dementé;
Plain vessel l'en a presenté
Et il en menja a plenté.
-
Ne se pout Frolles atenir
Que des auz ne feïst venir,   170
Tant por usage maintenir, [131ra]
Tant por Artur en sus tenir.
-
Franceis, qui devant lui esterent,
D'aler en l'isle se hasterent,
A quel que paine l'i menerent,   175
Laissierent le, si retornerent.
-
Frolles remest sor son destrier,
Artur vit venir fort et fier,
Lors n'out en lui que corrocier
Quant vers lui le vit aprochier.   180
-
Andui es estrius s'afichierent,
Si que, quant il s'entraprocherent,
Amedous lor lances bruiserent
Et lors chevaus s'agenouillerent.
-
Frolles acuit a menecier   185

Et Arthur trait le brant d'acier;
Quant Frolles vit le cop haucier
A terre se lessa cachier,
-
Et dist: 'Merci, Artur, beau sire!
Je sui recreant, ne m'ocire!'   190
Artur ne pout atremper s'ire,
Frolles ocist, n'en puis el dire.
-
Franceis furent espoenté
Quant lor rei virent graventé,
A Artur se sont presenté,   195
Que d'eus face sa volenté.
-
Et il, qui toz les voleit pendre,
Quant si humblement les vit
     rendre
Ne vout envers Deu tant
     mesprendre.
Par tote France fist defendre   200
-
Que nul n'en i eüst pendu, [131rb]
Vie et menbre lor a rendu;
En autre sens lor a vendu
Que vers lui se sont defendu,
-
Quer il les mist toz en servage,   205
Ou encor est tot lor lignage;
Iloc donna en eritage
Arthur as Franceis cuvertage.
-
Franceis en l'isle s'en passerent,
Lor rei, qui mort ert, enporterent,   210
En un grant feu le cors boterent,
Que por lui ardrë alumerent.

Frollo promulgated these laws in France, and the French took good heed of them; these days they are even worse, but I'm not telling you any more about that now.

When after some trouble he'd got his armour on, he beckoned to his chamberlain. 'Go quickly', said he, 'and busy yourself with making my breath really stink!' This man knew what he wanted, and that he was mad about garlic. He brought him a plateful, and he ate lots of it.[19] Frollo couldn't restrain himself from calling his men to him, as much to keep them on their toes as to keep Arthur down. The French, who were lined up before him, were in a hurry to go to the island. With a struggle, they got him there, then left him and came back.

Frollo sat on his war-horse, and saw Arthur coming strong and proud towards him. He felt nothing but anger as he watched his approach. Both braced themselves in their stirrups, so that as they met each other their lances shattered and their horses were brought to their knees. Frollo began to threaten, and Arthur drew his sword of steel. When Frollo saw him lift his arm for the blow, he threw himself to the ground, crying 'Mercy, Arthur, my dear lord! I surrender! Don't kill me!' Arthur could not control his rage, and killed Frollo. So that was that.

The French were horrified when they saw their king cut down. They yielded themselves to Arthur, to do with them as he liked. He wanted to hang them all, but when he saw them surrender so humbly he did not wish to put himself in the wrong with God. Throughout France he made it law that none of them should be hanged; he gave them back both life and limb. But he got his own back on them in another way,[20] for taking up arms against him. For he enslaved them all, and it's still the case with their descendants. So the inheritance they got from Arthur was to be in subjection.

The French went over to the island, and brought away their king who was dead. They threw his body onto a great fire they had lit to burn him.

---

[19] Frollo may be hoping that with breath 'like a rapier' (as the modern phrase has it) he may flatten Arthur.

[20] Lit. he sold them.

Deables furent en agait,
Qui d'enfer ourent le feu trait,
Donc il alumerent l'atrait,　　　　215
Qui por Frolles ardeir fu fait.
-

Mout out cel feu male ensuiance,
Que d'iloc avient, sanz dotance,
Qu'encor en art en remenbrance
Del feu d'enfer la gent de France.　　220
-

De Franceis prist Artur homage,
Et il establi par vitage
.iiii. deners de cuvertage
Por raaindre lor chevelage.
-

Assez trovent qui lor reconte　　　225
Cest hontage, mes rien ne monte;
De ce ne tienent plé ne conte,
Car il ne sevent aveir honte.
-

Ja Franceis celui n'amera
Qui bien et ennor li fera,　　　　230
Mes com il plus honi sera, [131va]
Et il .ii. tanz gorgeiera.
-

Quer savez que, liu u esrez,
Ja mar Franceis de rien crerrez;
Sel querez ja nel troverez,　　　235
Sel trovez ja prou n'i avrez.

The devils were lying in wait, who had brought the fire from Hell; it was they who set light to the pyre that had been built to burn Frollo. This fire had a dire consequence, because without doubt this is the fire of Hell that still burns in the memory of the French people.

Arthur took homage from the French, and to shame them he established an annual tax payment of four pence as if they were serfs.[21] There are plenty of people who remind them of this shame, but nothing comes of it. They don't give a fig or even a toss, because they're completely shameless. No Frenchman will ever love anybody who treats him well and honourably. Humiliate him, and he'll be twice as boastful. So take it from me, wherever you go never believe anything a Frenchman says. If you look for one you'll never find one:[22] if you find one he won't be honourable!

---

[21] Crouch reads 'vitage' as 'quitage' (a form of release payment); Holden as 'viltage' or shame. A penny was worth a great deal more than the modern 1p.

[22] That is, an honest one.

L'Apprise de Nurture[23]

> In your walk, posture, all external comportment, do nothing to offend anyone who sees you.[24]

This Book of Good Manners,[25] contrasting with the *Roman des Franceis* (above), contains a different kind of satire;[26] in its didactic intent it forms a link with the next piece, from *Maniere de Langage*. Here there are perhaps predictably few overlaps with lists of vices and virtues so common in the literature of lay piety, but it will be noticed that moderation is always stressed as of paramount importance, with the frequent injunction not to take part in gossip and slander probably coming a close second. My translation errs on the side of freedom, because a piece such as this, whose tone is 'Listen to me, my lad, if you know what's good for you!', must not be rendered in too solemn a manner.

Parsons' small volume (also available online) contains a number of Books of Courtesy and Nurture.[27] This text is pp. 432–7; it is briefly introduced on pp. 430–1, and see her main Introduction for general remarks and for the manuscript (Oxford, Bodleian Library, Bodley 9),[28] which may have been written in a nunnery (Parsons' p. 384). If so, we might guess that one of those gentlewomen who entered nunneries after becoming widowed may have set herself or her colleagues to thoughts of educational books for the young. There is no indication that any particular person or family was in the writer's mind; the instructions about how to treat women suggest a male author but do not rule out a female (the text could have been copied, not authored, in the place of the manuscript's origin). I follow Parsons closely, adding her notes. Although most of the verbs appear to be in second person plural (vous), 'tu' crops up quite frequently. There is a lack of distinction between the two in most forms of medieval French.[29]

---

[23] Dean 234.

[24] From the Rule of Augustine, cited in Whelan, 'Urbanus Magnus', p. 21 (and pp. 16–17, on the relationship between secular and monastic texts).

[25] 'L'Apprise de Nurture', ed. Parsons (*PMLA*).

[26] On women (see below).

[27] Whelan (cited above) further discusses 'courtesy literature'; and Arnould, 'Les Sources de *Femina Nova*'.

[28] Dean dates this MS to the second quarter of the fifteenth century. *Urbain le Courtois* (cited in Whelan) is her number 231.

[29] Medieval Latin shows a similar confusion of second-person forms (Woledge, 'The Use of *Tu* and *Vous*', *passim*).

Text

[f.61v]
Beau dulce, esgardés,
Dulcement si moy lisés,
Pernéz de moy guarde.
En quelle lieu vous venetz
Ales, esteetz, beal le guardetz,　　5
De nurture en avetz warde.
Si vous venetz entre la gent,
Portés vous honestement
Et en beale manere.
Soietz dulce en parlaunce,　　10
Simple et honeste en
　　counteynaunce,
Si emporterés la banere,
Si vous seietz a la table,
Od bealle nureture et amyable
Moustrés vous a toute gent.　　15
Si a vous viegne ascun amy
Qui vous reheite, responetz a luy
Et mercietz lui dulcement.
Tenet voz peedz en quiete
Et voz mains a vostre diete, [f.62r]　　20
Et ne parlez oultre mesure.
Ne lessetz vostre viaunde
Pur nulle autri demaunde,
Et ne bevetz a demesure.
Si vous veietz ascun manger,　　25
Ne lui devetz trop juger,
Hounte est, pur veritee;
Trop ne lui volez regarder,
Ne quei il fait a demaunder;
De nurture est un nyceté.　　30
Beau dulce fitz, si joesne juwe
Aqueu[30] jolyf, come faulk en mue,
Ne devetz pas mesdire luy;

A mal ne lui jugés, ceo est envie,
Et de nurture est vileynie;　　35
Juvente lui meyne, beau dulce amy.
Si soietz home de nurture,
Par nulle maner d'aventure
Chaungeable ne devetz estre de
　　coer.
Gard que ne soiez nounestable,　　40
Kar a Dieux ne homme ne serrez
　　covenable, [f.62v]
Pur ce que[31] ne savetz rien amer.
Dulce chose est de dulce amer
Et ceo dulceour fermement tener,
Sans nulle faillaunce.　　45
Nurture est, pur veritee,
De courtaisie estableté[32]
De tener la saunz flecchaunce.
Si ascun homme soit deshoneste
Ou en fait ou en geste,　　50
Ne luy juggez pur orguylous,
Kar vilaynie est, pur veritee,
Si tu juggez pur honesté
Le malnurri ou envious.
Si tu voils estre amé,　　55
Et de nulli estre blasmé,
Gard qeu soietz coumpaignable;
Einsi serretz vous sauns blasme.
Gardez bien vostre bone fame
Et ne soietz pas rogable.　　60
Si vous venetz en ascun lu
La ou vous n'estez pas cognu [f.63r]
Gardez vous dunke de rage.
De ryse auxi vous guardez,
La bouche trop ne ovrez,　　65
Ensi serretz tenuz pur sage.

---

[30] Corr. Auque.
[31] MS qui.
[32] MS estable.

Translation

Dear boy, look at this and read my words obediently;[33] pay attention to me. Whatever place you come into, walk or stand and hold yourself well, for you are the keeper of good upbringing. If you come among company, bear yourself like an honest chap and be well mannered. Be gentle in your speech, simple and straightforward in your looks, and you will win all hearts.[34] If you are seated at table, with fine good food before you,[35] be sure to show yourself to everybody. If a friend of yours should come up and hail you, answer him and thank him politely. Keep your feet still![36] And keep your hands by your food; and don't talk too much! Don't get up and leave your dinner for anybody's asking, and don't drink too much! If you see somebody eating, don't criticize him; it's a real shame to watch him too closely or pay attention to what he asks for. That is a foolish breach of good manners.

My dearest boy, if a youngster plays at something restlessly, like a moulting hawk,[37] you mustn't complain about him or think the worse of him, that's mean and ill-mannered. It's his youth that makes him behave so, dear friend. If you are to be a gentleman you must never, whatever happens, be fickle-hearted. Take care not to be changeable; this will please neither God nor man if you don't know how to love anybody. It is so sweet to love sweetly, and to keep firm hold of this sweetness without flagging. Good breeding is, indeed, the well-established courtesy that you maintain without fail.

If anybody behaves dishonestly, either by word or deed, don't judge him as proud; it's really bad manners to judge somebody as honest who is ill-bred or covetous. If you want people to love you, and not to blame you for anything, you must take care to be sociable; that way you will not get blamed. Guard your good reputation well, and never do anything to blush about.[38]

When you come into any place where they don't know you, watch your temper! Also, be careful how you laugh. If you don't open your mouth too far, they'll think you're wise![39]

---

[33] 'Dulcement', sweetly, kindly, gently, etc. Here 'like a good boy' is meant.

[34] 'Take the banner' seems to mean the kind of success that rewards good behaviour.

[35] 'nureture', variously spelt, means both food and upbringing (nourriture, and nurture). Here food is more likely to be the meaning.

[36] 'quiete'.

[37] 'jolyf' usually means merry or cheerful, but see Parsons' glossary; moulting hawks are said to be moody. 'mue' is there given as cage, but 'muer' means to change (sc. its plumage). See *AND* for the meaning 'intractable', in the context of hawks.

[38] Not in *AND*; Parsons' glossary gives two possible meanings, both with a query.

[39] This is timeless advice: cf. numerous modern sayings.

Et si la avetz estee devaunt,
Pur ceo ne soietz pas joiaunt
En fole countenaunce.
Qui trop s'affie en juyer   70
Pluis tost purra meserrer
Et faire a luy grevaunce.
Soietz dulce en parlaunt,
Amyable en reguardaunt,
Si en serrez vous amé,   75
Sues et beale maneyez;
Et prueement si vous juetz
Et ensi ne serretz blasmé.
Beau dulce fitz, entre la gent
Ne vous aletz lourdement,   80
Kar ceo est denorture,
Mais touzjours beale chiere
Faire devetz en vostre manere [f.63v]
Des fols conquereüre.
Si tu eyetz rien de courteysie   85
De nul homme en ceste vie,
Pensetz de faire guerdoun.
Pur poi ne serretz vous irretz
Envers toun amy ne enquerretz
Nule malveis enchesoun.   90
Devannt la gent ne tensetz,
Ne nulle homme ledengez,
Kar ceo est vileinye.
Nul encountre coer eietz,
Ne ses faitz reprovetz,   95
Ka[r] ceo vient de grant envie.
Tes mains devaunt la gent ne
        frotez,

Ne voz peedz mie discoveretz,
Kar n'est pas gentirise.
Vostre lange ne feynetz,   100
Ne vostre teste entour gettetz,
Kar ceo est une leide guise.
Si vous eitz ascun amy
Qui pur petit vous eit guerpi, [f.64r]
Et il de vous n'eyt cure,   105
Guardez vous en vostre vie
Qu'envers lui ne corroucez mye,
Kar il n'est pas nurture.
Si ascun homme vous eit mysdyt
Pur graunt chose ou pur petyt,   110
Ne pernetz nient en grief,
Mais moustrez toust en
        respoignaunt
Que nurri estez, noun pas enfaunt,
Par dulce parole et suef.
Si seignour parole, ne parlez nient, 115
Kar ceo malement avient
A homme nurri ou sage.
A primer boire et puis parler
Oultre le hanap et jangler —
Ceo moi semble outrage.   120
Si ascuny vous demaunde:
'Vuelletz rien de ceste viaunde?'
Ne le refusez, jeo vous empri;
Dulcement luy mercietz
Et pur ton sodal[40] le recevetz, 125
        [f.64v]
Et serretz tenu nurri.

---

[40] 'thi frend' written over the top in different hand and ink.

If you are placed favourably, don't crow about it or make a smug face. Don't get too involved in merry-making, because you can easily end up acting wrongly and causing harm to somebody. Always speak gently, and keep a pleasant countenance; you'll be well liked for this, and people will treat you gently and well. If you play fair, you won't get into trouble. Dear boy, when you go into company don't tread roughly, that's bad manners. But if you always try to look as pleasant as you can, then you'll be lord over all the fools. If you receive a courteous favour from anybody in the world, take care to reward them. Don't get annoyed with your friend, nor impute any bad motive to him. Never get aggressive with people, and never slander anybody; that's villainous. And don't hold a grudge against anybody, or criticize their deeds; that's bad manners.

Don't rub your hands in company, nor must you show your feet; this is not good manners. Also don't stick your tongue out,[41] or toss your head about, which is an ugly way of going on. If you have a friend who abandons you for some trifle, and no longer cares about you, try and lead your life so as not to get angry with him, which is ill-bred. If somebody has slandered you, in a big way or just a little, don't take it to heart. But always answer him with gentle and sweet words, to show you are well-bred and not a child. If a great man speaks, keep quiet! That's not the way,[42] if you are courteous and wise! First to drink and then to speak — between the cup and the chatter — what an outrage, I say![43] If anybody says to you 'Would you like some of this meat?' please don't refuse. Thank him warmly, and accept it for your companion;[44] this will be considered polite of you.

---

[41] Parsons' glossary has 'feynetz' with a query. It ought to mean 'use your tongue falsely' (feindre), but here the context is to do with irritating physical habits.

[42] This means, by ellipsis, that interrupting great men is not the way ....

[43] See Whelan, pp. 26–7: line 944 reads 'Avoid shouting "Weisheil" aloud unless instructed to'! The list is in Latin, but here is another English word (see below).

[44] 'thy friend'; another example of how languages interpenetrate: English appears in or commenting on a French text.

Ne voilletz estre avauntour
De toun sen ne de toun vigour
Entre congregacioun.
Nul home mokes, ne ne mentz   130
  mie,
Ne parléz rien de vilaynie:
Ceo de envie est l'enchesoun[45]
Sur la table ne vous souetz,[46]
Ne oud toun coutel ne juetz
Taunt come vous estez a maunger.   135
La hanap beale asseetz,
Et vostre viaunde beal trenchetz,
Et maungetz saunz daunger.
Ne encrachetz oultre la table
Si aultre lu soit covenable   140
La ou vous pouetz faire,
Ne vostre nees ne devetz pincer
Taunt come vous seetz al maunger,
Et la vous gardrez de pere.
Soiez franc de vostre doun,   145
Mais nïent oultre resoun, [f.65r]
Kar c'est nulle profit.
Vostre promesse replenetz,
Le doun de vostre amy ne refusetz,
Ja ceo qu'il soit petyt.   150
Devaunt la gent belement
  maungetz.
Sur le naperoun voz mains suetz,
Ne frotez voz gencies.
Od nulli ne parletz,
Ne od playn bouche ne bevetz,   155

Kar cestz soun vilaynies.
Si vous estez de age hault,
Pur ceo ne serretz vous trop bault
A nully de mesfaire;
Kar si tu soietz, tu serras notee   160
Pur denurri et desaffaitee,
Et ceo ne serroit affaire.
Si tu soietz pres de jangloures,
Ne soietz mye trop ragours
De parler vilaynie;   165
Kar ascun chose toi eschapera
Ke par aventure toi poisera [f.65v]
Tout temps de vostre vie.
Et pur ceo, bien vous guardez,
Si vous rien parler voulez   170
Od les escoymouses.
Dire devetz priveement
Et briefment vostre talent
Entre luy et vouse.
Si nulle femme jue od vous,   175
De vostre corps soietz gelous
Et de toun parlere,
Kar si rien faces a demesure,
Toi serroit dit a denurture;
A honte toi purreit turnere.   180
Si tu ne bien facez, ils ne lerrount
Que ascune chose ne pyncherount,
De dit ou de countenaunce,
Et de ceo vous mokerount,
Et aprés vous jugerount   185
Sans nulle defaillaunce.

---

[45] MS C. env. e. de l'e.

[46] Corr. pouetz.

Don't be a show-off in public, either of your wit or your strength. Never mock anybody, and never lie, for any reason of envy.[47] Don't lean on the table,[48] and don't play with your knife, when you are at a meal. Place your cup properly, and cut your meat neatly so as to eat without giving offence.[49] Don't spit towards the table if there is another place convenient where you can do so.[50] Don't pick your nose,[51] when you're sitting at table, and also take care not to fart. Be generous when giving, but not excessively; it's foolish to be extravagant.[52] You must keep your promises, and don't refuse a present from a friend however small it is. Eat elegantly when in company, wipe your hands on the napkin, and don't pick your teeth. Don't talk to anybody, or drink, with your mouth full; this is disgusting manners. If you are grown to manhood, don't therefore be too bold and do wrong to anybody; if you are, you'll get a reputation for being badly brought up and ill-taught, and that's undignified. If you spend time with gossips, don't be too quick to speak ill of people; you might end up saying something which could perhaps cause you regret for the rest of your life. That's why you must be careful how you talk to anybody who might be oversensitive. You must speak briefly and privately if you want to ask something [important], just between you and him.

If any woman plays with you, you must be careful what you do or say.[53] For if you do too much you will make yourself known as a bounder, and it could lead you into shameful ways. If you do anything naughty, people won't leave off making the most of it,[54] either by words or looks. They will make fun of you for it, and then they'll judge you and no mistake.

---

[47] The next line seems to begin a new subject, so one would expect a full or partial stop. The word 'souetz' is a problem, and corr. pouetz does not help. *AND* does not give the word, although 'pouetz' is cited for v. 141 of this text (meaning 'to be able'). If 'suetz' in v. 152, below, is the same verb then 'don't wipe yourself on the table' is possible but rather odd (*AND* gives no meaning 'tablecloth').

[48] Corrected from 'souetz'; 'pouer' means to lean on.

[49] 'daunger' has a range of meanings in Old French; here the safety of fellow-diners is probably not the point.

[50] 'oultre', here meaning across (or similar). There is an example of this instruction in *Urbanus*: don't spit 'beyond' the table. If you must spit, use a napkin, or if your chair will revolve then turn round and spit behind you (Whelan's pp. 13–14).

[51] 'pincer'; pinch is probably not exactly what is meant.

[52] Much is made of the virtue of moderation in all treatises of virtue; excess of generosity is a vice. Excessive largesse is ostentatious, and ostentation is a branch of pride.

[53] This part of the text deals with what in *Urbanus* is called 'satire on women' (p. 13).

[54] 'pyncherount' not in Parsons' glossary. The nearest in *AND* seems to be 'pincer', to exploit.

Pur ceo vous pri, beaulx dulce fitz,
Que vous ne ayetz de rien enviz
[f.66r]
De dame ou de damoisele.
Kar devaunt vous paisera,   190
Et en la chaumbre vous jugera;
N'i ad nulle que n'est hagernele.
Nulle femme mesdietz,
Ne nulle femme ne ferretz,
Pur rien qu'ele die.   195
Et si vous faicz, vous moustrez
      bien
Que vilans estez, et ne savetz rien
De nurture ne de curtaisie.
Jammés a counseil ne venetz
Si ne soietz appelletz,   200
Kar ce est mal presumpcioun.
Nule rien ne premettez
Fors ceo que doner voelez,
Kar ce est nulle reisoun;
Si vous avetz en nul amy   205
De par fortune soit empoevry,
Soietz naturel;
Ne luy despisez, ains lui aidetz
De vos biens, et lui counseilletz;
[f.66v]
Si fretz vous come droyturel.   210
Si vous eietz devaunt vous
Viaunde qui soit precious,

Od toun sodal partietz.
Aultre foitz od toi partira,
Et de toun partier toi mertiera[55]   215
Et nurri tenuz serretz.
Chiens et oisealx si ametz,[56]
A ches ou tables si juetez
Sauns hasarderie.[57]
Od toun veisyn tei aqueyntez,[58]   220
Od luy manger, vous devetez
Volountiers, s'il vous prie.
Devaunt la gent ne devetz
      reprendre
Nulle homme, mais devetz
      attendre
De dire toun talent   225
Jesques en un liu venetz
Ou vous a lui dire pouetz
Bien et privément.
Si vous estez a bras senestre,
Tener le devetz od la mayn destre   230
[f.67r]
Et enbracer bealement.
Et si vous karoler voulez,
Les mains trop ne movetz,
Mais les pedz jolivement.
Que ceste estorie sovent regard,   235
De nureture n'avera jamés warde
Certeynement.
Issi finist l'Apprise de Nurture.

---

[55] Corr. merciera.

[56] 'Par tens viande les donez' added in different hand and ink.

[57] 'le fetez' added in different hand and ink.

[58] MS te iaqueyntez.

For this reason I beg you, my dear boy, never to have ill-will towards any lady or girl. She will be quiet before you, but in her own rooms she will judge you; not one of them but is a two-faced witch.[59] Never speak ill of a woman, and never hit one whatever she might say to you! If you do, you'll demonstrate that you are unquestionably a low sort of fellow and know nothing of breeding or manners.

Never offer an opinion unless you're invited to do so, because that's presuming too far. Never promise anything, because that's foolish, unless it's something you want to give. If you have any friend who's had the bad fortune to become poor, act kindly![60] Don't look down on him, but help him by means of your own property and give him good advice. That's the right way to behave. If you have some delicious food in front of you, share it with your companion. Another time he will share his with you, and will thank you for your kindness; this way you'll be seen as good-mannered. You must be kind to dogs and birds ....[61] If you play chess or backgammon, you mustn't gamble.[62] Get to know your neighbour, and eat with him willingly if he asks you. You must never contradict somebody in public, but delay what you have to say until you are somewhere you can say it fully and privately. If you are by his left side, hold him with your right hand and give him a hug! If you want to dance, don't wave your hands about, but frolic well with your feet.

Whoever you are,[63] if you read this little book often you need never fear for your reputation, that's for sure. Here is the end of the Book of Good Manners.

---

[59] Glossary, with query, gives 'unstable, changeable' for 'hagernele'; see *AND* (citing this line).

[60] Lit. 'naturally'; 'kind' has a meaning 'natural, native' (*OED*).

[61] 'and give them their food at the right time' added.

[62] 'Do this!' is added, perhaps by an exasperated parent.

[63] This suggests the book was not written for a known youngster, but for anybody (or their parent) who will read it.

Grammar and Glosses

La Maniere de Langage[1]

> ... side by side we lay Fretting in the womb of Rome to begin our fray.
> Ere men knew our tongues apart ...[2]

This chapter presents some parts of a medieval 'Berlitz Guide', designed for Britishers to improve their foreign language skills.[3] 'The All Souls Continuation',[4] chosen for this book, is noted by Dean in her catalogue as one of several versions. With reference to the Cambridge text, the other published version, she remarks 'Kristol ... derives three *Manieres* from redactions and fragments in these six MSS and others'; this gives some idea of the complexity of the manuscript tradition.[5] All the passages in this All Souls (Oxford) version match passages in the version(s) edited by Kristol ('de 1396', page numbers noted below), but each is different enough to be worth reproducing and translating here. Of special interest is the passage about a mysterious 'Colin T' and the Brazen Head.[6]

Presentation of this curious and amusing work is complicated by the fact that Kristol's edition (1995) was published after the 'All Soul's Continuation' (1993); therefore Fukui, who edited the Oxford text presented here, could not know Kristol's edition. My inclusion of Fukui's version is designed to facilitate comparison of the two available versions, given that Kristol's notes are in French and thus perhaps not convenient for all readers.[7]

It will be seen that the speakers in the first dialogue address each other with what looks like excessive politeness; I am reluctant to omit any of the salutations, but have allowed myself some freedom in translating 'dear good sir', 'my very fair friend', and so on.[8] For the second dialogue, compare Kristol's pp. 24–5; the latter

---

[1] Dean 281; it was revised between 1396 and 1415, for the instruction of a well-born youth. 'The All Souls Continuation of *La Maniere de Langage*', in the ANTS *Essays* (OPS 2), is the version presented here; see *Manières*, ed. Kristol (searchable page-by-page online), for the alternative versions.

[2] 'France 1913' (in Kipling, *The Years Between*, pp. 15–16).

[3] Although French was being taught as an unfamiliar language by this date, Trevisa describes English as having to be taught in schools during the 1360s; see his addition to Higden's *Chronicle* (*The Universal Chronicle of Ranulf Higden*, Taylor, pp. 168–9 in Appendix II, p. 138, and *passim*).

[4] In Oxford, All Souls College, 182.

[5] See Kristol's Introduction.

[6] For Orleans and its tourist attractions, see Introduction to *The Mirror of Justices*, ed. Whittaker, whose author 'could never have been through proper law-school' (p. xxxiv). There is an excursus on Sorcery, on its pp. 15–16.

[7] New research on the *Manieres* is currently in train, towards a workshop in Oxford to be held in November 2017 (convened by Huw Grange and funded by the Leverhulme Trust); unfortunately, any proceedings will appear too late for inclusion in this book.

[8] Compare Kristol's pp. 32–4.

part of it is represented by the passage on Kristol's p. 36.[9] However, I reproduce Fukui's text as edited, with corrected readings only where they affect the sense, to save a good deal of flipping back and forth between editions. This second conversation reads less like a lesson in language practice and more like a piece of comic drama. The third and final section departs from imagined dialogue:[10] it is the author's explanation of and introduction to the foregoing work, instead of a preface; it may be compared with (for example) that of Wace or of *Clement's* author. Note that the author dedicates what s/he calls 'traitis' and 'livre' to an unnamed patron,[11] excusing any faults of language. It also casts an eye beyond the patron to the audience: all who will read the book. As with other writers, doubling of near synonyms ('traitee e compilee', 'entendu et apris', 'franceis ou romanz') is presumed to be for emphasis and nuance of meaning; I therefore translate such doublets as they stand.

The text follows Fukui very closely, but I have slightly modernized the punctuation of speech. Line numbers, including unnumbered line-breaks, are copied from that edition.

---

[9] His note on p. 88 is one in which he corrects Fukui's faulty reading.

[10] Compare Kristol's p. 45, which is headed 'The Author's letter to his Patron'.

[11] It is probable the author is male, because so many of the texts whose authors we know are written by men. But there is always the possibility that women may be among anonymous writers, and therefore I have tried to keep the habit of leaving their gender open. Neither Fukui nor Kristol pronounces on the subject; it is not known who wrote the *Maniere*, nor who the patron was.

Text

The First Dialogue

[314a]

'Mon tres gentil sire, Dieu vous beneit!'   1

'Mon tres doulz amy, je pri a Dieu qu'il vous donne bonne
encontre. [*vel sic*] Sire, Dieux vous beneit et la compaignie!'

'Beau sire, dont venez vous, s'il vous plaist? [*vel sic*] De
que part venez vous, mon tres doulz amy, mais qu'il ne vous   5
desplaise?'

'Vraiement, sire, je vien tout droit de Venyse.'

'He! mon amy, c'est une ville de Lumbardie?'

'Oil, vraiement, beau sire, si est.'

'Par mon serement, mon tres gentil sire, j'en ay grand joy de   10
vous que vous estez si bien travaillé, depuis que vous estez
si jones, car je pance bien que vous n'avez pas encore .xxx.
ans.'

'Si ay je vraiment et plus. Mais pour ce que je sui bien
sains et joliet ou cuer, la Dieu mercy, l'en me dit que je   15
sui plus jones que je ne sui pas.'

'Ore, sire, est Venyse une belle et grande ville?'

'Oil, vraiement, sire, c'est la plus bealle ville et la plus
noble port qui soit en tout le monde, si come m'a l'en dit en cel
pais la, qui out travaillé partout.'   20

'Et de que pais estez vous, beau tres doulz amy, mais qu'il ne
vous deplaise?'

'Vrayement, sire, je sui de France.'

'Et de que ville, s'il vous plaist?'

'De Parys, sire.' [*vel sic*]   25

'En que pais estiez vous nee, beau sire, s'il vous plaist?'

'Vraiement, sire, je fu nee ou roialme de France.'

'En que ville, beau sire?'

'En Parys, sire, si Dieu [314b] m'ait.'

'Vraiement, sire, je vous en croy bien, car vous parlez bien   30
et gracieusement doulz franceis. Et pour ce, il me fait grand
bien et esbatement ou cuer de parler avec vous de vostre
beau language, car c'est la plus gracieus parler que soit ou
monde et de tous gens mieulz prisee et amee que nul autre. Et
coment vous est a vis, beau sire, de tres bealle citee de Paris?'   35

Translation

The First Dialogue
'My good sir, may God bless you!'
    'My dear good friend, I pray God to grant your meetings will be fortunate!'
[or this:]
'Sir, God bless you and your company!'
'Good sir, where do you come from, please?'
[or this:]
'What part are you from, my good friend, if you don't mind my asking?'
'In truth, my friend, I've just come from Venice.'
'Oh, my dear fellow, is that a town in Lombardy?'
'Yes indeed, sir, it is.'
    'Well I must say, good sir, I am delighted for you, that you're so well travelled,[12] since you are so very young. I can't believe you are thirty yet!'
    'Oh yes I am, and more! But because I'm healthy and happy, thank God, people think I'm younger than I really am.'
    'Now, friend, is Venice a large fine town?'
    'Oh yes, sir, indeed it is! It is the most beautiful city, and the noblest port, in all the world; this is what people tell me there, who have travelled everywhere.'[13]

    'And what country are you from, my fine friend, if you don't mind my asking?'
'Indeed, sir, I'm from France.'
'From which town, please?'
'From Paris, my friend.'
[or this:]
'In what country were you born, sir, if you please?'
'Indeed, sir, I was born in the kingdom of France.'
'In which town, my friend?'
'In Paris, sir, as God is my guide.'[14]
    'Ah, yes, friend, I can well believe you, because you speak beautiful French so well and gracefully!'[15] This is why I'm so pleased and delighted to talk with you in your lovely language, because it is the most elegant in all the world. It is more beloved and prized than any other. And what do you think, my friend, of the fine city of Paris?'

---

[12] 'travailler' means 'travel', not 'work' as in modern French (see p. 157 of the edition). Another common word for 'travel' is 'errer'.

[13] It is possible that the same person continues the speech, asking a question in his turn, after the line-break.

[14] Lit: 'God help me', but (given what follows) the modern expression will not do here.

[15] One might speculate whether the other really speaks 'better' French than this one does.

'Vrayement, sire, il m'est a vis que ne vi oncques mais jour
de ma vie si belle citee come ce est, toutes choses acompteez,
car il en y a tant de si beaux chasteux, si grans forteresses et si
haultes maisons et fortes, et que sont si honestement
apparailliez que, si vous les eussiez veu, vous en seroiez   40
trestout esbahiz.'
'Vraiement, sire, il peut bien estre veritable ce que vous
ditez. He! pleust a Dieu et a la Vierge Marie, mon tres doulz
amy, que je seusse si bien et gracieusement parler franceis
come vous savez, car vraiement j'en feusse doncques bien aise   45
a cuer.'
'Par Nostre Dame de Clery, je vouldroy que vous seussiez.
Mais toutesvoies, vous parlez bien assés, ce m'est a vis, car je
pance bien que vous y avez demouree grand piece, depuis que
vous parlez si bien et plainement la language.'   50
'Par saint Pol, sire, je n'y fu oncques mais.'
'Et coment savez vous parler si bien donques?'
'Vraiement, sire, si come je m'ay acoustumee a parler entre
les gentils de ce pais [314c] icy.'
'Seinte Marie, j'en sui bien esbahis coment vous le pourrez   55
aprendre en ce pais, car vous parlez bien a droit hardiement.'
'Save vostre grace, beau sire, non fais.'
'Par Dieu, si faitez aussi bien et gentilment come se vous
eussiez demouree a Paris ces vint ans, car vraiement je n'oy
oncques mais Englois parler françois si bien a point ne si   60
doulcement come vous faites, ce m'est a vis toutesvoies.'
'He! sire, je vous remercy de ce que vous me prisez plus que
je ne sui pas dignes. Toutesvoies et pour ce, je sui tousjours
a vostre gentil comandement en quanque je pourrai faire pour
l'amour de vous.'   65
'Et vraiement, beau sire, vous estes tres bien venu en ce pais.
[*vel sic*] Et par m'ame, sire, vous estez tres bien venu ciens.'
'Grand mercy, mon tres gentil sire, de vostre grand gentilesse
et courtoisie. Beau sire, feustez vous oncques mais a Rouan en
Normandie?'   70
'Nonil, vrayement, sire, je n'y fu oncques jour de ma vie, mais
j'ay esté autre part en beaucoup de lieux, a Tours en Toureyn;
j'ay esté au Bloys, a Chartres et a Aurilians aussi bien.'
'A! Aurilians. Sainte Marie, c'est bien loins de cy, car c'est
bien pres au bout de la monde, si com nen dit en ce pais icy.'   75
'Vraiement, sire, ils sont bien fols qui le cuident, car c'est
ou mylieu du roialme de France.'

'Well, sir, I honestly think I have never in my life seen such a lovely city as that, in every way. For there are so many fine castles, great fortresses, big strong houses which are so bravely done up that if you'd seen them you would be absolutely astonished.'

'I'm sure it's true what you're saying, friend. Oh, if only it would please God and the Virgin Mary, my dear sir, to make me speak French as well and elegantly as you can! I'd be so happy if I could.'

'By Our Lady of Clery, I wish you could. But in fact you speak quite well enough, I think; it's my guess you've spent a long time there, because you speak the language so well and clearly.'

'By Saint Paul! I've never been there!'

'But how can you speak so well, then?'

'To tell the truth, I've made a habit of conversing with well-bred people of this country.'[16]

'By Saint Mary, I am astonished at how well you've been able to learn in this country. You speak accurately and confidently.'

'Excuse me,[17] sir, but really I don't.'

'My God, you do it as well and elegantly as if you'd been living in Paris these twenty years! Really, I've never heard an Englishman speaking French so well and so fluently as you do. That's what I think, anyway!'

'Oh, thank you sir! You praise me far more than I deserve. For this, anyway, I shall be at your very distinguished service, whatever I might be able to do for the sake of your friendship.'[18]

'Truly, my dear sir, you are very welcome to this country.'

[or this:]

'By my soul, friend, you are very welcome here.'

'Many thanks indeed, sir, for your great kindness and courtesy. Sir, have you ever been to Rouen in Normandy?'

'No, honestly not, my friend! Never in my life. But I've been to other parts, and many places: to Tours in Touraine ... and I've been to Blois, to Chartres, and to Orleans too.'

'Ah, Orleans! By Saint Mary, that's a long way off! It's just about at the end of the world, at least that's what they say around here.'

'Really? They must be mad to believe that, for it's right in the middle of the kingdom of France!'

---

[16] 'gentils' ought to mean 'gentlefolk', sc. upper class. It is a fair generalization to say that better-off people learned more French than the poorer classes did.

[17] 'Saving your grace' (note the English spelling) sounds too archaic.

[18] The Englishman speaks, thanking the Frenchman for his compliments. Therefore the next speech ought to be the same person welcoming the latter to England (the punctuation appears to show a change of speaker).

'Est Aurilians une beau ville?'

'Oil, sire, si Deu m'ait, la plus belle que soit ou roial[314d]me de

France aprés Paris. Et aussi il en y a un grand estude des loys,   80

car les plus vaillanz et les plus gentilx clers qui sont ou

cristiantee y repairent pour estudier en civil et canon.'

'Mon tres doulz amy, je vous en croy bien, mais toutesvoies j'oy

dire que l'anemy y apprent ses desciples de nigromancie en une

teste.'   85

'Pas voir, par saint Jaques. Toutesvoies, il y avoit jadys un

Englois qu'estoit fort nigromancien qui est a nom Colyn T., qui

savoit faire beaucoup de mervailles par voie de nigromancie.'

'Sire, ce n'est pas chose creable, mais qu'il ne vous desplaise,

car je say bien que n'y fut oncques mes estude de tel fatras. Mais   90

j'oy bien dire que souleit estre entre les Espaniols mescreans.

E pour ce, ne le croiez mie.'

'Sire, je vous croy bien.'

'Ore, alons boire, sire, s'il vous plaist.'

'Grant mercy, beau sire.'   95

'Bevez a moy, sire, je vous em pri.'

'Vous comencerez, s'il vous plaist.'

'Pur Dieu, non ferai.'

Et puis dit l'autre, quant il a bu:

'Sire, grand mercy de voz grans biens et despenses' [*vel sic*]   100

'Grant mercy de voz biens.'

'Il n'y a de quoy, beau sire.'

'Si est vraiement, car se je vous pourrai jamais veoir en mon

pais, je vous rendrai bien la grand gentrise que ore m'avez

fait par la grace de Dieu.'   105

'Ore, je recomande a vous et je pri a Dieu qu'il vous donne

santee et paix.'

'Mon tres gentil sire, a Dieu vous comande et vous donne

bon[315a]ne vie et longe.'

'Is Orleans a beautiful city?'

'Oh yes, friend, as God's my witness,[19] it's the loveliest in the whole kingdom of France except for Paris. And there is also a great law-school, for the worthiest and noblest clerks in all Christendom go there to study both civil and canon [law].'

'I believe you, my fine friend. But all the same, I do hear tell the Devil teaches necromancy to his disciples there, from inside a head.'[20]

'That's a lie, by Saint James! But indeed there was once an Englishman, a great necromancer called Colin T., who could perform all manner of wonders by means of his black art.'[21]

'This is quite incredible, I'm sorry! I'm certain there was never such a thing as courses teaching this nonsense! But I've heard it said there used to be some among those heathen Spanish. But for all that, don't you believe it.'

'No, but I do believe you!'

'Come on now, please let's go and have a drink!'

'Oh, thank you, friend!'

'Drink my health, I beg you.'[22]

'Oh please, you go first!'

'No, no, I insist!'

And then the other one says, as soon as he has drunk:

'Sir, I would like to thank you for your great kindness and generosity.'

[or this:]

'Many thanks for your kindness.'

'But not at all, dear friend.'

'But I mean it, because if ever I could meet[23] you in my country, I'd be able to repay the noble kindness you have shown me here, by God's grace.'

'Now I must take my leave of you.[24] May God keep you in health and peace!'

'My very dear friend, I commend you to God, and [may he] give you a good life and a long one.'

---

[19] 'God help me', see note above.

[20] Cf. Kristol, p. 34, 'une teste d'aresme', that is, the Brazen Head of legend (discussed in *The Brewer Dictionary of Phrase and Fable*). The head is not necessarily Roger Bacon's, the best known. Brewer's 'Speaking heads' mentions other forms of the legend (its invention was ascribed to Grosseteste even before Bacon; see Southern, *Robert Grosseteste*, p. 75). The Cambridge version does not mention the mysterious Colin T. and the miscreant Spanish (below), mentioned in Kristol's notes (his p. 87). Fukui, who had presumably not seen the Cambridge version, reads 'teste' to mean 'text' (p. 157). A 'head of brasse' in the romance *Valentine and Orson* (ed. Dickson) is crucial to the plot throughout. See, further, Tyson, 'Two Prophecies and a Talking Head'.

[21] Confusion between 'nigromancy' (from the word for black) and 'necromancy' (magic performed with the help of the dead) is common. *OED*, 'necromancy'.

[22] This must mean the speaker is offering to pay (see 'despenses', below), unless it is simply a polite tussle to yield precedence.

[23] Lit. 'see'.

[24] 'recomande'; there are several possible meanings, but in this context one speaker commends the other to God's protection (rather than recommending himself).

The Second Dialogue

De parler entre compaignons qi demourent ensamble en un hostel,   110
quant il se devent aler coucher.
'Guilliam, avez vous fait nostre lit?'
'Nonil.'
'Vraiement? Vous, bien meschant, que nostre lit est encore a
faire. Sourdez vous le cul e alez vous faire nostre lit, je vous   115
em pri, car je vouldroy estre endormy, [*vel sic*] car je dormisse
tres voulantiers, si je feusse couchee.'
'He! beau sire, me laissez vous chaufer bien les piés
premerement, car j'en ay grant froit.'
'Et coment le pourrez vous dire pour verité, quant il fait si   120
grand chaut?'
'Alumez la chaundelle e va traire de vin, se vous vueillez,
car je ne me bougerai ja.'
'Qu'il le meschie que vous en donnra a boire, car je m'en irai
querre du vin pour moy mesmes e pour Johan, e par Dieu, se   125
je puis, vous ne bevez mais huy, a cause de vostre malvaise
voulantee.'
'Vraiement, Perot, vous estes bien malvais. Je pri a Dieu qu'il
vous meschie.'
'Teis toy, senglant, hideus garçon, vilain mastin, meschant   130
paillart, cornart qui tu es, ou tu en avra des horions, que tu
les sentiras de cy as quatre jours.'
Doncqs, il lui donne un bon buffe sur la jouue, ainsi disant:
'Dieu met toy mal an quoy me respondiez vous ainsi!'
Et l'autre se comence a plorer e dit: 135
'Je pri a Dieu que tu peus rumpre le col avant [315b] que tu t'en iras
hors de ciens, ou bougeras de ciens.'
'Par Dieu, il te feust mieulx taiser, si ques tu n'as plus de
damage.'
'Vraiement, je ne suffrerai ja plus estre batu de vous. J'amasse   140
mieulx encore demourer la ou nul me cognoissoie qu'a rester plus
longuement icy.'
'He! Guilliam. Ne vous chaille! Je ne vous ferai ja plus de mal.'
'Ore, buvons nous tost et alons coucher!'
'Guilliam, ou alez vous?'   145
'Je m'en vais amont.'
'Beau sire, je vous em pri que vous couvrez le feu par moment,
et oustez ces busses et tysons tost, et boutez les carbons e les
breis ensamble, e mettez dessuz les cendres. E puis nous en irons
coucher.'   150

The Second Dialogue

This is for a conversation among companions who are staying in a lodging together, when it's time to go to bed.

'William! Have you made our bed?'

'Nope.'

'What? You are a slacker, when our bed still hasn't been made! Get off your backside and go and make our bed, if you please. I really want to go to sleep.'

[or this:]

'I'd go off to sleep like anything, once in bed.'

'Oh come on, boss, do let me get my feet warm first. They're freezing!'

'How on earth can you say that, when it's so hot?'

'Light the candle and go and draw some wine,[25] if you want; I'm not moving from here.'

'Bad luck to anybody who gets a drink for you! I'm going to get some wine, just for myself and John. By God, if it was up to me, you'd never drink again, you're in such a bad mood.'

'Oh Peter, you're impossible! God give you bad luck yourself!'

'Shut up, you bloody horrible brat, you ugly dog, beastly good-for-nothing, cuckold that you are, or you'll get such a bashing that you'll still feel four days from now!'

Then he gives him a savage blow on the cheek, saying:

'May God send you such troubles, for answering me back like that!'

The other starts crying, and says:

'God send you break your neck before you leave here — before you stir a step from here!'

'God had better make you shut up before you get worse coming to you!'

'Oh really! I won't put up with you beating me any more. I'd rather stay somewhere nobody knows me, than stay here any longer!'

'Ah, William! You can stop worrying, I won't hurt you any more.'

'All right then, let's have a quick drink and go to bed.'[26]

'William! Where are you going?'

'I'm off upstairs.'

'Friend, I beg you please to cover the fire now,[27] and quickly take out those logs and brands. And shove the cinders and the embers together, putting ash over the top. And then we can go to bed.'

---

[25] 'va traire' is the 'familiar' form, unlike the rest of this passage. There is a passage in second person singular below, before the speakers return to the 'polite' form.

[26] In Kristol's version, all three of these speeches are by the same person (sc. 'Perot', who has been bullying William).

[27] Kristol has 'premerement', thus meaning 'before you go'.

Et puis aprés, ils s'en vont a leur chambre amont. Et quant
ils seront la, l'un demandera a l'autre ainsi:
'Ou est Briket le petit chien, e Florette la petite chienne?'
'Je ne say my ou Briket est devenuz. Mais toutesvoies, Florette
s'en est couchee aval dessoubz les chesnes qui gisent ou jardyn.'[28]   155
'Guilliam, deschaucez vous tost e lavez voz jambes, e puis les
ressuez d'un drapelet e els frotez bien pour l'amour de puces,
qu'ils ne se saillent mye sur voz jambes, car il y a grand coup
gisanz en le poudre soubz les junx.'
Et puis il s'en vait coucher. Doncques dit il a l'autre: 160
'Traihez vous la, car vous estez si froit que je ne puis pas
endurer que vous me touchez point. Et dormeons, par Dieu,
car j'en ay grand mestier, a cause que j'ay veillez toutes ces [315c]
deux nuys passez sanz dormir.'
'Que, dea! vous estez bien chaut, ore que vous suez si fort!'   165
'He! les puces me mordent fort e me font grand mal et damage,
car je m'ay gratee le dos si fort que le sanc se coule. Et pour
ce je comence a estre roignous et tout le corps me mange
tres malement. Et pour ce je m'en vai demain pour estre
estufee sanz plus targer, car j'en ay tres grande necessitee.'   170
'He! Guilliam, que vous estez bien suef de corps. Pleust a Dieu
que je fus si suef et si nette come vous estez!'
'He! Perot, ne me tuchez point, je vous em pri, car je sui bien
chatilleus.'
'He! Guilliam, je vous chatoillerai tresbien.'   175
'Doncques, par Dieu, beau sire, finez vous, car il est hault
temps a dormir.'
'Mais huy, par l'amur Nostre Dame, toutesvoies c'en fait mon.'[29]
'Ore, ne parlons plus doncques, mais dormons fort et estraignez   180
la chandelle.'
'Guilliam, Dieu vous donne bonne nuyt, e bon repos a moy aussi!'
'Quoy? Ne dions nous noz orisons, si come nous sumez
acoustumee?'
'Il ne me souvenoit point.'   185

---

[28] The section ends here in Kristol's version, but on his p. 36 is a passage corresponding to, but
   shorter than, this pleasant bedtime chat. The All Souls version continues as follows.

[29] The edition is incorrectly lineated, probably because of a page-turn (there is no line 179).

After this, they go to their room upstairs. And when they get there, one asks the other:

'Where is Briket, the little dog, and Florette the little bitch?'

'I don't know where Briket has got to, but anyway Florette has gone to sleep downstairs under the oak-trees in the garden.'[30]

'William, get your trousers off quickly and wash your legs! Then you must wipe them with a bit of cloth and rub them well for the sake of the fleas. You don't want them jumping on your legs — there are loads of them in the dust under those rushes.'

Then he gets into bed. Now he says to the other:

'Push over, can't you? You are so cold I can't bear you to touch me at all! And let's go to sleep, for God's sake; I really need to, since I've been awake for the last two nights without sleeping.'

'What the Devil? You're quite warm enough, you're sweating so much!'

'Ah, those fleas are biting hard, and causing me such pain and discomfort! I've scratched my back so much it's bleeding. It's making me get really scabby, and my whole body is itching like fury. So tomorrow I'm getting myself a steam-bath without any further delay, I need it so much.'

'Oh, but William, you've got such a soft body! God, I wish I were as soft and clean as you are!'

'No, no, Perot, please don't touch me! I'm so ticklish!'

'Ha ha! I'll tickle you, then!'[31]

'Now for goodness sake, chum, cut it out. It's high time we went to sleep.'

'All right then, for the love of Our Lady, certainly by all means.'[32]

'Now then, let's stop talking and sleep tight. Blow out the candle.'

'William, God give you a good night; and let me sleep well too!'[33]

'What? Aren't we going to say our prayers, as usual?'

'Oh, I forgot.'

---

[30] Lit. 'under the oak-trees lying in the garden' (unless 'chesnes' is another form of 'chiens'). In the other version, she sleeps 'ov les autres chiens qui gisont ...'.

[31] Kristol's version adds 'doncques' to this line (p. 88).

[32] Fukui notes 'c'en fait mon' (p. 157) with a question mark, but see Kristol's glossary.

[33] Or: God give you good night and sweet repose, and me too (Kristol p. 88).

'Ore, nous dirons *De Profundis* en louent de Dieu et de
Nostre Dame, la benoite Vierge Marie, sa tresdoulce Mere, et
de tous les sains de paradis, et pour les ames de trespassez
que, la mercy de Dieu, attendant ou paines de purgatoire
qu'ils pourront le plus tost estre relesseez de leur paines a   190
cause de noz prieres, et venir a la joy par[315d]durable, laquelle
joye Dieu, qui maint en Trinitee sanz fin en cel eire delectable
et nous rechata de son precieux sanc, de sa grande misericorde
et pitié nous ottroit en la fin, s'il lui plaist! Amen.'[34]

The Author's Letter
Mon tres cher et tres honuré seignur, ore, Dieu en soit   195
regraciez, j'ay achevee cest traitis al reverence et instance
de vous. Et a mon esciens, je l'ay traitee e compilee si come
j'ay entendu et apris es parties dela la mer. Et se j'ay parlé
en mainte lieu oscurement et nient escienteusement fait cest
busoigne, je vous en supplie de vostre gentilesse, et tous   200
ceux qui cest livre en remirent, de m'avoir escusee, car, combien
que je ne sui pas le plus escienteux a parler et escripre doulz
franceis ou romance, neantmeins je l'ay fait selon ce que Dieux
m'a livree grace, raison, sens et entendement. Et vraiement, mon
tres doulz sire, s'il soit bien a point a vostre plaisance,   205
j'en ay tres grand joye et leesce ou cuer, entendans, s'il vous
plaist, treshonuré seignur et mon tres doulz amy, que je sui
et tousjours serai a vostre gentil comandement de faire voz
plaisirs en tous bons poins et honestes, sanz enfreindre heure.
Et Dieux me donne grace, s'il luy plaist, que je vous pourrai   210
rendre, ou temps a venir, du bien et de l'onneur pour les
grans biens, naturesses et courtoisies que vous m'avez fait et
mustree sans le mien desiert, [316a] et encore, s'il Dieu plaist, come
j'ay esperance de vous. Et je pri a nostre doulz Seignur Jhesu
Crist q'il vous donne bonne vie et longe, et vous en donne   215
santee et paix as toutzjours mais. Escript etc.

---

[34] The second dialogue ends here.

'Now, let's say a *De Profundis*,[35] in praise of God and the blessed Virgin Mary his sweet Mother, and all the saints in Paradise. And for the souls of the departed who are waiting for God's mercy among the pains of Purgatory, so they can be more speedily released from their pains thanks to our prayers, and come to everlasting joy.[36] This is the joy of God, who is in Trinity without end in that delightful place,[37] and who bought us with his precious blood, may he in his great mercy and pity grant us at the end, if it pleases him! Amen.'

The Author's Letter

My dear and honoured lord,[38] now (God be thanked!) I have finished this treatise, out of respect for you and at your instigation. To the best of my knowledge, I have drawn it up and compiled it according to what I have heard and understood in lands beyond the sea.[39] If there are numerous places where I have expressed something obscurely, or performed this task unskilfully, I pray you in your kindness — and all those who look into my book — to hold me excused. For, even if I am not the most skilful speaker and writer of sweet French or Romance,[40] nevertheless I have done as well as God has granted me grace, reason, sense, and understanding to do. Indeed, my very dear lord, if it pleases you at all I am overjoyed and glad at heart. Please understand, my honoured lord and very dear friend, that I am and always shall be at your kindly command, to do your pleasure in any good and honest business, without a moment's delay.[41] And may God give me grace, if it pleases him, that I shall be able to recompense you well and honourably in times to come for the great goodness, kindness, and courtesy you have shown me in spite of my undeserving; also, please God, as I have hopes of you.[42] And I pray the Lord Jesus Christ to grant you a long and happy life, giving you health and peace for ever. Written .... etc.

---

[35] This, Ps. 130 (129 in *LV*), is one of the Penitential Psalms (see, for example, *Cher Alme*, p. 237). Note (see Fukui, p. 157) that 'louent' is not a verb: it means 'praise' (the Cambridge version reads 'en l'onoure de Dieux ...').

[36] Souls in Purgatory may eventually be released, especially if the living pray for them; souls in Hell are lost for ever.

[37] Kristol, p. 88: 'en gloire delectable' (in delightful glory).

[38] 'Dear Sir' looks like a business letter. Although this is a 'business letter' I prefer to avoid the modern-sounding phrase.

[39] The writer does not suggest s/he is copying or translating, but that the book is compiled from experience and hearsay; this may or may not be true.

[40] See notes elsewhere, for 'romance' meaning 'French'; and Kristol's note on p. 89. The writer's modesty is probably no more than conventional.

[41] Kristol reads 'en faindre ...', meaning 'sans faillir un instant' (p. 89).

[42] Cf. Kristol: 'et encore ferez ... comme j'ay esperance de vous'. The writer hopes for future kindness from the patron.

Letters

Maud Mortimer's letters to the King[1]

The first letter is dated 1282, and was transcribed from the manuscript by Emma Cavell. She made a translation of part of the letter; the translation below is broadly my own. It is among a number of letters, from both men and women, that she has worked on. They are not from a letter-book or formulary, but exist as historical records of real correspondence rather than as patterns to copy.[2] It is possible some were transcribed into letter-books, as with the collection in which we find Christine's, below, but we have no record of whether these ones were so copied. I would have liked to publish a pair of Cavell's letters, that is, a letter together with its reply; unfortunately those she has worked on are (to my knowledge) all singletons. Since then, one was published in translation only in her article 'Intelligence and intrigue' (available online). Another from her collection is offered here together with (for want of a pair) a later letter from the same woman, both to King Edward I.[3] I have not added line numbers, not because they are prose but because they are so short. The first letter is Public Record Office SCI/19, no. 130. Maud Mortimer, widow of Roger Mortimer of Wigmore, writes to Edward I: although she cannot come to him, she asks for her inheritance.[4] The second letter, dated 1297, seems to follow the first in the source (see Tanquerey's heading); PRO, vol XIX, number 131. The story is that Maud, née de Braose, asks to be allowed to hold the land when her husband dies, and then for the same lands to revert to her after the death of her son William (to whom she had donated them).

One of Maud's sisters married a brother of Thomas Cantilupe,[5] and therefore her children were related to him. In 1290 another of her sons, Roger, benefited from a miracle in which his dead falcon, having been 'measured' for Thomas,[6] revived to full health next day. I owe this story to Ian Bass, whose paper on Cantilupe's miracles was presented at the Oxford Medieval Graduate Conference, 8th April 2016.[7] It is likely the Roger in question was the uncle of the Mortimer who was involved with Isabel, Edward II's queen.[8]

---

[1] These letters are not in Dean.

[2] Nat. Archives, Sp. Coll. 1.

[3] In *Recueil*, ed. Tanquerey (available online); number 70, pp. 69–70, dated 1297.

[4] Cavell's prefatory note says the page is very badly faded.

[5] In *ODS* he is called Thomas of Hereford.

[6] A string was stretched to measure the length of the body; then a candle was made, of that size, to offer to the saint.

[7] 'Miranda, Miracula'; I am also grateful for his email on the subject (the MS is in Oxford's Exeter College).

[8] See the second extract from *French Chronicle*, above.

Text

A sun tresnoble seygnur e treshonorable sire Edward, par la grace de Deu roys de Engleter, seygnur de Ireland e duc de Aquit'[9] la sue, si ly plest, Mahaud de Mortemer saluz ove quantke ele seist e peot de honur e de reverence humble e devoute cum a sun cher seygnur. Trescher sire asseez avez oy de autres, a ceo ke jeo antenk, ke mon seygnur est a Deu comande e jeo ne averoy pas mestre, si vus plust, sire, ke jeo feusse — tenue hors de mon heritage ke jeo claim tenire de vus pur chose ke jeo vus deyne fere cum a mon seygnur ky jeo su e tuz jure [so]y preste a fere quantke fere deveroy tut a vostre volunte; mes Deu le seist e vus sire savez une partie de ma feblesce e de mon estat ke jeo ne purroye audurer le cunsail de aler a vus la e[10] vus estes saunt trogrant meschef ne peril de moy par quey jeo pri e requer humblement vostre tres noble seygnorie kest tute esperaunce apres Deu si cum jeo me ay tuz jurs fye de votre bien voilance ke il pleise a vostre hautesce mettre en souffraunce e en respyt ceo ke jeo vus su tenue a fere taunt vus aproechez plus pres de nos parties ke jeo peusse venir a vus cum a mon seygnur e afere vestre pleisir [quant]ke fere vus deverey e vos lettres pri a vostre escheytur de Hereforsire e a autres ke mon clerc portur des lettres vus nomera si vus plest ke il me lessent aver le entre en mon heritage saunt lunz desturber mon trescher seygnur de vostre estat ke Deu sauvez averoye jeo, si vus pleist, grant joye e grant desir de oyr bones novels et vus en requer[11] ke mander le me deygnez ansamblement oud vostre pleisur de cestes choses e de tutes autres cum a la vostre lyge vaille e accresse vostre noble seygnorie tuz jurs en Deu. [Endorsed: A mon sire Edward roys de Engleter.]

---

[9] As in the letter below, the writer has abbreviated 'Aquitaine'.

[10] Read ou, u (where).

[11] MS aurequer.

Translation

To my most noble lord and most honoured sir, Edward by the grace of God king of England, lord of Ireland, and duke of Aquitaine. If you please, your [servant] Maud de Mortimer greets you with all she knows of honour and humble devout reverence as [is proper] to her dear lord. My dear sir, you must have heard it all from other people, I suppose, that my husband has been taken by God and I shall have no lord, if you please sir, and I may be kept out of my inheritance that I ought to hold from you, as I ought to do as my proper lord. And that I am and shall ever be ready to do what I ought to, according to your will. But God knows, and you know, my lord, something of my weakness and of my estate, and I could not bear to come to you where you are, as I have been advised to do, without harm and peril to myself. Therefore I beg and humbly pray your noble highness, in whom I have every hope after God, as I have always trusted in your goodwill, that it will please your highness to have tolerance and mercy[12] with regard to what I have asked you to do until you come nearer to these lands so that I can come to you as to my lord and carry out your command as I ought to do. And your letters, I beg your escheator[13] of Herefordshire and others whom my letter-clerk will name to you, if you please ask them to let me enter into possession of my inheritance without long troublesome business. My dear lord, of your good health, which God save, I shall have if you please great joy and great desire to hear good news, and I beg you will deign to send me [good news] together with your pleasure in these things and in all others as your worship deserves, and may your noble lordship increase daily in God. [To my lord Edward king of England.]

---

[12] 'respyt'; she would like him not to make a hasty decision, and to give her a respite until she can come to him.

[13] 'escheat' is to do with property that lapses to the king on the death of the holder without heir.

[The second letter]

A son tres honorable seingnur mon sire Edward, par la grace de Dieu roi de Engleterre, seingnur de Hirlaunde e duke de Aquit[aine], la sowe [si lui][14] plest, lige Mahaut de Mortemer, totes honurs e reverences cum a sun tres cher seingnur. Pur ceo, sire, ke vos eschetours unt seisi en vostre main terres ke jeo donay a Willam de Mortemer, mon fiz, a tenir a ly e a ses heirs de sun cors engendre, e trove est par enqueste ke les tenemenz furent en ycele manere done e ke Willam est a Deu comaunde saunz heir de sun cors, vous pri, si il vous plest, ke vous voillez comaunder a vos eschetours ke la seisine des avant dites terres me seit rendue solum la forme del estatut.

Vaille, sire, e accresse vostre Hautesce, longement en Jesu Crist.

---

[14] A hole in the parchment has caused these two words to disappear.

[The second letter]

To her most honourable sovereign, my lord Edward, by the grace of God king of England, lord of Ireland and duke of Aquitaine, her liege lord — if it please you — Maud de Mortimer, all honour and reverence as is due to her dearest lord.

Sir, since your escheators have taken into your hand the lands I gave to William de Mortimer, my son, to hold together with the heirs begotten of him, and it is found on examination that the holdings were in this manner donated and that William has gone to God without any heir of his body, I pray you, if you please, to command your escheators to return the possession of the said lands to me according to the form of the statute.

May Your Highness long flourish and increase in Jesus Christ.

[Tanquerey appends the following:[15] William de Mortimer, fifth son of Maud de Braose and Roger de Mortimer, died in 1297. The Close Rolls (1288–96, p. 73) contain the king's response to this letter, under the date 14th Nov. 1297. In it, the king orders the escheator not to pursue further the matter of the castle and lands that William de Mortimer held from his mother.]

---

[15] My translation (as is the footnote in the letter).

Christine de Pisan's letter to Isabelle of Bavaria

An Anglo-Norman version of this letter, critically edited in 'Christine de Pizan's *Epistre à la reine* (1405)', ed. Kennedy, is included here because it found its way into an Insular letter-book.[16] Legge's introduction describes the MS: letter-books of this kind were 'begun by clerks as note-books ... and continued as common-place books by the addition of material useful to them in their subsequent career.' Such letters as these are 'historical documents', because they were sent (as far as we know) as well as being copied into note-books. However, their subsequent use as models indicates that their 'audience' was much wider than just the original recipients. The importance of the letter among Christine's works may be gauged by reference to any bibliographical guide: *Christine de Pisan: A bibliography*, Yenal, and *Christine de Pizan: a bibliographical guide*, Kennedy. However, I have not so far found any modern translation of it, so this example of How to Write to a Queen is deemed to be of literary and historical interest for the present collection. The letter, which exists in a number of copies, is Yenal's number 32 (p. 49), headed *Une Epistre à Isabeau de Bavière*. Kennedy describes it thus: 'written in 1405 to persuade Isabeau de Bavière to mediate in the civil strife between the Dukes of Orléans and Burgundy, it marks Christine's emergence as a politically aware writer and represents the first of a number of prose epistles designed to comment on or influence contemporary affairs' (p. 253). The letter may have been meant for one or both of the adversaries as well as the queen: Louis d'Orléans was Isabelle's brother-in-law,[17] and Jean sans Peur of Burgundy was his cousin. A struggle for regency inevitably gave place to a mobilization of troops, upon which Christine drafted her compelling letter in the hope of sparing the nation from devastating civil strife. Not only does she evoke the horrors of war and fratricide, but also she correctly predicts foreign invasion of a weakened France; this indeed took place ten years later, at Agincourt. Orléans was killed in 1407, and Burgundy in 1419; the Dauphin was crowned finally in 1429 as Charles VII. One of the other MSS (Legge's MS C) is headed by a rubric which describes the political situation. It is thought that Christine's impassioned words probably did not influence her rulers, although she was in fact a noted figure in France, celebrated at court where all the players in the fateful game were among her supporters. She became an intellectual arbiter of her time, commanding esteem in aristocratic and learned circles alike.[18] Christine positions herself among the poor and humble suppliants, modestly stressing her own unworthiness but insisting on her own right as well as theirs to petition a queen.[19]

---

[16] Dean 324, miscellaneous collections of letters; the manuscript is Oxford, All Souls College, 182. This one is in *Anglo-Norman Letters and Petitions*, ed. Legge (ANTS 3), number 99 (pp. 144–50).

[17] A rondeau apparently addressed to Orléans ends the copy in Legge's MS A.

[18] Yenal's summary of Christine's life and works, pp. 3–25.

[19] This becoming modesty may have been a reason for regarding the letter as a model for others to emulate.

The Anglo-Norman letter-book is, according to Legge, haphazardly organized. She lists the chief sources for the French part of the collection as follows: Petitions to king and archbishop, Files or registers including correspondence about Richard II's second marriage, Similar files compiled by the Treasurer, Letters dealing with the archdiocese of Canterbury, Archbishop Arundel's correspondence, Letters concerning the diocese of Norwich, Henry Despenser's correspondence. None of these headings seems a likely filing-place for a Frenchwoman's letter to a French queen on the subject of averting war; one would like to know how it came to be included. I follow Legge's text exactly, including a few of her notes (Kennedy's critical edition may be consulted for variants). The letter appears in the collection with the following introduction:

Christine de Pisan to Isabelle of Bavaria. Paris, Oct. 5th, 1405 [An appeal to her to compose the differences between the Dukes of Orleans and Burgundy. Variants from B.N.F Fr: 580 (A), 604 (C), 605 (B).][20]

---

[20] Headed 'Une epistre a la royne de France' (A).

Text

A TRESEXCELLENTE, redoubtee et puissante princesse,
Madame Isabelle par la grace de Dieu Royne de France
etc.

[230d] Treshaulte, puissant et tresredoubtee dame, vostre
excellent dignitee ne vuille avoir en desdaign ou despris la 5
voix plorable de moy, sa pouvre serve, ains daigne encliner
a noter les paroles dites par affeccioun desireuse de toute
bonne adresce, non obstant que sembler vous pourroit q'a si
pouvre, ignorante et indisgne personne n'apartient soy
charger de si grans choses; mais, come ce soit de commun 10
ordre que toute personne souffrant ascun mal naturelment
affuye au remede, si come nous voions les malades pour-
chassier guerisoun et les familleux courrir a la viande et
ainsi toute chose a son remede, tresredoubté dame, ne vous
soit donques merveille se a vous, qui au dit et opinion 15
de tous pouéz estre la medicine et soverain remede de la
guerison de ce roialme a present playé et navré piteusement
et en peril de pis, on se traite et tourne, non mie vous
supplier pour terre estrange, mais pour vostre lieu et natural
heritage a voz tresnoblez enfens. Treshaulte et ma tres- 20
redoubté dame, non obstant que vostre bon sens soit tout
adverti et advisé de ce q'il apartient, toutesfoitz est il vroy
que vous, séant en vostre magesté roial, avironnee d'onneurs,
ne pouéz savoir fors par aultrui rappors le[s] communes
besoignes, tant en paroles come en fais, qui courrent entre 25
voz subgéz. Pour ce, haulte dame, ne vous soit grief [231a]²¹ de
oïr les ramentevences en piteus regraiz des adoulés suppliantz
françoys a present rampliz d'affliccioun et tristesse, qui a
humble voix plainne de pleures crient a vous leur sovereine
et redoubtee dame, priant pour Dieu mercie, que humble 30
pitié veulle moustrer a vostre benigne cueur leur desolacion
et miserie, par si que proschainnement paix entre ces deux
haulx princes germains de sang et naturelment amys, mais
a present par estrange fortune meuz a aucune contencioun
ensemble, vueilléz procurer et empetrer. Et chose est asséz 35
humainne et commune mesmement, souventesfoiz vient
entre pere et filz aucun descort, mais dyabolique est et
serroit la perseverance. En laquel vous pouéz noter deux
grans et horriblez maulx et dommages,

---

²¹ The editor omitted the next folio-marker (231b), which is therefore missing, below.

Translation

To you, most excellent, revered, and mighty princess, Madame Isabelle Queen of France by the grace of God [etc],

Your Highness, mighty and noble lady, your great dignity would not wish to disdain or contemn my tearful voice! I am your poor servant; please incline to take notice of my words, spoken affectionately and wishing to address you in all propriety, even if it may seem to you that such a poor unworthy and ignorant person should not meddle with such high matters. But, since it is common knowledge that anybody who suffers any misfortune must naturally hasten towards its remedy, as we see sick people in search of healing, and the starving in search of meat, so everything runs towards its cure. Do not be astonished if it is you, revered lady, who is said and well known to be the medicine and sovereign remedy for the healing of this kingdom, that is so wounded and pitifully injured and in danger of yet worse things, to whom one is drawn to turn. This is no supplication for a strange land, but for your own, that is the natural inheritance of your most noble children.

Highest and most revered lady, even though I am sure your good wisdom is well aware and advised of how the matter stands, nevertheless it is true that you, seated in your royal majesty and surrounded with honours, cannot know about common needs except by reports from others, in words and actions, about what is happening among your subjects. For this reason, Your Highness, let it not be too much trouble to listen to the reminders and pitiful complaints of the suffering and suppliant French people who are at present so filled with affliction and misery. With humble voices full of tears they cry out to you, their revered and sovereign lady, begging that by the mercy of God humble pity will show their desolation and misery to your benevolent heart, so that you may be willing immediately to procure and bring about peace between these two high princes, closely related by blood and naturally close friends, who are just now by some unusual fortune moved to evil contention one with the other. This is a natural and even a very common thing: sometimes discord arises between father and son. But if persisted in, it is and will be from the Devil.[22] And from this you can perceive two very great and dreadful harms, or evils, arising.

---

[22] Christine is referring to the well-known adage that to err is human but to persist in error is diabolical. Ultimately from Augustine, the idea was used by Seneca and Cicero and in more modern times by Pope (*An Essay on Criticism*) with the alternative ending 'to forgive, divine'.

                                             l'un que il couven-
droit en brief temps que le roiaume en fust destruit si come   40
nostre seignur dit en l'esvengille, 'le royaume en soi devisé
serra desolé,' l'autre que hainne perpetuelle serroit nee et
nourrie d'ore en avant entre les heires et enfans du noble
sang de France, lesquelx souloient estre comme un propre
corps et pillier a la defance de cestuy royaume, pour laquelle   45
cause d'ancien est apelee fort et puissant. Tresexcellent et
redoubtee dame, encore vous please noter et reduier a
memoire, troys tresgrans biens et proufiz qui par ceste
paix procurer vous ensuivront. Le primer apartient a l'alme,
a laquelle acquerréz tressouverain merite de ce que par vous   50
serroit eschevee si grant et si honteuse effusion de sang ou
tresgrant grif du peuple cristien et de Dieu establi le royaume
de France et la confusion que ensuivroit, se tielle erreur
avoit duree. Item, le second bien que vous seriéz porteresse
de paix et cause de la restauracioun du bien de vostre noble   55
porteure et de leurs loiaulx subgiéz. Le iij^e bien ne fait a
desprisier. C'est que en perpetuel memoire de los ramenteue,
recommendee et loé es croniques et nobles gestes de France
doublement couronné d'onneur seriéz avecques l'amour,
graces, presens et humbles grans mercis de voz loiaulx   60
subgiéz. Et, ma tresredoubtee dame, a regarder aux raisons
de vostre droit, posons qu'il fust ou soit que la dignitee de
vostre hautesse se tenist de l'une des parties avoir esté
aucunnement bleciee, par quoy vostre hault cueur fust
moins enclin a ce que par vous ceste paix fust traitee. O   65
tresnoble dame, quel grant sens c'est aucunnesfois mesmes
entre les plus grans laissier aler partie de soun droit pur
eschiver plus grant inconvenient ou pour attaindre a
tresgrant bien et utilité! [231c] Hee, trespuissant dame, les histoirs
de nos devanters qui deument se gouvernoient ne nous   70
doivent elles estre exemple de bien vivre, si comme il avint
jadix a Rome d'une trespuissante princesse, de laquelle le
filz par les barons de la citee avoit esté a grant tort et senz
cause bannys et chassiéz, dont aprés pour icelle injure
venger come il eust assemblé si grant ost que souffisant estoit   75
pour toute destruire, la vaillant dame non obstant la vilennie
faite, ne vint elle au devant de son filz et tant fist qu'elle
apoisa son ire et le pacifia aux Romains? Helas, honneuree
dame, doncques il en avra que pitié, charité, clemence et
benignité ne serra trouvee en haulte princesse, ou serra elle   80
donques quise?

One is, it must come to pass that the kingdom will shortly be destroyed, as Our Lord says in the Gospel: *Every kingdom divided against itself is brought to desolation.*[23] The other is that everlasting hate will be born and nourished from now on between heirs and children of the noble blood of France, those who ought to be as a true body and pillar in defence of this kingdom, for which reason it has from ancient times been called strong and powerful. Most excellent and revered lady, please also notice and remember three very great benefits or profits that will come to you as a result of procuring this peace. The first appertains to the soul, for which you will acquire the highest merit if, through you, there may be avoided a dreadful and shameful blood-letting and the terrible pain of Christian people in God's established realm of France, and also the devastation that would follow if such an ill-judged state of affairs had any duration. Next, the second benefit is that you will be bringer of peace and cause of the revival of the fortunes of your noble offspring and their loyal subjects. The third benefit is not to be despised. That is, in the perpetual record of praise commemorated, approved, and celebrated in the chronicles and noble epics of France,[24] you will be crowned with double honours, with love and thanks, with gifts and humble gratitude from your loyal subjects. And, my revered lady, with regard to reasons of your [personal] right, let us suppose it was or might be the case that the dignity of your highness attached to one of the parties being wounded in any way, by which your noble heart would be less inclined to allow that this peace could be arranged by you. O most noble lady, is it not wisest sometimes, even among the very greatest, to leave aside a little of one's right in order to avoid some worse trouble or to bring about some greater good or usefulness! Ah, Highness, ought not the history of our forebears, who governed themselves well, to be an example of how to live well? Thus it happened long ago in Rome, to a mighty princess whose son had been exiled and driven out, very wrongly and without due cause, by the barons of the city. For this insult, he wished to avenge himself by assembling a great host that was sufficient to destroy everything. However, in spite of this wickedness, did she not come before her son, and do such as would calm his fury and make peace between him and the Romans?[25] Alas, noble lady, when it comes about that pity, charity, mercy, and benevolence are not found in a noble princess, where then shall we seek them?[26]

---

[23] Matt. 12:25.

[24] 'gestes', lit. deeds; chansons de geste are meant.

[25] This could be a reference to Coriolanus and the efforts of his mother and wife to make peace (see *OCL*). It might also refer to Cornelia, the Mother of the Gracchi, although the incident is not described in *OCL*.

[26] The French makes 'it' singular; Christine means 'where shall we seek each of these?'

Car comme en feminines condiciouns soient
les dites vertues par raison doivent estre et habonder en
noble dame de tant qu'elle reçoyt plus de dons de Dieu,
et encores a cest propos qu'il appartiegne a haulte princesse
et dame estre moyenneresse de tratié de paix, il appert par   85
les vaillantz dames louees es sainctes escriptures; si come la
vaillant sage Royne Hester, que par son sens et benignitee
appaisa l'ire du Roy Assuaire, tant que revoquer fist la
sentence donné contre le peuple [231d] condampné a mort;
auxi Barsabee, n'apois elle maintesfoiz l'ire de David? Auxi   90
une autre vaillant Royne que conseille a son mari que puis
q'il ne pouoit avoir par force ses ennemys, q'il fist si comme
font les bons medecins, lesquelx quant ils voient que medicines ameres ne profitent a leurs paciens ils leur donnent des
doulces, et par celle voye le fist la sage Royne reconcilier a   95
ses adversaires: semblablement se pourroient dire infinies
exemples, que je laisse pour briefté, des sages roynes louees,
et par le contraire de perverses, crueuses et ennemis de
nature humainne, si come la faulce Royne Gyesabel et
autres semblablez qui pour leurs demerites sont encores et   100
perpetuelment serront diffamees, maudites et dampnees.
Mais des bonnes encor a nostre senz querir plus loign: la
tressage bonne Royne de France, Blanche, mere seint Louys,
quant ses barons estoient a descort pour cause de regenter,
la Royne ne prenoit elle son filz maindre d'ans entres ses   105
bras et entre les barons elle le tenoit disant: 'Ne vééz vous
vostre Roy? Ne faitez chose dont, quant Dieu l'avra conduit
en aege de discrecioun, il se doy tenir mal content d'aucun
de vous.' Et ainsi par son sens les appaisoit. Treshaulte
dame, mais que mon langage ne vous [232a] tourt a enuye,   110
encores vous dige que tout aussi come la Royne du ciel
"mere de Dieu" est appellee de toute cristianté, doit estre dit
et appellee toute sage et bonne royne "mere conforteresse
de ses subgiéz et de son peuple." Helas, doncques qui
serroit si dure mere qu[i] peust, se elle n'avoit le cueur de   115
pierre, veoir ses enfans entreoccire et espandre le sang l'un a
l'autre et leurs povres membres destruire et disperser!

These virtues are supposed to be found among the female of our kind, and should rightly exist and abound in a noble lady because she receives more of God's gifts, and more so because it behoves a noble princess and great lady to be the mediator in any peace treaty. This is proved by those gallant ladies who are praised in Holy Scripture, for example the brave and wise Queen Esther, who by her cleverness and good nature was able to appease the wrath of King Ahasuerus so that he revoked the sentence that condemned the people to death.[27] And Bathsheba, did she not often appease the wrath of David?[28] And there was another courageous queen, who advised her husband that since he could not take his enemies by force he must do as the best doctors do: when they see their patients are not benefiting from bitter medicines then they give them sweet ones. By this means the wise queen made him be reconciled with his adversaries. There are any number of similar examples to be told, which I shall leave aside for the sake of brevity, of wise and highly-praised queens; but on the other hand there are wicked and cruel ones, enemies of human nature, such as the false Queen Jezebel and another hundred like her who are still, and for ever shall be, defamed, cursed, and damned for their evil ways.[29] But we still have some good ones, no need to look far: there is the very wise Queen of France, Blanche, mother of Saint Louis. When the barons were squabbling about the regency, did not the queen take her youngest son in her arms and bring him among the barons? Holding him up, she said 'Do you not see your king? Do nothing that will make him discontented with any one of you, when God has led him to the age of discretion.' Thus by her wisdom she pacified them.[30]

Your Highness, without wishing to weary you with my words, I must speak to you about the Queen of Heaven. Just as she is called 'Mother of God' by all Christendom, so ought every good and wise queen to be called and spoken of as 'Mother comforter of her subjects and her people'. Alas, how can there be any such mother, unless her heart were of stone, who could see her children killing one another, spilling one another's blood, destroying and scattering their poor limbs!

---

[27] See the Book of Esther, and further chapters of Esther in the Apocrypha.

[28] Bathsheba was the wife of Uriah, whom David caused to be killed and then afterwards took her as his wife (II Sam. chapters 11 & 12, and I Kings chapters 1 & 2). Bathsheba is sometimes cited as an evil woman because she tempted David.

[29] Jezebel is a byword to this day for wickedness and treachery. Her story is found in the two Books of Kings: she was the wife of Ahab, and promoted the worship of Baal while also opposing and killing prophets of God; she was finally killed by Jehu. I have not succeeded in identifying the 'courageous queen' in the previous example.

[30] Louis IX of France, canonized for his crusading activites, is in *ODS*: Blanche was regent during his minority. She, as well as many of the good women cited above, is held up as a mirror by the Knight in ed. Offord, and ed. Wright (chapters 19 & 20, respectively). Some comparable 'advisory' material is found in *The Goodman of Paris*, tr. Power (and notes, in which the Knight's book is cited).

                                                              Et
puis qu'il venist par de costé estranges ennemys qui du tout
les persecutassent et laissassent leurs heritages! Et ainsi,
treshaulte dame, pouéz estre toute certaine couvendroit   120
qu'avenist en fin de ceste persecucion se la chose aloit plus
avant, que Dieu ne vueille, car n'est mye doubte que les
ennemys du roialme, resjouyz de cest aventure, vendroient
par de costé o grant armee pour tout parhonnir. Ha Dieu,
quel doulour a si noble royaume perdre et perir telle chiva-   125
lerie! Helas, qu'il couvenist que le pouvre peuple comparast
le peché dont il est innocent, et que les pouveres petiz
alleictans et enfans criassent aprés les lasses meres vefves
et adoulees, mourans de faim, et elles, desnués de leurs
biens, n'eussent de quoy les appaisier, lesquelles voix quant   130
a Dee avint, comme racontent les escriptures en plusours
lieux, percient les cielx par pitié [232b] davant Dieu juste et
attraient vengeance sur celx qui en sont cause. Et encores
avec ce, quel honte a ce royaume qu'il couvenist que les
povres, desers de leurs biens, alassent mendier par famine   135
en estranges contrees en racontent come celx qui garder les
deveoient les eussent destruiz. Dieu, comment seroit
jamais ce lait diffamé non acoustumé en ce noble royaume
reparé ne remis! Et certes, tresnoble dame, nous véons a
present les aprestes de ces mortelx jugemens, qui ja sont si   140
avanciéz que tresmaintenent en y a de destruiz et desers de
leurs biens, et en destruit on tous les jours de pis en pis, et
tant qui est cristien doit avoir pitié. Et oultre et encores
serroit a noter a celui prince ou princesse qui le cueur avroit
tant obstiné qu'il n'acompeteroit nulle chose a Dieu ne a   145
toutes si saintes douleurs, s'il n'estoit du tout fol ou folle,
les tresvariables tours de fortune qui en un seul moment se
peuent changer et muer. Diex, quants cops eust pensé la
Royne Olimpias, mere du grant Alixandre, ou temps qu'elle
veoit tout le monde soubz ses pieds et a elle subgit et obeis-   150
sant, que fortune eust puissance de la conduire au point ou
quelle piteusement fina ses jours a grant honte!

And then, that from the coast enemy strangers come, who will persecute and lay waste[31] their mother country! And so, Your Highness, you may be quite certain and agree what will come of this persecution, should it develop any further — which God forbid — for there is no doubt the enemies of the kingdom, rejoicing in their good luck, will come from the coast with a great army so as to put everything to shame. Dear God! What disgrace, that the chivalry of so noble a realm should perish and be lost! Alas, how could it be right that the wretched people must pay for a sin of which they are innocent, and that children and poor little babes at the breast should cry for their weary mothers who are widowed and suffering, dying of hunger, and those women who are stripped bare of their possessions have nothing with which to comfort them; when their voices reach up to God, as it says in several places in the Scriptures, they pierce the heaven for pity, before a just God, and bring vengeance upon those whose fault it is.[32]

And added to that, what shame on a kingdom where it is allowed for the poor people, denuded of everything, to go begging for very hunger into strange lands, telling how those who ought to have looked after them had destroyed them. Oh God, how should this hideous and unaccustomed infamy of our noble kingdom ever be repaired and put right! My noble lady, we can now see the preparations for these deadly judgements, which are now so far advanced that at present we see people destroyed and despoiled of their goods; every day more are afflicted from bad to worse, such that all Christianity must have pity. Even more, moreover, to any prince or princess whose heart is so obstinate they take no account of God or all his holy sufferings, unless he or she were completely mad, those swiftly changing turns of Fortune, that may at any moment alter and shift, should be pointed out. Dear God, could Queen Olympias, mother of Alexander the Great, have imagined such an overthrow in the days when she saw the whole world at her feet, obedient subjects to her: that Fortune had the power to lead her to the point at which she ended her days, pitifully, by such a shameful death![33]

---

[31] Another copy ('Christine de Pizan's *Epistre à la reine* (1405)', ed. Kennedy, line 103) has 'saississent' instead of 'laissassent'.

[32] The reference may be to the first part of Matt. chapter 18, in which Jesus commands the disciples not to sin against children.

[33] See the entry for Olympias in *OCL*.

Et sembla-
blement d'assés d'autres pourroit on dire, mais qu'en avient
quant [232c] fortune a ainsi acuilli aucun puissant seigneur ou
dame se si sagement n'a tant fait le temps passé par le   155
moyen d'amour, pitié ou charité qu'il eit acquis Dieu prime-
rement et bien vellans amys au monde toute sa vie, et ses
faiz sont conptés en publique et tous en reprouche, et tout
ainsi comme a un chien qui est chassiéz, touz lui queurent
seure, et est celui de toutz defoulés en criant sur lui qu'il est   160
bien employé. Tresexcellent et ma tresredoubtee dame,
infinies raisons vous pourroient estre recordees des causes
qui vous doivent mouvoir a pitié et a traitié de paix, lesquelles vostre bon sen n'ignore mie. Si fineray atant mon
epistre, suppliant a vostre digne magesté qu'elle l'ait aggré-   165
able at soit favorable a la plourable requeste par moy escripte
de voz pouvres subgiéz loiaulx françoys. Et tout aussi
comme est plus grant charité de donner au pouvre un piece
de pain en temps de cherté et de famine que un tout entier
en temps de fertilitee et d'abondance, a vostre pouvre   170
peuple veulléz donner en ce temps de tribulacioun un piece
de la parole et du labour de vostre haultesse et puissance,
laquelle come ils tiennent serra asséz souffisante pour les
ressasier et guerier du desir familleux qu'ils ont de paix.
Et ils prieront Dieu pour vous, pour lequel bien accomplir   175
et maints autres Dieu par sa grace [232d] vous vueille conceder
et ottroier bonne vie et longe et a la fin gloire pardurable.
Escript le v jour d'octobre l'an mil cccc et cinque.
Vostre treshumble et tresobeissante créature, Christine
de Puzan.

And the same may be said of many others. What happens when Fortune greets in this way any powerful lord or lady unless in the past, because of love, or pity or charity, he or she had wisely reached out first to God and then to well-disposed friends in the world, all their life. And their deeds are counted in public to their shame: just as with a dog that has been kicked out and everybody attacks it, and it is trampled down by everybody, who shout at it that it is rightly used thus. My most excellent and highly respected lady, please be reminded of the endless reasons that ought to move you to pity and to peace-making, which your good sense cannot ignore. Now I shall end my letter, praying your worthy majesty will find it pleasing and will favour the tearful request written by me on behalf of your poor loyal French subjects. Just as it is greater charity to give some of your bread to a pauper at times of dearth and famine, than it is to give a whole [loaf] in times of fertility and abundance, please give to your poor people in these troubled times some of your words and the labour of your eminence and power, so that when they have this it will be enough and sufficient to support and heal them in their ravenous hunger for peace. And they will pray to God for you, to accomplish this and many other things; may God vouchsafe and grant you a long and good life with an end in everlasting glory.

Written the fifth day of October, in the year one thousand four hundred and five.

Your most humble and obedient servant, Christine de Pisan.

Doctors, Lawyers, and Writers

This chapter gives a few examples of non-literary texts: these are envisaged as 'for use' rather than 'for enjoyment'. It has already been remarked that the boundary between these two groups of material can be problematic, for example in religious literature where prayers are for use rather than leisure activity. However, because Dean's catalogue barely touches the mass of material that was, for example, administrative and legal documentation, some recognition of the world outside 'literature' is included in this book. Doctors and lawyers are always with us (as is administration, whether we like it or not), and some popular sentiments on these subjects seem to be universal.[1] Here is Swift on the medical profession:

'Their next Business is, from Herbs, Minerals, Gums, Oyls, Shells, Salts, Juices, Sea-weed, Excrements, Barks of Trees, Serpents, Toads, Frogs, Spiders, dead Mens Flesh and Bones, Birds, Beasts and Fishes, to form a Composition for Smell and Taste the most abominable, nauseous and detestable, that they can possibly contrive, which the Stomach immediately rejects with Loathing'.[2]

And on the legal profession:

'It is likewise to be observed, that this Society hath a peculiar Cant and Jargon of their own, that no other Mortal can understand, and wherein all their Laws are written, which they take special Care to multiply; whereby they have wholly confounded the very Essence of Truth and Falsehood, of Right and Wrong; so that it will take Thirty Years to decide whether the Field, left me by my Ancestors for six Generations, belong to me, or to a Stranger three Hundred Miles off.'[3]

This chapter is also a place to add some comments made by (literary) writers about their work and their audience. A few such writers' voices are already heard elsewhere in this book, but there I have given all or part of their text as well. Instead of a separate chapter on audiences, together with writers' thoughts about their own work, I prefer to leave these clues to the Anglo-Norman Reader — whoever she was — scattered around the book. It has already been noted that not all Readers could read. A brief discussion of this point is included in the introduction to my *Edouard* (pp. 47–9), with a view to examining the probable audience of this saint's life only. Examination of all the audience for all the pieces in this book would be an impossible task, but it is well to remind modern readers of the ideas set forth by Joyce Coleman in her 'Aurality', in Strohm, ed. She offers the term 'prelection' for the consumption and enjoyment of literature whereby somebody listened to somebody else reading.

---

[1] The Knight complains about the men of law 'whiche sellen theyr talkynge ...' (ed. Wright, and ed. Offord, chapter 70).

[2] *Gulliver's Travels*, ed. Turner, p. 258. English recipes in the Harley collection are for making different kinds of colours ([Harley 2253] *Facsimile*, ed. Ker, items 10–17); a few receipts in this chapter are the kind of remedies intended to cure diseases rather than to purge the body.

[3] id. p. 253. See also the quotation from Naomi Mitchison, below, for the lay-person's bemusement at legal terminology; and Maud Mortimer's dread of 'long troublesome business' (her Letter, above).

Therefore this chapter is about professionals and their work. Most of the texts were written by somebody with interest and some knowledge in their field, if not always by a practitioner. Some may then have been copied by professionals who knew less about the field than they ought (the medical text below is an example). The copy of *Thèbes* excerpted above was made by an English scribe writing in Anglo-Norman; he didn't know French very well and so copied with extreme care. Many writers stress that they are using French because people understand it; the compiler of *Maniere* uses French because people don't understand it.

A Medical Compendium

> Excellent herbs had our fathers of old — Excellent herbs to ease their pain
> ... Anything green that grew out of the mould.[4]

Of the extant material on medieval medicine, much has been edited by Tony
Hunt. It is of great value for the history of science, vernacular lexicology,
botanical nomenclature, and even English art.[5] With his recent *Compendium*,[6] he
adds a further text from the important collection in Cambridge, Trinity College,
O.2.5 (1109), dated to the first half of the fourteenth century, to the corpus
available for study.[7] He points to the characteristic confusions and obscurities of
medico-botanical texts whose scribes were unfamilair with plant names and other
technical data. Putting such texts into print is an essential preliminary to the
work of collation and restoration needed for resolving these textual problems.[8]
The pseudo-Hippocratic work excerpted here appears in the Middle Ages under
a number of titles, see Hunt's Introduction (p. 1; he says the Anglo-Norman
translation is corrupt).[9]

In view of the above, I make no apology for presenting only small sections
of this intriguing material, tempting though it might be to amuse oneself rather
patronizingly at the quaint ideas our medieval predecessors had about how to look
after oneself and keep healthy.[10] The present book is not designed to elucidate
textual difficulties, nor to further research into special vocabularies,[11] but to raise
interest in the varied riches (and uses) of Anglo-Norman. The text excerpted
below is the most difficult among the three items mentioned; but the other two,
unlike this one, provide glossaries. As noted in my Introduction above, medical
practitioners, and medical information, may turn up as required in all sorts of
literary environments. Judith Weiss' essay on swooning in medieval literature
contains a very interesting commentary on the medical beliefs underlying not only
texts such as this but also the behaviour of characters in romance.[12] It will be

---

[4] Kipling, 'Our Fathers of Old'.

[5] 'Anglo-Norman Medical Receipts', pp. 179–85.

[6] *An Anglo-Norman Medical Compendium*, ed. Hunt (ANTS PTS 18). A useful sketch of these
texts is given in Pagan, 'Review: Tony Hunt, ed., *An Anglo-Norman Medical Compendium*'.

[7] For this MS, see Dean numbers 406, 414, 418, 423, 431, 433, 434 (the text excerpted here), &
440.

[8] *Receptaria* also gives much useful context for this 'inadequately studied' area (p. vi).

[9] For Hippocrates, and the later Galen (both historical figures), see *OCL*. The *Capsula* (below) is
not listed among works attributed to Hippocrates in the entry.

[10] I find two remedies in *Receptaria* still recognized today: coltsfoot for cough (as the Latin name,
tussilago, implies), and hot pepper for (the rare abdominal) migraine. But most, except perhaps
linseed to relieve constipation, are of the 'Do Not Try This At Home' variety.

[11] Hunt's notes, in this PTS volume and his other two items cited, refer further to his work on
medieval plant names; there are numerous other references essential for scholars of medieval
medicine.

[12] 'Swooning', pp. 130–34. See my reference in *Yder*, and comments about women's sexuality in *Des
Grantz Geanz*.

noticed that the recipe for curing stone, below, ends with a warning not to use too much of the herb; many recipes bear such warnings, and many others end with the words 'this is proved'. This was all useful protection, for careless practitioners were deemed to be criminals.[13]

I append a receipt for gout, taken from a Middle English saint's life, to the extracts presented in this chapter. As usual I have copied the texts from Hunt's edition as exactly as possible, omitting only the special references.[14] The compendium is entitled *Capsula eburnea*, A Coffer of Ivory.

---

[13] *The Mirror of Justices*, ed. Whittaker, p. 137, & Introduction p. xxxiv.

[14] For more in this vast field, see Hunt's apparatus in all three works cited.

Text

[*Capsula eburnea*]¹⁵

[f.98ra] Ipocras, le tresauge mire e que sour tutez altres sout la
nature de humeyne corps et cum il vist que il deust morer, comaunda
que l'en prist cest livre ou estoit escrit la nature de tut le cors el secrez et
que l'en mist a son chif en sepulcre ou il gist. Un jour passa Augustus   5
Cesar pardevant la sepulcre, quida que la gist grant tresour, si comanda
que l'en l'overist, et trova leuqes cest livere a son chif, e fu aporté a
l'Emperour; l'Emperour comandast son mire que il gardast dedeyns. List
ly mire, si trova au comensement:
    (1) Si li malade ad dolur ou emflure en la face et s'il tynt sa senestre   10
mayn a son piz et s'il frotet sovent son neez, a la .xx. et tressime jour
morra.
    (2) *Uncore.* Si li malade frentik est, que ad estordisons en le chif et
desus ambdeus genuls ad emflez rougez od sureemflure, et mult [ad] le
ventre soluble, en .ix. jor murra. Iceste enfermeté commence [a] aver   15
freides suurz et lez orailes freides et lé denz freidez.

For the Stone¹⁶

[f.103rb] (163) *Uncore.* Pernez le fulle de ere si grans cum un noiz de coudre et
le destemprez ov eisil chaud, si [f.103va] garra.
    (164) *Uncore.* Va la ou la centorie crest, si la environez treiz fetz tut
entour et un fietz, si li ditez: 'Joe te pren, herbe, en noun de Piere et de   530
Fiz et de seint Espirit, que tu seiez bone au medecine a celuy que joe te
durray.' Si ditez .iii. Pater Noster, et 'Sed libera nos a malo. Amen.' Si
l'estemprez et li donez a beivere en ewe douce, et quant il pissera, si
requillez en un bacin, si troveraz la piere menuement depecié, mez
gardez que vous ne li donez plus que ne poet arenger sus vus deuz deis.   535

---

¹⁵ p. 3.
¹⁶ p. 16.

Translation

[Introduction]

Hippocrates, the wisest of doctors, who knew better than anyone the nature of a human body, saw that he must die. So he commanded that this book, in which was written the nature of all bodies, should be taken secretly and placed by his head in the grave where he lay.

One day Caesar Augustus came by, in front of the sepulchre, and thought a great treasure must be lying therein. He ordered it to be opened, and this book was found by the [dead man's] head; and it was brought to the Emperor.[17] The Emperor commanded his doctor to look into it. The doctor did so, and this is what he read at the beginning:

(1) If the patient has pain or swelling in his face, if he holds his left hand to his chest, if he often rubs his nose,[18] then on the twenty-third day he will die.

(2) *Another*. If the patient is frantic, if he feels faintness in his head, and if he has red swellings and excessive swelling on both his knees, and if his bowels are very loose, he will die in nine days. This disease begins with cold sweats, and cold ears, and cold teeth.[19]

[For the Stone]

(163) *Another*. Take ivy leaves, as much as is equivalent to a hazel-nut, and mix them with heated vinegar. This will cure it.

(164) *Another*. Go to the place where centaury grows,[20] go all the way round it three times, and then once more, and speak to it thus: 'I take you, herb, in the name of the Father, the Son, and the Holy Spirit, that you may be good medicine for whomever I give you to.' Then say the Our Father three times, and 'Deliver us from evil, Amen.'[21] Then pound it, and give it him in fresh water to drink; when he pisses then gather it in a basin. You will see the stone has broken up into little pieces. But take care not to give him more than you can hold upon two of your fingers.[22]

---

[17] In *Receptaria*, Hippocrates gives the book personally to Caesar (p. 88).

[18] This may be 'assudualment', he rubs it hard (see Hunt's endnote; and compare his *Shorter Treatises*, p. 254 at [114]).

[19] This part of the book continues with further prognostications.

[20] This is probably *Centaurium umbellatum*, formerly used in medicine and said to have been discovered by the centaur Chiron.

[21] *Receptaria* contains a number of similar rituals for gathering herbs; among several found on p. 41 is: 'For tertian fever, gather three plantain plants after sunset, and say three Pater Nosters and three Hail Marys as you gather them; give this [to the patient] to drink at the onset of fever.' Some of the 'prayers' in this book look more like charms: mysterious letters accompanied by crosses are to be written, sometimes on the patient's body. It also contains numerous other remedies for the stone.

[22] There follows another receipt, before the writer turns to diseases of women.

Breathing Problems[23]

[f.104va] [379–410][24] Galiens reconte de une femme que [f.104vb] perdu aveit
l'aleine, et li polz esteit autresi cum mort, et nule semblant ne ost de vie
for un poy de chaud [qu'ele] aveit en cors entur le quer. Plusur dé mires
dient que ele fust morte, mez il pristrent leine carpie, sil mistrent au
bouche et al neis si veirunt muer un petit et par içoe surent que ele esteit   640
vive. Cest mal avint a femme de çoe que trop habunde de semence en ly
et de çoe que la semence est corrumpue et desnaturele. Içoe avint de çoe
qu'ele est trop longement sanz hant de home. Çoe avint a vevde velz que
sovent out esté enseintez et sovent out esté hauntez de home et dunt
sunt longement sanz hant. A le fetz avint a pucelez quant elez sunt venu   645
a le het qu'elez poent aver home e elez ne l'ont et habunde la semence
trop en ews que la nature vodreit gettre de cors altresi cum a home, mez
[de] cest semence, quant ele abunde en ele est corumpue et denaturé,
munte une fumé freide as corrnailes. Et pur çoe que lez corrnailez se
sunt jointez al quer et al pomon et as treiz est[r]ume[n]s que pertinent   650
al vois, ci en pert femme la parole.

To Make Rose Oil[25]

[f.107vb] (224) ... En ceste manere deit home
fere oyle roset. Pernez lez rose (?ment), c'est lez flors, une li[vre] ou .ii.,
si metez en un mortier, si triblez, pus metez en un vessel de verre ov .ii.
li[vre] de oile d'olive ou (?eu) une solunc çoe que metez lez roses, si
estupez le vessel, si metez pendre a solail .viii. jours. Al ixme colez lez   895
roses, si metez autretant frecche et metez regiers al solail. Içoe fetez deke
.xl. jours. Pus si lé metez en sauf. Iceste oile refreide tute chalurs. En un
autre manere li autres font plus legerement, car il prendrent une livere
de roses et un autre livere de oile de olive, sil metent ensemble en vessel
de verre et estupunt forment, pus si le metent pendre al solail .xl. jours   900
et aprés lez tuent, mez l'autre est plus freide.

---

[23] p. 19.

[24] The numbers in this section do not follow on from the previous text; they are in square instead
of round brackets. In the fourth passage, below, we return to the original numbering.

[25] p. 26, part of a receipt to cure rupture, from the Herbal section.

[There follows *De sinthomatibus mulierum*, an explanation of women's menstruation (a pollution caused by abundance of humours, pp. 16–17) and other ailments.][26]

Galen tells of a woman who had lost her breath, and her pulse was like a dead woman's; she had no sign of life except for a little warmth that there was in her body, around the heart. Many doctors said she was dead, but they took some combed wool and put it to her mouth and nose. They saw it move a little, and by this they knew she was alive.

This disease comes on a woman when she has too much seed in her, and the seed has become corrupt and unnatural.[27] This is because she has been too long without a man. It happens to old widows who have had many pregnancies and have been with a man many times, but now they have been without for a long time. It also happens to young girls when they come to wish for intercourse, but have had none yet; an abundance of seed builds up in them and Nature wishes to eject it, just as it happens with men. But [from] this seed, when it builds up and becomes corrupt and unnatural, a cold steam rises to the diaphragm. And because the diaphragm is joined to the heart and the lungs, and to the three organs belonging to the voice, so it makes a woman lose her speech.[28]

This is how to make oil of roses. Take roses, the flowers of them,[29] one pound or two;[30] put them into a mortar and grind them up. Then put them into a glass vessel with two pounds of olive oil, or one depending on how much rose you have used. Then stopper the vessel and put it to hang in the sun for eight days. On the ninth day, strain the roses, add as much again of fresh, and put them back into the sun. Do this for forty days, then put it away safely; the oil soothes all kinds of heat.

Others do this more easily another way, for they take a pound of roses and another pound of olive oil. They put them together in a glass vessel and bung it very firmly, then they leave it in the sun for forty days before siphoning off the oil.[31] But the other is more cooling.

---

[26] Compare Galen, in *Shorter Treatises* (pp. 91–2, & 121–2).

[27] A woman's own 'seed', joined to man's seed, was believed to be the requirement for conception.

[28] *Receptaria*, p. 18 (number 103) gives a simple remedy for a man in this predicament: 'Pound up three roots of red nettle, soak them in water, and give it him to drink' (the book contains others, mostly as straightforward as this one).

[29] The letters printed in brackets with a question mark (and below at line 894) represent unclear readings.

[30] Pounds (each equal to just under half a kilo) were used as measurement for a wide range of substances including liquids.

[31] 'tuent' must be a form of the word for tube (tuyau); *AND* cites several forms from *Chirurgerie* texts (although not this one).

A Miracle of Saint Cuthbert[32]

And atte laste he had the gowte in his kne   1
by colde that he toke in knelyng upon the
colde stonys when he seid his preyers, that
his kne bygan to swelle that the senews of
his legge were schronke that he myght not   5
go nor strecche oute his legge. And ever he
toke it ful patiently and seid when it ple-
sid oure lorde it shulde passe awey. And within a while aftir his brethren to do hym *com*-
forte bare hym in to the felde and there thei   10
met with a knyght that bade them 'Let me
se and handle this Cuthbert*is* legge.' And then
when he had felyd hit with his hondes he
bade them 'Take the mylke of a cowe of on
coloure and juse of smale planteyn and   15
feyre whete floure and sethe them al to gy-
der and ley hit therto hote like a plauster
and it wol make hym holle.' And anone
he was made *per*fite holle and then he thon-
kid oure lorde ful mekely, and knewe wel a-   20
none aftir that it was an angel sent fro heuene to hele hym of his (of his)[33] gret sikenes
and dissese by the purviance of god.

This late Middle English is easier than the prayers appended to Maurice de Sully's homilies, below. Translation is hardly necessary,[34] except for the receipt itself: 'Take the milk of a cow that is all the same colour, and juice of the small plantain,[35] and fine wheat flour, and cook them all together. Lay it on [the sore place] hot, like a plaster, and it will make him whole.'[36]

---

[32] This story is in a collection of saints' lives, in BL MS Add. 11565; I have transcribed the passage from a scan, sent me by the British Library, of f. 57ra. It is edited in *GL* (Supp), pp. 219–20; I have consulted, but not copied from, the edition. After becoming a monk, Cuthbert lived in great fasting and penance.

[33] The copyist wrote these two words twice. Italic letters in this passage indicate where abbreviated forms have been expanded.

[34] In Middle English 'go' means walk (cf. a child before it can speak or go: a child before it can talk or walk).

[35] Probably *Plantago major* (I can find no Lesser Plantain in this family). *Flora Britannica* gives details of the plantain's use in medicine, especially for bruising and crushing wounds (pp. 320–22). One MS calls the stuff 'sage'; perhaps the scribe was unfamiliar with it. *Receptaria* gives a recipe for sore feet (p. 27, number 220, in Latin); it was called *Plantago* because of the foot-like shape of the leaves. Many plants were used for things that their shape or colour were thought to resemble.

[36] This means the cow must not be brindled or black and white. The word 'seethe' has several meanings, but they all refer to some kind of cooking.

Legal Texts

> Un autre chien ad puis descouplé, qe Baudewyn est apellé, a pledours e a
> legistres e a contours, dount plusours sount chacez en enfer par baudour de
> lur sen.[37]
>
> 'Then he loosed another dog, called Boldy, at advocates and lawyers and
> pleaders; many of these were chased all the way to Hell because of the sheer
> audacity of their manner.'

Some of the texts of *Placita Corone*, if read without any knowledge of their
background and context, or of the law upon which the cases turn, seem to have
much in common with romance. I begin this chapter with a case from *Placita* that
illustrates this point; I present another below.

Paul Hyams recently provided the Oxford Anglo-Norman Reading Group with
one of these cases 'pledee devant justices'.[38] He was unable to attend the session, so
we read the text without his guidance. Here was a story about a woman who appeals
to the court against a most felonious felon who attacked her and her husband,
unprovoked. He drew his newly-sharpened sword of Cologne steel and murdered
the husband in the arms of his wife, who was trying to protect him. She raised a
hue and cry, and the court is now hearing her 'tale'.[39] One of the ways for the felon
to defend himself is by armed combat, acting the champion with shield and club.
This sounded more like something out of Malory's Arthuriad, than out of a real
law-court![40] However, on reading further we discovered that the felon could get
off on a technicality, by arguing that he never killed the woman's husband because
the 'husband' never married her. Only a woman whose (properly-wedded) husband
is killed 'in her arms' may summon a malefactor to court, otherwise women were
not allowed to 'call out' any man for any crime whatsoever.[41] Further, 'in her arms'
means merely that the couple live together 'as one flesh' (although it seems also to
have been necessary for her to witness the killing);[42] the dramatic scene of murder
amid a damsel's screams is also a construct based on the precise requirements for
such a case to be brought. *The Mirror of Justices* says the wife of a murdered man
may appeal, but only the wife in whose arms (that is, in whose seisin) he was

---

[37] [Bozon] *Les Contes Moralisés*, ed. Smith and Meyer, p. 32 (the fourth hound). Bozon dresses
the Devil in huntsman's clothes and sends him out with a pack of allegorical hounds in search of
sinners. See Grange, ed., 'The *Miserere* in Anglo-Norman' (pp. 46, 54, & 57), for priests as dogs
who are 'ferbalt' (keen).

[38] ed. and tr. Kaye (Selden Society). The cases date from the mid-thirteenth century.

[39] 'en conte contant' is the phrase used (to state one's statement); 'tale' is the Old English equivalent.
'The appellor having stated his case the appellee must traverse it word for word, point by point ...
the prolonged rigmarole of counting' (Introduction, p. xxvi).

[40] This may be because collections such as *Placita* were very conversational in their style, as Hyams
has explained, legal language not yet having crystallized at that social level (in the localities, away
from Westminster).

[41] In the Book of the Knight, a woman takes up arms in her husband's defence (ed. Offord, and ed.
Wright, chapter 92).

[42] *Placita* (Introduction), pp. xxviii–ix.

slain.[43] The felon, we then discovered, may also have purchased a pardon from the king, in which case he must carry it upon him at all times so that no judicial combat may ensue.[44] The cases in this collection are not real cases, but 'model pleas'.[45]

My departure from what is usually considered to be literature is encouraged partly by the popularity of this reading group among historians, who welcome the opportunity to practise medieval French. Furthermore, medieval law is as important as medieval medicine (which does feature in Dean's catalogue) for the understanding of medieval culture. Interdisciplinary studies are becoming a common thing at Oxford and elswhere, which is another reason for widening the scope of this book. These texts are not in Dean;[46] very few 'legal' texts are listed. Her numbers 32–5 (in the Historiographical section, unsurprisingly) are the very earliest law texts in French, and a translation of *Magna Carta*. *Magna Carta* is receiving a good deal of attention at the time of writing, which might have encouraged me to add an extract from it to this collection. However, the fact it is listed in Dean means it is better known and more accessible than so many others; further, by the time this book appears the limelight could have moved away from *Magna Carta*.[47]

> and not to ... any strange city, where they will be needing to explain
> themselves in precise words of a kind they are not handy with.[48]

The first passage in this chapter is from *Placita*. One reason for choosing it is because of its compelling bleakness (and because of the interesting use of the word 'prodhomme', discussed below). Another is because there did exist, in theory, a right for the starving poor to take what they needed in extremity; although secular law never recognized or implemented this right, it may have been in the mind of *Placita's* compiler when making the man complain of his poverty and distress.[49] In the late twelfth century, when canon lawyers and theologians were first 'inventing' this right, the Nun of Barking's Confessor explains to his aggrieved treasurer that the young servant who had made off with some money from the chest should not be pursued: 'He needed it more than we do', he says. The Nun makes more of

---

[43] ed. Whittaker. The supposition is that if he has many living wives (!) only the present one is so entitled: 'en qi braz qest ataunt adire cum en qi seisine il esteit occis' (p. 50). See also p. 112 for the order of combat, as mentioned earlier in this paragraph.

[44] The editor of *Placita* discusses the uncertainty of the effect of a charter of pardon (Introduction p. xi, and *passim*).

[45] '... a set of detailed precedents for the conduct of appeals of felony in the king's court', plus explanatory matter (Introduction, p. x).

[46] See her p. xi.

[47] For the general field, see introductions to the edited texts from which my three passages are taken; the *Oxford History of the Laws of England* may also be consulted. Articles on topics related to this chapter also include Hyams, 'Thinking Law'; his 'The legal revolution'; and his article cited below. The notes to these, together, provide more references for further reading.

[48] Mitchison, *The Bull Calves* (p. 108).

[49] Discussed in Hyams, 'Serfdom Without Strings'; the heading 'Necessity knows no law?' in Part II.

this incident than does Aelred, whose Life she is translating.[50] Hyams remarks 'One can imagine some ... landowner concealing a theft ... out of sympathy'.[51]

My second piece is an extract from the Statute of Winchester; perhaps this is almost as well-known as *Magna Carta*. It may be from reading stories about Robin Hood or other heroes, retold for children, that many remember learning how the forests had to be cleared back one bowshot from the sides of the road, so as to discourage robbers from lying in wait to ambush law-abiding travellers. I give only this one clause of the Statute, for want of space.

My third extract is from *The Mirror of Justices*, which (as will be seen) insists that law must be founded on scriptural teaching. It equates crime with sin, with predictably confusing results, and is not to be taken seriously as a law-book.[52] However, the passage rounds off the present Miscellany; its preoccupation with sin forms a link with the Religious writings in the third part of my book.

All this material, and other legal texts I looked at when compiling this book, is translated facing-page in the editions, but I offer the pieces here with my own translation because it is not the sort of thing we regularly encounter in our forays among literary texts, Anglo-Norman or not.[53] New translations are not intended to replace but to clarify the existing ones. For example, the word 'appeal' is used confidently by the translator of *Placita*, who knows that modern historians as well as contemporary readers will be aware of what sort of appeal is meant. To a non-specialist it could be confusing, because rather different from the modern meaning of 'appeal'. Better words in the context would be 'summon' or 'challenge' (to 'call out' renders the sense well). Therefore the opening of the case described above would read: 'Anneis de N, who is here, summons (challenges, accuses) Robert de C, who is there ...' (not 'Anneis appeals Robert', as the published translation has it). She is accusing him before the court, and not appealing against any previous decision of the court.

---

[50] *Edouard*, chapter 7 (Edward's Treasure).

[51] Hyams, 'Serfdom Without Strings'.

[52] A long introduction discusses the *Mirror* and its author. The editors call it 'an enigmatical treatise', that contemporary readers did not take seriously (pp. xxii–iii). I omit the riddling verses that head the text, because not much can finally be concluded from them.

[53] I am grateful to Paul Hyams, who has looked through my translations and suggested some useful notes.

Text

1) from *Placita* (pp. 16–17) De Cheval ou Boef Emblé

Nichole de E, ke ci est, apele Hue de M, ke la est, ke il vint teu jour tel houre
tel an etc, en les champs de E en un certein liu ke est apelé N et prist del sen
une Jumente neyr, de age de iii anz et del pris de xxs., a quatre dents de polain, et
hors del champ de memes tel liu certein le amena a sa meson demeyne en la vile
de M; et fist entendant a ses veysins et as bone genz de memes la vile ke son pere,   5
J par non de C, ly avoyt doné tel jumente a fere ent son preu et son espleit;
iloques la recetta felonessement com felon de teu jour iekes a tel jour ke il
lamena au marché de P et ilokes la vendi a un paysant pur un demy marc de
argent solement; et ke il la prist memes le Jour, memes le hure et memes le an et
en memes le liu certein en le champ avant dit, et en la manire avant dite la   10
recetta et puis la vendi en memes le marché de P pur un demy marc solement, si
com nos avoms vers li conté, felonessement com felon etc., cesti Johan, ki ci est
en present, prest est ke il puisse prover sur ly com sur felon par son cors ou par
quant la curt le Roy agarde ke prover le deyt.
'Hue,' fet la justice, 'avez entendu ce ke Johan ad vers vous conté?'   15
'Sire, oyl.'
'Ore li responés solom ce ke vous quidez ke bon seit.'

Translation

1) The Theft of a Horse or Ox

'[T]he itinerant justices ... would attempt to persuade the appellee to defend the matter ... by simply putting himself upon a jury for good and evil. Only a naïve, sanguine or innocent appellee would fall for this'.[54]

Nicholas of E, who is here [in the court], accuses Hugh of M, who is there, [saying] that he came on a certain day, at a certain time in a certain year, etc, into his fields [of E] which is in a place called N, and took a mare of his, a black one aged three years and valued at twenty shillings; and she had four foal-teeth.[55] And he led her out of the field in the said place, to his own house in the town of M. He gave his neighbours, and the good people of that place, to understand that his father, named J and from C, had given him this mare for his own use and profit.[56] So in this way he kept her, feloniously as a felon,[57] from that day, until the day he took her to the market at P. There he sold her to a local,[58] for no more than half a silver mark.[59]

(That) he took her on the same day and at the same time and in the same year, and in the same field in the same place as was said before, and that he kept her as was said, and then sold her at the said market of P for only half a mark, as we have alleged against him, feloniously etc. This Nicholas,[60] who is here, is ready to prove the case against him as a felon, if he can, by his body or by whatever means the King's court will adjudge to be appropriate to prove it.[61]

'Hugh', says the justice, 'have you heard what this man Nicholas has stated against you?'

'Yes, sir.'

'Now then, answer according to what you think is fitting.'

---

[54] Introduction, p. xxvi (my second epigraph of this chapter expresses the bewilderment, unchanging across the centuries, of country folk faced with matters of law). In the edition, no accents are used; I have added them where they help the sense. I have also added line numbers (from the beginning of the passage, not from the top of the edited page) to aid navigation when reading the translation.

[55] The state of a horse's teeth indicates its age, and therefore aids identification. Hence the expression 'Don't look a gift horse in the mouth', because such close inspection insults the giver.

[56] 'a fere ent son preu et son espleit' (tr. has 'to try out and make use of').

[57] This 'pleading formula', a typical common-form phrase, appears again and again throughout the cases in *Placita*.

[58] 'paysant', somebody of the region.

[59] The money value of a mark was two-thirds of a pound (that is, he sold her for a third of her value).

[60] 'Johan'. The notes show different readings in different MSS, but all show confusion among the names; I have adjusted them so they make sense. A real case would of course refer to real dates and places, too (thus: Hugh of Midhurst; on Friday 10th June 1250, at ten o'clock in the morning. His father was John of Chichester, he sold the mare in Petworth Market, and so forth). Furthermore, as the heading suggests, the animal could be an ox, whether black or not.

[61] 'par son cors' means by combat.

'Sire, pur deu, Je su un simples homs et nynt ay geres usé playe de terre,
paront Je me say meyns suffisaument defendre: et pur ce vous pri je, sire, ke je
puisse estre consillé de aukun prodhomme coment jeo me puisse meus defendre   20
en ceo cas.'
'Coment, Hue? Ce sereyt une deverie apertement encontre ley de terre
et encontre dreyture kar ki nous porra meuz certifier de vostre fet demeine ke
vous memes? Mes fetes com prodhomme, et com bon et leaus, et eyez deu
devant vous et reconnussez la verité de ceste chose et lem vous serra asez   25
merciable solom dreyture.'
'Sire, pur deu mercy. Ma grant poverté et ma grant meseyse, ke je ay
longtens suffert, me urent si gravez ke je quiday mout estre aleggé de mes
angoisses pur la value de ceste jumente: et pur ce, par atissement del maufé, la
pris je en autre manire ke fere devroye.'   30
'Johan, com bin avez vous usé tel mestir?'
'Verraiement, Sire, je ne usoy unkes le mestir, pur meseise ne pur poverté ke
je ay eu, avant ore.'
'Johan, ce fu trop partens, si deu le vou fist. Johan, vos avez reconeu ci en la
curt le Roy ke vous preistes autrement ke fere ne deussez?'   35
'Sire, oili.'
'Et pur ce ke vos saviez bin ke ele ne fu mye vostre, dité nous la manire.'
'Sire, verreyement je ne puys dedire ke je ne la pris larcenessement.'
'Deu le vos pardomt, si li plest. Ore, Johan, dité nos en peril de vostre alme si
vos aviez nul compaignon a fere tel larcin ou nul autre ke fet avez: si, nous diez   40
ky il est et ou il ert trové.'
'Sire, en peril de ma alme je vous di ke nen oy unkes compaignon a tel fet ne
a nul autre.'
'Baillif, fetes ly aver le prestre.'
'Sire, volantirs.'   45
Et suspendatur.

'Sir, by God, I'm a simple man and I'm not used to making legal pleas.[62] Therefore I'm sure I don't know how to defend myself properly. So I beg you, sir, to let me be advised by some gentleman, as to how I can best defend myself in this case.'

'What's that, Hugh? It would clearly be a departure from the law of the land and from justice, because who can best certify your own deed but yourself? Act like a gentleman,[63] as a good and loyal fellow. Have God before your eyes and acknowledge the truth of this thing, and you will be treated mercifully enough according to the law.'

'Sir, I thank you before God. My great poverty and my great distress, that I've borne for a long time, had so affected me I thought I'd be much relieved of my troubles by the value of that mare. So, through the tempting of the Devil, I took her in a way that I ought not to have.'

'Hugh,[64] how long have you been in the habit of doing this?'

'Truly, sir, I've never done this before, in spite of distress and poverty, until now.'

'Hugh, now was too soon, unless God [instead of the Devil] had been making you act.[65] Hugh, you have admitted here in the King's court that you took [something] otherwise than you ought to have done.'

'Yes, sir.'

'And since you knew she was not yours, tell us the manner of your doing it.'

'Sir, I can't deny that I took her thievingly.'

'God will forgive you, if it pleases him. Now, Hugh, knowing the peril to your soul, tell us whether you had any companion when you did this theft, or any other theft you may have done. If so, tell us who he is and where he can be found.'

'Sir, as I hope to save my soul, I tell you I never had any companion in this deed or in any other.'[66]

'Bailiff, fetch the priest for him.'

'Of course, sir.'

He is to be hanged.

---

[62] 'playe de terre' must mean pleas according to the law of the land, but this man does not know anything about them.

[63] 'prodhomme' has a number of meanings. It is a sad irony, in this case, that any 'gentleman' advising the accused would know how to help him lie; if he acts as a 'gentleman' on his own account the meaning will be 'as an honest man' (with predictable consequences). The translators give 'learned person' for the first and 'wise man' for the second.

[64] 'Johan' here too, until the end of the passage.

[65] 'si deu le vou fist'; the translators have omitted the phrase.

[66] Not only is God frequently invoked throughout this conversation, but also the accused is put upon peril of his soul; and he says he was tempted by the Devil. This overall tone is unlikely to be heard in a modern English court.

2) From the Statute of Winchester, 1285[67]

(The Statute begins) Pur ceo qe de jour en jour roberies, homicides, arsuns,
plus sovenerement sunt fetes qe avaunt ne soleyent ...
(Number V) Comaundé est ensement qe les hauz chemins des viles
marchaundes es autres viles marchaundes seient enlargiz, la ou
il iad bois, ou haies, ou fossez, issi qil nieit fosse, suthboys, ou
bussuns, ou lem peut tapir pur mal fere pres del chemin, de
deus centz pez de une part, et de deus centz pez de autre part,
issi qe cet estatut point ne estende as keynes, ne as gros
fusz, par qei ceo seit cler desuz. E si par defaute de seignur
qi ne vodra fosse, subois, ou bussons, en la furme avauntdite
abatre, e roberies seient fetes, si respoygne le seygnur: e sil
ieyt murdre, si seit le seignur reint a la volunte le rey. E si le
seignur ne suffist a suzbois abatre, si lui aide le pais a ceo fere.
E le rey veut qe en ses demeines terres, e boys dedenz foreste
e dehors, seient les chemins enlargiz cum avaunt est dit. E si
par cas park seit pres de haut chemin, si covendra qe le
seignur del park amenuse sun park, jeques ataunt qil ieyt la
leyse de deus centz pez pres del haut chemin, cum avaunt est
dit, ou qe il face tel mur, fosse ou haye qe meffesurs ne pussent
passer ne returner pur mal fere.

3) *The Mirror of Justices*, c. 1290, Preface[68]

[p. 1] Cum jeo maperceyvoie devers de [ceux] qe la lei deveroyent
governer par rieules de droit, aver regard a lur demeine
terriens proffiz, e as princes seignurages e amis plere, e
a seignuries e avoir amassier, e nient assentir qe les dreiz
usages fusent unqes mis en escrist, par unt poer ne lur
fuse toleit, des uns par colour de jugement prendre, les
autres exiler, ou enprisoner, ou desheriter, saunz peine
emporter, coveranz lur pechié par les excepcions de errour
e de ignoraunce, e nient ou poi pernante regard as almes
de peccheours sauver de dampnacioun par leaux jugementz,
solom ceo qe lur office demaunde,

---

[67] In *Stubbs' Charters*, ed. and tr. Stubbs (available online), pp. 463–9. The extract is so short I have
not added line numbers.

[68] ed. Whittaker, pp. 1–3. The text is edited with translation, like the others in this chapter; I have
supplied a new one for modern readers. I include or refer to editorial notes where appropriate,
and add acute accents to e where it helps the sense (as above); I have not added apostrophes or
adjusted word-divisions.

2) Because, day by day, robberies, homicides, and acts of arson are being committed more often than they used to be ...[69]

It is also commanded that the high roads between one market town and another shall be widened.[70] Wherever there are woods or hedges or ditches,[71] let there be no ditches, underbrush, or bushes where somebody might hide near the high road so as to do mischief; [this to extend] two hundred feet on the one side, and two hundred feet on the other. But the order does not include oak trees, nor any large timber, as long as it is light underneath.[72] And if through a lord's fault, who is not prepared to clear back ditches and undergrowth and bushes in the manner described, if robberies are committed then it is the lord's responsibility. And if murder is committed, then the lord shall be fined at the king's pleasure. And if a lord is unable to manage the clearing of undergrowth, then let people of the neighbourhood help him to do it. And the king wishes that in his demesne lands,[73] and woodlands within or outside of forests,[74] the roads must be widened as is said above. And if by any chance a park is near to a high road, it is important for its lord to reduce its size, so there is a width of two hundred feet beside the high road, as said above. Or he must make a wall, or ditch or hedge, so that no wrongdoer may come and go in order to do wrong.

3) As I perceived that many of those, who are supposed to administer the law by rules of law, have regard to the profits of their own earthly lands,[75] and to please princes and lords and friends, and to amass holdings and goods. They do not agree to right usages ever being put into writing, because power might be taken away from them. [This would be] for arresting some in a pretence of judgement;[76] others would be exiled, or imprisoned, or disinherited. Thus they do with impunity; they cover their sin with defences of error or ignorance,[77] thinking nothing or but little of saving the souls of sinners from damnation by means of lawful judgement, as the office of judge requires.

---

[69] There follows a list of six things to be 'actioned', as the modern saying goes. These include a curfew in walled towns, inquests to be made, and so on.

[70] It is likely that such roads are frequently used by merchants and their customers, all of whom will be carrying money and valuable goods.

[71] Naturally a ditch could be a barrier but could also be a hiding-place.

[72] 'futz'; the translation gives 'beeches' (*fagus*), and see also Larousse 'II. fou', but it seems likely that any tall tree (useful for timber so best left to grow) would qualify. 'fust' generally means wood for building and other such purposes.

[73] See *OED*, this includes a sovereign's own territory (from *dominicus*, belonging to a lord).

[74] A forest was not strictly woodland only, but included large spaces for hunting (for example); the New Forest is largely open space.

[75] 'terriens' can mean real land, not necessarily opposed to the heavenly (the author probably has both meanings in mind).

[76] 'colour de jugement'; see *French Chronicle* (the story of Rosamond, above) for this word meaning excuse or pretence.

[77] 'excepcions': the translators note that 'special pleas', or 'excuses' are meant, but that the author prefers to use a technical term (Larousse: 'mise a part, hors ligne').

                                    e eient usez en cea a
juger la gent de lur testes par abusion e examples dautres
erpanz en la lei plus qe par droites riules de seint escripture,
en arrerissement grantment de vostre [or: nostre] aprise, qi edefiez
sanz foundement e apernez a juger eins ces [ceo] qe vous vous
conoissez en jurideccion qest pié de vostre aprise, e en lei
de terre einz ceo qe en lei de persones, auxi come est de
[p. 2] ceux qe apernent arz avant les parz: — Je persecutor de
faus juges e par lur exsecucion fausement enprisoné, les
privileges le Roi e les vieuz roulles de sa tresorie, dount
amis me solacerent en mon soiour, cerchai, e le foundement e la nessaunce des usages dEngleterre donez por lei,
oveqe les gueredouns des bons jugez e la peyne des autres
i trovai, e a plus bref qe jeo savoie la necessité mis en
remenbraunce, a quoi compaignons meiderent destudier el
viel testament, el novel, el canon e en lei escrist.
[p. 3] E de nous usages fiz concordaunce a lescripture. E en
langage plus entendable en eide de vous e del comun del
poeple e en vergoigne de faus juges compilai ceste petite
summe de la lei des persones, des genz, en v. chapitres,
ceste assaver, en pecchiez countre la seinte pees, accions,
excepcions, jugemenz, abusions, qe jeo appellai Mireur a
Justices, solum ceo qe jeo trovai les vertues e les substaunces
embullées e puis le temps le Roi Arthur usez par seinz
usages accordaunce[78] as riules avantdites. E vous pri qe les
defautes voillez redrescier e aiouster solom ceo qe par verrei
garraunt enporrez estre garantiz e procurer a reprendre e
confondre les cotidienes abusions de la lei.

---

[78] Corr. accordauntz.

They have got used to dealing in such a way that they judge men out of their own heads, following the abuse and example of others who are mistaken in the law, rather than by the just rules of Holy Scripture. [This] goes seriously against our convictions,[79] that you build without foundation,[80] and undertake to judge before you have learned anything about the jurisdiction which is the basis of your knowledge. [You practise] land law before [learning] the law of persons,[81] just as those do who learn the arts before mastering the parts.[82] I, the persecutor of false judges, am falsely gaoled at their sentencing.[83] My friends, to comfort me during my prison term, brought Privileges of the King[84] and his ancient Treasury Rolls; I have searched in them, and found the foundation and birth of the customs of England given as law, together with reward for good judges and punishment of the others. As briefly as I know how, I have put the essentials on record; my companions have helped me to study in the Old Testament, in the New, and in the canon and written law.[85]

And I have made a concordance of our customs with the Scriptures, in a language more comprehensible [than Latin] so as to help you and the community of the people, and in order to shame the false judges; I have compiled this little *Summa* of the law of persons, or of the folk, in five chapters. That is to say: sins against holy peace, actions, defences, judgements, abuses; and I have called it the Mirror for Justices;[86] according to what I found of virtues and promulgated legislation ever since the time of King Arthur, used by holy custom according to the aforesaid rules.[87] And I pray you will correct my faults, and amend according to what can be guaranteed by true guarantee, and take care to correct and confound these daily abuses of the law.[88]

---

[79] A note in this line offers 'nostre' instead of 'vostre', allowing a different meaning.

[80] *sine fundamento*; see Luke 6:49 (and Matt. 7:24–7, 1 Cor. 3:10–11).

[81] The author regards his work as a treatise on 'the law of persons', which is more elementary than the law of land (editors' note).

[82] The translators note that the jingling contrast between *artes* and *partes* (you must learn the grammatical 'parts of speech' before you can write, essentially) was not uncommon.

[83] This may be a fiction, to arouse sympathy in readers (p. xxii).

[84] Perhaps in the sense of *privilegia* granted by the king — charters of immunity and the like (editors' note).

[85] I omit a long paragraph, mostly a list of Bible books from which the author finds himself able to glean legal precepts.

[86] Introduction, p. liv.

[87] 'embullées' must mean comprised in bulls or charters under seal, such as the 'privileges' referred to above (editors' note). The author will give us the virtues and substances, that is, the force and substance of charters and usages. His use of the word 'virtue' is significant in this context: he attempts to equate crime with sin throughout the book. The reference to Arthur indicates how widespread the fame of this legendary hero had become among writers and readers; this author takes it for granted that the basis of all good law comes down from him.

[88] The author does not make it very clear who is meant by 'you' in this preface (nor do we know who were his 'companions', above). It seems to include those who need correction and also those who will help with the correcting, not only of the writer's 'faults' (this is probably false modesty) but also of the faults of current law.

'En autre ovre' (Prologues)

'In other work ...': the author wishes to turn away from sinful poetry and provide something useful instead.[89]

Having looked at doctors and lawyers at work, this chapter includes prologues in which writers of another kind tell us what they are doing and why. For the prologue as a form, see *inter al.* Minnis, *Authorship*.[90] Ramey, 'The Poetics of Caxton's "Publique" ', offers insights about the construction of an audience (even though Caxton is 'selling' print); chapter 3 of Cerquiglini-Toulet, *A New History of Medieval French Literature*, tr. Preisig, in particular, is interesting on the subject of audiences. But it is wrong to say that villeins are 'unanimously rejected': villeins as potential audiences are specifically mentioned on her same page (51); see Denis (below), whose audience includes all from the greatest to the very least.

These Prologues may be compared with authorial comments elsewhere in this book, notably Wace's introduction to his work (historiography), and the final words of the nun Marie at the end of the story of Audrey (hagiography). There is a personal statement by the author of the *Maniere* (grammar, above), at the end of the treatise; Christine's opening words in her letter, and the preface to the law text *Mirror* (above), are also of interest. The prologue to *Rossignos* by John of Hoveden or Howden (below) is very short on personal detail, but he explicitly reaches out to the hearts of his readers. All such passages offer clues to what writers are trying to do, who their audience might be, and how they are going about the business of instructing and pleasing them. They stand as reminders throughout this book, to modern as well as to medieval readers, of a continuing exploration into the arts of presentation. The pieces included here are all prologues to saints' lives,[91] but each writer has a different view of the work in hand.

La Vie de seint Clement[92]

This Life survives in only one MS: Cambridge, Trinity College, R.3.46 (622), mid-thirteenth century. The writer, who is translating from Latin prose narratives, explains why he is not writing yet another learned new book but turning an old book (or books) into the vernacular so that unlettered people can understand the story. The stress is very much upon aiming one's work at readers or listeners, rather than showing off one's cleverness to other writers. Here is a comment on

---

[89] In v. 20, of the second passage below.

[90] And Spearing, *Medieval Autographies*, pp. 33–53 (in chapter 2).

[91] Besides the introduction to each edited text, more on these saints can be found in *ODS*. The purpose of this chapter is to look at the way authors think, rather than to present a piece of their work, which is why I have placed them separately from other religious material (and out of Dean's order).

[92] Dean number 517; ed. Burrows (ANTS 64–5, 66, 67). An account of Clement (pope and martyr; d. c. 100) may be found in *ODS*.

certain writers that he would vastly approve: '3e hald na wee of þe werd of witt worthe a mite, Bot he can practise & paynt & polish his wordis'.[93]

He assumes a listening audience who can probably not read for themselves, and also assumes that only the least educated will be unable to understand any French. Therefore his intended audience includes a wide range of people.

The text is copied from Burrows' edition; the passage is in vol. I (pp. 1–2), with introduction and notes in vol. III.

---

[93] *Alexander*, vv. 4555–6.

Text

Li clerc d'escole ki apris unt [122r]
Tant que aukes entendant sunt
Mult se peinent de livres faire
E de sentences en lung traire,   4
Que pur mustrer lur saveir,
Que pur los del siecle aveir.
Livres funt tut de nuvel,
Sis adubbent asez bel;   8
Bel escrivent e bel les ditent,
Mes li lai poi i profitent,
E clerc i sunt poi amendé
Ki en lettrure ne sunt fundé.   12
Li clerc meisme ki funt ces livres
Prest ne sunt ne delivres
De faire as nunlettrez aprendre
E en vulgar cumun entendre   16
Que ceo seit que il unt dit
En lur livres que unt escrit,
Kar ceo lur suffist asez
Que de autres clers seient loez,   20
E que ceo peusse estre dit:
'Bons clers est ki si escrit!'
Pur ceo que fous est tel purpens
De si despendre en nient bon sens,   24

E pur ceo que livres sunt asez
Ki bien suffisent as lettrez,
Al mien avis mult mieuz serreit
E a plus grant pru turnereit   28
Si li livre de antiquité
Ki sunt fait de verité,
E dunt l'um ad bien entendu
Que li auctur sunt bien de Deu   32
En tel language tresturné fussent
      [122v]
Que plusurs genz pru en eussent.
Ne sui pas de ces lettrez
Ki en clergie sunt fundez,   36
Nepurquant cel poi que sai
De si escrivre en purpos ai
Que clerc e lai qui l'orrunt
Bien entendre le porrunt   40
Si si vilains del tut ne seient
Que puint de rumanz apris n'aient.
Ki veut usdive eschiwir
Mette entente de cest oir   44
Que ceo que dirrai de seint
      Clement
Turner li peusse a amendement!

Translation

Those clerks studying at school, as soon as they have learned a little they are most assiduous at making books, and at drawing out maxims at length, either for showing off their knowledge or for winning the world's praise. They make brand-new books, well decorated; they write them beautifully and they recite them beautifully. But lay people don't get much out of them, and even the clerks are not much better off, unless they are well schooled in letters.[94] The clerks themselves who make these books are not ready and willing to help the unlearned to learn, or to make them understand in the vernacular what it is they've said in these books they have written. For it is enough for them to be praised by other clerks, so that it can be said of them 'What a good clerk he is, to write like this!' It is foolish to expend laudable knowledge in vain pursuits, and there are already enough books, which ought to be sufficient for educated folk. Therefore in my opinion it would be much better and more profitable if the books of old, which are written with truth, and we know for certain that the authors were good friends with God, were put into this language so that many people could profit from them. I am not among those learned men who are trained in wisdom. But nevertheless the little I know shall be written in such a way that any clerk or layman who hears it will be able to understand it, if they are not so thoroughly base that they have not learned any French.[95] Whoever wishes to avoid idleness, pay attention to this you are going to hear, so you may gain advantage from what I am going to say about Saint Clement!

---

[94] 'fundé en lettrure' means they would have to be trained in Latin (see notes to Wace's introduction, above). Otherwise they could not understand the beautiful books in Latin.

[95] 'rumanz'; the context generally makes clear whether this is the language, or something written in it. Cf. my note above (in *Maniere*) about lower classes not learning French.

La Vie seint Edmund le Rei[96]

This prologue to a saint's life contrasts with the previous one, because it is not about Latin versus French; it is interesting because of the author's comments on the sinfulness of lay literature. He is keen to be known and understood, giving his name early in the work and without undue modesty. Instead of claiming to be inadequate for the task of the present work, he insists on his own past wickedness. One suspects perhaps he is protesting too much; he is writing a saint's life in competition with the romances that are so popular these days. Instead of attacking would-be learned clerks, as the *Clement* author does, he is attacking authors and story-tellers (including himself) who put out impious texts. He is hoping to attract readers and listeners away from those wicked stories and towards morally profitable narratives about the good and the holy. The people who will, he hopes, benefit from his work are listed as kings and nobles; he says he began by making poems for courtiers (also noble). Therefore, to begin with, it is essentially the same audience he is aiming at. It is made explicit later, by a mention of 'good people', that a much wider audience is envisaged.[97] We may guess that an audience who enjoyed romances could be wooed into enjoying saints' lives, which are often very exciting and readable. The section of Prologue in which Denis discusses the fabulous verses composed by Dame Marie (and other such frippery) has been scrutinized extensively by scholars;[98] I give the rest of it, in which he tells us something of himself. As with the Nun's life of Edward, the author adds further personal information in a short chapter between the saint's life and his miracles.

Later in the text, Denis writes a brief prologue to his second book (vv. 3270–98). He reminds us what he has done: translated the life and death of Edmund. Then he tells us what he is going to do: recount the miracles God wrought through his saint. Apart from reiterating his name, he says little more about himself and his purpose, or about his audience, only remarking 'Translaté l'ay deske a la fin, E de l'engleis e del latin, Ke en franceis le poënt entendre Ly grant, ly maien et ly mendre' (vv. 3276–80). This is a reminder that his work is translated from both English and Latin, so that all can understand it: the great, the middling, and also the small.

---

[96] Denis Piramus, ed. Russell (ANTS 71); Dean 520. See also Legge p. 246, and her *Cloisters* pp. 6–12.

[97] It is possible that lay literature is envisaged as being attractive to the leisured classes, and that religious literature is by contrast aimed at all classes.

[98] Especially Short, 'Denis Piramus and the Truth of Marie's *Lais*' (2007), on p. xviii in the edition's bibliography. References within this text help to date both writers.

Text

Mult ay usé cum[e] pechere [3ra]
Ma vie en trop fole manere,
E trop ay use[e] ma vie
[E] en peché e en folie   4
Kant court hantey[e] of les curteis,
Si fesei[e] les serventeis,
Chaunceunettes, rymes, saluz
Entre les drues e les druz,   8
Mult me penay de tels vers fere
Kë assemble les puise treire
E k'ensemble fussent justez
Pur acomplir lur volentez.   12
Ceo me fist fere le Enemy,
Si me tync ore a malbaily,
Jamés ne me burderay plus.
Jeo ay noun Denis Piramus,   16
Mes jurs jolifs de ma joefnesce
S'en vunt, si trey jeo a veilesce,
Si est bien dreit ke me repente.
En autre ovre mettrai m'entente,   20
Ke mult mieldre est e plus nutable.
Dieus me aÿde espiritable,

E la grace Seint Espirit
Seit of moy e si [i] aÿt!   24
...
[3rb] Les vers que vus dirray si sunt
Des enfances de seint Edmunt,   80
E dé miracles autresi;
Unkes hom plus beals ne oÿ.
Rei, duc, princë e emperur,
Cunt[e], barun e vavasur   84
Deivent bien a ceste oevre
   entendre, [3va]
Kar bon ensample il purreit
   prendre.
Rey deit bien oÿr de autre rey
E l'ensample tenir a sey,   88
E duc de duc, e quens de cunte,
Kant la reison a bien amunte.
Les bon[e]s genz deivent amer
De oïr retreire e recunter   92
Des bons gestes e les estoyres
E retenir e[n] lur memoyres.

Translation

I have spent so much of my life as a sinner, wasting it like a madman; I have used up my life in too much sin and folly. I would haunt the court with the courtiers, making up satirical verses and little songs, rhymes and and love-debates between beloved girls and their beloved boys. I went to a lot of trouble, making these poems so as to bring them to one another; so they could be joined together in order to achieve their desires.

It was the Devil who made me do it! But now I consider myself mistreated, and I'll never make jokes again.

I am named Denis Piramus. The happy days of my youth are gone, and I creep towards old age; it's about time I repented. I shall set myself to another kind of work, which is much better and more important. May God's Holy Spirit help me,[99] and may the grace of the Holy Ghost be with me and aid my task!

The verses that I'm going to tell you are as follows: about the enfances of Saint Edmund,[100] and about his miracles too. Nobody has ever heard anything so fine! Kings and dukes, princes and emperors, earls and barons and nobles, they ought all to listen to this work of mine, for they will be able to learn from it.[101] A king ought to hear about other kings, and take the lessons to himself; a duke about dukes, an earl about earls,[102] when the sense of it is to the good. Good people ought to love hearing good deeds and histories told and retold, and keep them in their memories.[103]

---

[99] The editor notes that these 'two' persons of God are the same; fortunately there are two names for this being in English.

[100] 'enfances'; Denis is going to relate the whole life of Edmund, including the story of his childhood. Sometimes 'enfances' were written about well-known characters, after their lives and deeds had become popular, as a kind of 'prequel'.

[101] To take, and follow, a good example; *exemplum* is 'something taken out' as a specimen, or as an illustrative story (Gray, *Simple Forms*, p. 130).

[102] 'cunte' may also be translated as 'count'. The subject form, 'quens', gave way to the oblique form 'cunte' in the same way that subject 'ber' disappeared to leave 'baron' as the modern word.

[103] As with Wace's introduction to his work, Denis uses several words for the narrative ('gestes' are epic stories, 'estoyres' are story or history; also 'vers', oeuvre' ...) that he is going to tell and recount. Like Wace, he uses a pair of similar verbs, 'retreire' and 'recunter'.

La Vie des Set Dormanz[104]

'In other work', that is, in other Insular French texts, writers have a variety of prologue styles. Some are mentioned or described above.

Among romances, the Anglo-Norman *Alexander* begins with a short meditation on the evils of this life: this is why, Thomas explains, it is delightful to read about chivalry.[105] The romance of *Horn* begins with a mention of what the story is going to be about.[106] *Fouke le Fitz Waryn* begins, rather surprisingly, with one of those idyllic springtime meditations that often preface a dream-vision (such as the *Roman de la Rose*), before going on to narrate serious historical matters.[107]

Of the more homiletic or devotional genres, a few examples are: *Revelacion*, in which the writer goes pretty well straight into what Saint John saw in his vision;[108] and *Chant des Chanz*, in which the writer meditates on the love of Mary.[109] Both these are based on Bible books; other examples are the *Livre de Sibile*, which goes straight into enumerating how many sibyls there were.[110] *Le Petit Plet*, a debate by the same author (Chardri) as the *Set Dormanz*, announces a debate between an old man and a young one.[111] *Corset*, a meditation on the sacraments, begins with a short dedication to 'seignor Alain' on the part of Robert his chaplain; it then goes into a discussion of sin beginning with the story of Lot's wife.[112] None of these tells us very much about the intended audience for the work.

I choose the Prologue to the Anglo-Norman version of the Seven Sleepers story because it keeps the hagiographical theme of the texts in this chapter, and because it gives us the writer's views on various kinds of literature. The story of the Sleepers was very well known; among references in other literature, there is a charm to induce sleep that names all seven.[113] My text is taken from Merrilees' edition. See also Cartlidge's notes for Bible references; any audience, lettered or not, would have been familiar with biblical material. If church services were in Latin, priests told and retold Bible stories in their sermons (using English or French), or preached on selected passages from Old or New Testaments including what is now relegated to the Apocrypha. Chardri cleverly begins with a picture

---

[104] Dean 534. Chardri, ed. Merrilees (ANTS 35). *The Works of Chardri*, tr. Cartlidge, introduces the *Set Dormanz* on pp. 22–3; it is translated pp. 41–69 (prologue pp. 41–2).

[105] Thomas of Kent, ed. Foster and Short.

[106] [Horn] Mestre Thomas, ed. Pope. This romance is by another Thomas, not as far as I know identified with either the *Alexander* author or the Thomas (d'Angleterre) who wrote a *Tristan*. It is curious that Maries are conflated into one woman by scholars, but Thomases are not conflated into one man.

[107] ed. Hathaway *et al.*

[108] ed. Pitts.

[109] ed. Hunt.

[110] [Sibile] Philippe de Thaon, ed. Shields.

[111] Chardri, ed. Merrilees. For Chardri's work, see also Legge pp. 192–201.

[112] Rober le Chapelain, ed. Sinclair.

[113] *Shorter Treatises*, ed. Hunt, p. 223.

of British weather,[114] towards which British people are stereotypically phlegmatic, then leads us on from this into questions of cosmic significance. We would marvel, he says, if we were not so distracted by worldly things; he is going to tell us of a marvel. He contrasts 'adventure' with the 'misfortune' of the world and with the triviality of romance adventures. As do other writers, he uses a variety of words for narrating events: malaventure, aventure, cunterai, fables, mestre [s']estuide, parlerum, mettre [s']entente, escrit, dirrai ... he is interested in how to tell a story and how to get the attention of an audience.

---

[114] Compare a passage in *Alexander*: 'Ou[r] wil[l] is many ways wraiste as þe wedire skiftis ...' (v. 4751, and see note to v. 4750 on this commonplace).

Text

ICI COMENCE LA VIE DE
    SET DORMANZ

[216c]   La vertu Deu ke tutjurz
    dure
E tutjurz est certeine e pure
Ne deit pas trop estre celee,
Car quant it fet chaut u gelee,   4
Nues voler, escleir u vent,
De ceo n'unt merveille la gent,
Ne de la terre ne de la mer
Por ceo k'il sunt acustumer   8
De veer cele variance
Cum Deu le fet par sa pussance.
E neporoec mut esbaifs
I serrium, si ententifs   12
Pussum estre del penser
E Deu nus vousist itant tenser.
Ne porrum pas a chef venir
Si Deu nel vousist meintenir.   16
Ki porreit ore sanz encumbrer
Les esteiles del cel numbrer,
Ne la hautesce del firmamant
Ki tant est cler e tant resplent,   20
E la laur de tut le munde
E de la mer ke est parfunde?
Mut porreit l'en esmerviller
Ki weres en vousist parler.   24
Mes nus en pensum mut petit,
Kar aillurs avum le nostre affit
Enraciné par grant folie
En mauvesté e en tricherie.   28
Kar d'autre penser n'avum cure
For de cele malaventure
Ke en cest secle veum user.

[216d] Trop i delitum, seinnurs,   32
    muser,
Si n'avrum for hunte e dolur
Pur teu penser a chef de tur.
Cil ki de quor vout Deus amer
E retrere vout de l'amer   36
De cest mund ki tant travaille,
Mut se delitera sanz faille
Des uvraines Jesu Crist
K'unkore fet e tutjurz fist.   40
Lel serra ki par teu penser
Lerra sa grant folie ester.
Pur teus curages tenir
E le ben k'en poet avenir,   44
Une aventure vus cunterai
Dunt ja ren n'i mentirai,
D'un miracle ke fist Jesu
Ki pitus est e tutjurs[115] fu.   48
Ki Deus aime de bon curage
Or i tende, si frad ke sage.
    Ne voil pas en fables d'Ovide,
Seinnurs, mestre mun estuide,   52
Ne ja, sachez, ne parlerum
Ne de Tristram ne de Galerun;
Ne de Renard ne de Hersente
Ne voil pas mettre m'entente,   56
Mes voil de Deu e sa vertu,
Ki est pussant e tutjurz fu,
E de ses seinz, les Set Dormanz,
Ke tant furent resplendisanz   60
Devant la face Jesu Crist.
Car si cum il est escrit
Vus en dirrai la verité
[217a] De chef en chef cum ad esté.   64

---

[115] *sic.* See note to v. 1 in the edition.

Translation

The power of God that is everlasting, and is ever pure and certain, must not be concealed. For when the weather is hot, or freezing, when clouds fly,[116] or there's lightning or wind, nobody is astonished; neither at the earth nor at the ocean. This is because they are used to seeing such changes, as God performs them by his power.[117] Nevertheless we should be very surprised if we could apply our minds to conceiving it, and if God were willing to that extent to help us. We couldn't do it, unless God wished to support it. Who could now, without difficulty, count the stars of heaven, or [measure] the height of the firmament so clear and brilliant, and the breadth of the whole world, and of the sea that is so deep? If anybody wanted to speak of it at all, he might indeed marvel greatly at it.[118] But we think about it all too rarely, for our attention is elsewhere: it is so foolishly rooted in wickedness and treachery. So we don't care to think about anything else, besides this unfortunate business we see manifested in this world. Good people, we delight too much in musing upon it; but we'll have nothing but shame and suffering for such thoughts in the end. Whoever wishes heartily to love God, and who wishes to withdraw from loving this world of travail, they will certainly take the greatest delight in the works of Jesus Christ, that he has performed and performs still. It will be loyal of him to leave such folly alone by thinking like this.

So as to encourage such steadfastness, and the good that shall come of it, I'll tell you of an adventure without any word of a lie,[119] of a miracle the ever-merciful Jesus performed. Let all who love God with their whole heart pay attention to this, if you are wise.

Listen, people, I don't want to spend time studying the fables of Ovid.[120] Be sure we are not going to talk about Tristram or Galeron either.[121] I don't want to pay attention to Reynard or Hersent,[122] but to God and his power, who is mighty and ever has been. And of his saints, the Seven Sleepers, who shine so brightly before the face of Jesus Christ. For exactly as it is written I shall tell you the truth of it, the whole story of how it happened.

---

[116] The note cites p. 17 (Syntax, 9) in the Introduction.

[117] 'vertu' in v. 1, 'pussance' in v. 10. Cartlidge's notes cite Ps. 146 (147 in *AV*); he remarks on a theme of Creation exemplifying God's power in Chardri's work.

[118] I have broadly followed the editor's suggestion (notes to vv. 11–24, & 17) for this unclear passage; Cartlidge provides no note on it.

[119] 'aventure' (see note): adventures are usually the matter of romance. Chardri means to tell the story of one, using the word perhaps in opposition to 'malaventure' above, and perhaps to point up what he is going to say about romances presently.

[120] The classical author Ovid, in whose *Metamorphoses* many 'pagan' stories are recounted. His work was well known, and rewritten with moralistic Christian commentary.

[121] The Tristan romances are meant (note the English spelling of his name), and *Ille et Galeron*.

[122] Anti-hero, and victim, in the *Roman de Renart*: Reynard rapes the wolf's mate (aka Erswynde) in one of his vicious exploits. See also Cartlidge's notes for the proper names in this passage.

Religious Writings

'Mon père,' lui dis-je, 'quels sont ces gros volumes qui tiennent tout ce côté de bibliothèque?'
'Ce sont,' me dit-il, 'les interprètes de l'Ecriture.'
'Il y a un grand nombre!' lui repartis-je.[1]

Dean's sections 10 and 11 are entitled Biblical and Apocryphal respectively. Then follows Section 12, Hagiography. Finally there is a collection of Homiletic pieces, all found in her section 13.[2] For this part of the present book, it happens that the first two pieces (in the chapter immediately following here) complement each other even though one is listed by Dean as Biblical and the other as Apocryphal. The Saints' Lives naturally fall together into a group, although my passages were not chosen to illustrate the art of hagiography as such. In the final chapter, even though the *Sermon on Joshua* resembles biblical commentary, I have maintained Dean's ordering; how best to group texts generically is very much a matter of individual judgement. As discussed above, in the Introduction, the quantity of material under the general heading of Religious is enormous compared with everything of other genres that has come down to us.[3]

---

[1] Montesquieu, *Lettres Persanes*, ed. Roger, CXXXIV (p. 213 in this edition).

[2] There is not room to include anything from Dean's final group (devotional writings).

[3] However, scholars are no longer quite as anxious as hitherto, to separate sacred from secular. A text can be examined from both standpoints, removing 'the imperative to designate either register as dominant' (Gutt, 'Review: Barbara Newman, Medieval Crossover: Reading the Secular against the Sacred', pp. 327–8).

Biblical and Apocryphal

Proverbes de Salemon (chapter 7)[1]

Sanson de Nantuil wrote these Proverbs as a book of instruction, perhaps for the young Roger de Condet (aged about twelve).[2] Children's literature as we know it did not exist: children were taught from books we should now consider to be intended only for adults, or from primers when they learned Latin at school. Such books of instruction were not uncommon; this one differs from the *Apprise*, above, because that is about table-manners and not, as here, biblical exegesis. The writer does not address the child directly, except towards the end. He prefers to speak as if in the voice of Solomon. Legge offers a passage from Sanson's chapter 7 to illustrate the quality of his writing,[3] hence my choice. There is a list of vices in the Book of Proverbs (6:16–19), so Sanson's book of instruction could perhaps have been placed beside the *Deadly Sins* later in this book. A further note about the difficulty of generic grouping: Dean catalogues some Anglo-Norman proverb texts in her section 6 (entitled Proverbs); others, including this chapter, in section 10 (Biblical).

The following is number VII, corresponding to Prov. 7:1–23. I have not transcribed the Latin because it matches the text in *LV* exactly, and can readily be consulted there or in *AV*. The Litera translates the Latin (rather freely), and the Glose comments on it.

---

[1] Dean 458. Sanson de Nantuil, *Les Proverbes de Salemon*, ed. Isoz (ANTS 44, 45, 50), vol. I, pp. 143–56; notes in vol. III, pp. 110–11. A prose paraphrase of some fifty years later is *Les Paroles Salomun*, ed. Hunt.

[2] Legge (pp. 36–42) and Dean both date the work to c. 1150.

[3] vv. 4603–17, her pp. 40–41.

Text

LITERA

[34b] Ci amonestet li escriz:
'Garde mes paroles, cher fiz,
E mes comandemenz de lei
Remenbre e repun en tei.   4588
Garde ben ço que ai comandé,
Si vivras plus benü[e]ré.
Garde ma lei, kar mot le voil,
Com la purnele de ton oil.   4592
Fermement en tes deiz la lie [34c]
K'el ne te laist faire folie.
Es tables de tun queor l'escrif,
Si te garderat sain e vif.   4596
Sapïence apele seror,
Cointise amie par amor,
Ki te gard d'estrange moiller
K'el ne te puisset desvëer,   4600
E d'altrui femme ki parole
Est feinte e dolce e humle e mole.'
'Des fenestres de ma meison
Esgardai,' ço dit Salemon;   4604
'Par les chancelx gardai e vi
Les petiz que jo la choisi.
Les petiz vi, s'ei esgardé
Un damisel molt forsené.   4608
Par ces places le vi aler,
Joste un angle el vespre arester;
Lez la veie de sa meison
Alot regardant environ,   4612
El seir obscur, quant avesprout
E la nut alques s'espeisout.
Une moiller ad encontree
Ki putement ert atornee,   4616
Apareillé a almes prendre,
Solum ço que jo sai entendre.
Molt resemblot ben lecheresse,
Kar jolive ert e jangleresse.   4620
Ne poeit en maison durer

Në a nul repos arester;
Une sole hore ne se sist
K'el n'alast fors e revenist.   4624
Par ces angles alot guaitant,
Veies e places trespassant.
Un jovencel ateint e trove
K'el baiset mot, blandist e rove.   4628
Od humble vot dit: "Ami cher,
Pur salu deu sacrifier,
Hui ai jo ben mes voz renduz [34d]
Quant mis desir m'est avenuz.   4632
Encontre vos eissi pur tant
Ke de vos oi desirer grant
Ke jo vos peüsse vëeir.
Or vos ai trové, mun espeir.   4636
Ensemble aiuns hui mais delit.
De cordes ai teissud mun lit,
Tapiz depeinz ai estenduz
Ki de Egipte me sunt venuz.   4640
De mirre ai mun lit arrosé
E de canale e de aloé.
Venez! Alum nos deporter
De noz mameles enivrer,   4644
E tote nut nos delitons
Es enbraciers que coveitons,
Tant que li jorz seit esclarci,
Kar ja nulx ne nos savrat ci.   4648
Mis sire n'est pas en maisun,
Loinz est en altre regïon;
Sun sac portat e sa vitaille
Kë a pece ne li defaille.   4652
En pleine lune deit venir
A sa meisun e revertir."
Od bel parler e od blandir
Le lïet e fait enz venir.   4656
Aprés li vait d'altretel guise
Com li bos al sacrifise,
E com aignelét enveisé
Ki deit estre sacrifie;   4660

Translation

LITERA

This is what the Scripture tells us: 'Keep my words, dear son; remember and treasure up within you my commandments of the law. Keep well what I have commanded, and you will live more blessed. Keep my law, for I do wish it, as the apple of your eye. Bind it fast into your fingers, so that it will not let you do any foolishness. Write it into the tablets of your heart, and it will keep you alive and safe. Call Wisdom [your] sister, and make Understanding your lover,[4] who will guard you from the stranger so that she cannot lead you astray, and from the other woman whose talk is false and sweet, humble and soft.'

'I looked out at the windows of my house,' says Solomon, 'I looked through the lattice, and I saw the simple ones that I could perceive there. I saw the simple ones,[5] I saw a very foolish-looking young man. I saw him go around the streets, and stop by a corner in the evening. He went along towards her house, looking about him, in the dark of the evening as twilight fell and the night thickened. He met a woman who was dressed like a harlot, all ready to steal souls as far as I could tell! She looked every inch the lustful lady, being gay and flirtatious. She could not keep indoors, nor sit still to rest; never an hour could she stay, without going out and coming in again. She would go prowling round the corners, crossing the squares and the streets. She found a young man, and caught him; she fawned on him and cajoled him, making her command. Meekly she said,

' "Dear friend, I have just performed my devotions, sacrificing to the gods for my own good;[6] now my desires have come upon me! I have come out to find you, because I yearn for you so much, I wanted to see you. Now I have got you, or so I should hope. From now on we can have such fun together! I have wreathed my bed with ribbons, and I have spread decorated tapestries that came to me from Egypt. I have sprinkled the bed with myrrh, and with cinnamon and aloes. Come along! Let's go and enjoy ourselves, and get drunk at each other's breasts! We can take our pleasure all night, in the embraces we have longed for, until the daylight comes; nobody will know we are there. My lord is not at home: he has gone off to another part of the country, taking his bag, and his provisions which he won't run short of for a long time. He'll be back only at the full moon, when he'll return."[7]

'With sweet speech and coaxing she binds him and brings him in. He goes after her just like an ox to the sacrifice, or like the happy little lamb that is to be slaughtered.

---

[4] *LV amicam tuam*; *AV* 'thy kinswoman'. Sanson uses the vocabulary of medieval love: 'amie par amor'. In *Edouard*, the Nun of Barking uses the term 'fin' amur' for the love of God; this predates its use for earthly or 'courtly' love.

[5] The little people, 'petiz'; both Legge and *AV* have 'simple' here.

[6] This mention of sacrifice is ominous, given the image of sacrificial victims below.

[7] Here is an example of the husband who has gone away, perhaps on a pilgrimage, leaving a clear field for the sinful wife (cf. the Fabliaux, above).

Simple est e fol, ne set u vait,
Ne quë a lïens seit atrait,
Tresk'ele ait sun gisier perciét
De sun dart dun el l'at fichiét.   4664
Si com oisel ki est hastis
D'aler al laçon u est pris,
Ne set ne ne veit le peril
De s'alme qu'il met en peril.'   4668

GLOSE

[35a]   Ci ne nos esteot pas noter
Ço k'a sun filz suet regreter:
Si com dis ainz sovent regrete
Ço dunt velt plus qu'il   4672
    s'entremete.
El regreter k'il fait sovent
Velt que guard sun comandement,
Cure en ait de altretel baillie
Com de sun oil que pas n'oblie.   4676
Ne pot dreit vëeir ne choisir
Senz sun comandement tenir.
    Sapïence apelet seror:
Çö est d'eclesïal amor,   4680
E de fraternel alïance,
D'aveir en fei une creance
Kil guard de sieute d'eresie:
Ço est la moiller dun le chastie,   4684
Ki d'eclesïal casteé
S'estranget en male ordeé,
E de gesir en tel ordure
Se delitet a desmesure;   4688
Od dolce parole qu'el feint
Quiert k'a sun soil altres ameint.
    Mais Deus esguardet de toz
        l'estre,
E par cancelx e par fenestre.   4692
La fenestre de sa maison
Est l'ordre des clers que veüm.
Del cancel est li cielx notez

Dun il nos at toz esgardez.   4696
    Si com li Salmistre suelt dire:
'Del cel regardet nostre Sire.'
Les fiz des omes ad veüz
E com il se sunt contenuz.   4700
D'ileoc esgarde toz noz estres,
E des deciples e des meistres;
D'ileoc esguardet feble e fort,
Lor guarisun e lor confort,   4704
Les justes e les pechëors [35b]
Ki grant mester unt de socors.
    Un jovencel i veit desvé,
Avoiltre e senz estableté.   4708
Desvez est cil ki est en rage
E estrangez de sun corage.
Cil est de corage estrangié
Ki d'eresie est aprismé,   4712
E avoiltre est quant seinte iglise —
La bele espose qu'aveit prise —
Ad pur la siute d'eresie
Folement laissié e guerpie.   4716
    Par places le vit trespasser:
Ço est par errors del secle aler
Ki a mort meinent lor errant
Tresque vait s'espose fuiant.   4720
    Quant joste l'angle s'arestut,
De tenir fei lors se remut.
Ki en angle vait arestant,
Dejoste veie e regardant,   4724
Senblant mostret de repentir
Ke n'ait suen del chemin tenir,
Kar de veie de verité
S'est a malices encliné.   4728
    Ço qu'alout el vespre a seriz
Lez la meison la meretriz,
Quant li jor esteit avespré
E la nut ert en obscurté,   4732
Notet que peché vil e ort
Hastet celui kil fait a mort.

He is innocent and foolish, with no idea of where he is going, nor that he is being led into a snare, until his throat is pierced by the blade she sticks him with. Just as the bird is hasty to go towards the wire that will capture it, he neither knows nor sees the peril that endangers his soul.'[8]

GLOSE

There is no need for us to point out that he often admonishes his son; as I said before, he often repeats what he most wishes him to be concerned with.[9] The plea he so often makes is for him to keep his commandment; he should be concerned with it in the same way, and not forgetful of it, as if it were his own eye. He cannot see or perceive correctly unless he keeps his [father's] commandment.

He calls Wisdom [his] sister,[10] and that is churchly love and brotherly togetherness, to trust in faith to protect him from the following of heresy. That is the woman through whom he is chastised, who estranges herself from religious chastity by her horrible filth, and who delights outrageously in lying in such filth; she puts on a sweet voice in order to lead others into her pigsty![11]

But God watches over the existence of all, through the lattice and through the window. The window of his dwelling, that is the clerical orders as we know. The lattice, that means the heavens, from which he watches us all.

As the Psalmist says: *The Lord looked down from heaven.*[12] He saw the sons of men, and how they conducted themselves. From there he can see all our doings, of the disciples and of the masters. From there he watches the weak and the strong, their healing and their comfort; and the just, and the sinners who have such great need of help.

He sees a mad young man, adulterer, unstable. A madman is one who is raving, and stranger to his own heart. And if he is stranger to his own heart he is making friends with heresy. He is an adulterer, because he is mad enough to leave and abandon Holy Church — the lovely wife he had taken — so as to follow heresy.

He sees him wandering the city squares; that is, he is erring in the ways of the world, which lead their wanderers to death as they flee away from their wife. When he stops by the corner, that is when he leaves hold of his faith. Whoever goes to loiter at corners, looking about by the roadway, seems to be showing repentance without holding to his own path; for he has turned from the path of truth towards wickedness. That he was going stealthily[13] in the evening towards the house of the bawd, when the daylight was gloaming and the night was dark, means that vile and dirty sin hastens him who commits it towards death.

---

[8] Isoz notes the rhyme is suspect; a suggested reading is 'De s'alme quil met en eissil' (of his soul, that he puts into exile). It will be seen how far this *litera* differs from the text of the Old Testatment.

[9] Isoz notes that 'regreter' is used to mean 'beseech, call upon' (her note to v. 2999); her glossary gives 'admonish' for this line.

[10] Isoz notes that 'sa' is missing both here and at v. 4597 above.

[11] Isoz notes that 'soil' means both 'filth' and 'threshold'.

[12] Ps. 14:2 in *AV* (13:2 in *LV*).

[13] Isoz notes other possible meanings for 'a seriz'.

En tenebres se deit haster,
Kar a tenebres deit aler.   4736
Nuit de pechiét l'at esciwé
Quant de fei guerpist la clarté.
    Encontre lui vent la moiller
Ki li fait iglise avoiltrier.   4740
En sa manere est atornee
De enginz, e d'arz enloçunee,
Ki a putain sunt covenable [35c]
E dun el seit plus decevable;   4744
Apareillé a almes prendre
En quanqu'el lor pot feire
    entendre,
Kar li erites toz celz enble
K'a sa siute aünet e assemble.   4748
    Gangleresse est a conturber
Paiz de seinte iglise e meller.
    Vaie e jolive, e toz tens quiert
Com hom ki ja saols nen ert.   4752
Eglise queort a conturber
E genz a sa siute torner.
En pais une hore estre ne pot,
Kar feus de coveité l'esmuet.   4756
En maisun ore ne pot estre,
Tost cort a l'us u a fenestre;
Poroffret sei e sun servise
Pur vendre sa marcheandise.   4760
Sa meisun celx nos senefie
K'ele ad atraiz a eresie.
Cels ne li sunt pas soffeisanz
Se novels n'esteit decevanz.   4764
    Tost est defors, tost est es
    places,
Kar nient traçables sunt ses traces.
Les delitos es places prent,
Les paiens defors ensement.   4768
Es places solent cil hanter
Ki delit aiment seculer
De lecheries de moiller,
D'oïr chanter e fableier.   4772
Celx atrait a sei eresie
Par les deliz de puterie.

Par plusors vices le[s] sumont
Tant ke en lor siute de tot sunt.   4776
    Del defors not paiene gent
Ki lei n'unt ne doctrinement,
E telx pot l'um tost engingner
E a lor siute acompaigner.   4780
Fors sunt de lei de seinte iglise [35d]
D'enseignement e de justise.
Joste les angles sunt guaitant,
Lor sogez a mal enortant.   4784
    Le jovencel que la saisist
Est avoiltre, que tant blandist
Od le crimene de sun delit
Ke la l'ameine u el l'ocit.   4788
    Baisier enthoschet lechëor
E entalente de folor.
Tant sevent blandir li erite
Ke lor temptatïon delite.   4792
Debonairetéd vunt mostrant,
E de tant sunt plus soduiant.
    De ço que dit al lechëor
Ke sacrifier dut cel jor: 4796
Li erite unt costume e us
Ke de ço k'il desirent plus.
Ensorquetot de tot lor faiz,
Coment qu'il seient vilz e laiz,   4800
Pur lor salud funt sacrifise
Male de crimenes e de vice.
Sacrefice est al lor quider,
Purquant nel deit l'um si nomer,   4804
Kar ren n'i est sacrifiét,
Mais en pechez tot ordei[é]t.
De lor immolatïon dit
Li prophetes en sun escrit   4808
Ke Deus en s'alme la haeit
Ne ja lor dons ne recevreit.
Pur ço li dit la meretriz,
Solunc l'usage de ses diz,   4812
Ke ses voz out renduz el jor
Quant sun desirét lechëor
Poeit vëeir e enbracer
E d'avoiltre delitier.   4816

He must hasten in the shadows, for into shadows he must go. When he abandoned the light of faith, the night of sin blinded him.

The woman came to meet him, who made him unfaithful to the Church. She is apparelled from head to foot with tricks, and with studied arts proper to a harlot, that make her all the more deceitful. She is all set to entrap souls, those whose attention she can grab, for the heretic steals away all those whom she gathers and collects in her train.

She is gossipy, so as to disturb and confuse the peace of Holy Church.

She is flighty and frivolous, constantly on the prowl like one who can never have enough. She wants to disturb the church and make people follow her. She cannot sit quietly for an hour, because she burns with covetous longing. She cannot stay an hour in her house, but is for ever running to the door or the window. She offers herself and her favours, to sell her services. By her house, we understand that means those she has drawn into heresy. These are not enough for her, unless she can be ensnaring new recruits.[14]

Quickly outside, quickly into the streets! Her footprints are invisible; she catches lechers in the city's squares, and pagans out there too.[15]

Those places are frequented by people who love worldly delights, and frolicking with ladies, and hearing songs and fabulous stories. She reels these in, to her heresy, through their appetite for whoremongering. She incites them via their many vices, until they have totally become their followers.

Outsiders are called pagans, because they have no law or learning; it is easy for her to entrap such as these are, and add them to the entourage [of vices]. They are outside the law of Holy Church, and outside all teaching and justice. They lie in wait at the street-corners, exhorting their victims to evil.

The young man she snatched there is an adulterer, whom she so coaxed by criminal pleasures that at last she had him where she could kill him.

Kissing intoxicates the lecher, and sucks him into evil deeds. The heretics are so clever at flattery that their very temptations are a delight. They go about looking debonair, and thus they are even more seductive.

As for what she said to the lecherous young man, that she had to sacrifice that day — the heretics, in custom and practice, have anything they want. Especially for all their deeds, however vile and ugly they are, they make an evil sacrifice [involving] both criminal acts and vices.[16] Sacrifice is what they believe in, but nobody must call it so, for they do not sacrifice anything there! They just dirty everything with sin! Of their immolation, the Prophet says in his book that God hates them in his soul and will never accept their offerings.[17] That is why the harlot, following her usual words, told him she had done her vows for the day, when she could see and embrace her desired lover and pleasure herself with adultery.

---

[14] Isoz offers this rendering of the line (citing a passage from Bede).

[15] Bede is cited again in the editor's note.

[16] Isoz notes this line as slightly problematic; I have followed the suggested meaning.

[17] Is. 1:11–14.

Sacrefise en deveit doner
Quant lieu aveit de mal ovrer.
De l'achaison qu'ele a mostree [36a]
Pur quei contre lui ert alee: 4820
Dit que veier l'out desiré,
Pur çol quist tant qu'il l'out trové.
Ci volt noter e esclarier
Les treis maner[e]s de pecher: 4824
En pensé, en dit e en fait,
Ki alme a dampnatïon trait.

   De cordes ad teissu sun lit:
Repos par ço not e delit, 4828
Kar plus est molx e aësiéd
Ke lit de fust apareillét.
Des cordes pus senefïer
Ke om les fait pur traire e lier, 4832
E cil ki a erite assent,
Lïez est e traiz a torment.

   De tapiz peinz l'at portendu,
Ki d'Egipte li sunt venu: 4836
De tapiz peinz pöons noter
Lor grant facunde de parler.
Les arz dun il unt escïence
Lor est ornement d'eloquence. 4840
Dialetiche unt el gangler
E es raisuns d'argumenter.
Des arz orgoillos sunt e fiers
Dunt almes sevent engingner. 4844

   Des Ehnuchis unt lor sens pris
E en lor siute se sunt mis.
Ehnuchi sunt d'Ehsna nomé
Dunt lor non est pris e formé. 4848

Un mont suelt l'um Ehsna
   clamer
Ki toz tens suelt ardre e fumer,
Del feu d'enfern est sopirail
Ki jameis n'avrat definail. 4852
D'ileoc sunt nomé Ehnuchi
Ki entosché sunt e bruï
De l'enfernal feu d'averice,
Ki començail est de tot vice. 4856
Li erite dunt nos parlons [36b]
Tenent la siute a ces felons;
E comunelment lor merites
Partirunt putains e erites. 4860
Des tapiz not — ki bel sunt peint
—
Ke en lor parler sunt humle e
   feint.

   D'Egipte sunt; çö est boisdie
Kë en latin nos senefie. 4864

   Canele, mirre e aloé
Ad a odor sun lit poldré:
Ço est qu'il prametent pareïs
A celx que de lor siute unt pris; 4868
Celestïen odor prametent
Se de lor siute s'entremetent.
Od tel odor de traïson
K'il donent en abusïon 4872
Quant d'eresie traiter
Se quident si seintefier,
Quident que seit ben e justice
Tot lor delit e [lor] malice. 4876

She had to do sacrifice when she saw the opportunity to do evil. As for the reason she gave him, why she had come to meet him: she said she wanted to see him, and so had sought him until he found her.

Here we note and explain the three ways to sin: in thought, in word, and in deed. These lead to damnation.

Her bed was woven with ribbons; these mean repose and luxury, because such a bed is softer and easier than a bed made of wood. They signify cords that are made to bind and to draw, and those who assent to heresy are bound and dragged into torment.

She adorned it with pictured tapestries that came to her from Egypt. We may observe the great speaking power of these pictures.[18] The arts they demonstrate are their ornaments of eloquence. There is Dialectic in their gossip, and in their excuses for argument. These Arts are proud and arrogant, and clever at entrapping souls.[19]

They get their ideas from the pagans, and follow in their entourage. These pagans, or Ethnicans, are named from Etna; they are called that because of it.[20]

There is a mountain commonly called Etna, that used to burn and smoke ceaselessly; it was a vent for the fires of Hell that shall never be quenched. From it the Ethnicans are named, who are scorched and poisoned with the hellish flames of avarice. This is the root of all the vices.[21] The heretics we are speaking of are among the followers of these villains; their rewards will be shared among heretics and whores.

The tapestries, that are so beautifully painted, signify those whose speech is so humble and feigned. They are from Egypt, which means deception as we know from Latin.[22]

She has sprinkled her bed with cinnamon, myrrh, and aloes to perfume it: this means they promise Paradise to those who join their following. They promise celestial fragrance to them, if they undertake to join them. With such odours of treason,[23] that they improperly exploit and give out when they expound heresy, they reckon to sanctify themselves; they think all their wickedness and debauchery is just and right.

---

[18] The vivid pictures on Amphiarax' chariot (above) seem to leap off their painted surface, to move and shout and wage war. The chariot also had depictions of the Liberal Arts, here shown to be sinful. Note the slippage of the subject 'they' from the tapestries to the pictures to the arts to the pagans.

[19] These figures act like personifications.

[20] The editor notes this unusual 'derivation' (perhaps a garble of Latin *ethnicis*). Whatever source Sanson used for the Ehnucis, the connection between Etna and Hell was in fact well known, chiefly from Isidore of Seville's famous 'etymologies' (see, first, *OCL*).

[21] I Tim. 6:10.

[22] Isoz is uncertain whether Sanson is indicating an etymology or an association of ideas (for example, Is. 36:6), that Egyptians are untrustworthy.

[23] Isoz offers variant readings: 'around such people there is the stench of treachery'.

Come së od l'apostle Dé
Peüssent dire en verité
Ke de Crist fussent bon odor,
Mais il en sofferunt püor.   4880
   Si sunt coverz lor orz pechez
Com est li femiers ennegiez:
Defors unt bele coverture
E dedenz püor e ordure.   4884
   A tel coverte tricherie
M'est vis que la putain l'envie
Ki sun cors voldreit saziër
De la fain de sun desirer,   4888
De sa lecherie achever
Dunt molt se desire enivrer.
Par l'atrait des vices menors
Le puesset traire as nouaillors.   4892
   Si com li bevere ad delit
De beivre petit e petit
Tressi que tant s'est enivré [36c]
Ke de sun cors n'ad pöesté,   4896
Dunc est del tot pris e lacié
E aresté el vil peché,
Dunc ad acompli l'enbracier
Dun dist qu'ele aveit desirer,   4900
Kar a sa siute l'ad torné
Dunt en enfer serrad dampné,
E parmeindrat en itel guise
Tressi quë al jor de juïse: 4904
Jorz ert de pardurableté
Quant li bon serrunt enoré,
Li mal en tenebres obscures,
En aspres peines e en dures.   4908
   De l'home ki n'est en maisun
Solunc expositors noton —
Dunt la lecheresse ad parlé,
Ki longe veie esteit alé —   4912
Enmanüel Deu, Jesum Crist
De ki eresie banist,
Pur tolir nostre sacrament,

Kë il n'est pas corporelment   4916
En seinte eglise consacré
Solunc fei de cristïenté,
Ne de mort n'est resuscitez,
Ne sus el cel nen est montez,   4920
Ne d'espirit nes vint doctriner
A hues seinte glise garder:
Ço est la meisun que Crist laissat,
Ki cele longe veie alat.   4924
Del sac k'il portat entendum
Glorie de resurrectïun,
E quë il ad od sei porté
Enor de nient mortalité   4928
Dunt la cort del ciel fud goiose
E est de toz biens plentëose.
   En pleine lune deit venir
A sa maisun revertir.   4932
Pleine lune ert dunc veirement
   [36d]
Quant Deus vendrat al jugement,
Kar consummez serat cist mont
E les overaignes ki i sunt.   4936
   Cist mond n'est hore plus
     estable
Ke lune [ki] est defiesable.
Ne duret mie longement
Corot në esl[ë]ecement;   4940
Novelers est, kar sovent triche,
Tost i est l'um e povre e riche.
   De lune pleine renotum
Ke dunc serrat perfectïon   4944
Des esliz ki en Dampnedé
Avrunt lor parfite clarté,
Ki en obscurté sunt mundaine,
Si com est lune ki est pleine.   4948
   Veiet iglise — la moiller —
Quant sun espos deit repairer
Ne l'ait eresie avoltriee,
Kar ele en serreit corocié,   4952

It is as if, with the Apostle of God, they could say truly that they are a sweet savour of Christ,[24] but they will endure the stench of [their wickedness and debauchery]! They have covered up their filthy sins like a dungheap under snow: outside it is a beautiful covering, but inside it is stink and muck.

It seems to me that the harlot wanted just such covert treachery when her body wanted to slake the hunger of its desire, to satisfy the lechery with which she so badly wanted to intoxicate herself. By the temptation of smaller vices, she could drag him on to the worst of them.

It is like one who loves drinking, and goes from small sip to small sip until he is so drunk he has no control over his body, and is therefore taken and entangled and captured in vile sin.

Then she has carried out the embrace she said she desired so much: she has enticed him into her following, for which he will be damned in Hell. He will stay there, just like that, for ever until the Day of Judgement! That is the day of eternity, when the good shall be honoured. The wicked shall be [thrown] into darkest shadows, into harsh and bitter pains.

We note what the authorities say about the man who is not at home, the one the harlot talked about, who had gone on a long journey. Lord Emmanuel! Jesus Christ! Heresy proclaims, to take away our sacrament, that he is not consecrated bodily by Holy Church according to the Christian faith.[25] And that he did not rise from the dead, and did not ascend into Heaven, and his Spirit did not come to teach for the benefit of Holy Church.[26] [Holy Church] is the house Christ left, when he went on such a long journey. By the sack he carried, we understand the glory of resurrection; that he carried it with him, means the honour of immortality. The court of Heaven rejoices at it, and it is filled with all good things!

At the full moon he will return and come back to his house. The full moon is, indeed, when God will come in judgement. This world and all its works shall be consumed.

This world is never stable for an hour, like the moon when it is on the wane.[27] Neither anger nor joy can survive long; it is fickle, often deceptive, for a man may be suddenly poor and rich.

But let us explain that the full moon is when the chosen ones achieve their perfection, their perfect light in the Lord God, who had been in earthly darkness. This is like the moon when it is full.

Let the Church, that is the woman, see when her husband is due to come home; that she has not defiled herself with heresy. For this would make her anguished,

---

[24] II Cor. 2:15. This passage is cited in *La Vie seint Edmund le Rei*, ed. Russell, in a description of the saintly man (vv. 1857–66).

[25] See above, where the woman says her lord is away. This passage refers to the Church's tenet that the consecrated bread of the Mass is really, and bodily, God.

[26] Resurrection, Ascension, and Pentecost.

[27] Isoz notes that Sanson may have made up the word 'defiesable', perhaps conflating 'vanish' and 'faint'.

Ki de parler bel e mentir
La corrunt e fait mesbaillir;
Par bel semblant, par bel parler,
La feit de sun espos sevrer.   4956
     Li fols quidet que veir li die,
La putain sielt a eresie;
Ne plus que bof raisun n'entent,
Ainz vait a sa mort simplement;   4960
E com aignel mesconoissant,
Ki n'est saives ne entendant,
Ne set que l'um le deit lïer,
Trencher le col e escorcier.   4964
Sovent traient erite a mort
Les fiz d'iglese par tel sort,
Ki hastent lor perditïon
Come li oisel al laçon   4968
U il est pris e retenuz
E cil avoiltrez e perduz.[28]
LITERA
[37a]   Por ço dit enprés Salemon:
'Fiz, or m'oies e mun sermon;   4972
A mes paroles que jo di
Entent, filz, nes metre en obli,
Kë es veies de cel putage
Ne seit giens forstrait tun corage,   4976
Ne que tu deceüz ne seies
Par ses senters ne par ses veies.
Kar molt plaiez ad degetez
E tres forz ocis e tüez.   4980
Sa maisun sunt veies de bas;
Kis vait trebuche eneslepas,
Perçanz es entrailles de mort
Senz merci e senz nul confort.'   4984
GLOSE
     Ci voil vëeir e denoter
S'il i ad que determiner.

Sun fiz amoneste e aprent,
Si com vos ai noté sovent.   4988
Pur ço covent que melz retienge
Sun sens e ke plus l'en sovenge,
Ke par mals diz soduit ne seit
Del ben aprendre qu'amer deit.   4992
Par coveitise ad molt navrez
Ke pus ad a enfer getez.
     Tres forz ad soduiz e matez
E des tres saives des edez,   4996
Dunt uns fud cist reis Salemon,
Ki l'escrit fist dunt nos parlom,
     Par enging de moiller refud
Samson fortisme deceüd; [37b]   5000
E li tres saives reis David
En fud deceüz e traït;
E Origenes d'eresie:
Ço est la noualdre puterie.   5004
Navré en furent e ocis
E es peines d'enfern assis.
Asez est ocis ki la vait,
Mais alquant d'elx en sunt sotrait   5008
Ke le redemptïon de Dé
Ad par sa mort d'ileoc osté.
     De la maisun as bas degrez,
A la moiller dunt vos oëz,   5012
Denotuns d'enfer les tormenz
U plors ert e escroiz de denz
Kar molt est basse e tenebrose
E de toz tormenz angoisose.   5016
     Perçant es entrailles de mort,
Senz pïetéd e senz confort.
Ileoc prendrunt une merite
Ensemble e avoiltre e erite.   5020
Asez en sunt garni sovent:
N'i ad mais os chastïement.

---

[28] I omit the Litera in Latin, as above, which corresponds to Prov. 7:24–7 (in *LV*); f. 37a begins here.

whose fair speech and lies had corrupted her and put her in a sorry plight. A fine external show, and lies, that is what makes a breach with her husband.

The fool believed she spoke truly, and followed the harlot into heresy, understanding reason no more than the ox that goes innocently to its death. And like the unsuspecting lamb, which is neither wise nor intelligent, and does not realise they are going to tie it, and cut its throat, and skin it. The heretics often drag the sons of the Church to death the same way; they hurry towards their doom as the bird hurries towards the snare in which it is caught and held, and it is defiled and utterly lost.

[LITERA] This is why Solomon says, next, 'Son, now listen to what I say. Hear the words I'm speaking, my son, and don't forget them! So, don't ever let your heart be dragged into the way of such harlotry, and do not be deceived into her paths and byways. For she has destroyed many wounded, and she has killed and slaughtered the strong. Base are the ways to her house, and those who go there stumble immediately; they are pierced to the bowels by Death, without mercy and without any solace.'

[GLOSE] Here I want to see and comment, about what can be decided. He warns and teaches his son, as I have often shown you. Therefore it is important to retain his meaning properly, and to remember it, so that you will not be seduced by evil words and you will learn what you must love. Covetousness has wounded many who are then thrown into Hell. The strongest have been seduced and undone, and the wisest among the ancients. One of them was this King Solomon,[29] who made the book we are talking about; then the powerful Samson was deceived by the wiles of a woman.[30] The wise King David was deceived and betrayed by them; and Origen was deceived into heresy, which is the worst of filth. These men were wounded and killed, then assigned to the pains of Hell. Those who end up there are thoroughly dead, but some of them were taken out when God's redemption brought them away by his death.[31]

That house of infernal steps, belonging to the woman you have heard about; by this we mean the Hell of torments where there is weeping and gnashing of teeth,[32] for it is very deep and dark, and filled with every kind of agonizing torment. Without pity or comfort, Death having pierced them to the very bowels, they there take what they deserve together with adulterers and heretics. Many are often saved, for there is no further reason to chastise them.[33]

---

[29] Isoz gives a passage from Bede with which to compare these lines.

[30] A typically misogynistic cliché; a list of famous men destroyed by the wickedness of women (see, for example, the 'Wife of Bath's Prologue', in Chaucer, *Riverside*, ed. Benson).

[31] This is a reference to the Harrowing of Hell: an apocryphal story that Christ went into Hell, between his death and his resurrection, and brought out some of the souls who had been placed there before the coming of the New Testament (people in the Old Testament, however virtuous, could not believe in a Christianity that did not yet exist).

[32] Matt. 8:12.

[33] The next chapter begins: *Doth not wisdom cry, and understanding put forth her voice?* (Prov. 8:1). This is glossed as the 'espositor' attempting to make his voice heard.

The Creation, by Herman de Valenciennes[34]

The entry in Dean's catalogue does not list this piece independently, although it mentions de Mandach's edition of a part of the Geneva manuscript (formerly Phillipps 16378). The editor calls it an unpublished Mystery Play.[35] If indeed it is one, it would rank with Dean's short list of Anglo-Norman Drama (numbers 716–19, in her Homiletic section). *Creation* is not a very exact title,[36] since the piece is closer in its subject-matter to the *Jeu D'Adam.* Herman wrote twenty-two mystery plays, according to de Mandach (p. 251). His introduction gives further description of Herman's work: this is a 'chameleon' text that defies generic classification; the likelihood of stage performance cannot be ruled out,[37] and the dramatic character of Herman's *Bible* as a whole has often been pointed out. But there is little in the way of address to the audience. Our story is found in the first four chapters of Genesis, although the three angels are not named in that book: these appear *passim* elsewhere in the Bible. Other differences from the Genesis text are that the rebellion of the angels is added, not occurring in the Bible until the Book of Revelation;[38] further, God does not make coats of skins for Adam and Eve in Herman's version.

As is often the case in medieval French, verb-tenses are inconsistent compared with those in modern languages. Although it is impossible to follow the changes exactly in translation, I generally aim to reflect at least some of them so as to convey a feeling of the original. Of course if the text were actually set as a play, many of the tenses would be present-forms rather than past-forms. However, the use of 'tu' and 'vous' is more consistent than in many texts: God says 'tu' to Adam (unless talking to both of them), and he says 'vous' to God. The use of 'tu' is more likely between both speakers of differing rank in much though not all written speech. Adam and Eve say 'tu' to each other throughout, unusually; it is almost (not quite) a rule that close friends and lovers use 'vous' to one another.

For the manuscripts,[39] see de Mandach's introduction (no folio numbers are given in the edition).

---

[34] 'The Creation' (in ANTS *Essays*, OPS 2); Dean number 485 (section 11, entitled Apocryphal).

[35] The edited text is published in a collection of essays, entitled exactly as the work appears in my bibliography (and short-form running headings). Therefore, although listed bibliographically in this book by its title for ease of reference, it is not set out in the usual 'author-title' sequence.

[36] Dean lists it among 'Apocryphal', which is incorrect for this piece, but the larger *Roman de Dieu* that includes it contains much that is apocryphal.

[37] Narrative passages would be recited by a 'lector'; performances envisaged for this text would be open to a comparatively unrestricted public, young and old, lettered and unlettered.

[38] Rev. 12:7–9.

[39] Base MS formerly Cheltenham Phillipps 16378, supplemented from a twin copy in Pembroke College Cambridge.

Text

1
Cumencement de sapience, ce est la tumor de Deu,
Qui fist e ciel e terre, eve e fou, en tens breu;
Angles fist e archangles, mult les mist en bel leu.
Nus truvum en escrit de latin e de ebreu:
Partie en tresbuchast en leu malvei e greu,   5
Quant il voldrent regner, tolir li regne a Deu.

2
[L]'autre part qui remeist d'orgoil ne sout nent.
Ele remist en cel, si sert Deu bonement;
Al sun servise fere lui estait enpresent.
Nuns lur duna li Sire, par sun grant escient,   10
Michaël, Gabriël, Raphaël, si l'entent.
Provost fist Michaël sur cel asemblement.
Tuit sunt obeissant al son cumandement.

3
Quant furent trebuchez en enfer les cheitis,
Perdirent la clarté, si sunt tuit ennercis.   15
Mult unt malveis ostel, n'est pas bon lur deliz.
La se sunt herbergez; iloc meindrunt tut dis.
Apros nostre Sire sur tere paraïs
Arbres i ad plantez, qui tut tens sunt fluriz;
Idunc furmat Adam, iloc denz l'ad mis.   20

4
Quant de terre l'out fait, idunc si l'esgarda.
Fait l'out en sa figure, grant sens i purpensa.
Volt qu'il eit cumpanie, e il la li duna.
Une coste del lez del cors li desevra.
Adan s'i ert endormiz, pas ne s'en esveilla.   25
Dementers qu'il dormist, e Deus Evam furma.

5
Dunc s'esveilla Adam quant out asez dormit.
Deus l'at araisunet e mult bel li ad dit:
'Adam, ore as cumpanie, e as mult grant delit.
Tu feras mun cumand senz nul cuntredit.   30
Paraïs te cumand!' Adam li respundit:
'Volenters, le men Sire, trestut a vostre dit!'

Translation

The fear of God is the beginning of wisdom ...[40]

... God, who made heaven and earth, water and fire, in a short time. He made angels and archangels, and set them in a beautiful place. We find it written, in books of Latin and Hebrew, how some of them tumbled down into an ugly unhappy place, because they wished to reign, and to take the reign from God.

The others who are left know nothing of such pride; they stay in heaven, serving God faithfully. They were prompt in his service.[41] God gave them names, in his wisdom: Michael, Gabriel, and Raphael; this was his intention. He made Michael their high provost, and they are all obedient to his commands.

When the wicked ones had fallen into Hell, they lost their brightness and became all blackened. They have bad lodging there, and their delights are not delightful! That is where they are given to live, and will be for ever. After that, Our Lord planted trees in the place of Paradise, that were ever in flower. Next, he made Adam, and put him in it.

Having made him of earth, he looked at him. He had made him in his own image, which he thought was a wise decision. He wants him to have company, and so he gives it him: he took a rib out of the side of his body. Adam was asleep, and did not wake; while he was sleeping God made Eve.

When Adam had finished his sleep, he woke up. God addressed him, saying kindly 'Adam, now you've got a companion, and will have great delight! You must obey my commands without any argument. I commend Paradise to you!'

Adam replied 'With pleasure, my Lord! Anything you say!'

---

[40] Cf. Job 28:28; this is a common sentiment in religious writing.

[41] The verbs in this passage are singular, because their subject is 'one part' and 'the other part' of the host of angels.

6

'Adam, od ta cumpainne, paraïs garderas.
Del fruit de ces tuz arbres, si tei plest, mangeras,
Fors sul cest pumer; de cest ne gusteras!   35
Si tu bien le [me] gardes, mut grant pru i avras;
Si en manjües d'une, la mort en recevras.
Eva, ne l'entenz tu?' — 'Sire, nel tienc en gas.'
'Issi le te cumand sur la joie que tu as!'

7

Dunc s'en vet li Sauveres, n'i vot plus demurer,   40
Lasus en [sun] haut ciel ses angles visiter.
Li dïables d'enfern ne se volt ublïer:
De mut grant felunie se prist a purpenser.
'Cil hom ki [la] fait est, nus vot deseriter!
Si puis a lui venir e la dedenz entrer,   45
De cel fruit devehed lur ferai jo guster.'

8

Li culverd s'en issit de cel enfern pudlent;
Musçat se en paraïs, suz l'erbe cum serpent.
Al pumier est venuz ki ert mis en defens.
Tut entur s'avirunot, aguaitat en tuz sens   50
Que Adam nel i soust, ki ert de grant purpens.
Aperceut tres bien que Eva n'ert mie de grant sens.

9

'Eva, ça vien a mei! Parole al messagier!
Ça vien a mei parler desuz icest pumier!
Asmei ici que volz; pren de cest mangier!'   55
'Ne frai, kar il fu deved des hier.'
'[Manjüe], bele suer, nen avras desturber!'
'Nen os, pur mun Criatur, que nen aie encumbrer.
Jo l'eim de tut mum quor! Ne l'os pas curucer!'

10

'Eva,' dist li dïables, 'tu faz mut grant folie!   60
Tu dis que de cest fruit nen gusteras mie.
Ça vien plus pres de mei! Escute, bele amie!
Tei fist Deus e tun sire: or en ad grant envie.
Pur ço ad pris le fruit en la sue baillie,
Qu'il vul que tu perdes la permanable vie.   65
Mangüe! Nel duter! Ne te chalt k'il die!

'Adam, you and your companion are to look after Paradise. You can eat fruit from all these trees, if you like. All except this apple-tree — you mustn't taste any from it! If you look after it well for me, you will have great honour. But if you eat from this one, you will have death. Eve, did you hear me?'

'Sir, I don't take this lightly.'

'This is my command, by the joy that you enjoy!'

Then the Saviour,[42] not wanting to stay any longer, went away to the high heaven to visit his angels.

The Devil of Hell does not want to lose any time, and begins to plot a wicked felony.

'This man he's made here, he wants to disinherit us! If I can get to him, and get into him, I can make him have a taste of this forbidden fruit.'

The evil creature came out of his stinking Hell. He concealed himself in Paradise as a snake, under the grass. He arrived at the tree that had been prohibited, and coiled himself all round it. He kept watch in all directions so that Adam, who was very wise, wouldn't know [he was there]. He had realised quite well that Eve wasn't very wise.

'Eve, come over here to me! Talk to the messenger! Come and talk to me here under this apple-tree! Come close if you like, and take this food!'

'No, I'm not going to! It was forbidden, yesterday.'

'Eat, lovely sister, it won't do you any harm!'

'But I daren't, for my Creator, get into any trouble. I love him so much, and I don't dare make him angry!'

'Eve,' says the Devil, 'You're being a fool. You say you won't even taste this fruit. Come on, lovely friend, come closer and listen! God made you and your husband; now, he is very jealous of you. That's why he took this fruit under his own control, because he wants you to lose everlasting life. Eat! Don't be frightened! Pay no attention to what he says!'

---

[42] Here, as elsewhere in medieval writing, is an anachronism: God has not yet become the Saviour.

11

Saciez, bele suer, si tost cum tu mangeras,
De ma buche en la tue, e tu la receveras,
Perdras sanz demurance icest sen que ore as:
Ceo que ainz ne veïs, certes idunc verras!   70
Quant tu en avras mangied, a tun seinur en durras!
Il ferat tun cumand, certes, isnelepas.'

12

La lase prent la pume ke li fud deveé,
La parole de sun Meistre tut i ad ublïee.
Ad Adam est venue, en sa main l'ad portee.   75
Adam, quant vit la pume, mut l'ad esguardee;
Il li dist ducement: 'Que as tu, [mal] senee?
Ki te dunat la pume? — 'Ele me fu dunee!'
'Las! Jo criem que [tu] serras a curt terme enganee.

13

'Ma amie, jol sai bien, e vei a tun semblant,   80
Que [mangeras] del fruit dunt tu n'as cumant.
Ki te dunat la pume? Di mei! Jol te demand!
Certes, si la mangües, nus en serrum perdant.'
Ço repunt la chaitive: 'N'est pas al cuvenant!
Mangüe od mei, bel sire! Gred t'en saverai grant.'   85

14

'Certes,' ço dist Adam, 'mez nus vient obeir
A nostre Creatur, ne devum pas mentir,
Car aprés cest mesfet, tart ert del repentir.
Se mangües la pume que jo te vei tenir,
De cest liu u sumus, nus estuverad eissir.   90
Peines granz e travalz nus cuvendrat sufrir:
Ne voil certes, par veir, de cest liu partir?'

15

'Nenal,' ço dist Eve, 'ceo n'est pas cuven[an]z.
Ki le frut me duna, me dist tut autre sens:
Mangüe, frere, od mei! Nus remeindrum chaienz.'   95
'Volenters, bele suer!' Eh las, cum mal purpens!
Manjüent de la pume ki lur fud en defens.

16

Li dïables s'en turnet, quant les ot enganed;
Bien sot qu'il serrei[en]t de paraïs geted.
Nostre Sire i descent: tost les ad apeled: 100
'Dites, Adam, u estes? Purquei ne respunez?'

Understand, my dear, that as soon as you have received it — from my mouth to yours — and have eaten it, you'll immediately lose the feelings you have now. And you'll be able to see what you've never seen before! When you've had some, give some to your husband. He'll do what you tell him right away.'

The silly girl takes the apple that was forbidden, completely forgetting what her Master said. She comes to Adam, holding it in her hand. When Adam sees the apple he takes a good look at it. Then he says gently 'What have you got there, you idiot? Who gave you that apple?'

'I was given it.'

'Oh, horror! I'm afraid you'll very soon be caught in the trap! My love, I can tell, and I can see it in your face, you're going to eat that fruit you've been told not to. Who gave you this apple? Tell me, I insist! No question, if you eat it we'll be lost.'

The poor girl replies 'No, that wasn't in the agreement! Eat with me, dear husband, it would make me so happy!'

'Yes, I'm sure,' says Adam, 'but we'll have to obey our Creator and we can't lie to him. Because, after this sin it will be too late to repent. If you eat that apple I can see in your hand we'll be forced to leave this place where we are now, and we'll have to bear great pain and travail. Surely you don't want to leave this place?'

'No,' says Eve, 'but that isn't what it meant. Him, he who gave me the fruit, told me something quite different. Eat with me, dear brother, and we'll stay here!'

'With pleasure, dear sister!'

Alas, what a disastrous idea! They are eating the apple that was forbidden them!

The Devil went home once he had tricked them. He knew they were going to be thrown out of Paradise.

Our Lord comes down, immediately calling them.

'Speak, Adam! Where are you? Why aren't you answering?'

'Sire, chi sui, respuis, de fuille acuveitez.
Sire, jo ai mesfet. La vengance enprenez!'
'Certes, si ferai jo. Saciez: n'i remandrez!

17
Pur ceo que obeïstes a Eve plus que a mei,   105
Maleïçun te duins, si remandrat a tei.
Tu creïs lu dïables ki unques n'ot lei.
Il chaïd de lasus par sa malveise fei.
Is fors de paraïs, meine ta femme od tei!
Si en terre ne guaines, n'averas autre cunrei!'   110
'Sire,' ço dist Adam, 'certes ço peised mei.'

18
Dolenz s'en est essud Adam de paraïs.
Sa femme meined od sei, essilliez e mendis:
Des fuilles e de herbe sunt cuverz e vestiz.
Mut est grant [la] lur perte, quant ne lur est amis   115
Li Sires kis furmat, mut les ad enhaïz.
Tant od Adam dame Eve k'il en ot dous fiz:
Li uns ot num Abel e li autres Chaïns.

19
Mut [par] fud de Chaïn male engendreüre:
Unkes mere ne portat si male porteüre.   120
Quant il fud hume parfait, gueres de Deu n'ot cure;
A mort haïd Abel, la sainte crïature.
Tued l'ad li culverz par grant malaventure:
Mort le laissad gisant, cele sainte figure.

20
De lasus de halt ciel descendit li Furmiere,   125
Est venud a Chaïn: 'Diva', fet il, 'fel liere!'
Enemis Damnedeu, que as tu fet de tun friere?'
...
'Ne me fud cumanded, ne jo n'en sui gardere.'
...
'Maleite seit cel' ure que t'engendrat tis pere,
Que en terre nasquis del ventre ta mere!   130

21
Diva, traitre culvert! Tu es Deu enemis!
Tu as mort mun enfand, Abel, u l'as tu mis?
Mut m'as tu curucied: il ert mut mis amis.'
'Jo ne sai u il est,' ceo li respunt Caïnz.
'Ne me fud cumandet, ne en garde nel pris.'   135
...

'Lord, yes, I'm here answering you, all wrapped up in leaves.[43] Lord, I have sinned — now begin your vengeance!'

'Indeed I shall. Know that you cannot stay here! Because you were more obedient to Eve than to me, I give you a curse that shall remain with you. You believed the Devil, who has no law. He fell from on High because of his disloyalty. Get out of Paradise, and take your wife with you! If you can't get a living from the earth, you'll get no other provision!'

'My Lord,' says Adam, 'I am truly sorry.'

Out of Paradise went Adam in grief, leading his wife with him, exiled and beggarly. They covered and clothed themselves with leaves and grass.[44] Their loss is all the greater because they are no longer friends with the Lord who made them, and now hated them.

Adam took his lady Eve, and had two sons of her,[45] one named Abel and the other Cain. Cain was the begetter of a wicked race; never did mother bear such evil offspring. When he was grown to manhood, he cared nothing for God; and his hate for Abel, that holy creature, was deadly. This wicked man killed him in a dreadful way, and left the saintly body lying dead.

Down from the high heaven came the Maker, and approached Cain. 'What's this! Foul thing! You enemy of God, what have you done with your brother?'

'I wasn't told to look after him, so I'm not his keeper.'

'Cursed be the hour your father begot you, and that you were born of your mother's belly into the world! Ah, you treacherous monster! You enemy of God! You have killed my child Abel — where have you laid him? You have angered me greatly — he was my dear friend.'

'I don't know where he is,' says Cain. 'I wasn't put in charge of him, so I didn't take any notice.'

---

[43] The explanation, that they knew they were naked and so were ashamed, is missing here.

[44] These are protection against cold, and not for shame.

[45] Lit. 'Adam had her so much that ...' but this will not do. Use of 'to know' in its so-called 'biblical' sense is hardly better.

...
'Ki tun pere e ta mere getat de paraïs,
Tant fort t'ad enganed que tun frere as ocis.
22
Ne te sai que duner, fors ma maleïçun!
Tu seies maleït od tute ta possession,
Li enfand qu'engenderas, tuit cil de ta maisun!   140
Que laburras en terre, unkes nen ait fuisun!
Tu irras de cest siecle en grant perdicïun!
En enfern seit tis ostals, tut sanz remissïun!
Abel en paraïs seit od absoluicïun!'
23
Finad sa parole Deus, si [s'e]n est turnez;   145
L'aneme Abel en cunduit, e liu cors est remés.
Grant duel en fait li pere quant li enfés est truvez.
Li dui portent le tierz, dedenz terre est posez.
Del duel ne vus sai dire ki la fu demenez;
Asez i plured Adam, puis s'en est [re]turnez.   150
24
Od sa bele muiller puis cunversad Adans;
Par la volunted Deu ad engendrez enfanz:
Meschines e vatlés, de petiz e de granz.
Le frere prent la surur, de Deu en unt le cumand.
Dunc departent les terres, les forez e les chans: 155
De la terre a partir ne remist uns pans.
25
De la mort Abel forment Deu pesad:
A Chain ne a sun lignage amistied ne mustrad.
Lunkes meistrent sur terre, unc nes regardad.
Male vie menoent, puis [qu'Il] les adossad.   160
Puis qu'Il les maldist, unc plus nes amad:
Forment s'en repentid qu'Il unkes les criad.
26
Lunges vesquid Adam, e sa femme autretal.
Andui furent morz, n'i ot cuntrestal.
Quant paraïs guerpirent, a sei firent grant mal: 165
Quant turnerent del siecle, truverent mal ostal.
Andui trebucherent enz al feu enfernal:
Tuit cil ki de lui naistrent reçourent altretal.

'The one who threw your father and mother out of Paradise has so beguiled you that you have killed your brother! I can't think what to give you except a powerful curse: you shall be cursed with all that is yours, the children you engender, everybody in your household! Whatever work you do in the earth, may it never come to harvest![46] You shall quit this world, utterly damned, and your dwelling shall be in Hell without any pardon! Abel shall be in Paradise, with remission of all sins!'

God ceased speaking, and turned away. He took the soul of Abel with him, leaving the body there. The father made great mourning when the son was found. The two of them carried the third, and put him in the earth. I don't know how to express the sorrow they felt; Adam wept many tears before he came away.

Then Adam communed with his beautiful wife, and by God's will he made children. There were boys and girls, large and small. The brothers took the sisters [to wife], as God had given them permission.[47] Then they shared out the lands, the forests and fields, until there was not a scrap of earth left to be divided.

God was bitterly unhappy at Abel's death. He showed no love for Cain or his lineage; they lived long in the earth but he never looked at them. They led a vile life, since God had turned his back on them. Since he had cursed them, he never cared for them again. He bitterly regretted ever having created them.

Adam lived for a long time, and so did his wife. Then they died, because there was no help for it. When they left Paradise they did themselves no good, because when they left this earth they found a worse place. Both fell down into the infernal fire, and all those born of him will do likewise.[48]

---

[46] Cain was a tiller of the soil, and Abel was a shepherd.

[47] Albina and her sisters had children who coupled brother with sister, without God's permission (*Des Grantz Geanz*).

[48] This ending is rather abrupt, with no suggestion that one day the children of Adam will be redeemed. See de Mandach's p. 253 for continuation of the 'cycle'.

Hagiography

Passages from three saints' lives have been chosen to represent this important corpus.[1] They are all by women, making a neat set,[2] but I have not attempted to compare them as specifically women's writing, which I feel would be reductive.[3] Instead, I am taking passages from each that differ widely in genre within the life and miracles of the saint in question. From the first, I have chosen a miracle that is not one of the saint's own; for the second, I have focused on the writer's historical passages; from the third I extract passages illustrating the protagonist's rhetorical brilliance. The three saints in this chapter are extremely different from one another, representing a variety of saintly 'types' as well as authorial styles, as will be seen. There is not space here to give a summary of each, but *ODS* may be consulted, as well as introductions to the edited texts. A creative attitude to historical truth is to be expected and even celebrated in medieval saints' lives; see for example Bouchard's *Rewriting Saints and Ancestors: Memory and Forgetting in France, 500–1200.*[4]

---

[1] Prologues from another three are included in the preceding 'Miscellany' section.

[2] They appear together with other Lives in the Campsey manuscript (see notes below), but not exclusively.

[3] See, *inter al.*, Legge, *Cloisters*, pp. 49–51, for these three nuns.

[4] Grange, 'Review: Bouchard, Rewriting Saints': rather than think about forgery or authenticity, we appreciate these attempts to revivify the past in the present by the exercise of 'creative memory'.

La Vie d'Edouard le Confesseur, by a Nun of Barking[5]

The story of Mellit and the Fisherman is inset among passages about Edward's vow
to make a pilgrimage, and about his re-founding of Westminster Abbey. He carries
out the latter, instead of the pilgrimage, because his people are afraid to let him
go to Rome in case he never comes back. It complements the passage chosen from
the *Roman de Rou,* above, because Wace does not give us this story as part of his
account of Edward.[6] The Nun introduces it by saying Edward had heard of many
wonders that took place 'in the good old days that were now passed away', and
she wants to digress from her main narrative so that we can enjoy this favourite of
hers. Her style is much more conversational and personal than that of her primary
source, which was written for a reading rather than a listening audience. This
miracle differs from other miracles in saints' lives because it is not performed by
the saint in question but is a flashback to a miracle, performed by somebody else,
that took place in legendary history.[7] The Nun admits it does not belong to her
'matire', but is confident that 'Nuls nel purra senz joie oïr Pur quei qu'il ait de Deu
desir'.[8] She envisages a pious (and mixed) audience who will delight in this good
story.

This is not the place for a detailed study of Edward's Lives, but some contextual
remarks may be of interest. The Nun's version was until recently considered a mere
translation of her original, the *Vita* by Aelred of Rievaulx. I have shown elsewhere
that she certainly had other sources, and some details of her version have come
through into later English lives of Edward.[9] It is clear she knew a life of Edward
the Martyr that Aelred, if he knew it, did not use. There is also the possibility
she knew Old English poetry, because of a couplet that looks very like an echo
of lines in the *Battle of Maldon.*[10] Both these details reappear in a much later
Life: the writer of *GL* (Supp) knows that Edward the Martyr was said to have
been murdered at the behest of his step-mother;[11] and its description of Edward's
dying sentiments resembles that in the Nun's version.[12] Some of her differences
from Aelred may be because she used different manuscript(s) from the one edited
in *PL;*[13] some recent work on this is described in my translation of the Nun's life
cited here.

---

[5] Dean 523.

[6] In later times, Washington Irving added this very same story to his article about Westminster
Abbey (*Sketch Book,* pp. 184–200, at 196–8).

[7] Legge, pp. 60–66 (and 246–7).

[8] vv. 2477–80.

[9] *Edouard,* p. 50.

[10] Although it sounds proverbial, all efforts to track it down in Dictionaries of Proverbs have been
in vain (discussed in my short 'Old English *Gnome*').

[11] p. 3, lines 11–13; *Edouard,* p. 23.

[12] *GL* p. 23, lines 819–20; *Edouard* p. 147. The sentiment with its poetic antithesis, in both
vernacular versions, is not present in Aelred.

[13] See the *GL* introduction to Edward (p. 1).

The text is copied from *La Vie d'Edouard*, ed. Södergård;[14] the translation is my own, almost exactly as previously published in *Edouard*,[15] except that it was without the text on each facing page as here. My Introduction to it may be consulted for further background; I have included a number of my footnotes here. The chapter comprises two 'sections', each marked in the edition with a capital in bold and a line-break.

---

[14] Folio numbers are those of the base manuscript (Vatican, MS Reg. Lat. 489). I include some variants from other MSS (but not rejected readings); minor corrections from the online version (https://uwaterloo.ca/margot/) are silently added.

[15] It has been slightly modified here and there.

Text

[f.7c] Al tens lu bon rei Edelbert
E al tens sun nevu Sexbert,
Ices reis furent cunverti
Par Augustin, le Deu ami;   2484
Li uncles reis en Kent esteit,
Li nevus en Lundres maneit.
De sun regne ert le mestre sié.
Puis fud li reis acuragié   2488
De dens les murs faire une iglise
Ki el num seint Pol fust asise.
Sié d'evesquë i vuleit faire
Pur l'iglise a grant onur traire.   2492
Saint Mellit ad evesque fait
Od grant onur e od grant hait. [f.7d]
Saint Mellit fud forment
        produmme,
Od saint Augustin vint de Rume,   2496
Ki Engletere a Deu turna,
Le quel saint Gregorie envea.
Li reis Sexbert fud pruz e sage
E si refud de grant curage.   2500
Puis vint al rei en volenté,
Si cum saint Pol ot honuré,
Que saint Piere honurer voleit,
Une eglise en sun num fereit.   2504
Dehors les murs de la cité
Vers le west ad li rei fundé
Une eglise en l'onur saint Piere
La quele a tuz jurz puis out chiere.   2508
Li reis i ad granz teres mises
E mult riches rentes asises.
Puis vint un tens que a Deu plout
Qu'ele dedïee estre dut.   2512
Vienent i genz de pres e de luin,
Aparaillent quanqu'ad busuin
A l'uvrainne de si halt jur

Pur le liu e pur Deu amur.   2516
Saint Mellit fud mult pensis
E tute la nuit ententis
D'ordener e d'aparilier
Qu'al demain li avreit mestier.   2520
Li poples fud liez endreit sei,
Ja seit qu'il fussent luinz de fei.
Le dedïement attendirent,
Ja seit qu'il en Deu ne creïrent,   2524
Plus pur la merveille veer
Que pur devocïun aveir
Ne qui qu'unkes mais le veïssent
E pur ço de plus s'esgoïssent.   2528
Icele nuit dedenz Tamise
Aveit un peschur sa nef mise,
Ki curt tut dreit suz le mustier.
Cil i fud entrez pur peschier.   2532
Vers l'altre rive estiet alee [f.8a]
Sa nef e pres fud arivee.
La li est saint Piere aparu,
Cume pelerin fud vestu,   2536
Dist lui qu'il avreit bon luier
S'ultre l'eve le vult nager.
Cil li ad volentiers granté,
Saint Piere est puis a lui entré.   2540
Quant de l'altre part sunt venuz,
L'apostle est de la nef eisuz,
Puis est dedenz l'eglise entrez,
Li peschur l'ad tut esguardé.   2544
Puis que l'apostle entrez i fu,
Se demustra tost la Deu vertu.
Del ciel decent une clarté,
Ki le liu ad enluminé.   2548
Tant fud ample sa resplendur
Que la nuit est turnee en jur.

Translation

In the time of good King Edelbert and of his nephew Sexbert, these kings were converted by Augustine, the friend of God. The uncle king was in Kent; the nephew stayed in London. It was the principal seat of his realm. There the king was inspired to make a church within the walls, to be established in the name of Saint Paul. He wanted to make it a bishop's seat, so as to bring great honour to the church. He made Saint Mellit bishop, with great honour and great joy. Saint Mellit was a very good man: he came from Rome with Saint Augustine, whom Saint Gregory sent and who converted England to God. King Sexbert was worthy and wise, and also he was of great virtue. Then the king had an idea, that as he had honoured Saint Paul he wanted to honour Saint Peter: he would make a church in his name. Outside the walls of the city, to the west,[16] the king founded a church in honour of Saint Peter, which he ever after held most dear. The king granted it great lands and established many rich rents. Then came the time when it pleased God it should be dedicated. People came from near and far; they prepared whatever was necessary for the proceedings of such a high day, for the place and for the love of God. Saint Mellit was very thoughtful, and all night was attentive to the ordering and preparation of what he would need next day. The people were happy about it all, though they were far from true faith. They attended the dedication, even though they did not believe in God — more to see the marvels than out of devotion — and because they had never before seen anything like it they were the more joyful.[17]

That night a fisherman had put his boat into the Thames, that ran right there beneath the church. He got into it, to go fishing. The boat went towards the other bank and arrived quickly. There Saint Peter appeared to him, dressed like a pilgrim, and told him he would have a good reward if he would take him across the water.[18] He willingly agreed, and Saint Peter got in with him. When they came to the other side, the apostle got out of the boat, then he went into the church — the fisherman saw it all. When the apostle had entered, he soon showed the power of God. From Heaven came a brightness that lit up the place. Its splendour was so abundant that night was turned to day.

---

[16] The abbey was originally built on Thorney Island. Södergård notes 'west' as an anglicism, but French 'ouest' sounds the same so not much can be made of it; Wace uses 'west' in his own account. In another chapter of *Edouard*, I translated 'Tornei est de jadis numé' (v. 2168) as 'it is changed from its former renown'. This was probably wrong (Södergård is also wrong when he locates Thorney in Cambridge, see his IPN); I ought at least to have put a footnote with the alternative. I thank Richard Howard, of the Thorney Island Society, for alerting me to this.

[17] Although the Nun translates Aelred's text fairly closely much of the time, she allows herself a good deal of freedom. The result is often more personal and descriptive; here, she makes more than Aelred does of Mellit's sleepless night and the people's ignorant wonder. For this chapter, see 'Vita S. Edwardi Regis et Confessoris', Aelred of Rievaulx, ed. Migne, 755D–7C; and *The Historical Works*, ed. Dutton, ch. 14.

[18] 'nager' is to transport, or be transported, in a boat (not 'swim').

A l'apostle vint en aïe
Cele tres noble cumpanie   2552
Des citeens del ciel la sus
Les quels maintent li reis Jesus.
Li angle e li saint vunt devant
Od grant clarté e od dulz chant.   2556
En tere n'ad buche ki die
Cum fud dulce la melodie,
Cum cele joie fud plenerie,
Cum bele fud cele lumiere.   2560
Ki puet dire cele dulçur
De la celestïene odur,
Quant les nobles celestïens
Furent asjuins as terrïens?   2564
Tute la tere en fud joiuse
E des glorïus glorïuse.
Li angele i muntent e descendent,
Le chant del ciel a tere rendent.   2568
[Li lieus fu toz saintifiés
Et des sains angeles dediés.]¹⁹
Quant saint Piere od sa cumpainie
Ot bien dedïé l'abbeïe
E fait quanque il faire dut
Qu'al dedïement afferut, [f.8b]   2572
Dunc s'est vers la nef returné
Al peschur qui l'aveit passé.
Cil avait tel poür eü
Que pur poi out le sens perdu.   2576
Sun fieble cors ne pot suffrir
Tel chose veeir ne oïr.
Dunc le conforte dulcement
Saint Piere e sun sens puis li rent.   2580
Cil ad sa nef vers tere trait
E l'un peschur od l'altre vait.
Li dui peschiere i sunt entrez
Mais de diverses poëstez.   2584
L'un peschot pur anemes guarir,
L'altre pessuns al cors nurir,
Li uns les anemes de la gent,
L'altre del cors sustienement.   2588
Mult furent divers lur voleirs

Et nun semblables lur pueirs.
A saint Piere est dunc suvenu
Des duz diz sun maistre Jesu.   2592
Cument poust ses diz ublïer
Qu'il sot tant dulcement amer?
Cument poust ubliance aveir
De ço u tut fud sun vuleir?   2596
Tant li fud dulz li dulz Jesu
Que sun quoer si addulci fu
Que l'amertume de pechié
N'i prist puis la dulçur sun sié.   2600
Pur ço ne pot metre en ubli
Les duz diz de sun duz ami.
Sun cumpaignun prist a reigner,
Si li dit: 'N'as tu que mangier?'   2604
'N'aie par fei,' cil respundi.
'Rien ne pris, kar ci t'atendi.
Cert fui de mun pramis luier,
Pur ço ne me vuoil travaillier.'   2608
De rechief li ad dit saint Piere
Od dulz semblant, od piue chiere:
'Lasche tes reis, met les em prise!'
          [f.8c]
Cil ad fait sulunc sa divise.   2612
Tost fu chargiee si la rei
Qu'a peine la pout traire a sei.
Les pessuns a la rive trait,
En sa nef les met od grant hait.   2616
Saint Piere ad dit al pescheür:
'Prens des pessuns le tut greinur,
A saint Mellit le porteras.
De ma part li presenteras.   2620
Les altres seient tun luier
Que te promis pur tun nagier.
Jo sui numé Pieres, ami,
Od mes piers del ciel descendi   2624
Pur dedïer la meie eglise,
Ki ci est en mun num asise;
E par la mei' auctorité
Ai jo cest liu sanctefié.   2628

---

¹⁹ This couplet is added in one of the other MSS.

To join the apostle came that noble company of citizens of Heaven above, over whom reigns King Jesus. The angels and saints go ahead, with bright radiance and with sweet song. In earth there is no mouth that can tell how sweet was the melody, how complete was the joy, how beautiful was this light. Who can tell the sweetness of this heavenly fragrance, when the celestial nobles accompanied the terrestrial?[20] All the earth rejoiced at it, and gloried in the glorious. There the angels go up and down,[21] and give back the song from heaven to earth. [The place was sanctified from top to bottom, and dedicated by the holy angels.] When Saint Peter with his company had dedicated the Abbey, and done what he had to do that pertained to the dedication, then he turned back to the boat of the fisherman who had transported him.

This man had been so frightened he was nearly out of his wits. His frail body cannot endure to see or hear such things. So Saint Peter gently comforts him and brings him back to his senses. He brought his boat to land, and one fisherman went with the other.[22] The two fishermen went into the boat — but with differing powers: one fished to cure souls; the other, fish to feed bodies. One, sustenance for the souls of the people, the other for their bodies. Very different were their intentions, and their powers were not the same. Then Saint Peter remembered the dear sayings of his master Jesus. How could he forget his sayings, whom he knew how to love so sweetly? How could he lose the memory of that wherein his whole desire lay? So sweet was the sweet Jesus, his heart was so sweetened that the bitterness of sin nevermore took the place of the sweetness. Therefore he cannot but remember the sweet sayings of his sweet friend.

He addressed his companion and said to him: 'Haven't you anything to eat?'[23]

'No, indeed,' he replied. 'I caught nothing, because I was here, waiting for you. I was certain of my promised reward, and so I didn't want to go to work.'

Immediately Saint Peter said to him, with gentle look and kindly manner: 'Let out your nets, put them in position.'

And he did so, as [Peter] wished. Quickly the net was so laden he could scarcely draw it towards him. He pulls the fish to the bank, and puts them in the boat with great satisfaction. Saint Peter said to the fisherman:

'Take the very biggest of the fish — you shall carry it to Saint Mellit. You are to present it to him, from me. The others shall be your reward, that I promised you for your crossing. I am named Pierre, friend; with my peers[24] I came down from Heaven to dedicate this, my church, which is established in my name; and by my own authority I have sanctified this place.

---

[20] This question-form, with the notion of inexpressibility, is an example of the Nun's dramatic style (as is the play on 'glorious, below).

[21] Aelred has 'as if on Jacob's ladder' (Gen. 28:12); the Nun prefers the idea of giving back the song.

[22] The Nun makes much of this point, following Aelred (Matt. 4:19), but she goes on to elaborate the contrast.

[23] This conflates episodes in Luke 5:1–7 and John 21:5–11.

[24] Aelred's Peter mentions 'fellow-citizens' without punning.

Plus de l'evesque me hastai,
Kar einz de lui la dediai.
Tut li dirras demain, ami,
Quanque veü as e oï.   2632
Tel enseigne el mustier verra,
Par quei les tuens diz bien crera.
N'estueit mais que la main i mette
Ne del dedïer s'entremete,   2636
Mais tant qu'il face le servise
Demain cel jur desdenz l'eglise,
Puis die al pople le sermun,
Si lur duinst ma beneïçun.   2640
Bien les acert e bien lur die
Qu'il en cest liu avrunt m'aïe.
Des feeilz Deu ki ci savrai
Les prïeres suvent orrai,   2644
Si overai a mes amis
La grant porte de pareïs.
Ceos ki chastement ci vivrunt
Ja close ne la truverunt,'   2648
Saint Piere a itant s'en ala,
Aprés ço tost l'albre creva. [f.8d]
Saint Mellit est matin levé,
Ki mult aveit la nuit pensé   2652
De faire le dedïement
Qu'il plust a Deu e a la gent.
Li peschieres l'ad encuntré,
Le peisun li ad presenté.   2656
Puis li ad tut par ordre dit
Que de saint Piere oï e vit.
Li evesquë en fud mult liez,
Forment s'en est esmerveilliez.   2660
Les us del mustier uvrir fist,
Vit que veirs fu que cil li dist.
Les deos abeces unt truvez,

Ki furent mult bien cumpassez.   2664
Les .XII. cruiz truvees unt,
Ki del saint' olie uintes sunt.
Des dudce cirges unt truvee
La remasille as cruiz fermee.   2668
De l'evoe beneite jetee
Fud l'iglise encore arusee.
Des que tut cest ourent veü,
Si unt tut l'altre bien creü.   2672
Nuls ne poeit aveir dutance
Dunt Deu lur fist aseürance.
Saint Mellit est al pople alé,
Cest miracle lur ad cunté.   2676
Trestut cum ala lur dit,
Puis lur fait veeir ço qu'einz vit.
Le rei del ciel trestuz aürent
E de joie e de pité plurent,   2680
K'il par cel saint dedïement
Ad duné creance a sa gent.
Le peschur e tut sun linage
Soleient par dreit eritage   2684
Le guain de lur pessuns dimer
E a Westmustier aporter.
Mais nepurquant uns le retient
[f.9a]
Ki de sun guain issi avint   2688
Qu'unques ne pot prendre peisun,
Desqu'a saint Piere enquist
    pardun.
Despuis que saint Ædward oï
Le miracle qu'ai conté ci   2692
Par escrit e par recunter,
Mult se pena del liu amer.
Fist le mustier, fist maisuns faire,
Riches rentes al liu atraire.   2696

I hastened more than the bishop did, for I dedicated it before him! You will tell him tomorrow, friend, all you have seen and heard. He will see such a sign in the church, by which he will believe your words. It will no longer be necessary for him to set his hand to it, nor undertake to dedicate it, but as soon as he performs the service that day — tomorrow — in the church, and then says the sermon to the people, thus he gives them my blessing. Let him reassure them and tell them that in this place they shall have my help. I shall often hear the prayers of God's faithful, whom I know to be here; and I shall open the great door of Paradise to my friends.[25] Those who live here chastely shall never find it closed.'[26] With this, Saint Peter went away; soon afterwards, the dawn broke.

Saint Mellit rose in the morning; he had thought much during the night about performing the dedication so as to please God and the people. The fisherman met him and presented him with the fish. Then, from beginning to end, he told him what he had seen and heard of Saint Peter. The bishop was overjoyed, and marvelled greatly at it. He had the doors of the church opened, and saw that what he had told him was true. They found the two alphabets, which had been properly set out. They found the twelve crosses, that were anointed with holy oil. Of the twelve candles, they found the remainder fixed to the crosses. The church was still wet with the scattered holy water.[27] As soon as they had seen this, they believed all the rest completely. None could have any doubt, now God had assured them of it. Saint Mellit went to the people and recounted this miracle. As soon as he went, he told them, then he showed them what he had already seen. Straightaway they praised the King of Heaven, and for joy and piety they wept — that by this holy dedication he had given faith to his people.

The fisherman and all his lineage, father and son, thenceforth used to reckon the tithe of their fish and take it to Westminster.[28] But nevertheless one of them held this back, for his own gain, and it so happened that he was never able to catch fish again until he had begged for Saint Peter's pardon.[29]

When Saint Edward heard of the miracle I have told here — by writing and by re-telling — he took much trouble to cherish the place. He made the church, and he had houses built, to draw rich rents for the establishment.

---

[25] Aelred cites Titus 2:12 here; the Nun's mention of friends is a typical theme with her.

[26] Edward was celebrated for his chastity (*Edouard, passim*).

[27] This conforms to the ritual of consecrating a church. The alphabets may have been painted or drawn (one MS has 'Les letres mult bien painturé'). The crosses are incised, not free-standing, and candles stuck onto them; 'the remainder' indicates they had been lit, by no mortal hand, and had been burning all night.

[28] A tithe was properly a tenth of one's income, supposed to be offered by everybody to the Church as a matter of course.

[29] Aelred's chapter ends here; he begins the next with a rather longer account including several Bible references. The Nun ends with a typically personal comment.

La Vie Seinte Audree, by Marie[30]

The Life of Saint Audrey contains extensive historical passages, claiming to be taken from Bede. I have chosen it for this reason, in accordance with my preference for selecting passages untypical of their genre: history can be found in fiction. Its author names herself Marie, and it has recently been attributed to 'Marie de France'.[31] However, Richard Trachsler has even more recently examined the development of this composite 'author' and her stubborn resistance to being dismembered.[32] Although I would naturally prefer to see two (or more) women writers instead of one, it is not my intention to involve myself further in the question; the field of Marie studies is already very well covered by numerous scholars.[33]

For an introductory discussion of this work, which exists in only one MS, see first Legge (pp. 264–6). Like that of the Nun of Barking, this nun's style is chatty and personal; our third nun Clemence says much less to her audience than either of these two do. The Life can be found, with others in the 'Campsey' manuscript, online (https://uwaterloo.ca/margot/). This collection was put together for the purpose of mealtime readings in a nunnery; whatever the original audience envisaged, this version of the text had an audience of nuns together with their household and any guests. Religious houses were much more open than might today be supposed: visitors both clerical and lay came and went, bringing news, letters, books.[34] There are numerous appeals to a listening audience, where the writer addresses them in the second person, or makes chatty explanations. Like other religious women who produced saints' lives, Marie is literate in Latin and has translated from a Latin source or sources. The saint is Etheldreda, a nun of Ely and a queen.[35] It begins with what purports to be historical narrative.[36] However, it

---

[30] ed. Södergård; Dean 566.

[31] I have consulted *The Life of Saint Audrey,* ed. and tr. McCash and Barban; I continue to use the older edition because I am not convinced of the author's identification with Marie de France (see also Wogan-Browne, 'Wreaths of Thyme', for doubts about this still-contentious attribution).

[32] Seminar paper delivered to the Oxford Medieval French Seminar, 28th April 2015: 'Comment naît un auteur médiéval: le cas de Marie de France'.

[33] *Inter al.,* McCash, 'A Fourth Text?'; Griffin, 'Gender and Authority'; Landolfi's essay in *Anglo-français: philologie et linguistique*; and Burrows, 'Review: *Marie de France: A Critical Companion,* Sharon Kinoshita and Peggy McCracken'. There has also been a move to identify 'Marie de France' with the abbess of Barking who was Thomas Becket's sister (Rossi, 'Name of Marie'). But Marie was a very common name, so the chances that all persons called Marie must be one and the same are somewhat remote; there may well have been more women writers than is generally supposed even now.

[34] See *Edouard,* for the Nun of Barking and her audience.

[35] The text begins 'Ici comence la vie seinte Audree, noneyne de Ely', but the first mention of her at vv. 17–18 is of 'la royne bonuree'.

[36] See Bede, *History,* tr. Shirley-Price *et al.* (and notes below); Leyser, *Beda,* gives some historical background.

is clear from a glance at Bede's *History* that Marie cannot be drawing directly from it,[37] especially since a glance at *Liber Eliensis* shows a much closer similarity in the arrangement and style of the narrative.[38] It is also interesting for the story behind our word 'tawdry', and for the author's name (rarely found among women writers for a number of reasons) placed at the end of the text. Three passages are therefore reproduced here, with translation and notes. References are to *ODS* as well as to text and notes in the edition; Södergård provides both Analyse and IPN.[39] The spelling of names in modern English, not to mention Södergård's French, varies from one source-book to the next, so I have generally adopted spellings given in *ODS*. The table in *The Life of Saint Audrey*, ed. and tr. McCash and Barban, p. 11, is useful; reference to notes in this volume are added with an asterisk, as they are marked on the page.[40]

---

[37] *History*, tr. Shirley-Price *et al.*, also cited frequently in notes below; here, see for example pp. 236–9, and notes on p. 372.

[38] tr. Fairweather, cited *passim* in my notes below. The story is found on pp. 12–16; even to the comparison of Anna's daughters with the wise virgins of the Gospel.

[39] Blank lines in the edited text are reproduced here as a row of dots.

[40] Variant readings in their edition (see also their Appendix 1) do not in my view affect the sense of the text, therefore I have added only those of special interest. Some asterisks are missing from their text; it may be advisable to go straight to the endnotes beginning on p. 249, but I have copied the sense of the most useful ones.

Text

Audrey's Family and Birth[41]

Pour sainte Audree la roine
Cui bien ne faut ne decline
Hay comencé ce livre a faire. [f.100d]
Ici m'estuet dire et retraire   32
De quel linage ele fu nee
Et com deus foiz fu mariee.
Ainz ke paroil dou mariage,
M'estuet moustrer de son linage.   36
    Solom l'estoire as anciens
En icel tens ke Marciens
Hout de Rome la seignurie,
L'empire et tute la baillie,   40
Une genz, Engleis sunt nomez,
En Bretaine sunt arivez.
Cinqante sis et bien cent anz,
Si come saint Bede est disanz,   44
Ainz ke saint Austin venist,
I furent les Engleis, ceo dist,
Treis maineres de compaignons,
Godlondeis, Engleis et Seixons.   48
Furent icil qui de Germaine
Esteient venuz en Bretaine.
De la lignee as Godlondeis
Furent engendreis li Kenteis;   52
L'autre partie des Estreis
Furent engendrez des Engleis,
L'autre partie des Seixons
Ke Seixons Estreis apelons.   56
Estaungle a non cele partie
Dont Engleis eurent la seignurie.
De cele genz fu engendree

La glorieuse sainte Audree   60
Ke mut fu de grant sainteté
E de real dignité.
Redwald fu en icel tens reis,
Ce dist l'estoire des Kenteis.   64
Titulus out son pere a non, [f.101a]
Ulf son aol, issi le trovom.
De cest Ulf furent apellé
Ulfinges li reis et nomé.   68
Aprés icel rei Redwald
Regnat un sen fiz Erkenwald
Ke par le bon rei Edwine
Se torna a la ley divine.   72
Cist Edwins estoit reis,
Sire et mestres de Norhombreis.
Par son seint amonestement
Converti cist liu et sa gent.   76
Occis fu, poi de tens dura.
Sigilberz,[42] son frere, regna,
Bons cristiens fu sanz dotance,
Cist jeta le pais de errance   80
Par saint Felix, un sen ami.
Eveskes fu, mut le crei.
En France ert a lui acointez,
Dementres qu'il fu eissilliez.   84
Kant de son essil vint ariere,
Felix manda, par sa priere
Vint a lui et eveske le fist
De Dounemoc ou il le mist.   88
Par precher et par sainteté
Converti il cele cité.
...

---

[41] vv. 29–228; pp. 57–62 in the edition. New sections are marked by capitals in bold type and a space on the page.

[42] *MS 'Sire gilberz'.

Translation

Audrey's Family and Birth

I have begun to make this book for Saint Audrey the Queen, who never fails or fades. Here I must tell and record what lineage she was born from, and how she was married twice. But before talking of marriage, I must show her lineage.

According to the history of ancient time, in the days when Marcian was lord of Rome and held the empire and dominion over all,[43] a people called the English[44] had arrived in Britain. A hundred and fifty-six long years, as Saint Bede says, before Saint Augustine came, there were said to be three companion peoples: Jutes,[45] Angles, and Saxons. These were the people who came from Germany into Britain. From the Jutes, the Kentish people sprang. One section of the Eastern people were engendered by the Angles; the other section by the Saxons, whom we call the East Saxons.[46] East Anglia is the name of the region where the Angles were in power.[47] These are the people from whom the glorious Saint Audrey was born, who was so saintly and so royal in her dignity. Redwald was king at that time, as the history of the Kentish tells us.[48] His father was Titulus and his ancestor was Ulf, as we find there. From this Ulf, the kings [who followed him] were called by the name Ulfings. One of Redwald's sons ruled after him; this was Earpwald,[49] who was converted to Christianity by the good king Edwin. This Edwin was king, and he was lord and master of the Northumbrians; by his holy admonition he converted this region and its people.[50] He did not rule long, for he was killed.[51] His brother Sigebert reigned;[52] he was a good Christian without any doubt! He led the country out of sin with the help of his friend Saint Felix. This man was a bishop, I'm certain. He got to know him in France while he was in exile.[53] When he came back from exile, he sent for Felix, who came to him at his bidding and he made him bishop of Dunwich. By his preaching and by his saintliness he converted the city.

---

[43] (Eastern) Roman Emperor 450–57.

[44] *In Old French this word was used for both English and Angles.

[45] 'Gotlanders'.

[46] Essex; the sentence is confusing because Marie calls both lots 'Estreis'. Audrey was of Anglian (not Saxon) stock.

[47] Compare this with *Description*, above.

[48] See Bede, note to p. 171 (on p. 369), for dates of Redwald and his immediate successors.

[49] The IPN says he was son of Redwald and brother of Sigebert. Bede (note on p. 369) does not give this relationship, but see the genealogy on p. 380.

[50] See *ODS* for Edwin (584–633).

[51] *After the death of Edwin, the East Angles reverted to paganism.

[52] vv. 77–8 must refer to Earpwald (Sigebert's brother), not to Edwin. Such confusion of pronouns, or failure to restate the subject, is common (see, for example, *Piety and Persecution*, ed. and tr. Boulton, p. 59).

[53] *ODS* contains entries for both these figures. Felix of Dunwich was a Burgundian by birth. Sigebert returned from exile in 630 to rule over the East Angles.

En icel tens que ge vus di
Sigilberz son regne gerpi.   92
En Bedrichesworde l'ai oi[54]
Qu'a moinage se rendi,
Egeriz, le suen parent,
Dou reiaume la cure rent   96
Ki en cel tens une partie
Del reiaume avoit en ballie.
Mut soffri cist bataillie et guerre
    [101b]
D'un rei Penda qui en la terre   100
Vint ocians de Merchenelande;
Sa pousté vout qu'ele espande.
Quant Egeriz ne pout contendre
Ne la terre vers eus defendre,   104
Sigilberz voleient faire issir
De son moinage et partir
Pur eus aider et conforteir
Et lur corages afermeir.   108
De sa abeie le geterunt
Et a force ou eus le menerunt
En la bataille ou cil esteient
Ki encontr'aus se combateient,   112
Membra lui par religion
De sa sainte profession.
Autre armeure ne voloit
Fors une verge ke il tenoit.   116
Occis fu en cele bataillie
Et Egeris li reis sanz faillie.
Totes lur hoz et leur mainees
Hont occises et detrenchees.   120
Trente set anz furent passés
Et sis cenz puis que Deus fu nees.
Quant ceste aventure avint si
Que jeo vos ay cunté ci.   124
...
Le fiz ainnez, un noble vassal,

De noble linage et de real
Regna aprés le occision.
Anne le rei l'apelloit hom.   128
Cex rois fu pere sainte Audree,
La roine bonnuree.
Kant le regne out bien en justise,
Si honura mut une eglise   132
Que en Cnaresburc estoit [f.101c]
Ou Phurseus manoit,
Ke par la grace et par la aie
Sigilberz out cele abbeie.   136
...
Anne ert reis de la cuntree,
Sainte vie et bonnuree
Mena et tint mut sagement,
Femme prist al lou de sa gent.   140
De ceste dame trovom nous
Ke digne fu de tiel espous
Et de linage et de honesteté
Et de bone moralité.   144
Tant furent de Deu espiré
Ke tost s'estoient aturné
A Deu servire, lur creatur,
Et a poveres doner de lur.   148
Tres noble engendrure et digne
Heurent ensemble et mult
    benigne.
Deuz fiz e quatre fillies haveient,
Norir les firent cum meuz pooient. 152
Li uns fu Aldulfs apellez,
Jurmins fu li autres nomez;
Des fillies ert Sexburg l'ainznee,
Tres noble dame et alosee.   156
La secunde out a non Edelberge
En qui toz[55] meint et herberge.
La tierce avoit a non Audree,
Saintiesme virge et honuree.   160

---

54 *Notes here and *passim* (for example, to v. 99) discuss the scribe's spelling.
55 Södergård notes (p. 182) a word missing here.

At this time I'm telling you about, Sigebert abandoned his kingdom. I've heard it was at Bury Saint Edmunds that he went into retreat in a monastery.[56] He left the care of the realm to his kinsman Ecgric, who was then partly in charge of it. This king suffered dreadfully from war and attacks by a king called Penda, who came slaughtering into the land from Mercia. His power wished to extend itself! When Ecgric could stand no more of this, and could no longer defend the land against him, he and his people wanted to get Sigebert to leave his monastic life, to come out in order to help and comfort them, and strengthen their courage. They hauled him from his abbey and dragged him forcefully along with them to the battle they were in, against those who were attacking them. But he was mindful, religiously, of his holy profession: he would not have any weapon of war, except only the staff he carried. He was killed in the battle, together with King Ecgric of course: all their hosts and their armies were killed and cut down by the enemy. Since the birth of God it was six hundred and thirty-seven years, that the wonderful things happened which I've related to you here.[57]

The eldest son, a fine young man of noble and royal lineage, reigned after this killing. They called him Anna the King. This king was the father of Saint Audrey, the blessed queen. When he had got the kingdom under control, he paid great honour to a church at Burgh Castle. Here lived Saint Fursa, who had the abbey by Sigebert's grace and favour.[58] Anna was king of the land, and he led a blessed holy life, behaving himself wisely. He took a wife on the advice of his people.[59] We read of this lady that she was worthy of such a husband, both in lineage and in honesty, and of good conduct. They were so inspired by God that they quickly turned to serving him, their Creator, and giving their goods to the poor. Together they were blessed with most worthy and noble offspring. They had two sons and four daughters, bringing them up as best they knew how.

The first was called Eadwulf, and the next one was Jurmin.[60] Of the daughters, Sexburga was the eldest — a very noble and praiseworthy lady.[61] The second was named Ethelburga, in whom all [...] lives and has dwelling.[62] The third was called Audrey, most famous and holy virgin.

---

[56] IPN has Bury St Edmunds, but see below; and *ODS* 'possibly at Burgh Castle'.

[57] *The note discusses 'aventure' as a favourite word used by Marie de France. However, it is a favourite word used by many medieval writers (a rough count in this book yields about a dozen).

[58] The saint left for France after Sigebert's death (*ODS*, Fursey). The site was indeed Burgh Castle, in spite of the name's similarity to modern Knaresborough.

[59] *The note (p. 250) refers to other 'Marie de France' texts in which a young man is urged to marry by his people. But this topic is not exclusive to texts by 'Marie': according to legend, Edward the Confessor was likewise urged. Unlike romance heroes, certain high-placed men who were thought to prefer the holy life needed persuading that an heir would become necessary.

[60] See *ODS* for the latter. It is doubtful whether Anna had any sons, in spite of what *Liber* says, although it is reasonably clear that Audrey was Anna's daughter.

[61] This saint also appears in *ODS*.

[62] Ethelburga became a nun at Faremoutier-en-Brie. The missing word is probably 'goodness' or similar, since she too was a saint (in *ODS*). 'the second' is more commonly written as 'l'autre'.

La quarte suer Withburc out non,
Mut fu de grant religion.
Sachez ke ceo quatre soers
Deservirent bien en lur jurs   164
Ke ou les cointes virges pristrent
L'oille k'en lur lampes mistrent
Ke ja meis ne seient estaintes
    [f.101d]
Dont les nonsages font les   168
   pleintes.
Et Aldulfs, fiz al rei l'ainznee,
Dist saint Bede qu'ot grant
   bontee.
En Jurmins out grant sainteté,
Devotion et honesteté.   172
De ceste dame dist ici
Dont si bon linage issi
Ke Hereswide out a non,
Fillie Herici un baron.   176
Cist fu nefs le rei Edwine
A ki Norhomborlond acline.
Sexburg, la fillie Anne l'ainnee,
A Herchenbert fu mariee,   180
Sire rois de Kent, si come nos dit
Saint Bedes ke le livere fist.
Aldulfs fu rois puis le decés
Et Edelwold regna aprés.   184
La mere Aldulf, Hereswid,

Fu suer, ceo conte li escrit,
Sainte Hilde, une bone dame,
Abesse mult de noble fame,   188
Et furent fillies Herici.
Ceo havé vos bien devant oi.
Alvriz out lur aol a non,
Fiz Edwine le baron.   192
Hereswide, dont jeo vous di,
Out heu un autre mari
Dont ele out une fillie bele,
Sedrete out non, virge et pucele.   196
Sexburg par le conseil sa mere
Al quint an del regne son pere
A Erchenberc fu mariee
Ky l'a en Kent ou li menee.   200
Eldeberge virginité [f.102a]
Promist a Deu e chasteté,
Rendi sei en religion.
En icel tens, dont nos parlom,   204
Out en Bretaine meinte eglise
Fundé e faite a Deu servise,
Ou plusors lur fillies metoient,
A Deu esposer les fesoient,   208
Si come il ooent les lois
E les costomes des François.
Fillies e neces e parentes
Fesoient noneines ou grant rentes.   212

The fourth was named Withburga, who was very religious.[63] You are to understand that these four sisters in their time richly deserved to take oil with those clever virgins; they put the oil in their lamps so that they should never go out, unlike the foolish virgins who bewailed theirs.[64]

Eadwulf, the king's elder son, was a very good man according to the holy Bede. In Jurmin too was great holiness; he was devoted and honest. Of this lady from such a fine lineage, he says here she was called Hereswith.[65] She was daughter of a baron named Hereric; he was the nephew of Edwin, the king to whom Northumberland was subject. Sexburga, Anna's eldest daughter, was married to Erconbert; he was lord king of Kent, as Bede says who made the book. Eadwulf was king after the death [of his father], and Æthelweald reigned after him.[66] The written document says that Eadwulf's mother, Hereswith, was sister to Saint Hilda. She was a good lady and a famous abbess; they were daughters of Hereric. You have heard all about this before.[67] Eadfrid was the name of their kinsman, and he was son of the noble Edwin.[68] Hereswith, whom I've been telling you about, had had another husband and from him had a lovely daughter called Saethrith, a virgin maid.[69] On the advice of her mother, Sexburga was married to Erconbert in the fifth year of her father's reign, and he took her to Kent with him.

Ethelburga promised her virginity, and chastity, to God: she took the religious life. In those days I'm telling you about there were many churches in Britain, founded and built for the service of God. Many people put their daughters into them, making them brides of God, as if they understood the laws and customs of the French.[70] They made nuns of their daughters and nieces and other female relations, which raised good rents.[71]

---

[63] All Anna's supposed children (see Jurmin, above) are in *ODS* except the eldest.

[64] This refers to the parable of the wise and foolish virgins, in Matt. chapter 25. 'cointes', an unusual word for the former, is more expressive than 'wise'.

[65] Södergård notes (p. 182) that the lady was Æthelhere's wife, not Anna's (a mistake already in the Latin text). 'Edelher' appears at vv. 702 & 807 as Anna's brother, and is mentioned in *ODS* under the entry for Jurmin. The *note, in the later edition, remarks on this confusion.

[66] Södergård notes (to v. 184) a mistake here: Æthelweald succeeded his brother Æthelhere, who therefore succeeded Anna rather than Eadwulf. He gives dates of Anna's brothers' reigns in his IPN: Æthelhere 654–5; Æthelweald 655–64. A *note in the later edition suggests there may be a lacuna in or around this line.

[67] See *ODS* for Hilda; this is the first time she is mentioned in the Life.

[68] This Eadfrid 'lur aol' was their father, according to the IPN; but we have been told that Hereric, Edwin's nephew, was their father (Edwin's son was Eadfrid, and his nephew was Hereric). Södergård's Analyse makes Eadwulf's mother the sister of Hereswith (p. 8), which must be a mistake. Eadfrid is not the same as Edfrith of Lindisfarne (in *ODS*). The copyist may have confused the couplets about Hereswith and Hilda with the couplets about Sexburga and her marriage.

[69] According to *ODS* the girl was said by Bede to be Anna's daughter, although modern scholars make her his step-daughter. If the latter, Marie is right.

[70] This appears to suggest that marriage with God was a French idea, but it probably refers to the next few lines about nuns being sent to French houses. See *Liber*, p. 15: there were not many monasteries, so people used to go to the monasteries of the Franks.

[71] In theory, a woman brings a 'dowry' to the nunnery when she enters it.

A Calke, a Briges e alliors
Furent rendues des meilliors.
A Briges fu mise Sedree
Ky de l'autre seignur fu nee   216
Et Eldeberge ensemble ou li
Ky fu del naturel mari.
Wythburg, ki la puisné fu,
Espiré estoit de vertu.   220
Fiz des rois la voleient prendre,
Mes ele ne voleit mie entendre.
Richesce e parentee despit,
En solitaire liu se mist.   224
Pur avoir la Deu compagnie
Voit avoir solitaire vie.
Aprés la mort son pere Anna
A Dereheam se herberga.   228

Audrey's Death[72]

[f.114b] En cel tens furent mut seuz
Signes et miracles veus   1872
De la roine, sinte Audree,
Et de cele seinte assemblee.
En cors ou erent li dieble
Delivra la virge mirable   1876
Et de plusurs enfermetez
Delivra Deus les enfermez
Et cil ki loinz furent de ly[73]
Par li nomer furent gary.   1880
De totes gens estoit amee
Ceste roine et honoree.
Par la devine demoustrance
A ses noneines dist en oiance   1884
Ke une pestilencie vendroit

Ke suer la maison decenderoit.
Pur ce lur a devant moustree
Ke lur quers seient affermee   1888
Et ke lur poors soient mendre
En cele pestilence atendre.
En Elge ou icele abbeie
Fu ordenee et establie,   1892
Sainte Audree ki dame fu
Par seinteté et par vertu
Tint le covent en honesteté
Et garda bien tot son heé.   1896
Pur une grant dissencion
Ke nos ici vos mostrom
Que fu entre le rei Egfrid
Et le ercevesque, seint Wolfrid,   1900
Ki le roy de son sé geta, [f.11c]
Ou seinte Audree sejorna
Treis anz com en exil fu.
Ceo est par seint Bede coneu.   1904
Sainte Audree enveia a Rome
Pur lur bosoignes ce seint home
Pur lur abbeie amender
Et lur dignitez comfermer.   1908
Come seint Wolfrid de Rome vint
Par Suxesse son chemin tint.
Cel pais par unt i passa
A crestieneté atorna.   1912
Saint Wolfrid quant fu veneu,
En Ely fu bien receu.
Tel previlege i aporta
Ke tut tens iert et durera.   1916
En meisme cel an finy
Seinte Audree ke tint Ely.

---

[72] vv. 1871–950; pp. 106–8 in the edition.
[73] *d'Ely.

At Chelles, at Brie, and other places, they were sent the best of them! Saethrith, the one who was daughter of the other husband, was sent to Brie. And Ethelburga went with her, who was the daughter of the current husband.[74] Withburga, the youngest, was inspired by virtue. The sons of kings wanted to take her, but she would not hear a word from them. She despised riches and family, and took herself off to a solitary place. To have the company of God, she wanted to live a solitary life. After the death of her father Anna, she made her home at Dereham.

Audrey's Death

In these days there were many well-known signs, and miracles seen, of Saint Audrey the Queen and also her saintly company.[75] The marvellous virgin delivered many bodies that were possessed by devils, and God delivered many sick people of their afflictions; those who were far away [from Ely] could be cured just by saying her name![76] This queen was loved and honoured by everybody. Thanks to a divine warning, she was able to tell her nuns, for all to hear, that a pestilence was imminent and was going to descend upon their house. This is why she told them about it beforehand, so their courage would be fortified and their fears would be alleviated, while they awaited the coming of this pestilence.[77] In Ely,[78] where this abbey had been ordained and established, Saint Audrey who was their abbess kept the convent honestly thanks to her saintliness and virtue; she kept it well all her days.

Because of a dreadful quarrel, which we shall now tell you about, between King Egfrith and the archbishop Saint Wilfrid, the king threw him out of his see, and for the three years of his exile he stayed with Saint Audrey.[79] Bede knows all about it! Saint Audrey sent this holy man to Rome on their affairs, to help the abbey and to confirm their privileges. When Saint Wilfrid came [back] from Rome, he took his way through Sussex, and he converted to Christianity all the country through which he passed. When Saint Wilfrid came to Ely he was warmly received; he brought privileges with him that will be and endure for all time. In this same year Saint Audrey, who held Ely, died.

---

[74] 'naturel mari' sounds as though Saethrith was the daughter of an 'unnatural' marriage, although there is no hint of irregularity elsewhere in the text. Marie means that this husband is the one who concerns us here in Audrey's story.

[75] These are her nuns; the previous passage describes the convent of Ely (see also the Analyse, p. 15).

[76] This line may have been miscopied by Södergård: the later edition prints 'd'Ely' without noting a different reading in the appendix. I have adopted the correction, as it makes more sense.

[77] Södergård's Analyse says the women could comfort one another, and also take the necessary precautions in good time; this reading between the lines is not unreasonable. For the whole passage, cf. *Liber* pp. 48–50.

[78] *Note to this line (on p. 253) discusses Marie's use of 'Elge' meaning Land of God. See *Liber*, p. 3: the name came first from the abundance of eels in the place, and later the meaning was changed 'by way of improvement ... a house worthy of God' (here Elge refers to eels, Ely to God).

[79] *ODS* does not mention Audrey in connection with Wilfrid. *Liber* agrees that he spent time at Ely (p. 49), but a footnote warns that this is not in Bede (for which see Bede p. 225).

...

Le mal dont la dame moreut

Fu d'une grant enfleure ke li creut. 1920

Soz la gorge entur le col fu,

Dont la dame a tel mal eu

K'ele jeut et fu en languor,

Tant fu grevee en la dolur   1924

Ke tuz furent desesperé

De sa vie et de sa saunté.

La virge en oroison manoit,

Sa char dantoit et destroinoit.   1928

A Deu rendi grace et merci

De la dolur qu'ele sueffri.

Ele entendi ke Deu flaele

Ceuz k'il eime et ke il repele.   1932

Les riches homes sunt tant mari

Et les povres tut autresi:

Les riches pur lur seingnorie,

[f.114d]

Les povres pur lur grant aie   1936

De ceo ke lur donoit suvent

Ses asmones mut largement.

La seinte virge ert mut heitee

Et de son mal joieuse et lee   1940

Et dist sovent par son deserte

Li ert ceste dolur aperte

Pur les nuesches k'ele portoit

D'or, ou sovent se delitoit.   1944

Entur son col creoit seinte Audree

Ke par cel malfeit fust grevee.

Mes ele espera et crei

Que par cel mal espeni   1948

Le suerfait et la vanité

De l'or qu'ele avoit porté.

...

Marie's Sources, and her Name[80]

[f.134a] De un bon moine reconte   4540
    ci[81]

Ke estoit del covent de Ely

Ke leut la vie seinte Audree

En un livre ou il l'out trovee.

En engleis ert la vie escrite   4544

Ou li moine mut se delite.

Un bieu miracle i a trovee

Ke il a bonement recontee

De la roine, seinte Audree,   4548

Ki primes fu a Tonbert donee,

Un duec ke ert de grant valur

Et mut bien de nostre seigniur.

Ensemble furent seintement   4552

En bone vie et chastement.

Par un jur la roine estoit

En sa chambre ou ele entendoit

As puceles ke la servoient   4556

Et as overes ke eles fesoient.

Le duc ala a li parler

Par une bosoigne mostrier.

Kant il li out dist et mostré   4560

Et conseil quis et demandé,

Pur ce ke ele ne vout otreier,

La prist le roi a manacier.

La seinte virge en pes suffri   4564

Si que un seul mot ne respondi.

Homblement et en pes se tint,

De l'ewangelie li sovint

Ke dist ke pacience veint   4568

Malice et tres grant ire esteint.

La seinte virge estoit pensant,

[f.134b]

En son quer Deu orant.

---

[80] vv. 4540–620; pp. 179–81 in the edition.

[81] This line is numbered 4545 in the later edition; see their p. 15 for lines skipped in the earlier one.

The lady was dying of an illness in the form of a great swelling that grew upon her: it was on her throat and around her neck.[82] It gave the lady such pain that she lay powerless. She was so racked with this pain that everybody was in despair for her life and her health. The virgin remained in prayer, and she daunted and disciplined her flesh.

She gave praise and thanks to God for the suffering she was going through; she understood that God scourges those he loves and calls to him. All the rich were in distress, and so too were all the poor: the rich because of their right to receive rents,[83] and the poor [were in distress] because of the great help she gave them by frequently donating generous alms to them. The saintly virgin was well content; she was glad and joyful in her sickness. She often said she deserved this malady that had come upon her, because of the ornaments of gold she used to wear and delight in. She believed she was being punished around her neck for this sin. But she hoped and believed she was expiating, through this very sickness, the pride and vanity of the gold she had worn.[84]

Marie's Sources, and her Name

Here I shall tell about a good monk who was of the convent of Ely, and how he read the Life of Saint Audrey in a book where he found it. He delighted in the book, which was written in English. He found a beautiful miracle in it, which he retold very well. It was about Saint Audrey the Queen, who was given first to Tondbert. He was a duke,[85] most valiant, and beloved of Our Lord. They lived a holy life together, both good and chaste.

One day the queen was in her chambers, where she was listening to the girls who served her and supervising their work. The duke came in to speak to her about something that needed doing. When he had told her and explained it, he asked for her help and advice; then because she didn't want to agree with him he began to threaten her. The holy virgin suffered him calmly, not answering him a single word. She stayed quietly and humbly, remembering the Gospel where it says Patience conquers Malice and restrains furious Anger.[86] The holy virgin stood there, thinking, and praying to God in her heart.

---

[82] 'Soz' ought to mean 'under', but 'on' makes more sense in the context, unless the meaning is 'under her jaw'. Anglo-Norman sometimes confuses the forms 'sur', 'sus', and the like (see *Trinity Apocalypse*, ed. Short, p. 130).

[83] 'seingnorie' is their position; the abbey had been generous to them. 'The populace was afraid of losing its lady ...' (*Liber* p. 50; their 'lord' is female).

[84] The finery referred to was sold at Saint Audrey's Fair (*OED*, 'tawdry').

[85] Later in this passage Marie calls Audrey's first husband 'roi' (v. 4563); the 'prince' (in Bede) is called 'ealdorman' in *ODS* and *Liber*.

[86] *Note remarks that the Book of Proverbs (chapter 15) is a better source for this passage than the Gospels. Here, as often, Vices behave as if personified.

Ses ganz a de ses meins hostés,   4572
Si les a par devant li getez.
Seur un rai de soleil avint
Ke amedeuz les ganz sostint.
En pes i ont les ganz geu.   4576
Cel miracle a le duc veu
Et tut cil ke ou li vindrent
Ke a grant miracle le tindrent.
Le duc de ce ke il a leidi   4580
Mut durement se repenti.
Merci li cria bonement
Ke ele ne out ver li maltalent
Et bonement li pardonast   4584
Ke vers li ne se corouçast.
Ducement pur humilité
Li ad la virge pardoné.
Icist coruz dont ge vos di   4588
Ne vint pas de ovre de enemi,
Mes pur mostrier de Deu la gloire
Et de la virge la victoire.
Cist moine ke leut en sa vie   4592
Ce miracle ne creoit mie.
La nuit aprés, quant il se geut,
Seinte Audree li apareut
Et dist li ke il n'out dotance   4596

Del miracle ne mecreance
Ke il avoit en livre trovee.
Bien le seut pur veritee
Et ce estoit ele, seinte Audree,   4600
Ke a li estoit demoustree.
L'endemain le moine le dist
Et al covent saveir le fist. [f.134c]
De cele revelation   4604
Mercierent Deu et son non.
...
Issi ay ceo livere finé,
En romanz dit et translaté
De la vie seinte Audree   4608
Si com en latin l'ay trové
Et les miracles ay oy,
Ne voil nul mettre en obli.
Pur ce depri la gloriuse   4612
Seinte Audree la precieuse
Par sa pité ke a moy entende
Et ce servise a m'ame rende
Et ceus pur ki ge la depri   4616
Ke ele lur ait par sa merci.
Mut par est fol ki se oblie.
Ici escris mon non Marie,
Pur ce ke soie remembree.[87]   4620

---

[87] *Note (p. 257) that the last couplet is incomplete, and there is no 'amen' or other formal ending. It has been suggested that Marie left it thus deliberately, to focus attention on the word 'remembree'.

She took her gloves off her hands, and tossed them away in front of her. Then it happened: there was a ray of sunshine, and it supported both the gloves so that they hung there quietly![88] The duke saw this miracle, and so did all those who had come in with him; they thought it the greatest of marvels! The duke sincerely repented the hard things he had said to her, and he gently begged her forgiveness, so that she would not feel badly towards him, and that she would generously pardon him and not be angry with him. In her humility, the virgin most sweetly forgave him.

This Anger I'm telling you about did not come from the Devil's works, but in order to show the glory of God and the virgin's victory.[89]

The monk who was reading this miracle in her Life did not believe it! But the night after, when he was in bed, Saint Audrey appeared to him; she told him not to doubt the miracle, nor disbelieve what he found in the book. So he knew it was true, and that it was Saint Audrey herself who had been shown to him. He told the story in the morning, and made it known to the whole convent. They all praised God and his Name for making this revelation to them.

There, I have finished this book. I have translated it, telling in French the Life of Saint Audrey, just as I found it in the Latin; and the miracles, as I heard them.[90] I don't want any of it to be forgotten. Therefore I pray to the glorious and precious Saint Audrey, to listen compassionately to me, rendering this service to my soul and to those on whose account I pray to her, to help them in her mercy.[91] It would be very foolish to let oneself be forgotten, so I am writing my name here — Marie — so that I shall be remembered.

---

[88] This delightful idea is not unique to Audrey: there are two examples in *GL* (Supp), one for Saint Bride (pp. 144–5) and one for Saint Aldhelm (p. 187). See also Leyser, *Beda* (pp. 234–5 & 257) for this trait (common in Irish hagiography); the garments in question are those of Cuthman, Bridget, and Aldhelm. In *Sir Ferumbras,* ed. Herrtage, pp. 184–6 (the end of the poem is missing, so the final section of the French source is supplied), Charles 'tests' the relics wrested back from the Saracens by seeing if they will hang unsupported in the air — they do.

[89] It is an interesting comment here, that a sin is not caused by the Devil.

[90] It is clear that if she was a nun of Ely Marie heard the miracles told orally, including perhaps this last miracle from the monk himself, as well as reading the Life in Latin. 'romanz' means French (she does not call her story a 'romance').

[91] She is asking not only for herself but also for her companions in the convent.

The Life of St. Catherine, by Clemence

This text, Dean's 567, is Clemence of Barking, *The Life of St Catherine*, ed. MacBain (ANTS 18).[92] It survives in three manuscripts: MacBain edits from MS A (Paris, Bibliothèque Nationale, nouv. acq. fr. 4503); W is Welbeck, now known as the Campsey Manuscript; P is Paris, Bibliothèque Nationale, fr. 23112.[93] I have copied MacBain's text very closely, but I have not reproduced variants printed at the bottom of his page.

The focus of this life is very largely on the saint's intellectual abilities, and my passages are chosen to reflect the fact. Much of the text is dialogue; little is concerned with miracles, posthumous or not, compared with (for example) the Nun's life of Edward. *Catherine* has attracted a good deal of scholarly interest, and the published translation is now out of print and hard to obtain. This saint is among those admirable women who are held up as an example, in books of instruction and nurture: in the Knight's book she is used an an argument for sending girls to school to get an education, in spite of the fact that she came to what most would consider to be a sticky end.[94]

MacBain's introduction comments on the sub-genre of a Saint's Life built around a disputation, although we cannot positively identify the origins of the apologetic material in this legend of Katherine (pp. xi–ii).[95] He also remarks on a particularly nuanced portrait of the Emperor (p. xiv); other scholars have identified the influence of Tristan stories, especially in versification that recalls the poem by Thomas.[96] However, courtly influences notwithstanding, I no more identify the Nun of Barking with Clemence than I identify one Marie with all the others.[97] Katherine's arguments about God and Man, in which she plays on the paradox of the tree in the Garden of Eden and the tree that was the Cross, are comparable with arguments on this subject in *Piers Plowman*, passus XVIII.[98] This is a favourite theme, and can be traced in a number of places: for example *Golden Legend*, Jacobus de Voragine, tr. Ryan (vol. I, p. 209, in ch. 53).[99]

---

[92] Legge, pp. 66–72. Clemence of Barking, 'The Life of St Catherine', tr. Wogan-Browne and Burgess, has been consulted but not copied.

[93] See pp. xv–x of the edition.

[94] ed. Wright, and ed. Offord, chapters 90 & 89 respectively.

[95] Her name is spelt with a K where it appears in the text, although spelt with a C in the edition's title; I use Clemence's spelling for the saint (and the other for the edition).

[96] Thomas d'Angleterre, *Tristan*, ed. Wind; and Legge, p. 67.

[97] See my introductions to the Nun's work, and to *Audree*, above.

[98] [Piers] *The Vision of Piers Plowman*, ed. Schmidt; and *Piers the Ploughman*, tr. Goodridge (and their notes). Cf. also the 'sermon' preached to Ferraguz by Roland in *Pseudo-Turpin Chronicle*, ed. Short, pp. 50–54.

[99] I Cor. 15, esp. 21–2.

Text

Introduction to Katherine

[44v] D'escripture la fait aprendre,
Opposer altre e sei defendre.
El munt n'out dialeticien
Ki veintre la poust de rien.   144
Sages ert de mult de choses
    mundaines,
Mais sun desir ert as suvereines.
[En Deu mist tute sa entente ...[100]

The Convocation[101]

[47r] 'Ço sachent tuit e pres e loin
Que l'emperur ad grant besoin
— E meimement rethorien
Ki parler seivent e bel e bien —   332
Que tuit a l'emperur viengent,
S'onur e sa lei maintiengent,
Kar une plaideresse ad forte
Ki de sa lei guerpir l'enorte.   336
Si [il] ceste poent cunfundre,
Que ne lur sache mais respundre,
Que devant tuz seit recreante
Del desputer dunt tant se vante,   340
De ses cunseilz les frad privez
E sur tuz serrunt honurez.'

The Battle[102]

[52r] 'Segnurs, cumbien sufferum
    nus
Ceste fole ci entre nus?
Malement a noz deus rendum
Le bien que nus de els recevum,   740
Se nus tost nes venjum de li
Ki lur nun ad si escharni.
De lui quidai grant sens oir,
E pur ço nus fist l'um venir.   744
La fable nus dit de Jhesu

Ki ja[dis] fud en croiz pendu.
Un suen disciple le trahi
Ki as mals Judeus le vendi.   748
Par esguart le crucifierent
E meins e piez li encloerent.
Il ne pot de sa mort fuir
Car destresce li fist suffrir.   752
Al tierz jur pois resuscita.
Aprés ço el ciel munta.
Iço vunt crestien disant
E sil tienent pur tut poant.   756
Ceste recreit en lur errur,
Si dit que cist est criatur.
De lui sa raisun cumença,
Mais d'altre finer l'estuvera.   760
Ele ad tel chose cumencie [52v]
Dunt guaires n'iert avancie.'
    Quant ço out dit, ele respunt,
Oant ices ki oie l'unt: 764
'Par Deu, fait ele, 'si cume entent,
De lui oi bon cumencement,
De lui ki criad tute rien
E cumencement est de tut bien.   768
Bon cumencement oi de lui,
Par ki tu es e par ki sui.
De ço ne me deis tu pas reprendre
Se tu vels raisun entendre.   772
Pur ço me vels mes diz falser
Quant tu les tuens ne sez pruver.
Puis que mes diz tiens a fable,
Mustre dunc pruvance raisnable   776
Pur quei me vels issi blasmer,
Quant tu ne me sez amender.
Or m'en di la veire pruvance,
Car jo l'escut senz dutance.'   780

---

[100] MS W adds a few lines of extra description at this point.

[101] When Maxence, the pagan emperor, realises he cannot win Katherine over, he sends for learned clerks to oppose her.

[102] The whole exchange is very long, but very informative about many questions of medieval theology; I give the last part. One of the clerks bursts out in exasperation ...

Translation

Introduction to Katherine

He [her father] made her learn her letters, and to put questions to others, and to defend herself against them. There was no dialectician in the world who could overcome her. She was wise in all worldly things, but her desire was for heavenly things: she bent all her thoughts upon God.[103]

The Convocation

'Be it known to all far and wide that the Emperor is in dire need — of rhetoricians, especially, who can talk well and convincingly. Let them all come to the Emperor, to uphold his honour and his law! For there is a powerful orator here, and she is urging him to abandon his faith! If they can manage to confound her so that she can never answer them, and make her admit defeat in front of everybody, and deny this litigiousness she is so proud of, then he will make them his privy counsellors and they shall be given the highest honours.'[104]

The Battle

'Gentlemen, how long must we put up with this madwoman in our midst! We do our gods a disservice in return for the benefits we receive from them, unless we can take vengeance for them upon her for the way she has vilified their names! We thought we'd hear great wisdom from her, and that's why we were sent for. But she tells us fairy stories about Jesus! Who was hung on a cross long ago, because one of his disciples betrayed him and sold him to the wicked Jews. They decided to crucify him, and stuck nails through his hands and feet. He couldn't run away from his death; it was necessary for him to suffer. Then, on the third day, he came alive again; after that he went up to Heaven. This is what the Christians go round saying, and they call him Almighty. This woman believes it too, and calls him Creator; her arguments begin with him. But she'll have to think again before she's finished! She's started something, and not got very far with it!'

When he had said this, she replied in the hearing of all who listened to her: 'By God,' said she, 'as I understand it I've had a very good start: from him. From him who created all things, and who is the beginning of all good things, I've had a good beginning from him by whom you are, and by whom I am. So you have no right to contradict me, if you will just listen to reason. For you are trying to falsify what I say, when you can't prove what you say! Because you think what I say is fairy stories, now show me sufficient proof why you should blame me when you've no idea how to correct me. Go on, prove it; I'm listening!'

---

[103] It is notable that her education and skill in dialectic and rhetoric are forcefully stated first, before the fact of her Christian persuasion.

[104] Once the fifty learned clerks arrive, they are scornful of being set against a mere woman.

Cil li respunt par mult grant
   ire,
Car a peine li sout que dire:
'Par fei,' fait il, 'par ço te pruis
Qu'en tes diz verté nen truis.   784
Se il est cum tu nus diz,
E Deu e hume e a Deu fiz,
Cument pot le fil Deu murir
Ne nun mortel la mort suffrir?   788
Murir ne peut pas par dreiture
Quant nun mortele est sa nature.
Se hume fud, dunc est mortel
E nient a nun mortel uel.   792
Murir ne pot se il fu Deus
Ne revivre se fud mortels.
Cument puet hume veintre mort?
E se Deu murut ço fu tort.   796
Mortel ne puet mort eschiver
Ne nun mortel la mort user.
Cuntre nature te desleies,
C'ors de raisun te forveies. [53r]   800
Deu u hume granter le puis,
Kar d'ambure le dreit nen truis.
L'un u l'altre estre l'estuet,
Car l'un e l'altre estre ne puet.'   804
   Quant cist out sa reisun finee,
Ele li dist cume senee:
'Ci empire ta subtilité
De cuntredire la verité.   808
Pur ço que creire ne volez,
Unes cuntraires nus mustrez.
Se il est huem, dunc n'est pas
   Deus.
Se il est Deus, n'est pas mortels.   812
Granter ne vels que ço seit dreit,
Que Jhesu Deu e hume seit.
Se saveir vels la verité,
Oste la superfluité,   816
Le grant orgoil de tun fals sens,
Car n'as pas dreiturier defens.
Devien diciple pur aprendre
E jo te frai le dreit entendre.   820
D'oil ne de cuer ne veiz tu gute

Quant tu de ço as nule dute.
Or esguardez ses criatures
E lur estres e lur natures,   824
Kar par els purras saveir
Le suen nun disable poeir.
En tutes mustre sa poissance;
Il sul est a tuz sustenance.   828
Des qu'il tute rien fist de nient
E tute rien par sei maintient
E sur tute rien est poissant
E tut ad fait a sun talant,   832
Ne pot cil dunc hume devenir,
Ki tut puet faire a sun plaisir?
E ne pot il faire de sei
Ço qu'il fist de mei e de tei?   836
Par poesté, nient par nature,
Devint li faitres criature.
Hume devint a tuz mustrable,
Kar en sei fud Deu nun veable.   840
   [53v]
Se huem ne fust ne poust murir,
E se Deus, ne poust revesquir.
Briefment te dirrai ci la sume:
L'ume fu en Deu e Deu en l'ume.   844
Le fiz Deu en charn mort suffri
E la char en Deu revesqui.
Ne pot il sei resusciter
Ki mortels morz fist relever,   848
Li quel erent mort par nature
E par destresce de dreiture?
Lepruz e desvez esmunda,
Enferms e avoegles sana.   852
Si tu ne creis que Jhesu Crist
Ses miracles el mund feist,
Crei sevels nun que el nun Jhesu
Unt plusurs eu ceste vertu.   856
Plusurs par lui morz raviverent
E par sun nun enferms sanerent.
Bien deit estre cil Deu creu
Ki dune as suens tele vertu.   860
Mult est la vertu grande en sei
Quant hume l'ad tele par sa fei.

He replied very angrily, hardly knowing what to say: 'Faith,' says he, 'this is how I shall prove to you why I find there's no truth in your words. If it is as you tell us, he is God and man and son of God, how can the son of God die, or any immortal suffer death? It stands to reason, if his nature is immortal. If he was man, then he was mortal and in no way like an immortal. He couldn't die if he was God, and nor could he come to life again if he was man. How can a man conquer death? And if God died, that would be wrong. No mortal can escape death, and no immortal can experience it. You are arguing against nature, because you are wandering from the truth. God, I can accept, or man. But I can't see any sense in both; he's got to be one or the other, because both one and the other is not possible.'

When this man had finished his argument, she spoke to him wisely: 'It does harm to thy subtlety, when thou sayest against the truth.[105] Because you refuse to believe, you must show us a counter-argument. If he is man, he is not God; if he is God, he is not mortal. You don't want to believe this is the case, that Jesus is God and man. If you want to know the truth, get rid of the dross which is great pride in your false wisdom, for you have no justifiable defence. Become a disciple, so as to learn, and I shall make you understand the right. You can't see with your eyes, or your heart, if you have any doubt about this. Now, consider his creatures, their being and their nature, for by them you can know his ineffable power. He shows his power in them all; he alone sustains them. Since he made all things from nothing, and sustains all things himself; since he has power over all things, and made everything as he wished, cannot he then become man, since he can do everything he wants to? Cannot he do for himself what he did for thee, and for me? By power, not by nature, the creator can become creature. He became man, manifest to all, for in himself he is invisible. Had he not been man, he could not have died; had he not been God, he could not have come back to life. I tell thee again, in a few words: the man was in God, and God was in the man. The son of God suffered death in the flesh, and the flesh came back to life in God. Could he not resurrect himself, who resurrected mortal men? They had died, as was meet and right, under the constraint of natural law.[106] He cleansed lepers and madmen; he healed the sick and the blind. If thou canst not believe that Jesus Christ performed his miracles in the world, at least believe that many had this special strength in the name of Jesus.[107] Many were they who brought the dead to life, and many who healed the sick by his name. This God surely must be believed in, who gave such strength to his own. How great must be the strength in himself, when man has such strength through faith in him!

---

[105] Katherine's speech varies between 'tu' and 'vus' forms. Sometimes she is addressing the whole group; here she is clearly attacking just one of her antagonists. I do not reproduce every switch, but the occasional 'thou' is very forceful. The clerk calls her 'thou' throughout.

[106] The editor notes the Campsey MS (W) makes more sense than the base MS here.

[107] Katherine is leaning hard on this one clerk, directing much of her argument against him alone. 'vertu' means virtue, and also strength.

Bien la puet cil en sei mustrer
Ki as altres la puet duner.   864
Ci te pruis jo apertement
Que Jhesu est Deu veirement.
Car bien set l'um, si Deu ne fust,
Que ço pas faire ne poust;   868
E bien set l'um que hume fu
    Jhesu;
Ore est Deu e huem par vertu.
E se Jhesu la mort senti,
Par fei, pur ço mort nel venqui.   872
La mort n'ocist pas Jhesu Crist,
Mais Jhesu en sei mort ocist.
E si tu as d'iço dutance,
Encore te frai altre pruvance.   876
Se vus mei creire ne vulez,
Les enimis sevels creez,
Ki mes diz testimonient
E Jhesu fiz Deu estre dient,   880
Quant par sun nun sunt cunjuré,
    [54r]
Que de li dient la verité.
Mult heent a dire le veir,
Mais sa vertu tolt tut lur poeir,   884
Que le veir ne po[en]t celer;
Cuntre voleir lur fait mustrer.
Chaitif, mult as orrible errur
Quant tu ne creis al criatur,   888
El quel neis li enimi creient
Ki sa vertu criement et veient.
Par Deu mult me merveil de tei
Pur le grant sen que jo i vei,   892
Que tu nostre Deu si denies
E lui e sa croiz escharnies.
Dous essamples te musterai
Que jo en voz livres truvai,   896
Que Platun li sages escrist
De la sainte croiz Jhesu Crist.

Il dist que Deu se mustreit
Altrement que dunc n'esteit   900
E un signe avreit tut runt;
Ço est la croiz ki te cunfunt.
Sibille de la croz redit;
— Ço sai, ses diz avez escrit.   904
Ço dit: "Cil Deu est boneuré
Ki pent en halt fust encroé."
De sa venue profetiza,
De sa naissance assez parla   908
E de sa croiz e de sa mort.
Si ço ne creis, dunc as tu tort.
Des tuens oz tu ci regeissance
E de verité veire pruvance.   912
Il dist que Deus el mund vendreit,
En semblance d'ume appareit.
Sibille dist: "Boneuré fud
Cil Deu ki el fust est pendu."   916
Pur ço boneuré le diseit,
Kar bien sout que la mort
    veintreit.
Pur ço vus di les diz de voz,
Car pas ne crerriez les noz   920
Ne en nostre seinte escriture
Ki nus mustre tute dreiture. [54v]
Se les voz creire ne vulez,
Les noz malement dunc crerrez.'   924
    A tant se taist la Deu amie.
Cil l'ad derechief envaie.
'Certes,' fait il, 'si ço est veir
Que tun Deu seit d'itel poeir,   928
Ne se laissast ja en croiz metre.
D'iço desdi tei e ta letre.
Quel mestier ot cil de murir
Ki tuz poeit de mort guarir?   932
Cument pot mort lui dominer
Ki morz poeit resusciter?

'It must be clearly manifest in himself, who can give so much of it to others! So I prove to thee, openly, that Jesus is truly God. We know full well that if God were not then nobody could do such things. And we know full well that Jesus was man; he is God and man by this strength. And if Jesus suffered death, by God, death did not defeat him, death did not kill Jesus Christ but Jesus in himself killed death. Dost thou still doubt? I have other proof!

'If you don't want to believe me, then at least believe the demons![108] They can bear witness to what I say, that Jesus is the son of God, when they are conjured by his Name; they tell the truth about him. They utterly hate telling the truth, but his strength robs them of all their power so they cannot hide the truth; it forces them to testify aganst their will. Thou wretch! What hideous error, not to believe in the Creator, in whom even the demons believe, who both see and fear his strength! By God, I am amazed at you, for I can see your great wisdom; that you deny our God and scorn both him and his cross! I shall give thee two examples, that I found in your books that Plato the Sage wrote about the holy cross of Jesus Christ. He said God would show himself other than he was then, and there would be a clear sign:[109] the cross that confounds thee!

'The Sibyl also spoke of the cross — as I know, because you have her written words.[110] She said "This God is blessed, who hangs nailed up on the high wood." She prophesied his coming; she spoke much of his birth, as well as of his cross and his death. If you don't believe this then you are in the wrong; you have this confession in your own [books],[111] and it is a true witness of the truth. The Sibyl says God would come into the world, appearing in the form of a man. She says "Blessed was this God who was hung on the wood." She called him blessed because she knew he would conquer death. So, I am telling you about these writings of yours, because you will not believe ours, nor our Holy Scripture, that shows us all righteousness. If you won't believe your own, then you're hardly going to believe ours.'

Then the friend of God was silent; immediately this man attacked her.

'Oh yes,' says he, 'if it's true that your God is so powerful, then he would never have let himself be put on the cross. Therefore I despise you and your learning. What need had he to die, who could cure everybody from death? How could death take him, who could revive all men from death?

---

[108] 'Enemy' is a common word for evil spirits, or the Devil (cf. the Hebrew noun 'satan', which means adversary). It is used for the incubus who engendered Merlin; in *Des Grantz Geanz* (above, and see my note for Merlin) such spirits are called 'maufez' or 'deables'.

[109] The editor notes this is a difficult line even if 'runt' is taken to mean 'plain'; it could mean 'round', in which case the sign might be a cross within a circle.

[110] The Sibyl is masculine in gender, but most readers know of this legendary prophet as a female. MacBain's IPN spells her 'Sybil', but see *OED* and *OCL*; the latter gives an account of 'prophecies' surviving into the Christian era. Weiss, 'Emperors and Antichrists', contains an overview of Sibylline material in the Middle Ages.

[111] 'regeir' usually means to confess (one's sins); here it means to confess to a faith (cf. holy men and women known as 'confessors').

Ço desdi fiançusement.
S'il est Deu, ne murut naent.   936
S'il fud hom e mort senti,
Sa resurrectiun dunc desdi;
E si ço vels vers mei defendre,
Dunc t'estuet d'altrui sens   940
    aprendre.'
    Il est teü, ele li dit:
'De tei ai jo apris petit.
Sage te tinc, ore i met mais,
Car encuntre dreit es trop engreis.   944
Nul mestier n'ai de ta science,
E si cuntredi ta sentence.
Par tun sens iés tu ci deceu,
Kar tu n'as pas [bien] entendu.   948
Ço que enceis dis, uncore dirai
Ja seit que mes diz einz pruvai.
Jo di que Deu nostre salvere
Est par nature uel al pere,   952
E des qu'il est al pere uel,
Dunc n'est il pas en sei mortel.
Il ne pot en sei mort suffrir,
Ne dolur ne peine sentir.   956
Pur ço que murir ne poeit
En la nature u il esteit,
Se vesti de char e de sanc
Qu'il reçut d'un virginel flanc.   960
Sa nature pas ne muad, [55r]
Mais nostre par soe honurad.
La sue ne pot estre enpeirie,
Mais la nostre par soe essalcie.   964
Le pere ki lui enveiad,
Ki tute rien de nient furma,
Quant hume e femme aveit crié,
De mal de bien poeir duné,   968
Cist hume par le fruit pechia
Del fust que Deus li deveia.
Par cel fruit fumes nus dampnez
E a cruele mort livrez.   972

Pur ço que Deus ne velt suffrir
Que hume doust issi perir,
Reçut la fraile charn de l'hume
Pur guarir le fait de la pume.   976
Par le fruit del fust deveé
Fud tut le mund a mort livré.
Jesu fud le fruit acetable
E a tut le mund feunable.   980
Icist bon fruit fud en croiz mis,
Si ramenad en pareis
L'ume ki en fu hors geté
Par le fruit ki fud deveé.   984
Par cest froit fumes nus guariz
Ki par l'altre fumes periz.
N'est tei avis que ço dreit fust,
Que cil ki venqui par le fust,   988
Que par le fust fust pois vencu,
Par le fruit ki fud pois rependu?
Se l'Enimi l'ume enginna,
Qu'il le fruit del fust esraça,   992
E l'ume enginna l'Enimi
Par le fruit qu'el fust rependi;
E se Deus a l'hume n'aidast,
Ja hume le mund ne salvast.   996
Mais pur ço que Deus hume fist,
Fud dreit que l'ume maintenist,
E que par hume venjast l'ume [55v]
E par le froit vengast la pume.   1000
Bien poust Deus par poesté
U par sule sa volenté
Guarir le mund de l'Enimi,
Mais par greinur dreit le fist si,   1004
Que un hume l'ume venjast;
Ço que hume forfist, hume
    amendast.
Saciez que icest amendance
Nus dune de vie esperance   1008
De revivre aprés ceste mort.
S'ore ne me creis, dunc as tu tort.'

'I can confidently refute that! If he is God, he can't die; if he was man and underwent death, then I deny his resurrection. If you want to argue with that, you'll have to learn another way to do so.'

He fell silent, and she said to him:

'I have not learned much from you! I thought you were wise — now I'll qualify that, because you are so violent against what is right. I don't need your knowledge, and I defy your conclusions. You have been misled by your own thought, because you have not understood a thing! What I said before, I'll say again, even though I have already proved it.

'As I said, God our Saviour is by nature equal with the Father. Because he is equal with the Father, he is of course not himself mortal. So he cannot himself suffer death, and nor can he feel pain and torment. Because he could not suffer death in his own nature, as he was, he clothed himself in flesh and blood that he received from a virgin's body. He did not change his nature, but honoured ours with his own. His own could not be brought low, but ours is exalted by his. The Father who sent him, who created all things from nothing, when he created man and woman he gave them the power to know good from evil.[112] This man sinned by the fruit of the wood that God had forbidden. We were damned because of this fruit, and delivered to cruel death. But because God did not wish to allow man so to perish, he took on the frail flesh of man, to cure the effect of the apple. The whole world was delivered to death, for the forbidden fruit of the wood. Jesus was the acceptable fruit, fertile for the whole world. This good fruit was put on the cross, and so brought man back into Paradise, who had been thrown out because of the forbidden fruit. We are healed by this fruit, as we perished by the other. Don't you see it would be right, that he who would conquer by the wood, would be conquered afterwards by the fruit that was hung back up on the wood?[113] If the Devil tricked man, so that he pulled the fruit from the wood, then man tricked the Devil by the fruit when it was hung up again. If God did not help man, then man could never save the world. But because God made man, it is right he should protect man, and that by man man should be avenged; by fruit the apple should be avenged. God might well, by his might or simply by his will, save the world from the Devil; but he did it with better justice: a man avenged man, and a man redeemed what a man forfeited. You must understand that this redemption gives us hope of life, to live again after this death. If you don't believe me now, you are wrong!'

---

[112] This is a slight but interesting variation on Gen. 2:16–17: God told them not to eat of the tree of knowledge of good and evil.

[113] Katherine is not only playing with ideas of fruit and wood (or tree), she is punning on 'fust' (imperfect subjunctive of verb 'to be'), as well as the meaning 'wood'.

Ele s'est teue a itant.
Merveillent sei petit e grant   1012
De ço qu'ele ad issi parlé,
Sun dit issi par dreit pruvé.

Victory[114]

[56v]

Un des clers li respunt a tant
Ki sages iert e mult vaillant.   1076
'Certes,' fait il, 'dreit emperere,
Unques puis que nus porta mere,
N'oimes femme si parler,
Ne si sagement desputer.   1080
Ne nus mostre pas choses vaines,
Ainz sunt de verté tutes pleines.
Le plus dunt ele ad desputé,
Ço est de la divinité.   1084
Un[c] mais ne nus pot cuntrester
Nul a qui deussum parler.
Tel se tint sage a l'envair
Qui se tint fol al departir.   1088

Unc ne vi clerc si vaillant,
Que nel rendisse recreant.
Mais ses diz desdire ne puis
Kar falseté nule n'i truis.   1092
Ce n'est pas petite chose
Dunt ceste dame nus opose.
Del faitre parole del mund,
E par verté nos deus cunfund.   1096
Nus ne li savum mais que dire
Car false est la nostre matire.
En sun Deu creum veirement
Ki tute rien fist de neent.   1100
Puis que ceste dame nus dist
De la sainte cruiz Jhesu Crist,
De sun nun, de sa puissance,
De sa mort e de sa naisance,   1104
Trestut li sanc nus enfui
E tuit en sumes esbai.
De tus nos cuers en lui creum;
Altre chose ne te dirrum.'   1108

---

114 Predictably, Katherine has won over all fifty of the learned clerks. The emperor demands to know how on earth a little woman can have got the better of them; later he will have them all put to death.

Now she stops speaking. Everybody, great and small, marvels at how she could speak thus, and prove that her words are right.[115]

Victory

One of the clerks, who was wise and worthy, then replied to him.

'Indeed, good Emperor,' said he, 'never since we were born of our mothers have we heard a woman speak like this, nor debate so cleverly. She shows us no foolish trifles, but things filled full of truth. Most of what she argued was about divinity. Never before could anybody to whom we spoke oppose us. None of us who felt so wise at the outset, but felt fools by the end. I have never seen such a brilliant advocate, who can make anybody admit defeat. But I can't throw doubt on anything she said, for I can find no falsehood in any of it. It is no small matter, what this lady was disputing with us about: she spoke of the Creator of the whole world, and she has confounded all our gods with her truth. We don't know what more to say, for our case was false. We believe truly in her God, who made all things from nothing. When the lady told us of the holy cross of Jesus Christ, of his name and his might, of his death and of his birth, all our strength[116] drained out of us and we were left stunned. With all our hearts we believe in him, and there is no more we can say to you.'

---

[115] The passage continues with a description of the conversation that follows, with people arguing, and with Clemence's own thoughts. Katherine's account of the Fall differs very markedly from that in the *Creation* (above): two writers are treating the subject in different contexts and for different purposes.

[116] Literally, 'our blood ran away'.

Homiletic

Maurice de Sully: *Credo* and *Pater Noster*

Maurice de Sully, bishop of Paris, composed a series of homilies between 1168 and 1175. The manuscript from which this text is taken is listed by Dean (number 587) as Anglo-Norman, and dated to the middle of the thirteenth century.[1] I am grateful to Tony Hunt for allowing me to use his unpublished edition of these two pieces, and for his diligent rechecking of the MS as well as going over my drafts. Oxford, Bodleian Library, MS Ashmole 1280 (first half of the thirteenth century) is one of the earliest copies so far to have come to light.[2] Dean lists Insular manuscripts;[3] the edition by Robson is of a Continental MS (the Sens Chapter MS, Paris, BN, fr. 13314).[4] I have added line numbers to Hunt's text.

I conclude this section with a version of the same prayers in early Middle English, for comparison. These prayers are in the same hand as Scribe 1 of the *Middle English Physiologus*, and are printed as an appendix to it.[5] The manuscript is dated around 1300. This is not to say that the text was written at this date; it might be a good deal earlier. The language is certainly earlier and more difficult to read than that of the saints' lives copied in the mid-fifteenth century.[6] In the body of the *Physiologus* text, there is mention of 'pater noster and crede' (p. 5, v. 87, in the *Significacio* of the Eagle).[7] The eagle's bill is twisted so that, or because, he cannot yet say them!

---

[1] Homily ii and Homily iii, from the Ashmole MS.

[2] Reeves, *Religious Education*, p. 81; see also Meyer, 'Les manuscrits français de Cambridge (pt. ii)', 342.

[3] It will be noted that the *incipit* she gives for number 587 is slightly different from what is reproduced here, because it is from a different MS.

[4] My footnotes below cite *Maurice's French Homilies*, ed. Robson, where appropriate: pp. 70 & 75 for the MS, pp. 83–7 for the text.

[5] ed. Wirtjes, pp. 47–8 (for editorial procedure see p. xcii). I have consulted but not copied the edition; the text is transcribed directly from the MS.

[6] An example from a saint's life is given above, appended to the Anglo-Norman medical receipts.

[7] See also the *Bestiary* in *An Old English Miscellany*, ed. Morris (p. 4, vv. 111–13, dated to mid-thirteenth century), at the same point, though the remark is not in the appended Latin version. The prayers may have been copied here as a reminder to readers. Master Richard's eagle has a beak that is twisted because of pride (*Bestiary of Love*, tr. Beer, pp. 31–2).

Text

Credo

[f.19ra] *Credo in Deum patrem omnipotentem, creatorem celi et terre, et in*
Jesum Cristum filium eius unicum Dominum nostrum, qui conceptus
est de Spiritu Sancto, natus ex Maria virgine, passus sub Pontio Pilato,
crucifixus, mortuus et sepultus. Descendit ad inferna, tercia die resurrexit
a mortuis, ascendit ad celos, sedet [ad] dexteram Dei Patris omnipotentis.   5
Inde venturus est judicare vivos et mortuos. Credo in Spiritum Sanctum,
sanctam ecclesiam catholicam, sanctorum communionem, remissionem
peccatorum, carnis resurrexionem et vitam eternam, Amen.

Nus creuns la Sainte Trinité, le Pere et le Fiz et le Saint Espirit. Nus creuns
que le Pere, le Fitz, et le Saint Espirit sunt uns Deus tutpuissant et pardurables.   10
Nus creuns que le Pere et le Fiz et li Saint Espirit fist le cel et la terre et tutes
choses de nent. Nus cre[f.19rb]uns que le Fiz prist carn en la Virgine
Marie, ke il suffri passion el tens Pilate et ke il murist en la croiz pur hume
reindre de[s] peines d'enfer et que il fud mis en sepulture et ke il au
terz jorn resuscita de mort a vie et que il munta al cel et que il set a la destre   15
sun Pere, et que il vendra al jor de juise pur juger les visf[8] et les mort[z]
et rendra a checun ceo k'il avera deservi. Nus creuns que li Pere et le Fiz
et od le Saint Espirit est aurez et glorifiez. Nus creuns en Sainte Iglise et el
saint baptesme. Nus creuns la resurrectiun des cors al jur de juise, a la
pardurabele vie, Amen, ceo est verrement. Ceo est la creance par que[i]   20
Sainte [Eglise] creit et cunuit Deu. Qui [ad] ceste creance ad bone creance
et si fet bone ovre pur quei il seit tels ke il vuille regarder vers sun [pecché,
le] benfait [f.19va] su(n)lun k'il avara fet serra rendu devont Deu et si
li fra estuié desque algrant bosoing si il nel forfet entre ci et la. Seingnurs,
ceste creance que Sainte Glise ad en Deu est fundiment et cumencement   25
de tuz bens, kar sicume li apostre dit 'Sant fei ne poet nul hume pleisir
[a Deu]', ceste devét vus tenir et garder[9] que vus ne maumetez
les bens que en vus sunt par nule mescreance ne par sorceries ne par
karettes ne par nule autre chose que seit contrarie a la creance de Sainte
Glise, kar ceo sachez certeinement que cil qui sunt crestiens et   30
creient en Deu et funt sorceries ke il malmetent et destruirent del tut
en tut la sainte creance ki est en eus. Pur ceo dit li apostre a tele manere
[de] gent

---

[8] *sic,* for vifs.

[9] MS quarder.

Translation

Creed

I believe in God the Father Almighty, maker of Heaven and earth, and in Jesus Christ his only son Our Lord, who was conceived of the Holy Ghost, born of the Virgin Mary, suffered under Pontius Pilate, was crucified, dead and buried. He descended into Hell, on the third day he rose again from the dead, ascended into Heaven, and sits at the right hand of God the Father Almighty. Whence he shall come again to judge both the quick and the dead. I believe in the Holy Ghost, the Holy Catholic Church, the communion of saints, the remission of sins, the resurrection of the body, and the life everlasting. Amen.

We believe in the Holy Trinity, the Father, the Son, and the Holy Spirit. We believe that the Father, the Son, and the Holy Spirit are one almighty and everlasting God. We believe that the Father, the Son, and the Holy Spirit made heaven and earth, and all things from nothing. We believe that the Son took flesh in the Virgin Mary, that he suffered in the days of Pilate, and that he died on the Cross to redeem mankind from the pains of Hell, that he was put into the sepulchre, and that on the third day he rose again from death to life and that he ascended into Heaven, and that he sits at the right hand of his Father. And that he will come at the Day of Doom to judge both the quick and the dead, and will render to each person what they have deserved. We believe that the Father and the Son, with the Holy Ghost, is worshipped and glorified. We believe in Holy Church, and in holy baptism. We believe in the resurrection of the body on the Day of Judgement, to life everlasting. Amen, that means truly.[10]

This is the creed by which Holy Church believes in God and knows him. Whoever has this belief has good belief, and if he does good works in such a way as to pay attention to his sin, the good by which he has acted will be given up before God,[11] and it will be stored up for him against his great need, if he does not forfeit it between now and then. Good people, this faith Holy Church has in God is the foundation and beginning of all good things, for as the Apostle says: 'Without faith no man can please God'.[12] You must hold and guard this, so as not to misuse the good that has been placed in you by any wrong belief, nor by sorceries or enchantments, nor any other thing that is against the creed of Holy Church, for you must understand fully that those who are Christians and believe in God, but who perform sorcery, they corrupt and destroy completely the holy faith that is in them. Therefore the Apostle says to such people:

---

[10] The writer has altered the Latin of the Creed quite substantially in his translation.

[11] Meaning 'offered up'; S reads 'receüs' (received).

[12] Heb. 11:6.

Dies, inquid, observatis et tempora et annos ad facienda opera
vestra. Timeo ne frustra [f.19vb] *laboraverim in vobis.* Oez seignurs,
metez la sainte creance ki est fundement de tuz bens en vos currs, en tele   35
manere que vus la pussez gaurder[13] fermement et asurement et
establement et desur edefier les vertuz et les bones ovres *et crescere in*
habitaculum Dei in spiritu sancto.

Pater Noster

[f.19vb] *Pater Noster qui es in celis sanctificetur nomen tuum*
Nostre Pere, qui es el cel, sanctificé seit tun nun.
Adveniat regnum tuum
Avenge vostre regné.
Fiat voluntas tua sicut in celo et in terra   5
Seit feit vostre volunté; sicume ele [est] feit el cel, si seit ele feit en tere.
Panem nostrum cotidianum da nobis hodie
Nostre pain de chescun jur nos dunez.
Et dimitte nobis debita nostra sicut nos dimittimus debitoribus nostris
Pardunez nos meffaez sicum nus pardunun a ceus qui mesfeit nus unt.   10
Et [f.20ra] *ne nos inducas in temptacionem*
ceo est a dire, ne suffrez que nus seuns tempté ne par male temptation
al de(l)able ne per malveise char mené a mal.
Sed libera nos a malo, Amen,
ço est verrement, mes deliverét nus de mal. Amen.   15

En trestutes les paroles qui furint unches establies ne dites en tere, si est
la plus sainte et [la] plus aute et la meudre[14] la Pater Noster, kar ceste
numément establit Deu meimes et comanda la a dire a sez apostres et
eus a dire a ceus qui creient en lui. Pur ço qu'ele est dit et plus deit estre
dit en Saint Glise que nule autre, pur ceo devez vos saver que ele es[t] haut et   20
que ele amunte plus que nul autre oreisun, kar ço sachez certeinement
que tel poez vus estre, que plus demandét vos mal a vostre oes que ben
quant vos dites la Pater Noster et pur ço nus volens [f.20rb] que vus sachez que
vus dites et que vus demondez a Deu quant vus dites la Pater Noster. Si
vus dirruns et mustreruns ço que la letre ad en sei et ço que ele nus enseigne,   25
en tele manere que vus la puissét entendre, kar quant nus diuns la Pater
Noster, si feisun set requestes, ceo sunt .vii. peticiuns, a Deu.
Ore dirruns la premere peticiun que nus requeruns a Deu quant nus diuns la
Pater Noster: 'Nostre Pere, qui es el cel, sanctifié seit le tun nun.' Tels apele
Deu 'pere' quant a dit la Pater Noster que il vaudreit melz que il ne la deist,   30
kar il n'est pas(t) le Fiz Deu par nule bone ovre k'il face ne par nule bone
vie que il meint ne Deu nel reconuist a sun fiz pur le peché u Deable l'ad
mis,

---

[13] For guarder.
[14] MS la m. si est.

You observe days, he says, *and months, and times, and years* [for doing your deeds]. *I am afraid of you, lest I have bestowed upon you labour in vain.*[15] Listen, good people, put into your hearts the holy faith that is the foundation of all good things, in such a way that you may hold it firmly and surely and steadfastly, and upon it build virtues and good works, and grow in the habitation of God through the Holy Spirit.[16]

Pater Noster

Our Father, who is in Heaven, may your name be sanctified.[17]
May your reign come to pass.
May your will be done, as it is done in Heaven let it be done on earth.
Give us our daily bread.
Forgive us our misdeeds as we forgive those who have done wrong to us.
That is to say, do not allow us to be tempted by evil temptation of the Devil, nor led into evil by the wicked flesh.
This means, truly, but deliver us from evil. Amen.

Of all the words that were ever established or spoken on this earth, the holiest and the highest and the best is the Pater Noster, because it was established by no less than God himself; he commanded it to be said by his apostles, and to be told by them to all who believe in him. This is why it is is said, and must ever be said, in Holy Church more than any other. Therefore you must know that it is a high prayer and it rises up more quickly than any other. But you must understand that, whoever you are, you may be asking for evil as well as good when you say the Pater Noster. So we want you to understand what you are saying and what you are asking God when you say the Pater Noster. We are going to show you and demonstrate what the words mean in themselves and also what they teach us, in such a way that you will be able to understand. For when we say the Pater Noster we make seven requests, that is, seven petitions, to God.

Now let us say the first petition we make to God when we say the Pater Noster: 'Our Father, who is in Heaven, may your name be sanctified.' Some people call God 'father' when they say the Pater Noster though it were better they didn't say it, because they are no son to God through any good works they have done, nor by any good life they have led; nor does God recognize this person as his son because of the sin that the Devil has thrown him into.

---

[15] Gal. 4:10–11. I give the *AV* text, since the writer does not translate into French. For a similar passage, but in the context of Covetousness, see *Cher Alme*, pp. 332–3.

[16] Eph. 2:19–22. For further references, see Robson p. 196 notes 1–6 (heading ii).

[17] The Latin uses 'tu' for God, the French uses the formal 'vus' (in modern French churches God is called 'tu').

kar li maveis hume qui despit Deu et ses comandemenz e fet icels
choses que li Deable aime n'est [f.20va] pas fiz Deu, mes fiz al Deable, sicume
dist Nostre Sire as Gieus, qui de lui ne de ses paroles n'aveint cure: *Vos,*   35
inquid, ex parte[18] *diabolo estis* [John 8:44], 'Vus estes de cel pere qui est
Deable.' Ore bosoigne dunches celui qui veolt que Deus li oie et sa preere qui
il face teles ovres que Deus par sa grace a sun fiz le conuisse, et lores pura il
dire a dreit Pater Noster et l'orra et il frad ceo qu'il li demandera s'il veit qu'il
seit a sun profit. Et se cil ke prie n'est fiz Deu et il nel reconuist a sun fiz par   40
la sainte vie qu'il deit demener, sa preere ne serra pas oïe, kar sicume dit la
Scripture: *Peccatores non exaudit Deus* [John 9:31], 'Deus', ço dit, 'n'ot pas
les pecheurs.' [Ceo est] ceus[19] que de lui [n']unt cure et plus volenters
funt les ovres al Deable que les comandement Deu. Cheun hume se deit amender
[et] par bone vie demener deit il fiz Deu [f.20vb] devenir et lores l'orra Deus,   45
lores purra il dire 'Nostre Pere qui es [es] cels, saintifié soit le tun nun.' N'est
le nun Deu saint et saintefiez tut jorz en sei meimes ne plus ne poet estre
saintifié en sei meimes qu'il est? Mes vus devez saver que [quant] nus diuns
'saintefié seit le tun nun', nus ne preuns pas que li sons nuns seit
saintefié en lui meimes, kar il [est] parfitement saintefié, mes nus preuns   50
qu'il seit saintifié en cels en qui il n'est pas encore saintefié, e en qui il est
saintefié seit encore plus saintefié, kar quant li hume meuz creit tant est li
nuns Deu en lui plus saintefié. *Sanctificetur nomen tuum*, ceo est a dire 'Sire
Deus, saintifiez seit le tun nun es coers as paens e as Geus, as mescreanz,
a tuz ceus que tu as purveu a sauveté, qui il creint veirs Deu et   55
veirs Seignurs et que il plus fermement te anment.'

...

[f.21ra] *Adveniat regnum tuum*, 'Advenge le tun regné.' Damnedeus est
reis et guverne le sun regné totes ores *quia ipse gubernat omnes creaturas*
suas que sunt in celo et in terra, in mari et in omnibus abyssis. Ja seit iceo   60
que il seit reis et que sun regné seit tutes ures, nequedent si priuns que
avenge le suen regné pur ceo que meint hume ad en tere qui quide que
Deus [n]e[20] regne mie, mes li Deable regne par peché et qua[n]t nus
disuns *Adveniat regnum tuum*, si dep[ri]ons nus Deu que il destrue en tele
manere le regné et la pousté al Deable et de sa gent et que il mette einces la   65
bunté et la saintee que il ad mis en cels que lui aiment et en qui il regne par
sa grace et priuns nus uncore qua[n]t nus disuns *Adv[eniat] re[gnum] t[uum]*,
'Que avenge la fin del secle', que enemi vei[e]n[t] [f.21rb] et sachent que
est veirs[21] Deus et tuz puissant et veirs reis et que tute Seinte Iglise qui est
le sun regné mei(i)nnement seit eshausé et glorifié en cel et en tere, en tuz ses   70
fiz et en tutes ses files

---

18 The Vulgate reading is *patre*, but it is often deformed to 'parte' in commentators.
19 MS De vous que.
20 MS est.
21 MS verirs.

For the bad man who despises God and his commandments, and who does things the Devil loves, is no son of God but he is son of the Devil, as Our Lord said to the Jews who took no notice of him and his words: 'You are from that father who is the Devil.' Now it is necessary for anybody who wants God to listen to him, and to his prayer, to do such works that God in his grace will recognize him as his son. And then he can rightly say the Pater Noster and he will hear him, and will do what he asks of him if he sees it will be to his benefit. But if he who prays is no son of God, and is not recognized as his son by the holy life he ought to be leading, his prayer will not be heard. For it says in the Scriptures 'God does not listen to sinners.' Those who take no notice of him are more willing to do the Devil's work than do God's commandments. Such a person ought to mend his ways, and by living a good life become a son of God. Then God will listen to him; then he can say 'Our Father, who is in Heaven, may your name be sanctified.' Is not the name of God sacred, and sanctified every day, of itself, so it cannot be sanctified any more than it is already? But you need to know that when we say 'may your name be sanctified', we aren't praying for his name to be sanctified in itself, because it is already perfectly sanctified. But we pray for it to be sanctified in people where it is not yet sanctified, and in those where it is already sanctified for it to be sanctified even more. For the more you believe then the better is the name of God sanctified in you. The petition means 'Lord God, may your name be sanctified in the hearts of pagans and Jews, in unbelievers, in all those whom you have provided with salvation, that they may fear the True God and True Lord, and may love you more thoroughly.'

'May your kingdom come'; the Lord God is king, and governs his kingdom always. For he himself governs all his creatures that are in heaven and earth, in the sea and in all the depths. Even though he is king, and his kingdom is for ever, yet we pray that his kingdom may come because there are many on earth who believe that God does not reign; but the Devil reigns through sin, so when we say 'Thy Kingdom come' we pray to God that he will destroy in this way the reign and the power of the Devil and all his creatures, and that he will put into them the goodness and holiness he has put into those who love him, and in whom he reigns in his grace. And also when we make this petition we pray: 'May the end of the world come.' And let the enemy see[22] and know that he is true God, and all-powerful, and true king; and let all Holy Church that is his kingdom be especially exalted and glorified in heaven and in earth, in all his sons and all his daughters.

---

[22] MS vein; S has 'si anemi voient'.

Quia finito hoc seculo solus Deus regnabit quia ipse erit
omnia in omnibus. Cum evanuerit[23] *omnem principatum et potestatem*
et virtutem nec amplius angelus angelo vel homo homini vel demon demoni
dominabitur.

...

Fiat voluntas tua sicut [in celo] et in terra. 'Seit feit ta volenté en terre sicume   75
ele est feit el cel.' Seignurs, el cel est feit la volenté Deu parfitement *Quia*
angeli, archangeli, principatus, potestates, virtutes, troni, dominationes.[24]
Cherubin, Seraphin, patriarche, prophete, apostoli, martyres, confessores,
virgines et omnes electorum anime[25] que sunt el cel devant Deu,
obeissante [f.21va] a lui e funt parfitement sa volunté et sun   80
comandement, mes en terre ad mut de seus qui funt teles choses que Deus
ne voldrat mie. Et pur ceo priuns nus et disuns *Fiat voluntas t[ua] s[icut]*
in c[elo] et t[erra], ceo est autresi cume nus disuns 'Sire Deus, sicume
ceus qui sunt el cel sulunc la grandesce del ben que tu lur dones funt ta
volenté parfitement, issi doinges tu que li hume mortel la facent en terre   85
sulunc la grace que tu lur dones. Sire Deus, tu doinges que la face li apostoile
archiepiscopi, presbyteri et omnes ordinati ecclesie, reges, principes, comites,
milites, agricole, femine, pusilli cum maioribus.'

...

Panem nostrum cotidianum da nobis h[odie]: nostre pain de chescun jorn
donez nus hui. Hume qui est de deus natures, de nature corperel et de   90
spiritel [...][26] pain a l'alme. [f.21vb] Li pains a l'alme est sainte doctrine et la
predicatiun del comandament Deu par quei ele est ben enseigne sicume dit
li pains est la guareisun al cors.[27] Ceo savez vus ben, ceo li quer[e]z
volenters, l'un et l'autre demandét a Deu, si fereiz saveir et plus le pain a
l'alme que le pain al cors, kar si le cors ad ceo k'il veolt et alme murge   95
de faim, ceo est a dire si ele n'est enseignee, et fait iceo que deit, si irra
l'alme et le cors en la glorie pardurable.

...

---

23 S reads *evacuaverit.*

24 Col. 1:16.

25 See Richard de Saint-Victor, *Liber Exceptionum* (ed. J. Chatillon, Paris, 1958), p. 450, lines 25ff.
    For Richard, see *Cher Alme*, pp. 72 & 294.

26 Haplography: 'ad mester de deus pains, de pain corporel et de'.

27 MS paens en. See Robson p. 86 for a correct text.

For at the end of this world God shall reign alone, for he shall be all in all. So shall all Principalities and Powers and Virtues vanish;[28] no more shall angel be above angels, nor man above men, nor devil above demons.

May your will be done on earth as it is in Heaven. Good people, in Heaven the will of God is done perfectly, for angels, archangels, principalities, powers, virtues, thrones, and dominions ... cherubim and seraphim, patriarchs and prophets, apostles and martyrs, confessors and virgins, and all the chosen souls who are in Heaven before God are obedient to him. They do his will and commandment perfectly, but there are many on earth who do such things as God does not want at all. This is why we pray, saying 'Thy will be done', that is as if we say 'Lord God, just as those who are in Heaven do your will perfectly by the great goodness you give them, so grant us that mortal men may do your will on earth according to the grace you give them. Lord God, grant that the Pope[29] may do it, and archbishops and priests and all those ordained in the church, kings and princes, counts and knights, farmers and women, small as well as great.'

Give us this day our daily bread. Man who is of dual nature, body and spirit, [needs two kinds of bread: earthly bread for the body and spiritual] bread for the soul. Holy Doctrine, and the preaching of God's commandments, are bread for the soul, by which it is well taught that bread is good for saving the life of the body. Know this, you must ask for it eagerly, ask God for both this kind and that, but I want you to ask more for the spiritual than for the corporeal. Because if the body has what it needs but the soul dies of hunger, meaning it is not taught, [then both body and soul will go to the fire of Hell. But if the soul is well taught,] and does what it ought to, [and knows what it ought to know,] then soul and body will go to everlasting glory.[30]

---

[28] These are some of the orders of angels (see *Cher Alme*, p. 14).

[29] 'apostoile' means both Apostle and Pope.

[30] Passages in square brackets translated from S.

Dimitte nobis d[ebita] n[ostra] s[icut] n[os] d[imittimus] d[ebitoribus] n[ostris]:
et pardune nos meffaiz sicume nus pardununs a cels qui meffez nus unt. Ci
poet oir celui qui volt que Deus li pardune ses pechez, si cuvient que   100
il parduinge a celui qui meffez li ad meimment se cil que meffet li ad, crie
merci et li offre dreit avenable. Si lores [f.22ra] ne li pardune, pur nent dit la
Pater Noster, kar il demande a sa dampnatiun la u il die *Dimitte etc* car si li
vaudreit meuz tesir(e) qui Deus preer desque il ne veolt autri parduner si cume
deverat, pardune dunches a autri meiment quant il vus crie merci e il   105
vus offre dreit avenable, si vus volez que Deu vus pardoint vos pechez, kar
sicume Deus dit *eadem mensura quam mensi fueritis remetietur vobis*
[Luke 6:38], 'Sulunc la mesure que vus suffrez a autri, sulunc cele vus
remesura il.'
...

Et ne nos inducas in temptationem: et ne nus meinés en temptaciun. Ceo est   110
a dire, ne suffrez que nus par temptement seuns mené a mal. Li D[e]able
veit envirun et asaie la gent, saveir mun s'il purra ren prendre. Il tempte les
bons moines et les chanoines et les hermites et le[s] reclus, les humes et les
femmes, les [f.22rb] povres, les reches pur eus atraire al ma[l], kar il sunt
tost trebuché en peché, mes li produme et prodefemmes se defendent   115
vertuosement et pur ceo *accipient coronam vite quam repromisit
Deus diligentibus se* [Jac. 1:12].[31]
...

Libera nos a malo: delivre nus de mal et de tuz maus del cors et de l'alme,
ceo est del mal de cest secle et de l'autre, ceo est del mal que vus apelez
peché et del mal qui est apelé peine. Amen ceo [est] veraiment. Ceo aferme   120
tutes choses que nus demanduns a Deu en la Pater Noster, Amen vaut
autretant cume si nus deisons a Deu 'Sire Deus, veraiment nus otriez ceo
que nus avuns demandé en la Pater Noster. Veraiment seit saintefié le tun
nun, avenge le tun regné, veraiment seit feit la tue volunté en terre sicume
ele est [f.22va] feit el cel, veraiment nus dune hui nostre pain de cheun jor,   125
veraiment nus pardunez nos pechez sicume nus pardunum a ceus qui
meffeit nus unt, veraiment ne suffrez tu que Deable nus tempte a mal faire,
veraiment nus deliverés de mal.' *Libera nos a malo. Pater, da nobis bonum
anime, bonum corporis in hoc seculo, bonum in futuro, bonum quod est
justicia, bonum quod est gloria.*   130

---

31 Richard, *Liber*, p. 454, lines 11ff.

And forgive us our sins, as we forgive those who have sinned against us. Hear this, then: whoever wants God to pardon his sins, it behoves him to pardon the one who has sinned against him, even if that one who sinned against him has begged his pardon and offered him suitable compensation.[32] If he will not forgive him then, he says the Pater Noster in vain, for when he says 'forgive' he is praying for his own damnation; he would do better to keep quiet than pray to God thus, since he will not forgive another as he ought. Therefore forgive others, especially if they beg your pardon and offer suitable compensation, if you want God to forgive your sins. For as God said, 'According to the measure you allow to others, so will he measure unto you.'

And lead us not into temptation. This means, do not allow us to be led into evil by temptation. The Devil goes around trying people, to ascertain whether he can grab anybody.[33] He tempts the good monks and canons and hermits and recluses, men and women, the poor and also the rich to draw them towards evil, for they are easily tumbled into sin. But good men, and good women, defend themselves virtuously; therefore *they receive the crown of life, which the Lord hath promised to them that love him.*[34]

Deliver us from evil, and from all ills of body and soul, that is ills of this world and the other. In other words, from the ill you call sin and from the ill that is called pain. Amen, this means truly. This affirms all the things we ask of God in the Pater Noster: Amen is as if we were saying to God 'Lord God, grant us truly all we have asked for in the Pater Noster. May your name truly be sanctified, and your kingdom come. May your will truly be done in earth as it is in Heaven. Please really give us our daily bread today, and really forgive us our sins as we forgive those who have sinned against us. Please really do not allow the Devil to tempt us to do evil, and please really deliver us from evil.' Deliver us from evil. Father, give us the good for souls and bodies, in this world and the next; give us the good that is justice and the good that is glory.[35]

[Hunt continues: 'This [the Pater Noster] is followed by Richard de Saint-Victor's Commentary. At ff. 26va–29ra there is a commentary on the Credo.'[36] I append the following,[37] transcribed from a scan sent me by the British Library, of BL MS Arundel 292.]

---

[32] The reasoning here seems rather strange, but S says the same. It probably means that one ought virtuously to refuse compensation.

[33] 'ren' or 'rien' can mean anything, or nothing, but is also used of people.

[34] I use the *AV* text (emphasized), copied here since the writer does not translate the Latin.

[35] For further references, see Robson pp. 196–7, notes 1–18 (heading iii).

[36] These two items have not been transcribed. The transcription reproduced above places *Pater Noster* before *Credo*, but I have restored them to the order in which they appear in the manuscript.

[37] See my introduction to this section, above.

Text

CREED

[f.3r] Ileue in godd almicten
faðer,[38]
Ðatt heuene &[39] erðe made to
gar,
& in ihesu crist his leue sun,
Vre onelic louerd ik him mune,
Ðatt of ðe holigost bikennedd　　5
was,
Of marie ðe maiden boren he
was.[40]
Pinedd under ponce pilate,
On rode nailedd for mannes sake.
Ðar ðolede he deadd wiðuten wold
I biriedd was in ðe[41] roche cold.　　10
Dun til helle licten he gan;
Ðe ðridde dai off deadd atkam;
Toheuene he steg in ure manliche;
Ðar sitteð he in hijs faðeres riche.
O domes dai sal he cumen agen　　15

To demen dede & liues men.
I leue on ðe hali gast,
Al holi chirche stedefast,
Men off alle holi kinne,
& forgiuenesse of mannes sinne,　　20
Vprisinge of alle men,
& echelif ileue. Amen.

THE LORD'S PRAYER

Fader ure ðatt art in heuene blisse,
Ðin hege name itt wurðe bliscedd;
Cumen itt mote ði kingdom;　　25
Ðin hali wil it be al don
[f.3v] In heuene & in erðe all so,
So itt sal ben ful wel ic tro;
Gif us all one ðis dai
Vre bred of iche dai　　30
& forgiue us ure sinne,
Als we don ure wiðerwinnes;
Leet us noct in fondinge falle,
Ooc fro iuel ðu sild us alle. Amen.

---

[38] Each prayer is headed by a title written to the right of the first line, thus: || Credo in deum; and || Pater noster. Letters in italic denote the expansion of abbreviated forms.

[39] 'and' is written as a nota.

[40] This line is lacking in the edition.

[41] MS de. Several of these letter forms could be either d or eth.

Translation

Creed

I believe in God the Father Almighty,
That caused heaven and earth to be made,
And in Jesus Christ his dear Son,
Our only Lord, I grieve for him,[42]
That was begotten of the Holy Ghost;
Of Mary the maiden he was born.
He suffered under Pontius Pilate,
And was nailed on the Cross for Mankind's sake.
There he underwent death, out of this earth,
And he was buried in the cold stone.
Then he descended down to Hell;
The third day he came back again from death,
And he went up to Heaven in his Man's body,
Where he sits in his Father's kingdom.
On the Day of Doom he shall come again,
To judge both live and dead men.
I believe in the Holy Ghost,
The all-holy established Church,
All men of saintly life,
And forgiveness of Man's sin,
In the resurrection of all Mankind,
And I believe in eternal life, Amen.

Lord's Prayer

Our Father who art in the bliss of Heaven,
May thy high Name be blessed,
May thy kingdom come,
And may all thy holy will be done
In Heaven and in earth likewise,
So it shall be truly, I believe.
Give us all today
Our daily bread,
And forgive us our sin
As we do our enemies.
Let us not fall into temptation,
But shield thou us all from evil, Amen.

---

[42] 'mune' usually means to think or to consider; it can also mean 'grieve', which is appropriate here.

Sermon on Joshua[43]

ANTS Plain Texts have no glossary, as previously mentioned, so a translation of some samples may prove useful. Here is Sermon 4 (in PTS 13, *Sermons on Joshua*, pp. 18–23): *The Walls of Jericho*. It is headed 'Origen (Homilies 6–7)';[44] my text follows it very closely, although I have added line numbers to aid navigation and made very minor changes to punctuation. Because the lines in the edition are longer than is convenient for this book, I have taken the unusual step of presenting them in five-line groups as prose; this preserves the beginning of every fifth line. I have signalled breaks on the edited page by inserting dots, to separate the long paragraphs.[45] Further to aid navigation, page numbers of the edition are signalled in my footnotes.

The Latin in the text is translated closely and immediately by our author into French; I translate the Latin only if it differs enough to give extra meaning. Jesus Navé, or 'fils Navé', is the name given to Joshua throughout the Sermons. Joshua son of Nun prefigures Jesus son of Mary.[46] I am grateful to Matthew Albanese for providing me with the relevant passage from the Greek Septuagint (Jos. 1:1), which clearly shows the form which has been transliterated as 'Naue': Ἰησοῖ υἱῷ Ναυή.[47]

The manuscript is Oxford, Bodleian Library, Douce 282 (mid-thirteenth century); variants in Hunt's notes are from C (Cambridge, Trinity College, O.2.14, mid-thirteenth century) and P (Paris, Bibliothèque Nationale, fr. 19525, second half of the thirteenth century). Because the text is very dense on the page, making it difficult to read, I have taken the liberty of omitting the references to 'Rufinus' embedded in the edited text; these are explained in the Introduction (PTS 12, p. 1).[48] Origen's Homilies are extant only in the translation by Rufinus; however, the writer of this Sermon departs repeatedly from the source. The Bible references in Hunt's text are to the Latin Vulgate, and have been copied here as they appear on the edited page (the writer uses the Rufinus version of the Latin Vulgate text). My translation provides corresponding Bible passages from *AV* (in italics) only when they match the writer's French wording closely.

---

[43] ed. Hunt (ANTS PTS 12, 13); Dean 595.

[44] The source is *Origène, Homélies sur Josué*, ed. A. Jaubert, Sources Chrétiennes 71 (Paris, 1960).

[45] My own paragraphs in the translation match the sense, if not the layout, as closely as possible.

[46] See Sermon 1 (PTS 12, p. 9).

[47] *Nave* is the Greek form of the Hebrew proper name Nun; Joshua is an alternative form of the (Greek) name Jesus.

[48] Hunt points out that the writer is inspired by the source rather than translating directly from it, following the choice of episodes and scriptural quotations but not the commentary itself. Exegetical vocabulary is discussed briefly on p. 4.

Text

[f.47v] *[Cum] autem esset Jesus in agro urbis Jericho, respexit oculis et vidit hominem
contra se et evaginatus gladius erat in manu eius et cetera* [Jos. 5:13]. Ço cunte l'estorie
de la lei: [Q]uant Jesus Navé fud el champ de la cité Jericho, il regarda des oilz e
vit un hume ester encuntre lui ki tint une espee nue sanz waine en sa

main. E Jesus aprimat a lui si li dist: *Noster es an adversariorum?* [Jos. 5:13], 'Es-tu   5
de noz u de noz adversaries?' E cil li dist: *[E]go sum princeps milicie Domini. Nunc
adveni* [Jos. 5:14], ço est 'Jo sui prince de la chevalerie Deus. Ore vinc.' Quant Jesu
ço oid, aurat le e dist: 'Sire, quei cumandes tu a tun serf?' [Jos. 5:14]. E cil li dist
'Deslie tun chalcement de tes piez, le liu u tu estas

pur veir est terre sainte' [Jos. 5:15]. E dist li sire a Jesu: 'Jo t'ai duné en ta main   10
Jericho' [Jos. 6:2]. Dunc pristrent .vii. prestres .vii. busines sicum Deu lur aveit
cumandé e alerent devant l'arche Deus avirunant la vile Jhericho e sunant les busines
sis jurz prés a prés. Al setime jur liv[er]ent par matin e avirunerent la cité set feiz.
Al setime jur sune une busine lunge e clere. Dunkes dist Jesus al pueple Israel,
dunt une partie alat devant

l'arche, une partie aprés: 'Criez. Deus vus ad duné ceste cité. Seit la cité maldite e   15
tutes les choses ki la dedenz sunt fors sule Raab, ele vive e saluee seit [f.48r] od tutes
ses choses ki en sa maisun sunt' [Jos. 6:16–17]. E dit Jesus: 'Guardez des choses
maudites, ke vus ne facez la maisun Israel maldite, parunt vus seez destruite e tute
Synagoge' [Jos. 6:18]. Li pueples dunkes cria e les busines sunerent e li mur de
Jericho

chairent e li fiz Israel munterent en la cité, chascun par cel liu ki encuntre lui ert,   20
e issi fud tute Jericho reversé fors sule cele putain Raab ki od tute sa maisnee fud
salué. *[E]t adicta est in Israel usque in odiernum diem* [Jos. 6:25], 'E Raab', ço dit
l'estorie, 'est ajustee a Israel desque al jur de ui.'

...

Tute ceste aventure avint par figure e fud mis en escrit pur assenser nus ki sumes
en la

vespree del siecle. E pur ço ke nus ne suffisuns neent a esclairer la raisun de cest   25
escrit par nus, requeruns ententivement le Seint Esperit k'il nus duinst sa grace en
aie ke dignement puissuns remuer la cuverture de la lettre, ke li tresors ki desuz
tapist al pru de noz almes en la lumiere del Seint Esperit seit esclairé.

Translation

The history is recounted thus in the Old Testament:[49]

When Joshua was in the field at the city Jericho, he looked around and saw a man coming towards him holding a naked sword, unsheathed, in his hand.

And Joshua went to him and said 'Are you one of ours, or are you one of our enemies?' And he said to him 'I am the Prince of the Chivalry of God. Come now!' When Joshua heard this, he worshipped him and said 'Lord, what do you command of your servant?'

And he said to him 'Undo the fastening of the shoes off thy feet, for truly the place where thou standest is holy ground.' And the Lord said to Joshua *I have given into thine hand Jericho.*

Then seven priests took seven trumpets, as God had commanded, and went before the Ark of God around the town of Jericho, sounding the trumpets, for six days once every day. On the seventh day they arose in the morning and went around the city seven times. On the seventh day a trumpet sounded loud and long.

Then spoke Joshua to the people of Israel, part of which went before the Ark and part after it, 'Shout! God has given you this city. May the city be accursed, and everything that is within it, excepting only Rahab;[50] let her be saved alive, and everything with her that is in her house.' And Joshua said 'Beware the accursed things, or you will make the house of Israel accursed; by which you and all the Synagogue will be destroyed.'

So the people shouted, and the trumpets sounded, and the walls of Jericho fell down. And the sons of Israel went up into the city, each going in the way nearest to him.

Thus was the whole of Jericho brought low, except for the harlot Rahab who was saved with all her household. 'And Rahab', says the story, 'was united with Israel, from that day to this.'

All this adventure happened figuratively, and was put in writing as instruction for us who are in the evening of the world.

And because we are incapable of explaining the sense of this writing by ourselves, let us pray devoutly to the Holy Spirit to send us his help of grace, so we can fittingly remove the veil of the text.

Thus the treasure hidden underneath may be illumined for the good of our souls by the light of the Holy Spirit.

---

[49] 'la lei' means 'the law'; The Old Law and the New Law are the Old and New Testaments respectively. See, in this context, Jos. 1:8, *This book of the law.*

[50] Rahab helped the Israelites by hiding their spies (Jos. chapter 2). She appears in lists of good women in texts such as the Knight's book (ed. Offord, and ed. Wright, chapters 87 & 88 respectively).

Dunt jo, pecheres(se) plus ke autre hume ki neent ne (ne) sui digne de enquere la
parfundesce de si grant segrei

Damnedeu, devant tuz autres rende graces a Deu de sa demustrance, ke puisse   30
veraiement dire od le Prophete: *[E]cce veritatem dilexisti incerta et occulta s[apientie]
t[ue] m[anifestasti] mihi* [Ps. 50:8], ço est a entendre 'Estevus veirement verité
amastes, les choses dutuses e celees demustré m'avez en apert.' Ço dit en l'estorie
ke li fiz Navé vit el champ de Jericho un hume encuntre lui ki tint une espee

nue. Cest champ signefiat les quors de cels ki creirent ke [f.48v] Jesu ert a venir   35
pur le[51] mund salver. Quors de hume veirement sunt ensement cume champ dunt
Deus, ki cultivur est celeste, esrace carduns de vices e de mescreance e seme greins
de vertuz e de veire creance. En cest champ devant ço k'il prist humanité fud Jesu
Crist par desir de ses esliz es desirus quors de cels sulunc la purveance sun pere en
une manere ja

furmé hume. Le vit le fiz Navé al regard de ses oilz esperitels par creance e par   40
entendement. Il le vit, ceo dit, ester encuntre sei, kar ço fud avis al pueple Israel e
a lur princes ke Jesu Crist estut contre eals quant il quiderent ke il volsist lur lei
abatre. Mais il ne l'abati nent, einz le parempli. E pur ço est escrit en l'estorie li fiz
Navé aprima a lui. Cument? Esmerveilant, enquerant, prophetizant. E dist: 'Es-tu
nostre u de

noz adversaries?' e il respundi: 'Jo sui prince de la chivalerie Deu. Or vinc.' Par   45
ço devuns entendre ke tuzdis se presente Deus a cels ki pur lui e pur sun dreit
cumbatent e travailent. Le fiz Navé regarda des oilz e vit un hume. Dun n'out il
anceis gardé e veu humes asez? Oil. Mais a cest regard vit il un hume de autre
vertu ke ainz n'out veu. Cest regard ert des oilz del quor ki sunt apelé raisun e
entendement. De ces oilz vit il

ke il n'ert neent sulement hume cume autre, einz ert plein de vertuz. Mais uncore   50
ne sout il neent lequel ces vertuz furent de Deu u de diable. E pur ço enquist
ententivement e demanda humblement ki il ert. E quant [f.49r] il fud acerté de li
mames, dunc se laissa chaer a ses piez e devotement le aura e dist: 'Sire, ke cumandes
tu a tun serf?'

---

[51] End of p. 18.

And I,[52] a greater sinner than any man who is wholly unworthy to enquire into the depths of so great a secret of the Lord God, above all others I render thanks to God for his manifestation to us, to be able truly to say with the Prophet 'Behold, truly you love truth; you have openly shown to me the things that are cloudy and hidden.'[53]

It says in the history that the son of Navé saw a man approaching him in the field of Jericho who held a naked sword. This field signified the hearts of those who believe that Jesus was coming to save the world.

Human hearts are truly just like a field where God, the heavenly husbandman, roots out the thistles of vice and wrong belief, and sows seeds of virtue and right belief. Jesus Christ was in this field, before he became a man, through the desire of his chosen ones, in their desiring hearts, according to the will of his Father in a manner he was already made man.

The son of Navé had sight of him by his spiritual eyes, through faith and understanding. It is said that he saw him coming against him, for it was the belief of the people of Israel and their princes that Jesus Christ stood against them when they thought he wanted to tear down their law.

But he did not tear it down, he fulfilled it! Therefore it is written in the history that the son of Navé approached him. How, then? By marvelling, questioning, and prophesying. And said 'Are you ours, or of our enemies?' and he said 'I am the Prince of God's Chivalry. Come!' By this we must understand that this is how God always shows himself to those who fight and work for him and his justice.

The son of Navé lifted up his eyes and saw a man. Had he not seen and looked at enough men already? Yes, of course. But with this look he saw a man with more power than any he had ever seen. This look was with the eyes of the heart, which are called Reason and Understanding. With these eyes, he saw that this was not just a man like any other, but one who was full of power. But he did not know yet which of these powers were from God or from the Devil. This is why he enquired cautiously, and asked humbly who he was.

And when he was certain within himself, then he fell down at his feet and devoutly worshipped him and said 'Lord, what do you command your servant?'

---

[52] The editor has corrected the MS 'pecheresse'; it is remotely possible the text was intended for a woman but subsequently rewritten, although there are no further clues. If so, it is more likely that the writer used a female persona (to show the text is for female use) than that the writer was in fact female; but cf. 'A Woman's Prayer' in *Cher Alme*. Women used religious literature abundantly; some may have been able to read books such as this to their illiterate families.

[53] *LV* Psalm numbers differ slightly from *AV*; this is Ps. 51:6.

Estevus desque il cunut k'il fud veirs Deus, e neent einz, ert il prest de

faire sun cumandement. Ensement avint de Jesu nostre Salveur e de plusurs Gius   55
e de autres poestis humes del siecle. Il furent lunges en dute del Salvur, mais
desque il le cunurent en la lumiere de ses granz miracles e k'il paremplirent[54] la lei
esperitelment, dunc aprimes se convertirent il a lui e reçurent ses cumandemenz.

...

Par ceste ententive enqueste sumus nus apris ke nus ne devuns neent estre trop
hastifs

de creire ne ço ke l'uem a l'oil veit ne ço ke l'um des oreiles ot, kar oil pot estre deceu   60
par adubement u par fantasme, oreille par mençunge. De creance dist li Apostre:
[N]olite credere omni spiritui, sed probate spiritus si ex Deo sunt [I Joh. 4:1], ço fait a
entendre 'Ne creez nent ço ke chascun vus dit. Pruvez primes si ço ke l'em vus dit
vienge de bon esperit.' Le fiz Navé aurat cel hume neent pur ço ke il ert

de part Deu, mais pur ço k'il fud maime Deu. Autrement ne l'eust il nent auré se   65
il nel cunust e cert fust ke il ert Deus. Veirement est Jesu Crist, ki est veirs Deus e
veirs hom, prin[ce] de la chevalerie Deu, kar tute la chevalerie celestiene, angeles,
arcangeles, vertuz e dominatiuns, poestez e principatés sunt tuzdis en la chevalerie
Jesu Crist, kar il est Prince des princes e Poestif sur poestifs, e il dune les poestez

sicum il dit par example en l'Ewangelie: *[E]sto et tu potestatem habens supra .x.*   70
civitates [Luke 19:17], ço est 'E tu aies poesté sur dis [f.49v] citez.' L'espee ke nostre
Prince tient traite e nue en sa main est la parole Deu. La waine de ceste espee fud
la lettre de la lei. Ceste espee fud deswainee e desnuee des icele ure, ke en la lumere
de vertuz e de miracles furent aparisantes tutes les choses ke furent de

Jesu Crist prophetizees en figure e en umbre. Ço ki les enemis Deu furent uncore   75
en Jericho e nepurquant dist Deu al fiz Navé 'Le liu u tu estas est terre seinte' nus
dune a entendre ke en quel liu ke Deus se presente, la sue presence sein[te]fiet le
liu. La presence Deu est confusiun de deable e de felun.[55] Ço ke Deus dist devant
al fiz Navé 'Deslie tun chalcement' [Jos. 5:15] fud dit pur nus assenser ki sumus

menbres Jesu Crist. Chaucement est fait de la pel de morte beste e signefie mortel[56]   80
pecché dunt le curs a l'alme ki se haste vers le celestien pais est encumbré.[57] Si
nus dunkes avuns en purpos de aprimer al Prince de la chevalerie Deu, ceo est a
Jesu Crist, il nus dira: 'Desliez vostre chalcement', ço est deliez e ostez les mortels
pecchiez ki encumbrent les pez de voz almes. Deske ces serrunt desliez e arere dos
jetez,

---

[54] paremplireit, P.
[55] MS felum.
[56] End of p. 19.
[57] MS menbre; encombrez, P.

Behold, as soon as he knew he was the true God and none other, he was ready to do his command. Thus it came about with Jesus our Saviour, and some of the Jews and some of the other powerful men of the world. They were long in doubt about the Saviour, but once they knew him in the light of his great miracles, and that he fulfilled the law spiritually, then straight away they converted to him and received his commandments.

By this careful enquiry we are taught that we must never be too hasty in believing either what the eye sees or what the ears hear, because eyes can be deceived by adornments or by phantoms, ears deceived by lies.

On the subject of faith, the Apostle says 'Do not believe what any person says to you.[58] First try them, to find out whether what they say comes from a good spirit.' The son of Navé worshipped this man not because he was of God, but because he was God himself. Otherwise he would never have worshipped him, unless he recognized him and knew for certain he was God.

Truly Jesus Christ, who is true God and true man, is Prince of God's chivalry, for all the celestial chivalry — angels, archangels, virtues and dominions, powers and principalities — are always of the chivalry of Christ, for he is Prince of princes, Power above powers, and he gives power as it is said (for example) in the Gospel: *have thou authority over ten cities.*

The sword that our Prince holds, drawn and naked in his hand, is the word of God. The scabbard of this sword was the letter of the law. The sword was unsheathed and bared from this moment, so that by the light of power and miracles all those things that were prophesied figuratively and shadowed forth of Jesus Christ should be made apparent. The enemies of God were still in Jericho, and nevertheless God said to the son of Navé 'The place where you stand is holy ground'; this tells us that wherever God shows himself his presence sanctifies the place.

God's presence is confusion to the Devil and to the wicked. What God said before to the son of Navé, *Loose thy shoe,* was spoken in order to show us that we are members of Jesus Christ. Shoes are made from the hide of dead animals, and signify the mortal sins with which the body, whose soul is hastening towards celestial peace, is encumbered. Therefore if we wish to approach the Prince of God's chivalry, that is Jesus Christ, he will tell us 'Loose your shoe';[59] that is, undo and take off the mortal sins that encumber the feet of your soul. As soon as they are unfastened and thrown away behind us,

---

[58] I Joh. 4:1, cited opposite, is not the Gospel but the First Epistle of John. *AV* says *believe not every spirit*; the writer translates *omni spiriti* as 'chascun' (anybody, or everybody).

[59] The command, above, was in the singular 'tun chalcement'; the writer wishes to differentiate between Joshua and the rest of us.

erraument avrum Crist en aie pur descunfire malignes esperiz e vices ki sunt noz   85
enemis mortels. La raisun suentre nus aprent cument nus devuns descunfire noz
esperitels enemis e reverser lur forcelés. Ço dit ke set princes pristrent set busines e
alerent devant l'arche Deu envirun Jericho sunant les buisines. Al setme jur leverent
par matin e les murs de Jericho dechairent en la manere ke il ad devant dit en
l'estorie.

Jericho signefie cest mund sicume vus avez [oi] en [f.50Ar] l'Evanglie la u il dit 'Uns   90
huem descendi de Jerusalem in Jericho e sei embati entre larruns' [Ex. 3:5]. Cel
hum ert Adam ki descendi de Parais en cest peccherus mund e se embati entre
pecchez e vices ki a larun suppernnent hume. Devant ço k'il se dune garde pur
reverser les bailz e les murs de ceste cité ne fud unkes espee traite ne dart lancé

ne de picois feru. [S]ulement par les suneiz des buisines as pruveres furent li mur   95
reversé.

...

Ore veuns quels furent les bails e les forcelés dunt li munz ert ensemble cume
des murs purceint devant l'advenement Jesu Crist. Li cultivement des ydles, la
decevance des divinurs, la sorcerie des enchanturs, de tuz icés ensemble cume murs
ert avirunez li

munz. Fermé enteimes cume chastel de ses maistres turs ert li mund dé diverses   100
sciences dé philosophes e de lur desputisuns de aperte pruvance. A la parfin vint
Jesu Crist nostre Salvere, ki venu signefiad Jesu le fiz Navé, e enveiat prestres, ço
furent apostres e evangelistes, ki porteren[t] la predicatiun de la celestiene doctrine
ensemble cume busines bien sunantes. Matheu li Evangelistes suna premer sa
buisine en

preschant. Marcus ensemble. Lucas e Johan a haute voiz preecherent ensemble   105
cume li prestre ki des buisines entunerent. E Peres e Jacob les buisines de lur
epistres sunerent. Al derain, de plus grosse e clere buisine, cil ki dist: *[P]lus omnibus
laboravi* [I Cor. 15:10], ço est a dire 'Jo ai travaillé plus ke tut li autre.' Ço ert li
bers sein Pol, kar par la doctrine de ses quatorce [f.50Av] epistres ensemble cum par
fuildrant sun de

haut e lunge buisine chai le[60] cultivement des ydeles e falsee fud la decevable   110
doctrine des philosophes. [E] notez ke les murs de Jericho dechairent nent sulement
par le sun

---

[60] MS les.

so soon shall we have the help of Christ to discomfit the wicked spirits and vices that are our mortal enemies. Reason will then tell us how we can baffle our spiritual enemies and destroy their trickery.

It is said that seven princes[61] took up seven trumpets and went before the Ark of the Lord around Jericho, sounding the trumpets. On the seventh day they arose in the morning, and the walls of Jericho came tumbling down as it was told earlier, in the history.

Jericho signifies this world of ours, as you have heard in the Gospel where it says 'A man came down from Jerusalem into Jericho, and fell among thieves'.[62] This man was Adam, who came down from Paradise into this sinful world and fell among the Sins and Vices that attack men like thieves.[63]

Because of this, let him take care to throw down the fortifications and the walls of this city, without any sword drawn nor dart hurled, nor piercing by any lance. Only by the sound of the priests' trumpets were the walls thrown down.

Now let us see what were the fortifications and the snares that the world had around it, as those walls were surrounded, before the coming of Jesus Christ. The cult of idols, the deceptions of soothsayers, the sorcery of enchanters, all these things together are like walls around the world.

Above all, the world was closed in, like a castle by its strong towers, by numerous philosophical sciences and their disputations about open proof.[64]

At last came Jesus Christ our Saviour, whose coming was signified by Joshua son of Navé; and he sent priests — that is, apostles and evangelists — who would carry forth the preaching of celestial doctrine just as if it was the sound of well-blown trumpets.

Matthew the Evangelist sounded his trumpet first, by preaching; then Mark; Luke and John both preached with a loud voice, like priests playing trumpets. Peter and James sounded the trumpets of their Epistles.

Last of all, the loudest and clearest of trumpets, he who said *I laboured more abundantly than they all*. This was the noble Saint Paul, for by the doctrine of his fourteen epistles together, like the thundering sound of loud long trumpeting, the cult of idols fell and the deceitful doctrine of philosophers was proved false.

You must observe that the walls of Jericho did not fall only by the sound

---

61 'princes', not 'prestres' as above.

62 This is not Ex. 3:5 but a close rendering of Luke 10:30. There may be a special connection, which I have so far been unable to identify, to explain the unlikely reference.

63 Abstract nouns of this kind hover on the verge of personification.

64 The writer seems to mean that these pseudo-sciences are easily seen to be worthless (see below, for the 'proof').

des buisines, einz firent par concordable cri del pueple ensemble od les buisines.
Ço nus signefie ke si nus voluns acraventer les forcelesces e les enginz al diable, il
cuvent ke nostre vie e noz volentez en unité se cuncordent a la seinte doctrine des
apostres e

des ewangelistes. A chascun Cristien ki volt les forcelesces al diable abatre cuvent   115
ke ait Jesu Crist a duiur e si il est letré, k'il face buisine des Seintes Escriptures.
En cels sei ause de tutuler, en celes chante; tutule es salmes, chante es ymnes e
esperitels chançuns [cf. I Pet. 2:9]. Se il n'est lettré, chante sa Crede, chante sa
Pater Nostre, loe Deu en seinte devotiun, porte u suive cels ki porterent l'arche del

testament, ço est a dire les cumandemenz Moyse ensemblement od seinte Ewan-   120
gelie tienge[65] e face esperitelment, e od iço gard ke la multitudine de ses pensers e
de ses sens, ki el quor creis[s]ent tutdis cume pueple, od une volenté nent od duble,
od estable nent od flotante, parmaigne e concordable seit a Seinte Escripture. Sun
quor e sun semblant aient en sei veraie unité e concordance, ne feigne neent fine
chere e ait

falsine al quor, neent a la fie die veirs e a la fie pur losenge de hume poestif se suille   125
de[66] mençunge, ne seit nent orgui[f.50Br]lus e de surfait vers les basses persones e
umbles, e vers les haultes persones e orguiluses cuard e lasche.

...

En la signefiance de tele concordance se concorda le cri del pueple as busines des
pruveires en la ruine de Jericho. [E]n la venue Jesu fud Jericho reversee e par la
venu

Jesu Crist fud li mund vencuz sicome il mames de sa buche dist quant il enortat   130
ses chevalers a esperitel bataille par cestes paroles: *[C]onfidite, ego vici mundum*
[John 16:33], 'Aiez fiance, jo ai vencu le mund.' [P]uis ke Jesu Navé out escumegé
e entredit Jericho e or e argent e quantque dedenz ert, dunc dist il as fiz Israel:
'Gardez vus de choses maldites, ke vus ne facez les herberges de tuz les fiz

Israel entredites par unt vus seez destruit e tute Synagoge' [Jos. 6:18]. Ceste parole   135
afiert especialment a ceals ki se convertissent del siecle a religiun ensement cume
ki deist a eals 'Vus ki avez le siecle guerpi e pris vus estes a religiun, gardez ke n'aez
en vus secularité', ço est a dire ke vus ne hantez en religiun les wisches del secle
sicum nus truuns escrit: *[N]olite conformari huic secolo* [Rom. 12:2], ço est

'Ne [vus] conformez[67] el secle.' Entredit vus seit cuntenement del secle e vus,   140
persones e prestres ki devez la maisun e la maigné Deu garder e guverner
esperitelment, ne entremellez neent seculers afaires od esperiteles.

---

[65] MS & C vienge.

[66] End of p. 20.

[67] MS confortez; confirmez, C.

of trumpets, it was achieved by the massed shouting of the people and the trumpets together. This means that if we want to crush the wiles and trickery of the Devil, it is necessary for our life and our will to be united in accord with the holy teaching of the apostles and the evangelists.

Each Christian who wants to smash the Devil's trickery must have Jesus Christ as his guide, and if he is educated let him make his trumpet of Holy Scriptures. For some of these, let him practise blowing; in others, sing. Tootle the Psalms! Sing the hymns and spiritual songs![68] If he is not educated, let him sing his Creed and Lord's Prayer, praise God in holy devotion, carry — or follow those who carry — the Ark of the Testament, that is, the commandments of Moses and the holy Gospels. He must hold and perform this spiritually; he must take care that his myriad thoughts and senses, which multiply in his heart as populations multiply, should be of one single purpose and not duplicated, be stable and not floating, must persevere and be in accordance with Holy Scripture. His heart and his outward looks should be in true unity and concordance; never feigning a sweet expression with treachery in the heart. He must not speak truth at the same time as soiling himself by speaking lies to powerful men to flatter them. He must not be arrogant and presumptuous towards lowly and humble people, nor cowardly and cringing towards the high and proud.

In the meaning of such concordance, the crying of the people and the trumpets of the priests combined to be the destruction of Jericho. With Joshua's coming Jericho was thrown down; with Jesus Christ's coming the world was conquered, as he said with his own lips when he exhorted his knights to spiritual battle with these words: 'Have faith, for I have conquered the world!'

When Jesus Navé had placed an interdict and excommunicated Jericho,[69] and gold and silver and everything that was therein, then he said to the children of Israel 'Keep yourselves from the accursed things, so that you shall not make the dwellings of all the children of Israel forbidden, by which you and the Synagogue will all be destroyed.'

This saying is specially apt for those who convert from the world to religion, just as him who says to them: 'You have abandoned the world and betaken yourself to religion, take care there is no worldliness left in you.' That is to say, you do not practise in your religious life the vices of the world, as we find written: *And be not conformed to this world.* Let the world's way of life be forbidden; and you, the parsons and the priests whose task it is to take care of God's house and household, and to govern them spiritually, never mix secular affairs with spiritual ones.

---

[68] Col. 3:16 seems closer, here, than the Epistle of Peter.

[69] 'The Anglo-Norman "Hugo de Lincolnia"', ed. Dahood, says 'escomenge' can mean simply 'accursed', rather than 'excommunicated'; recorded as mid-fourteenth century, it could be as early as late thirteenth. Our text here is from a mid-thirteenth century MS (see PTS 12, p. 2), so 'escumegé' predates the above. Boulton (*Piety and Persecution*, p. 135, note 3) remarks on the use of 'escumegé' for non-Christians: 'ecclesiastical judgments do not apply to those outside the Church ... a Christian-centric attitude.'

[V]us ki devez par ureisun a Deu plaisir, n'enplaidez neent [vostre] prosme, e ki
devez a Deu merci crier pur le pueple e messes chanter ne devez nent[70] marchandises
[faire] sulunc le dit seint Jeronime: 'Cil

ki ço funt, il atraient en la maisun Deu [f.50Bv] l'entredit de Jericho'. Vienge vus en   145
memorie le fait Jesu Crist meimes. Il mist hors del temple les marchanz e espandi
le metal as changeurs. Par ço nus duna a entendre ke cil ki sunt atitelés[71] de aver
lur sustienement en Seinte Eglise ne deivent nent estre changeur, ço est afermer
verité a mençunge, ne mençunge a verité, ne acunter ben a mal, ne mal a bien, kar
cel

change n'est pas reisnable. Ne ceals ki marchandise demeinent ne deivent corperel   150
benefice par personage ne par pruverage en Seinte Eglise aveir. A peine puent
marchanz vivre sanz peril de lur alme de lur purchaz seculer.

...

Seint Jeronime nus mustre enteimes cument li fol prestre suillent sei en Seinte
Eglise de l'entredit de Jericho, quant li prestre, ço dit, ki deivent le pueple pur lur
pecché

chastier se funt trop debonaire vers cels ki mesfunt, u pur dute de male lange u   155
pur crieme de poesté u par guain, e mettent arere dos pruveral severité e ore ne
volent ore n'osent faire ço ke ceste Escripture cumande: *[P]eccantem coram omnibus
corripere ut ceteri metum habeant* [I Tim. 5:20], ço est a dire 'Chastiez celui ki pecche
a veue de tuz, ke li autre en aient pour' e derechief: *[A]uferte malum de vobis*

[I Cor. 5:13], ço est 'Ostez le mal de vus.' Li prestre dussent prendre garde e   160
esample de l'Apostre ki dit: *[T]radidit huiusmodi hominem Sathane in interitu carnis
ut spiritus salvus fiat* [I Cor. 5:5], ço est en rumanz 'Jo ai livré hume de tele maniere
a Sathanas en mortefiement de la char par [f.51r] tele devise ke sun esperit seit sauf.'
En la devandite manere volent esquanz prestres fere sei trop

benignes vers lur peccheurs parossiens. Jo crei k'il n'entendent nent ço ke est escrit: 165
*[S]acerdotes populorum iniquitate dampnantur si eos aut ignorantes non erudiant aut
peccantes non arguant,*[72] ço est en rumanz 'Li prestre pur la felunie del pueple
sunt dampné se il n'enseignent les nunsavanz e chastient les pecchans.' De ço dist
Deus al Prophete: *[S]peculatorem dedi te domui Israel [...] Si non fueris locutus ut se
custodiat*[73]

impius a via sua, ille vero in iniquitate sua moriatur, sanguinem eius de manu tua   170
requiram [Ezek. 3:17–18], ço est en rumanz 'Guardien te fis de la maisun de Israel,
se tu ne diz ke felun se guard de sa felunesse veie, pur quei il more en sa felunie, jo
requerrai sun sanc de ta main.' En ceste manere fud Hely le prestre dampné pur la

---

[70] Ne demenez m., P.
[71] MS auteles.
[72] Isidore, *PL* 83,714C; cf. *PL* 102,640A; 105,870C; 134,83A.
[73] End of p. 21.

You who must please God by your prayers, do not persecute your neighbours; and you who must cry to God for mercy on the people, and must sing the Mass, you must never do as the merchants do, according to the word of Saint Jerome:

'Who does this will bring down the Interdict of Jericho upon the house of God.'

May the memory of what Jesus Christ did come to your minds. He threw the merchants out of the temple, and scattered the metal [coins] of the money-changers.[74]

By this, he gives us to understand that those who are supposed to have their sustenance in Holy Church must never be changers. That is, to affirm truth for lies, or lies for truth; nor to account good for evil or evil for good. For this changing is against the right. Nor may those who practise commerce receive any worldly benefits from being a parson or being a priest in Holy Church. Merchants can barely live without danger to their souls, from their worldly earnings.

Saint Jerome even shows us how the wicked priests within Holy Church soil themselves by infringing the Interdict of Jericho. He says the priests, who ought to be reproving the people for their sins, are too gentle with those who do evil, because nervous about their reputation, or afraid of powerful men, or hopeful of gain; they throw their priestly severity behind them and either will not or dare not do what this Scripture commands:

Them that sin rebuke before all, that others also may fear; and above all 'Root out evil from among you.'

Priests should pay attention to the example the Apostle gives, in French:

'I have given up this kind of man to Satan, for mortification of his flesh so that in this way his spirit may be saved.'

In this way, as I've said before, some priests try to make themselves too kindly towards their erring parishioners.

I don't think they have understood what is written, in French:

'Priests shall be damned for the wickedness of their people if they do not teach the ignorant and punish the sinful.'

God speaks of this to the Prophet, in French:

'I have made you guardian of the house of Israel; if you do not warn the evildoer to leave off his wicked ways, because he will die on account of his wickedness, I shall require his blood of your hand.'

In this way Eli the priest was damned for the

---

[74] Matt. 21:12–13 & Mark 11:15–17; cf. Jer. 7:11.

felunie de ses fiz. Est ço dunkes deboneireté? Est ço misericorde, ke l'em esparnie a
un e par ço prennent plusurs achaisun de peccher? Mais puet cel estre alcuns 175
pensera: 'Quei afiert ço a mei se cist[75] mesfait u cil mesaut, puis jo tuz reprendre?
Puis jeo tuz chastier?' Ço n'est el a dire ke si le chef deist: 'Ke apartient a mei si la
main se dolt?' u se oil deist: 'Ke puis jo si le pié mesvait?, 'Si vus estes blescé, dei jo
dunkes de vostre blesceure estre trublé?', 'Ai jo dunkes ke faire de vostre servise?'
Gart prelat e prestre

ke ço ne die, ke ço ne pense, mais tutdis ait devant ses oilz ke pur une berbiz malade 180
est tute la faudee entuschee. Ensement ço dit seint Jeronime: 'par un luxu[f.51v]rius
u par un vicius est tute une maisnee suillee.' Dun ne savez vus ke nus tuz feeilz
sumes menbres de un cors desuz Jesu Crist, ki est nostre chief? [J]esu Crist ki est
uns meimes Deus en unité de verraie creance nus contient e ensemble juint. De
cest cors est oil

chascuns ki est mis a garder Seinte Eglise. Si tu dunkes a ço es mis, veille, esgarde 185
par tut, purvei[76] les perilz ki poent avenir. Tu es pastur e veiz les oeilles tun seignur
es gules des leuns [de]vurables e nes vulez rescure. Tu les veiz waer[77] el mareis e la
mer munte e tu ne te volz mettre en lur cuntre ne pur els hucher ne els par cri de
chastiement rapeler. Quant tu es si negligent, ben pert ke tu ne prenz nent esample
del

suverain pastur ki guerpi nonante noef oeilles es celestienes muntaines e descend[i] 190
a terre pur une sule ki forsveiat. E quant il la truvat, sur ses espaulles al ciel la porta.
Par esample de cest suverain pastur deiz tu estre amonesté de duner grant entente
a cels ke tu as a garder. E si alcuns de ta garde amonesté e chastié une fie e altre e
terce, neent ne s(a)'amende, fai dunkes ço ke fait sage mire. Uigne l'emflure de sa
duresce de oile

de misericorde, ço est requere[z] Deu pur lui e mettez a sun mal emplastre de 195
chastiement apert. Si l'emflure dunkes ne amolie ne asiet, n'i [a] autre medecine
fors sul le malveis membre par rasoir de escuminicatiun del cors de Seinte Eglise
del tut trencher sicum nostre Sire cumande: *[S]i manus tua scandalizat te, abscide*
[f.52r] *eam et proice abs te* [Matt. 18:8], ço est 'Si ta main te verguine,

retrenche la e gete de tei.' Mais gart ke ço ne facez pur leger pecché, kar nuls hum 200
en cest siecle ne vit senz pecché.

---

[75] MS est.

[76] par unt, C.

[77] waier, C; vair, P.

wickedness of his sons.[78]

Is this kindness? Is this merciful, to let one off so that others will take the opportunity to sin? Suppose somebody like this will think 'What is it to me if this person does wrong or that one goes astray? How can I reprove them all? Have I got to punish everybody?' It's as if the head were to say 'It's not my problem if the hand hurts', or if the eye said 'What can I do if the foot goes wrong?' or 'If you are injured, must I be troubled with your wounds?' or 'Haven't I got better things to do than be at your service?' No prelate or priest must ever say that, or think it. They must always keep in mind that one sick sheep may infect the whole flock. Just so, Saint Jerome says 'One lustful, or one vicious, can pollute a whole household.'[79]

Don't you know that all we faithful are members of one body, under Jesus Christ who is our Head? Jesus Christ, who is one God in unity with true faith, contains us and joins us together. Of this body, the eye is the man who is stationed as guardian of Holy Church. If you are the one so stationed, keep watch and look around everywhere, prepare yourself against the dangerous things that could happen. You are the shepherd, and you see your lord's sheep in the jaws of the ravening lion, and you don't want to rescue them! You see them wallowing in the marsh — the tide is coming up, and you don't want to go towards them, neither shouting at them nor recalling them with cries of reproach. You are so careless, it really seems you won't follow the example of the greatest Shepherd of all, who left his ninety-nine sheep in the celestial mountains and went down to earth for just one that was straying. And when he found it, he carried it on his shoulders back to heaven.[80]

The example of this sovereign Shepherd ought to teach you to take good care of those who are yours to guard. And if one of those who is taught and chastised once, twice, three times but does not mend his ways, then you must do what the wise doctor does.

Anoint the hard swelling of his puffed-up obduracy with the oil of mercy; that is, pray to God for him, and apply a poultice consisting of manifest chastisement. If the swelling does not soften and ease, there is no other medicine except only to cut the diseased member off completely from the body of Holy Church by the razor of excommunication, as Our Lord commands: 'If your hand shames you, cut it off and throw it from you.' But of course you must not do this for small sins, for no man on this earth lives without any sin.

---

[78] I Sam. 2:27–36.

[79] I have been unable to locate this reference. If the writer does not give the Latin, a concordance is no help; the French may be worded very differently from the original.

[80] This refers to Ps. 23, and to the story of the lost sheep in Matt. 18:12–13; see also the Prodigal Son in Luke 15.

[N]e quidez nent ke ço seit cumandé de la main corporele, einz est sicume seint Jeronime dit: *[S]i ego videor esse ecclesie quasi manus dextra et presbiter nominor et verbum Dei ad refectionem ecclesie debeo seminare, si ego, inquam, contra ecclesiasticam regulam et evangelicam gessero*

disciplinam ita ut contempnens corrigi scienter scandalum ecclesie faciam, unanimi consensu et conspiratione universa ecclesia digne et juste me putativam dexteram suam abscidere et proicere ab se. Expedit enim ecclesie absque scandalizante manu introire in regnum celorum quam cum illa mitti in gehennam. Cest lunc cunte fait seint Jeronime entendre en rumanz 'Si jo par semblant sui ensement   205

cum la destre main de Seinte Eglise e prestre sui numé e la parole Deu a la refectiun   210
de Seinte Eglise dei semer, si jo dunkes cuntre l'ordenement de Seinte Eglise e la doctrine de l'Evangelie oevre en scient dunt Seinte Eglise seit par mei vergundee e jo ai sur ço chastiement en despit, tute Seinte Eglise od uns asens e od cunseil par vive raisun deit en veie trencher mei sa fause destre e jeter de sei. [M]elz vient a Seinte

Eglise sanz sa huntuse main entrer el regné del ciel ke de estre jetez od li e par li el[81]   215
sulphurin feu d'enfern.' Mult besuigne ke chascun se gart, se est oil u poin u pié de Seinte Eglise, ke il chose ne face par quei [f.52v] il seit par reignable excommunicatiun en veie colpé, kar tant cume la main u l'autre menbre sei tent cument ke seit a sun cors, tut sei[t] li menbres malades, tut le cors purtraite sa cure e

nel puisse il del tut guarir, il le uint, il met emplastre, il a sun poeir le coist. Mais   220
desque il est del cors trenché n'est k'il coisse ne enprenge bone cure, lores est livré as chiens u as oisels u a purreture. Ensement est de pecchur. Ja pur tant cum il gist en pecché, pur ki il est en reignable excomunicatiun desevré de la comune de Seinte Eglise devant ce k'il seit repentant e pensif de sei reconcilier, n'est establi en Seinte

Eglise ki de li prenge cure ne par almones ne par ureisuns faire ne il en tantes biens   225
de Seinte Eglise partire ne puet. De l'autre part si aucun menbre ki a sun cors se tient senz esperance de garir ne fine de purrir, li saives le fait retrencher. Autrement purreit tut le cors par la pureture de l'un menbre tost enmortir. Ensement avint en la ruine de Jericho. Pur ço ke li fiz Israel se cumunierent a un pecchur ki amender ne se volt, tut

ensemble furent entredit de Deu e perdirent sa grace e par ço furent puis vencuz   230
de lur enemis. En ceste reversiun de Jericho sule la pute Raab od sa maisnee est salvee e par Jesu Navé vivifié e a tuzdis mais ajustee a la maisun Israel. Oez, vieus gent maleuree, cument ceste pute femme Raab est ajuinte a la maignee Israel.

---

[81] End of p. 22.

Nor must you think that the commandment applies to the bodily hand; it is as Saint Jerome says.

This long passage means,[82] in French:

'It is as if I were like the right hand of Holy Church, elected priest, and it was for me to sow the Word of God at Mass;[83] if, then, I knowingly do against the commands of Holy Church and the doctrine of the Gospel, so that Holy Church is put to shame through me, and I deserve chastisement and contempt for that; then Holy Church with one accord and advisedly for the best of reasons must in judgement cut me off, as its false right hand, and throw me out. It is better for Holy Church to enter the Kingdom of Heaven without its shameful right hand than to be thrown, with it and because of it, into the sulphurous fires of Hell.'

It is essential for every one of us to take care, whether they are eye or hand or foot of Holy Church, not to do anything for which they can be reasonably judged guilty and excommunicated; for as long as the hand or other member holds on in whatever way to its body, even if the member is sick the whole body performs its cure. And if it cannot heal everything, it anoints it and plasters it up, cauterizing as best it can. But as soon as it is cut off from the body, it cannot be cauterized or given good healing; consequently it is thrown out to the dogs or the carrion-birds, or to rot.

So it is with a sinner. As long as he wallows in sin, and is therefore rightly excommunicated and cut off from the community of Holy Church; until he becomes repentant and thinks of making peace with it, Holy Church does not allow care to be taken of him: not by alms, or prayers for him, and he may not take part in the good things of Holy Church. At the same time, if any member holds onto his place in the body without hope of healing, nor stops putrefying, the wise ones will have him cut off. Otherwise the whole body will quickly putrefy into dead flesh, because of one putrid member.

So it was with the ruin of Jericho. Because the sons of Israel had converse with one sinner who would not mend his ways, they were all excommunicated by God and lost his grace, and so they were overcome by their enemies. In this destruction of Jericho, only the harlot Rahab was saved with all her household; she was given life by Joshua Navé and added to the House of Israel for ever.

O ancient and accursed people, hear how this harlot woman Rahab was joined with the company of Israel!

---

[82] The French follows the Latin, so I have not translated the meaning twice.

[83] 'la refectiun': the Church's holy meal.

Esgardez cument [f.53r] l'om recolpe les secches branches del bon oliver e en cel meimes estoc cument l'uem

ente les branches de l'oliver parhaine[84] e celes branches par la force del natural   235
estoc portent bon fruit. Par ço poez vus entendre ke nus ki sumes estrait de fole
gent de avoiltrine creance, ki parhaine furent, senz fruit de bones vertuz, quant il
cuiltiverent fust e peres e ydeles ensement cum Deu, sumes ore par la destre al
celestien cultivur, ço est par Jesu Crist, enté en la verraie creance Abraham, Ysaac
e Jacob u nus faimes

fruit de uveraines ki a Deu plaisent. Dunc vus maleurez Jueus estes recolpez   240
ensement cume de humurs de bones vertuz desechiz. Sicum dit avuns, ert Raab
sule salvee en Jericho par Jesu. [D]eu, ço dit l'estorie, fut od Jesu e sun nun fud
denuncié e depueplee en tutes terres e li disciple Jesu Crist alerent par universe
munde preechant sun seint nun e sa creance. E Deus en els uvra e lur predicatiun
par signes conferma. Dunt en

cest nun Jesu li celestien nostre Salvur supplient e terriens e enfernals a lui sunt   245
aclin cume cil ki genuil plient. Ore, bone gent, ostuns les encumbremenz des piez
a l'alme, desliuns les enlacemenz de pecchiez, ke nus puissuns a delivre aprocer al
prince de la celestiene chevalerie. Destreinum nus par le cumandement Jesu Crist de
chascun vice Jericontin, ke nus puissuns sauvement siure l'arche Deu par esperitele
garde des

cumandemenz de la lei e de l'Evangelie e par son concordable cri de ureisuns   250
[f.53v] e Deu loer e od voiz de une bone volenté fames trebucher la malice de cest
mund e metuns peine de garder nus de chascun entredit de cest siecle, ke nus
en l'embracement Raab, ki est notre laür, ço est Seinte Eglise, seruns ajusté a la
maignee Israel, ço est a esperitels humes ki de quor veient Deu, parunt od els seruns

refait de la visable veue Deu el ciel pardurablement en sa glorie. Ço duinst nostre   255
Seignur Jesu Crist ki ad honur e cumandement de secle en secle senz fin, AMEN.

---

[84] *id est* barhaine.

See how the dry branches of a good olive-tree are cut away, and how onto this same trunk are grafted branches of a barren tree, and these branches bear good fruit thanks to the strength of the natural stock. By this, you may understand that we who are descended from foolish people of adulterous faith, who were barren and without the fruit of good virtue, when they pursued wood and stone and idols all as if they were God; now by the right hand of the celestial Cultivator, that is Jesus Christ, we are grafted into the true faith of Abraham, Isaac, and Jacob, where we produce the fruit of good works that are pleasing to God. So you wretched Jews are cut off, just as the sap is from withered good virtues.

As we have told you, Rahab alone was saved out of Jericho by Joshua. The story says that God was with Joshua, and that his name [Jesus] was announced and made known in all the lands; and the disciples of Jesus went through the whole wide world preaching about his holy name and his faith. And God worked through them, and confirmed their preaching by signs. So Our Saviour's celestials pray to this name of Jesus, and those on earth and in hell bow down to him as on bended knees.

Now, good people![85] Let us shrug the encumbrances off the feet of the Soul, and undo the bindings of Sin, so we can quickly come close to the Prince of Celestial Chivalry. Restrain ourselves, by Jesus Christ's commandment, from all Jericho's vices, so that we may safely follow the Ark of God in the spiritual guard of Old Testament commandments and of the Gospel.

In a massed shout of prayer, praising God with a voice of good will, let us topple down the wickedness of this world! And let us take pains to keep ourselves from all the interdicts of the age.

And so in the embrace of Rahab — our model, which is Holy Church — we may be added to the house of Israel, that is, to spiritual men who see God with their hearts, through which we shall be refashioned in the visible sight of God and forever in Heaven, in his glory. May Our Lord Jesus Christ grant this, who has honour and dominion for ever and ever, world without end, AMEN.

---

[85] Hunt remarks that this is the only direct address to the audience in this sermon (PTS 12, p. 4).

Rossignos[86]

This verse homily on the life of Christ was written for Eleanor of Provence, mother of Edward I, by John of Howden, probably before 1282.[87]   There is only one manuscript (Cambridge, Corpus Christi College, 471), dated to the second half of the fourteenth century. The prose Prologue explains the title; I present it together with the first section of the text (vv. 1–144). This long poem later includes among other things a list of heroes that seems to anticipate the canon of Nine Worthies.[88] The extended roll of honour includes figures both historical and legendary. It has already been noted that Tristan was not originally attached to the Arthur legend; he does not appear in the list, although Lancelot does (another figure who 'arrived' after the earliest stories had become current in Britain). Historical figures include William the Conqueror, who is listed as 'li Bastard plain de value' (the worthy Bastard, v. 3993). It is unusual to see William called both Bastard and 'worthy', as has been noted in the twelfth-century Nun's life of Edward the Confessor.[89]

The text is copied from the edition; I adjust only a few items, such as quotation marks, to conform to the overall format in this book. Initials in bold indicate a coloured initial in the manuscript (space was left for one at the first C below but it was not executed). I have not reproduced all the editor's notes, many of which discuss fine detail of the MS readings.

---

[86] Dean 626; see Legge, pp. 232–5.

[87] *Rossignos*, John of Howden, ed. Hesketh (ANTS 63), p. 10.

[88] Editor's note to v. 3969.

[89] Translated in *Edouard*, p. 17.

Text

[1r] CI comence la pensee Johan de Houedene, clerc la roine
d'Engleterre mere le roi Edward, de la neissance e de la mort e
du relievement e de l'ascencion Jhesu Crist e de l'assumpcion nostre
Dame. Et a non ceste pensee 'Rossignos', pur ce ke, sicome li
rossignos feit de diverses notes une melodie, auci feit cest livres de
diverses matires une acordaunce. Et pur ce enkores a il non
'Rossignos' que il estoit fez e trové en un beau verger flori ou
rossignol adés chauntoient. Et pur ce fu il faiz que li quor celi qui le
lira soit esprys en l'amour nostre Seignour. Benoit soit qui le lira!
Ceste oevre comence. Ci comence li 'Rossignol'.

...

Alme, lesse lit de peresse
E ta langor e ta tristesse;
Apreng d'amour la parfondesse
E a penser d'amour t'adresse!   4
Oste de toi delivrement
De vaine amour le marrement,
Apreng d'amer entierement
Et parlier d'amor docement!   8
Jhesu, des saintz la drüerie,
Leur quor, leur amor e leur vie,
Fai a moun povre engin aïe
Que ta parole enpreigne e die!   12
Li seint feu de t'amour m'espreigne [1v]
Si ke de toi penser m'enseigne
Fai de ma langue riche enseigne
Que ta louange ben enpreigne!   16
Li seint angle vint a Marie
E disoit que le Rei de Vie
Enfanteroit. Ele le prie
Que la manere enseigne e die;   20
Cil li respont sanz demoree:
'Ne soiez pas espöentee,
Enfant avras, Virge sacree,
Du Seint Espir[i]tz aombree.'   24
Lors s'asenti la pucelete,

Translation

Here begins the dream of John of Hoveden,[90] clerk to the Queen of England who is mother of King Edward, about the birth and death, about the resurrection and ascension, of Jesus Christ, and about the Assumption of Our Lady.[91] This dream is called Nightingale because, just as the nightingale makes one melody out of many notes, so this book makes a concordance out of diverse materials. It is called Nightingale also because it was made and invented in a beautiful flowery orchard where nightingales endlessly sing.[92] Further, it was made so that the heart of whoever reads it will be overcome with love for Our Lord. Blessed be all who read it![93] The work begins. Here begins the Nightingale.

O Soul, leave your bed of idleness, and your languor and sadness![94] Learn about the depths of love, and set yourself to thoughts of love! Quickly strip off the sadness of vain love; learn to love wholly and talk of love sweetly! Jesus, beloved of saints,[95] their heart and love, their life, help my limited intelligence so that I may learn and speak thy Word! May the holy fire of thy love inflame me, if thou teach me to think of thee; make of my language a powerful battle-cry, so that I undertake thy praise![96]

The holy angel came to Mary, and said she would bring forth the King of Life.[97] She begged him to tell and teach her how this could be, and he answered her without delay: 'Do not be afraid. You shall have a child, Holy Maiden, from the shadow of the Holy Spirit.'

Then the young maiden assented.

---

[90] 'pensee', thought. I translate 'dream' because of the romantic setting in a garden. In such a garden, with beautiful flowers and birds, the narrator of many a dream-vision falls asleep before encountering the wonders that the following story will contain. There are no line numbers to this prose section in the edition; I have retained the length of each line exactly without adding numbers.

[91] For the latter, see an annotated and translated version in *Cher Alme*.

[92] 'trové', found or 'invented' (that is, made up). Latin *invenio, inventio*, means either or both. Here is another 'doublet' or pair of words meaning the same thing (cf. Wace's first passage, above). It is clear that the repetition adds nuance and emphasis, so I do not conflate into a single word.

[93] Properly this should be in the singular ('he who reads'), but clearly both male and female are intended — including (but not exclusively) Queen Eleanor.

[94] A sinful and self-indulgent *tristitia* was a branch of *Accidie* (see note in Sloth, in *Deadly Sins* below).

[95] 'drüerie' is a word used of earthly lovers; it strengthens the intensity of heavenly love described here (cf. 'fin' amur').

[96] Much of the second-person speech is singular, 'tu' or 'thou'; this sounds cumbersome to a modern reader (especially when the writer switches from this to 'vous' without apparent reason), so I use it sparingly.

[97] For the Annunciation, see Luke chapter 1.

E meintenaunt en la chambrete
De sa poitrine chaste e nete
Entras, com en pré vïolete,   28
E tu sa purté tote entiere
Gardas par ta grace plenere,
Que raison vout ke la lumere
Ne blesce ja verine clere.   32
Reis ke le ciel ne poet
       comprendre,
Par noef mois i vousis atendre;
Lors des angles te fesoit mendre
Amor ki ose tot emprendre.   36
Quant fuites né de la Pucele [2r]
Qui tote joie renovele,
Des angles cumpanie bele
Chantoit de pes chanzon novele.   40
Tu qui donez les fines joies,
De quel amor suspris estoiez
Quant a bender t'abandonoies
E en la creche demoroies?   44
Ta creche de petite afaire
Nos est livréz pur exemplaire,
Et nous aprent le quor retraire
De tot orgoil, Rei debonaire.   48
Tantost te mez a la bataille
Contre orgoil, e la vains sanz faille,
Et veus ke ta creche nos baille
Le large ciel sanz definaille.   52

Et tu, Pucele benuree,
Ta mamele seinte et sacree
As a ton fitz abandone[e].
Hei! Dieu, quel joie as assenee!   56
Li pains de pardurable vie
Dount la court d'angles est servie,
Li pains qe le ciel resazie
De toi se pest, virge Marie.   60
De douzor la fonteine vive, [2v]
La qui douzor toz tens desrive,
Qui les quors amortis ravive,
De ton seint piz porprent la rive.   64
De totes douzors la plus fine
Suche douzor de ta poitrine;
Trestote la court celestine
Esmervailler de ce ne fine.   68
Seule as a droit joie trovee,
Ele est en toi seule comblee
Quant cil de tei prent sa livree
De qui tote joie est livree.   72
Ce qui li done ta peitrine,
Quant il la tent en sa seisine,
A li est nur[e]ture fine
E a nous droite medecine.   76
Countre la pome envenime[e]
Qui si mort humene lignee
Est ta mamele tresacree
Trïacle, c'est chose provee.   80

Now you entered into the little space of her chaste and pure breast, as if into a meadow of violets; and by your abundant grace you preserved her purity absolutely. For reason shows us that light can never hurt clear glass.[98]

O King, whom Heaven could not contain, you were content to wait nine months there. You made yourself less than the angels, O Love that dares all! When you were born of the Virgin, who is the renewal of every joy, a glorious company of angels sang a new song of peace.

You, Giver of exquisite joys, what was the love that ravished you when you abandoned yourself to swaddling clothes and rested in a manger?[99] This manger, such a lowly thing, is given to us as a lesson: it teaches us to withdraw our hearts from all pride, O gentle King. Soon you take up the battle against Pride, and unquestionably you win it; you want your manger to give into our possession the infinite width of Heaven. And you, blessed Virgin, you made your holy sacred breast fully available to your son. Ah, God! What joy you have achieved! The Bread of everlasting life that is provided for the court of angels, the Bread that satisfies the heavens, feeds from you, Virgin Mary.[100] The living Fount of sweetness whence sweetness ever overflows, that revives dead and dying hearts, has its brim at your holy breast.[101] The Sweetest, above all sweet things, sucks sweetness from your breast. The whole celestial company never ceases to marvel at this! Only you have found joy rightfully; it is entirely fulfilled only in you, when he who furnishes all joy took from you his daily food.[102] What your breast gave him, when he held it in his grasp, is exquisite nourishment for him and sovereign medicine for us.[103] Against the poisoned apple, that condemned the human race to death,[104] your thrice-holy breast is proved to be the remedy.[105]

---

[98] This is a common explanation for how the Virgin was able to conceive without losing her virginity: the Holy Spirit entered her as light shines through glass without breaking it. Compare Katherine's discussion of the mysteries of Godhead (above); she does not dwell on this particular point.

[99] See Luke chapter 2 for the birth of Christ.

[100] John 6:32–51.

[101] For the unusual meaning of 'rive' (here lip, brim) see editor's note.

[102] 'livree' also means 'livery' (as in *Piers Plowman*: dress, uniform, sc. man's flesh).

[103] Treacle (and v. 80), see *OED*: the meaning was originally that of an antidote against wild beast venom; it came to mean simply medicine, and was frequently used of godly remedies against sin.

[104] Editor's note: 'mord' appears above the line as an alternative, meaning to bite. But the word 'mort' (to kill) is equally possible. In the Genesis story of the Fall, the fruit is not said to be poisoned; nor is poison mentioned in the *Creation* piece, above.

[105] 'tresacree' means 'very holy', but my pun is allowable given the quantity of untranslatable word-play in this text.

Quant vie suche [a] ta peitrine,
De nostre mort moert la racine;
Li dampnéz recovrent seisine
De fine joie qui ne fine.   84
Hautesce estoit lors avalee [3r]
Et tote longor abreggee,
Tote puissance humilïee
Et tote laour estrescee.   88
Quant plorer ton douz fitz vëoiez,
Trebien apeser le savoiez;
Lors par ton douz let l'adouzoiez
Qui seule sa douzor estoiez.   92
Dame qui donez joie entiere
A celi qui en est rivere,
Puis ke tu en es botellere,
Ne soiez pas a moi avere.   96
Celer de vin est ta peitrine
En qi boit la vigne devine;
La boit la sapïence fine
Trefine douzor qui ne fine.   100
E puis, quant fuis entalente[e],
Endormi l'as, Virge sacree,
De ta chanson savoree
Ke rossignous n'i out duree.   104
De ton douz chant la melodie
Fist endormir le chant de vie.
Hareu! Com fu doce e serie
Puis ke tant plout a plesancie!   108
Ceste pucele est si aprise [3v]
A chaunter en si douce guise
Ke cil s'endort qui touz justise
Les chanz du ciel e les devise.   112
Quant en chanter metoit sa cure,

Vers sa chanzon, tant estoit pure,
Cithole n'out envoiseüre,
Viele n'est fors k'arroüre;   116
Harpe vers li n'ad melodie,
Daunce de gige est amortie,
Li chalemeaus ne chante mie,
Et le flejol descorde e crie.   120
Des doz chanz d'angles que diroie
Ki adés chantent de la joie
Ke Dieu de Gloire leur envoie
Quant son visage leur desploie?   124
Ben sei que leur chanzon est bele
Ke touz jours est freche e novele,
Mes meauz me pleroit oïr cele
Chaunter qe mere est e pucele,   128
Kar si douce est la vïelure
De la gorge a la Mere pure
Ke d'estre endormi bien endure
Li Rois de tote envoiseüre.   132
Cil qui li ciel ne poet comprendre
        [4r]
De gré se venoit prison rendre
A ceste pucelete tendre,
Tant le pout sa chanzon sospendre.   136
Jeo croi ke la court celestine,
Quant en chantant plus fort
        s'affine,
A ceste chanzon si trefine
Volunters e de gré s'encline.   140
Ne sui pas dignes qe descrive
Cest chaunt dont la dozor est vive
Et tant soronde e si desrive
Ke je n'i troez ne fonz ne rive.   144

When Life sucks at your breast, he kills the root of our death. The lost ones will recover possession of the fine joy that is infinite.[106] Pride is then brought low and length is made short; all power is humbled, and all breadth is narrowed. When you saw your son crying, you knew how to comfort him: now you sweetened him with the sweet milk that was all the sweetness he knew. Ah, lady who gives abundant joy to him who is the River of joy, since you are joy's Butler, do not be ungenerous with me! Your breast is a wine cellar where drinks the Vine of heaven. This is where fine Wisdom drinks fine sweetness that is without end.[107]

And then, Holy Virgin, when it pleased you, you sent him to sleep with your delicious song that even the nightingale cannot resist. The melody of your gentle song sent the Song of Life to sleep. Ah, Heaven! How sweet and delightful it was, so to please Pleasure himself! The maiden was so skilful at singing so softly: she could send him to sleep, who rules and creates all the songs of Heaven. When she set herself to her singing, her song was so pure that the citole no longer held any delight. The vielle sounded only harsh, the harp no longer had melody; the dancing fiddle fell dying, the bagpipe chanted no more, and the flageolet screamed discord.[108] What can I say about the sweet songs of the angels, who sing ceaselessly of the joy vouchsafed to them when the God of Glory reveals his countenance to them? I know their song is beautiful, and is ever fresh and new. But it would please me more to hear her sing, who is both mother and maiden. For the throat of that pure Mother is such a sweet instrument, that the King of all Delight allows himself to be lulled to sleep by it. He whom the Heaven cannot contain, willingly came to render himself prisoner to this tender little maiden, so strongly can her song captivate him. I believe that the court of Heaven, when it excels itself in singing at full voice, willingly and with pleasure bows down to this finest of songs. I am not worthy to describe this song,[109] whose living sweetness so flows and overflows that I can find no ground, and no shore, to it.

---

[106] Lit. 'damned', but no damned soul can ever be released; unless the writer is thinking of the Harrowing of Hell.

[107] All these nouns, metaphors for God, resemble personifications.

[108] See editor's notes for these instruments; their exact equivalents are uncertain (some glossaries give 'fiddle' for 'viele', others give 'viol' or even a kind of hurdy-gurdy).

[109] The author's modesty, rather than the idea of inexpressibility, causes his (or her) pretended silence on the subject.

Eight Deadly Sins, attributed to Robert Grosseteste

... nought but the names of the sins but never how folk could come to be sinning them.[110]

Dean's entry for this piece is marked as forthcoming by Tony Hunt; I am most grateful to him for providing me with his transcription, and for his corrections (as for the Prayers, above).[111] The Seven Deadly Sins in *Cher Alme* may be consulted for comparison (pp. 277–85). The sins are there listed as follows: Pride, Envy, Anger, Sloth, Avarice, Gluttony, Lechery. The order may differ slightly from one text to another, but Pride conventionally heads medieval lists; also in the Bible. The Old Testament book of Proverbs tells of six things the Lord hates; *yea, seven are an abomination unto him* (Prov. 6:16–19).[112] A commentary on this chapter is found in Sanson de Nantuil's *Proverbes* (chapter six; I give his chapter seven, above). Grosseteste was Bishop of Lincoln; a number of works were ascribed to him without any definite attribution.[113] After his death he was regarded as a saint, though never canonized.[114] The present text describes eight sins, adding Homicide (rather a catch-all) at the end of the list.[115] For homicide, *The Mirror of Justices* includes reasoning about the different times of Christ's death reported in the Gospels: he was killed in three different ways.[116] The act of confession could be difficult for both priest and penitent: the former had to know what questions to ask and how best to ask them; the latter had to understand the meaning of each sin.

The text below is not strictly a manual of confession, being a list of sins to bear in mind when preparing to confess but not telling the penitent what to say. It goes 'If you have done this, or this ...' with the final instruction, 'You must confess it', understood. The manuscript, Oxford, Bodleian Library, Rawlinson C. 485, is dated by Hunt as thirteenth century and by Dean as early fourteenth. As with the Prayers (above), I have added line numbers to Hunt's edited text.

---

[110] Mitchison, *The Bull Calves* (p. 40). Such questions are universal, in eighteenth-century Scotland as in medieval Europe.

[111] *La Manere de sey Confesser*, Dean 662 (she states there are nine, without listing them).

[112] A proud look, a lying tongue, hands that shed innocent blood; wicked imagination, swiftness to mischief; false witness, and sowing of discord.

[113] See, for example, Rigg, *Anglo-Latin Literature*, pp. 125–7, on Courtesy Books and a manuscript of Urbanus Magnus ascribed to 'magister Robertus Grosteste' (*sic*); cf. *Apprise*, above, for Urbanus. See also Rigg's index, references in *Cher Alme*, and Thomson, *The Writings of Robert Grosseteste*; and Southern, *Robert Grosseteste*, esp. p. 28.

[114] See also McEvoy, *Robert Grosseteste*, and a brief account in *Robert Grosseteste, Bishop of Lincoln 1235–1253*, Srawley.

[115] For the eighth Capital Sin as a branch of Sloth, see *Cher Alme*, pp. 17–18; Newhauser and Ridyard, eds, *Sin in Medieval Culture*.

[116] ed. Whittaker, pp. 22–3.

Text

[f.79r] Ici comence la manere de sey confesser des mortels pecchez e de lur
especies solum mestre Robert eveske de Nichole.

Orgoyl: Si vous eiez Dieu corucee en parlaunt que est grant orgoyl. Le
primer orgoyl est de partyr de Dieu e la dreynere humilytee est a Dieu
repeyrir; si vous quidez aver de vos mesmes les biens qe vous avez u   5
si voz creez qe Dieu les vus ad donee pur vostre deserte; si vus
eiez avauntee d'aver ço ke vous n'avez nient; si vus eiez despyt les
autres e voliez estre veu ceo qe vus n'esteyez nent; si vus eiez folement
jugee les altres pur vostre fole presumpcioun; si vus eiez esté coveyrus de
veyneg[l]orie; si vous eiez pecché par ypocresye; si vous eiez eu delyt en   10
vesture q'est une manere de lecherye; si vous eiez esté inobedient a Seinte
Eglyse e a ses prelaz e ensement a vos seygnurs e a lurs baillifs e ensement
femme espousé a sun barun.

De Ire: Si vous eiez esté enmeu ver vostre proume par trop de ire; si vous
eiez blescee akun par tençouns u leidengee u par blame; si vous eiez hay vostre 15
prume; si vous eiez provoké nul hom a coruce; si vous ayez desiree autri mort u
damage; si vous eiez provoké nul hom a coruce en overaunt u conseilaunt u
engrutaunt u en altre acune manere semblable; si vus ayez esté tretre u ayez oÿ
les tretours; si vus ayez maudit e voylét la execucion de vostre malesçoun;
si vus ayez eschinee u degabee; si vus ayez blastangee.   20

[Envie]:[117] Si vous ayez en deol par akune manere d'envye de la propretee
de vostre prome; si vous eye[z] envye a vostre peer qe il vus est semblable en
acune chose; si vus ayez amenusee u estudiee d'amenuseer [f.79v] la
prosperitee de vostre prume par akune manere d'envye u par conseil u
par overe u par aide; si vus eiez esté seynur de descord.   25

---

[117] MS De ire cūm dist', but the text is about envy. Envy is traditionally placed before Anger, but
this list reverses them.

Translation

Here begins the form of confession, of the deadly sins and their branches,[118] according to Master Robert Bishop of Lincoln.[119]

Pride: If you have angered God in speech, this is great pride. The first pride is to part from God, and the ultimate act of humility is to come back to him. If you believe the good in you is from yourself, or if you believe God has given it to you because you deserve it [that is Pride].[120] If you have boasted of having something that you have not; if you despise others, wanting to be seen as something that you are not; if you have foolishly judged others through your own foolish presumption. Have you been desirous of vain glory, or have you sinned through hypocrisy? If you have had delight in fine clothing, that is a kind of lechery. If you have been disobedient to Holy Church or its priests, or also to your overlords and their servants; or if a married woman, to her husband.

Anger: Have you been moved to excessive anger against your neighbour? If you have wounded anybody in a quarrel, or harmed or blamed them; if you have hated your neighbour, or have provoked anybody to fury. If you have wished for somebody's death or injury; if you have provoked anybody to fury, either by deeds or by words, or by grumbling, or anything at all like that. If you have been a traitor, or if you have listened to traitors; if you have ill-wished anybody and wanted that evil thing to happen to them; if you have mocked or laughed at somebody; if you have blasphemed [you must confess to these branches of Anger].

Envy: Have you been miserable in any way, through envy of your neighbour's belongings? If you have felt envy of your equal, because he is like you in some way; if you have taken away — or tried to take away — from your neighbour's prosperity through any kind of envy: by words, by deeds, by aiding or abetting? Have you been a sower of discord?

---

[118] The main sins are frequently divided up into many sub-sins, sometimes known as their 'children'. In *GL* (Supp) they are called 'spices' (a form of the word 'espece', or kind; 'What the Church Betokeneth', p. 108).

[119] As noted earlier, the spelling of Lincoln as Nichole is typical of Anglo-Norman.

[120] Each item could be rephrased as a question; I vary the formula *passim*.

De accide: Si vous ayez par necligence tressaylli hors la creaunce en la pater
Nostre; si vus ayez esté necligent d'orer; si vous ayez esté necligent d'aler
a mustier en tens due; si vous donastes poy de oyr les paroles Dieu;
si vous ayez esté ennuyé de bien; si vus ayez amee mult udiuesce;
si vous ayez fet necligentement le uvere Dieu; si vus ne ayez pas honuree   30
vos parenz; si vous ayez fet vow qe n'est pas avowable e tele vow eiez pursuy;
si vous eiez fet vou q'est a vower e ne l'avez pursuy; si vous eiez en trop de
tristesce; si vous ayez esté en desperaunce e eyés pou prisé l'ame e la vye; si
vous ayez esté necligent governour de Seinte Eglise en seynant, en amendant,
en eydant, en servant.   35
De Avaryce: Si vous ayez estee coveytous en purchaçaunt e chinches
en retenaunt; si vous aiez esté foularge en donaunt; si vous ayez nule chose
emblé u ravy; si vus ayez consentu as laruns e as robbours; si vous eiez celé u
retenu chose qe vous ad estee baillé a garde; si vus eiez retenu a vostre serjaunt
sun luer; si vous aiez celee chose trovee u prop[r]es us turnee; si vus ayez   40
prestee an usure; si vus ayez en akune manere fet symonye; si vus aiez deceu
vostre proume par akun contract; si vous aez donee faus jugement; si vous
ayez la fey blescee; si vous ayez faus juree; si pur fausine eiez mentu; si
vous eyez porté faus temoyne; si vos eiez esté losengeer; si vous eiez estee
tretre; si vus n'eyez pas pleinement [f.80r] rendu vos dymes e vos   45
offrendes; si vous n'eiez pas donee dymes de totes les choses que se
renovelent par an; si vus eiez fet trescherie en dymaunt en celaunt u en
changaunt les meillors; si vus aiez estee en acune ayde u servise par
covoytyse.

Sloth: If you have wavered through negligence, from belief in the Lord's Prayer; or if you have been lazy about praying, or about going to church at the right time; or if you have not given ear to the Word of God. Have you been bored of goodness, or loved idleness too much? Or you have done the works of God negligently? Have you honoured your parents? If you have made a vow that is not proper to be made, and have pursued that vow; or if you have made a proper vow and have not pursued it. If you have been in too much sadness;[121] if you have been in despair, prizing too little the soul and its life; if you have been neglecting the rules of Holy Church, in making the sign of the Cross,[122] in improving, in helping, in serving.

Avarice: If you have been covetous in your buying, and mean about holding onto money; if you have been foolish in giving.[123] Have you taken or snatched anything? Or connived at theft and robbery? Have you hidden or held back anything that was entrusted to you to look after? If you have withheld from your servant his hire; or if you hid something you found, and diverted it from its proper use. Have you lent money usuriously, or done any kind of simony? If you have deceived your neighbour in any contract, or given false judgement, or broken faith or sworn falsely; if you have lied about an untrue thing, or borne false witness. Have you been a detractor, or a traitor; have you failed to pay your tithes and offerings? If you have not given tithes for everything that is due annually, if you have cheated in your tithes by hiding, or substituting the worse for the better; if you have done anything in the way of help or service because of covetousness.

---

[121] For sadness (*tristitia*) as a sin, cf. *Rossignos*, above; *GL* (Supp) p. 108; and *Cher Alme*, esp. p. 18.

[122] 'en seynant' could be a mistake for 'en [en]seignant'; 'teaching' would be appropriate in this list of neglected actions.

[123] Virtuous moderation stipulates that excessive largesse ought not to be considered as generosity.

De Glotonye: Si vus eiez mangee avaunt hore u eiez en custume sovent 50
manger u boyvre; si vous ayez en custume aver delyt en trop diversitee de
mangers e de boyvre; si vous ayez estee trop custoumer ferventement manger
u boyvre; si vus ayez passee mesure; si vus ayez encustoume de quere
deliciouses mangers e chieres; si pur glotonye eiez vomy; si vus eiez
provoké les autres a exces par malice u par veyneglorie; si vus aiez fet larcyn 55
de manger u de boyvre pur glotonye.

De leccher[ie]: Si vus aiez fet fornicacion; si vus aiez estee avouteres; si vus
eiez eu afeere a vostre parente charnelment u ové deus procheines parentes
u oveske acune altre k'en en acune manere a vous ateneit; si vus vus eiez
suyly en puteyne; si vus eiez pucele depucelee; si vus eiez [e]u afere de 60
femme malade; si vus eiez en acune manere donee entente de conseiller u
aider u consentyr a fornicacioun; si vus [eiez] esté de destable corage u de
cors; si vus eiez eu delyt de suyre les caroles u acune de tens[124] maneres veins
jues.

De Homicide: Si vus eiez consentu al homicide par conseil u par uvere; si 65
vus vousistes unkes estrangler u occire; si enfaunt eiez tuee u conseil u
aide a tel occisioun donee; si vus eiez estee present la u enfaunt ad pery
sanz bapteme; si vus ne savetz la furme de baptesme; si vus eiez fet
sacrilege u sorcerye eiez procuree u a tele chose eiez affiaunce donee;
si vus eiez levee acun dé funz avant qe vus seustes la creaunce; si vus 70
eiez estee necligent d'enseyner [f.80v] a vos filz esperitels
la Creaunce e la Pater Nostre; si vus eiez esté necligent de quere
confirmacioun; si vous eiez poy prisé d'estre confés aprés trespas; si vus
eiez feintement venu a confessioun; [s]i vous eiez lessé vos pecchez
dehors e eiez retenu les circunstances dedenz; si vous n'eiez pas fet la 75
penaunce qe vous fust ajoynt; si vus eiez pris le cors Nostre Signur en
mortel pecchee u prestre en mortel pecchee aydee a chaunter u si vous
estes prestre e eiez en mortel pecché chauntee; si vous estes clerk e eiez
fet nul contrakt; si vous eiez mys mayn en clerk en malice.

---

[124] Read 'teus', tels (such).

Gluttony: If you have eaten before it's time, or if you are in the habit of eating and drinking often; if you make a habit of enjoying too much variety in things to eat and drink, or if you too often eat or drink voraciously. Have you over-eaten? Do you often seek out the most delicious and expensive food? If you have made yourself sick with your greed; if you have incited others to excess either maliciously or out of vanity; if you have ever stolen food or drink because of gluttony.

Lechery: Have you fornicated? Are you an adulterer? If you have had carnal relations with your female kin, or with your near relations, or with any other [woman] who is in any way connected to you;[125] have you dirtied yourself with a prostitute, or taken a virgin's maidenhead? Have you had relations with a sick woman?[126] If you have in any way intended to counsel or to help or to consent to fornication; if you are inconstant in your heart or your body. If you love following the round-dance, or any such kind of vain games.[127]

Murder: Have you connived at murder, by word or deed? If you ever felt like strangling or killing somebody; if you have killed a child, or helped in any way in such killing by counsel or assistance; if you have been there when a child died without being baptized; if you don't know the proper form of baptism. Have you ever done sacrilege, or arranged for sorcery to be done, or put faith in any such thing? If you have ever stood godparent to somebody before knowing the Creed;[128] if you have been lazy about teaching your godchildren the Creed and the Lord's Prayer; if you have been negligent about seeking [their] confirmation. Do you delay going to confession after sin, are you reluctant to come to confession? You may have left your sins outside but kept the occasion of sin within you, if you have not done the penance that was enjoined upon you. If you have taken the Body of the Lord in mortal sin, or helped a priest who is in mortal sin to sing the office; or if you are a priest have you sung the office while in mortal sin? If you are a clerk, have you fulfilled your office? And have you wickedly laid hands on a clerk?

---

[125] Sex with relations, to some considerable degree of remoteness, counted as incest.

[126] This could be a reference to the sin of making love even with your wife while she has her periods.

[127] As with the sin of vanity in clothing, such wickedness as dancing was considered to lead to lasciviousness.

[128] 'levee acun dé funz'; this refers to baptism.

Nicole Bozon, from *Contes Moralisés*, 128: Bad Company[129]

This little homily contains a story well known from Branch IV of the *Roman de Renart*, although it differs in certain details.[130] Many of Bozon's moralized tales are taken from natural history and illustrated by fables, exempla, and biblical references. These appeal to a public with a deep knowledge of the Bible through hearing it in church, and whose life involved a good deal more natural history than ours does. There are two manuscripts listed in Dean, both fourteenth century. Both the edition used here, and Rose's translation, are based on London, Gray's Inn, 12 (768).[131] It is a trilingual text, containing Latin, French, and English. These tales are among the sources for *Gesta Romanorum*, and the exemplum of the dogs that are vices appears in *Gesta*'s Tale CXLII.[132]

The Bible citation in the text below is of interest, giving as it does the name of the book and the chapter (although incorrectly, in this case).[133] Many medieval writers cite the Bible in a much more general way, referring simply to the presumed writer. The Apostle is Paul; The Prophet is Isaiah, or another; The Evangelist refers to one of the four Gospel books; Solomon can be any of the 'Wisdom' books; The Psalmist, or King David, means the writer of the Psalms. Further, the division of Bible chapters into verses is a comparatively modern phenomenon, dating from approximately the fourteenth century; Wyclif writing his *Trialogus* towards the end of that century is still citing books and chapters without verses.[134]

My aim throughout this book has been to point up connections and reflections, as topics and themes recur in the variety of texts I have chosen. The *Conte* is placed here at the end of the book so that this animal story forms a link through to the Appendix below, where a werewolf is invoked. Another of Bozon's *Contes* (number 22) is about how the Devil hunts souls with his accursed hounds, seven in all: the

---

[129] Dean 695. [Bozon] ed. Smith and Meyer; and [Bozon] *Metaphors of Brother Bozon*, tr. R[ose]. The former may be viewed online in its entirety; my extract is so short readers may wish to read more. The latter is also available online. Legge gives c. 1320 as a probable earliest date for his *Contes* (her p. 232).

[130] *Le Roman de Renart*, ed. and tr. Dufournet and Méline. The Middle English version (*The History of Reynard the Fox*, ed. Blake) relates a similar story as a 'flashback' in Number 33 (see note 91/11ff. on pp. 136–7). Cf. also The Fox and the Wolf, number V in *Early Middle English Verse and Prose*, ed. Bennett and Smithers. Douglas Gray discusses beast fables (*inter al.*) in his *Simple Forms*, esp. ch. 8. In *Uncle Remus*, story number XVI (Old Mr Rabbit he's a Good Fisherman), Brer Rabbit fools Brer Fox.

[131] As usual, the reader is referred to the introduction and notes of the edition, for further discussion. See also Legge, pp. 229–32; and her *Cloisters*, pp. 86–7.

[132] ed. Oesterley, pp. 248–9, entitled 'Of the Snares of the Devil'. The named dogs there number eight, as do (no doubt coincidentally) the *Deadly Sins* in this book. See also *Gesta Romanorum*, ed. Herrtage, pp. xii & 524.

[133] Cf. the reference to Aristotle, and my footnote below.

[134] I thank Justin Stover for pointing this out (division into chapters was made in the late twelfth or early thirteenth century, by Stephen Langton).

fourth hound is called Baudewyn, and it is loosed at all manner of lawyer-figures, who are hunted to Hell by the boldness ('baudur') of their mind and speech.[135]

It is sheer coincidence that the evil creature in the Alderney story below is called 'tchen bodu'. The creature, which never in fact appears on the night in question, has been traced to the building it was said to haunt, the Villa Baudu in Guernsey. This was once a slaughterhouse, on the site of an ancient monastery. It is entirely probable that locals, coming home late from the pub and seeing a beast with blood-stained jaws, should take a hungry thieving dog for a werewolf. The building at or near the monastery may have been named for some church notable (monk, bishop, abbot) called Baldwin, but I have been unable to establish this for certain. Or it could simply have been named after its builder, perhaps a local landowner by the name of Bodu or similar.

The name Baldwin means Bold (in a good sense, of course, unlike Bozon's hound), no more and no less than Stephen means Crowned. My main point is illustrated in this example: a house and a name belonging to the Baskerville family would have held no terrors for anybody until a famous and terrifying dog-story was written about it. The word 'bodu' cannot be traced as meaning anything to do with darkness or death or shape-changing in any of the languages historically current in the Channel Islands, although some folklorists are convinced such a meaning must exist because of the animal's baleful reputation. But the *word* Baskerville does not mean 'deadly'![136]

As usual, I copy the edited text closely. I have added line numbers and simplified editorial marks (I note the latter if they are of special interest); anything in square brackets was supplied from the other MS.

---

[135] Cited as epigraph to my chapter of legal texts.

[136] A reference in *Jersey Folklore* is unsatisfactory. Having declared Bodu means The Abyss, this author remarks that the animal haunted the Ville Bodu. It is therefore clear the dog was named for this house 'of the Abyss' and was not itself from Hell (in Bois, ch. 1, pp. 39–40; the 'meaning' is not referenced).

Text

[f.43]

128 *De mala societate fugienda.*
Aristotil dit en son livere qe si poleyne [en ju-
vente] seit del let de asne norri, qe cely quant vendra
en age guerpira sa nature demeigne, e par la noris-
saunce del let le asne qe en juvente ad receü, se joyndra   5
al asne. Auxint meynt homme par fol compaignie en
juvente est hony en age, si com avent a Roboam.
Pur ceo dit le seint Espirit: 'Si vous recevez en com-
paignye [homme] de estraunge nation, il bestor-
nera vostre manere e vous amenera hors de la dreit   10
veie.' *Si admittas alienigenam, subvertet te et alie-*
nabit te a viis propriis. PROVER. XI.

Translation

Fleeing from bad society.

Aristotle says in his book[137] that if a foal in its babyhood is fed with the milk of an ass, when it comes of age it will abandon its true nature. And because of the food of asses' milk it received in its youth it will become like an ass.[138] In this way, many a man who frequents mad company in youth will be shamed by it in his maturity, as happened to Rehoboam.[139] Therefore the Holy Spirit says 'If you receive into your company a man from a strange land, he will pervert your nature to wickedness and lead you out of the right way.'[140]

---

[137] We are not told which book is meant, and there is no way of tracing whether the saying is even Aristotle's. The editors' note offers 'Arist. VI, xxix?' Sometimes such things can be located, but usually by sheer luck; any attempt to search a database is likely to fail because the keywords may not be 'correct'. An idea of the frequency and inexactitude of citations from *auctores* in medieval writings may be gleaned from *Cher Alme*, in which they are numerous.

[138] In the Arthurian stories, an explanation for Kay's boorish behaviour is that Arthur was given his foster-mother's milk when he was taken away from his real mother; consequently, his foster-brother Kay was suckled by a peasant woman who was naturally deemed to be without chivalric virtues. He is at his worst in the romance of *Yder* (above).

[139] A Concordance gives several references for Rehoboam; the most apposite is I Kings 12:8, about the foolish young men with whom he grew up. When consulting these books of the Bible, it is useful to remember that *LV* has Reg. I, II, II, IV for *AV*'s I & II Sam. and I & II Kings; I & II Chron. are there known as I & II Paralipomenon.

[140] The passage is not in the Book of Proverbs. See Ecclus. 11:34 in *AV* (11:36 in *LV*). The words are not exactly the same, but close: *Receive a stranger into thine house, and he will disturb thee, and turn thee out of thine own.* 'Holy Spirit' clearly means 'Holy Scripture'.

Fabula ad idem.
Le gopil dit al moton: 'Amez poynt de fur-
mage?' 'Nanil,' dit l'autre, il ne me vient   15
poynt de nature.' 'Non?' dit le gopil, 'venez od
moy, e jeo vous aprendra de [amer] chose qe unqes
ne amastez.' 'Et loez issint?' dit le moton.
'Oyl,' fet l'autre, 'en bon fey.' 'Ou le trouve-
rons?' dit le moton. 'Jeo vy un homme porter   20
furmage,' [dit le gopil,] 'pres de un fontaigne, e
le homme cesta, e un furmage lui eschapa e chey en
le fontaigne.' 'Et coment le averons?' dit le mo-
toun. 'Jeo descendray' dit le gopil 'en un dez bo-
ketez.' Quant le gopil fust descenduz jesqes al fond,   25
le moton demanda 'Pur quoy demorrez tant?'
'Le furmage' fet l'autre 'est si graund q'i moy covient de aver eyde. Saillez' dit il al moton 'en
l'autre boket; si averoms [fet de] meyntenant.'
'Veiez moy ci', dit le moton en descendant en la bo-   30
ket. Et le gopil vynt sus en l'autre boket mountant,
e saut a terre e dit al moton en riaunt 'Est le furmage bon e savoree?' 'Veire!' fet l'autre, 'hony
seiez vous de Dampne Dieu!
"Was it nevere my kynd   35
Chese in wellez grond to fynde"'
Pur ceo dit SALOMON, Prov. I: 'Si lui mauveis
homme te prie de aver ta compaignie, veietz qe
vous ne assentez mye.' *Si te lactaverint peccato-*
res, ne adquiescas illis; si dixerint: Veni nobiscum,   40
etc.

Fable for the same.

The fox said to the sheep 'Don't you like cheese?' 'Of course not,' said the other, 'it's not in my nature to do so.' 'No?' says the fox. 'Come with me, and I'll teach you to like something you have never liked before!' 'Do you recommend it?' asked the sheep. 'Oh yes,' says the other, 'by my faith!' 'Where shall we find it?' says the sheep. 'I saw a man carrying cheese,' says the fox, 'near a well, and the man stumbled, and a cheese escaped his grasp and fell into the well!' 'But how shall we get it?' says the sheep. 'I'll go down,' says the fox, 'in one of the buckets.'

When the fox had got down to the bottom, the sheep asked 'What's keeping you so long?' 'This cheese,' says the other, 'is so huge I'm going to need help. Jump', says he, 'into the other bucket and we'll soon have hold of it.' 'Here I come!' says the sheep, going down in the bucket.

And the fox comes up in the other bucket which is ascending, and jumps out onto dry land; laughing, he says to the sheep 'Is that cheese good and tasty?' 'Oh really!' says the other, 'May the Lord God damn you! "It was never my nature to find cheese in the bottom of a well!" '[141]

This is why Solomon says 'If the wicked man begs to have your company, take care never to consent.'[142]

---

[141] This couplet is in English.

[142] Prov. 1:10–11. *My son, if sinners entice thee, consent thou not. If they say, Come with us, let us lay wait for blood, let us lurk privily for the innocent without cause* ... the passage continues with more about the terrible things planned. In this story, the fox gets nothing but a good laugh because of course there is no cheese. The Middle English couplet may be a trace remaining from a lost English version of the story (editors' notes, p. 282).

Appendix

'Et pis y avait quat'e: enne histouaire de ma graond'mé', an adventure story

My appendix presents Insular French of another kind, as it survives into modern times: here is one of the stories told to Royston Raymond of Alderney by his grandmother;[1] he is writing them down for interested colleagues. Although the Alderney patois, or 'parler', has effectively died out, Raymond remembers his grandparents' speech. On first looking into Wace's *Roman de Rou*, he said to himself 'This is the language of my grandparents!' He tells me his grandfather boasted of speaking the language of Duke William. Now retired, he is compiling a dictionary of Alderney vocabulary (the language differs from that recorded in the other islands), and working with the local school to bring knowledge of the language to the next generation. He has transcribed his grandmother's speech as exactly as he can, from memory. This was a spoken language only, and as far as we know was never written down;[2] the Island administration used standard French in official documents until 1948. The stories have been studied in the Oxford Anglo-Norman reading group, because of notable similarities to the extant Anglo-Norman of medieval times;[3] and also recorded, when he visited Oxford. One or more of them are to appear in the *Alderney Society Bulletin*; some are in Raymond's *Fishermen's Tales*.[4]

A comparatively recent essay on Island patois is illuminating because it demonstrates correspondence between a medieval language and a modern dialect or

---

[1] He is working on more of these.

[2] Local gossip at one time believed the language (of Guernsey in this example) to be that of witches: Edwards, *Ebenezer Le Page*, p. 317.

[3] In the 1860s Le Cerf said, of Wace, 'De nos jours encore ses chants pourraient etre compris dans les chaumières des iles' (*L'Archipel des Iles Normandes*, Paris 1863, p. 29). This was written around the same date as events in the story presented in this book, less than a century before its recital in the 1940s. The name of our hero, Sebire, is still current in Alderney.

[4] The latter (Raymond, ed., *Fishermen's Tales*) includes the story presented here, with minor differences, in Raymond's own translation and without the original French. This same one has now been published in the *Bulletin* (Raymond, 'And then there were four'), again with minor differences. I am very grateful to him for allowing me to include it in this book.

dialects.[5] Unfortunately Daffyd Evans omitted Alderney from his study because, he said, the local dialect died out when the island was completely evacuated at the beginning of the Second World War. He seems to be unaware that at least six of the returning evacuees still spoke the patois, after 1945. The last one died in the early 1980s. In Darmesteter, *La Vie des Mots*, remarks on patois remain useful when researching old forms of a language.[6] A similar dialect is alive and well in [Cap de la] Hague; Raymond corresponds with native writers and speakers in their own language; Fleury noted its closeness to Aurignais (or Aourgniais).[7] The present volume is called *An Anglo-Norman Reader*, and it must be remembered that Insular French does still exist outside the medieval field.[8]

The distinctive spelling, below, represents Raymond's effort to render his memory of what the language sounded like. Neither this, nor his pronunciation on the recording, sounds much like Old French as medievalists are taught to pronounce it. He prefaces his current work as follows: '[This] is merely an estimated reconstruction of Alderney patois based on amateur research and 65 year old memories from the late 1940s when my grandmother told me this story. It cannot claim to be 100 per cent accurate.' Elsewhere, he notes 'li' is masculine (as in Old French) and 'lé' is feminine.

---

[5] Evans, 'The Taxonomy of Bird-Naming in Anglo-Norman and Channel Island Patois'.

[6] For example, note 1 p. 170. See also Hogg, ed., *The Cambridge History of the English Language* (ch. 3), p. 68, for the value of dialect in tracing the history of a language.

[7] *Essai sur le patois normand de la Hague*.

[8] I am grateful to Ian Short for further material on the subject of Island languages (his 'Mainland and Insular Norman' provides a number of references).

Text

A daeux milles au norouet d'Aur'ni y a en p'tit ilôt noumai Burhou. Dans lé laoungawge des Vikings che veurt dire 'Ilôt dove enne caumine'.

Réel'ment enne p'tite caumine ou maisounette en pierre se tint au milli de l'ilôt quai fut bastie y a laoungtemps a l'assinant de Chretiannetai p'tête coumme en ermitawge pour en anacorite irlandais.

Depis des chentoines d'onnoaies les paissouniers et pis les Etats d'Aur'ni ont moint'nu che bastiment coumme abri pour les mariniers nawfrawgés ou des coilliers d'ormés durant les graound's maraies. En d'dans y avait terjours en coffre de biscuits de mé et enne barrique d'eau a bere.

Choque Ernouvoi en guoing de treis d'ouveriers, en tcherpentier, en machaon et en peintre fut enviai a Burhou pour faire les reparaciaons tch'il faout. Y em'noient en dedans lé maisounnette tous leurs outi's; des sacs de chiment et de caue sans oubilloi en amas de mang'rie, enne barrique de cidre et des bouteilles de rhom.

Enne foueis durant les onnaies sessantes de lé dix-neuvième siecle au mouais d'avril mon arrière graond onc'e, Daniel Sebire, en tcherpentier, s'est atterri a Burhou dove les autres ouveriers pour faire les travaux coumme de couteume.

Oprès chinq jours leurs tâques furent finies et y se sont mis à préparai pour li r'tour en Aur'ni. Par malheur en Nordvouestin fut arrivaïe et y furent abandonnaïe acore treis jors sur l'ilôt.

Che seir law y furent assis a sen aise d'vant en gros fouaie de bouais rammassaïe sur lé banque. En graond bachin de croc fut a mitounniair et les treis hoummes fumaïent leurs pipes et craquiaïent tandis tche dehors le vent heurlaïe et lé maisounette tchatchaïe sous les bourdèques.

Translation

And then there were four! A story of my grandmother's[9]

Two miles to the north-west of Alderney[10] there is a tiny islet called Burhou. In the language of the Vikings this means 'Islet with a Hut'.

In truth, a little hut or tiny house of stone stands in the middle of the islet; it was built long ago at the dawn of Christianity perhaps as a hermitage for an Irish anchorite.[11]

For hundreds of years the fishermen, and then the States of Alderney, have maintained this building as a shelter for shipwrecked mariners or for the ormer-gatherers during the great spring tides.[12] And inside there was always a chest full of ship's biscuit and a barrel of drinking-water.

Every spring a gang of three workmen — carpenter, mason, and painter — was sent to Burhou to do the necessary repairs. They took all their tools into the hut, and sacks of cement and lime, not forgetting a stock of provisions, a barrel of cider, and bottles of rum.

One time, during the sixties in the nineteenth century, in the month of April, my great-great uncle Daniel Sebire was the carpenter; he landed on Burhou with the other workmen to do the repairs as usual.

After five days, their tasks[13] were completed, and they began to prepare for the return to Alderney. But unfortunately a north-wester had blown up, and they were marooned for another three days on the islet.[14]

On that evening they were sitting comfortably in front of an enormous fire of driftwood gathered at the water's edge. A great pot of bean stew was simmering,[15] and the three men smoked their pipes and chatted while outside the wind howled and the hut shuddered in the blasts.

---

[9] The translation is broadly my own, though I have consulted Raymond every step of the way with this unique material.

[10] The French name for Alderney is 'Aurigny'.

[11] Legend has it that Alderney, with the other islands, was converted by Celtic missionaries in or around the sixth century (see my 'Vignalis, or Guénaël, of Alderney: A Legend and its Medieval Sources').

[12] The ormer (oreille de mer) is a univalve shellfish much prized in the Channel Islands: a kind of northern abalone. *OED*: the Ormer (Fr. Ormier, Lat. *auris maris*, 'Sea-ear', in Alderney patois 'ormé') is *haliotis tuberculata*. It is difficult and dangerous to gather, and very good to eat when properly cooked; the shell, pictured on the back cover of this book, is beautiful.

[13] 'tâques' (pronounced 'tork'); Raymond alters the spelling of 'taches' so as to represent the long drawling 'a' sound, and the hard final consonant, of the local pronunciation as he hears it.

[14] A century and a half after these events took place, Burhou remains inaccessible in bad weather: it has no harbour or landing-place.

[15] Locals are proud of their 'bean jar' (this appears in Island recipe books, and no two households make it the same way); it is not unlike cassoulet.

Soudain'ment y aont ouï en grattement affaiblli a li hus. Li sang a g'laie dans leurs voines. Durant tchitchuns secaonds y furent paralisaïe par lé crointe. Enfin Daniel s'est butaïe. 'N'ouvre por Daniel!' ont criaie les aout's, 'ch'est li tchen bodu!'

'Ach foutu feignaonts! Ne porle por du bavin!' il a répondu, mais tout de maesm il a gardaïe en graond couté a lé moin destre quand il a ouvaert li hus.

Law sur li peraon était en houmme, ses hardes en nocq de nocq et erachiaïes, les moins et gambes ensanguinaïes.

Y l'ont trognaïe en d'dans, ont degraïe ses hardes et l'ont enveloppaïe dans en bllanquet et l'ont mis près de faeu. Nou l'a dounnaïe en graond bolaie de croc brulant arrosaïe de rhom.

Li landemoin matin li naufrawgaïe a pu leur racontaïe sen histouaire. Son baté, enne barquentine en passage de Birdeaux a Li Havre, par enne faoute de navigaciaon fut naufrawgi sur lé greune de Renonquet.

Par en miraclle il a pu nouaïr enviars l'ilôt de Burhou et a grimpotaïe a tchique bord sur lé banque ou les houlingues n'étaient paw trop fortes. Enne fwais a terre y a vu li lueur d'lé lampe a huile dans lé f'nête d'lé caumine. Naette paumaï il a catounaïe enviaers li.

R'venu en Aur'ni il fut mis a l'hôpital des paoures et pllus tard lé paraesse a payaïe son retour en Angllectaire.

Ma graon'mé m'a terjours assaeuraïe tche chutte histouaire était vraïe, mais jo ne l'ai jomais trouvaïe racontaïe dans lé Presse de Djernesi.

Suddenly there was a feeble scratching at the door! The blood froze in their veins ... for several seconds they were paralyzed with terror. At length Daniel sprang up. 'Don't open it, Daniel!' cried the others. 'It's the werewolf!'[16]

'You bloody feeble lot! Don't talk such balls!' he retorted ... but, all the same, he kept a big knife in his right hand as he opened the door.

There on the threshold was a man, his clothes torn to rags, and drenched to the bone, his hands and legs bloodied.

They hauled him inside, pulled off his clothes and wrapped him in a blanket, and put him in front of the fire. Then he was given a big bowl of hot stew laced with rum.[17]

Next morning, the castaway was able to tell them his story. His ship, a barquentine on her way from Bordeaux to Le Havre, had been wrecked on the reef of Renonquet through a fault of navigation.[18]

By a miracle, he had been able to swim towards the islet of Burhou, and crawled ashore at a point where the breakers were less ferocious. Once landed, he saw the light of the oil-lamp in the window of the hut. Almost fainting, he had dragged himself towards it.

Back in Alderney, he was put into the paupers' hospital, and later the parish paid his passage back to England.

My grandmother always assured me this story was true, but I have never been able to find it reported in the Guernsey press.[19]

---

[16] This creature was reputed to be a dog (see my introduction to Bozon's *Conte*, above).

[17] A word looking like 'nous' is in fact third person singular; it means 'on' ('oun' reversed) and may be used either thus or to indicate a passive.

[18] The waters around Alderney are littered with wrecks, over untold centuries; the rocks and reefs are deadly, and the tidal currents surging past the island are among the fiercest in the world (a tidal-power project is currently in development).

[19] The scribe, Raymond himself, speaks. The site of this wreck, at least (together with numerous others), may be identified on a map in the Alderney Museum.

Bibliography

Primary Texts

1066 and All That, Walter Carruthers Sellar and Robert Julian Yeatman (1930; repr. Harmondsworth, 1960).

Aelred of Rievaulx, *The Historical Works*, ed. Marsha L. Dutton, tr. Jane Patricia Freeland (Kalamazoo, 2005).

'The All Souls Continuation of *La Maniere de Langage*', ed. Hideka Fukui, in Short, ed., *Anglo-Norman Anniversary Essays* (q.v.), pp. 149–57.

Anglo-Norman Anniversary Essays, ed. Ian Short, ANTS OPS 2 (1993).

'The Anglo-Norman *Description of England*', ed. Alexander Bell, in Short, ed., *Anglo-Norman Anniversary Essays* (q.v.), pp. 31–47.

The Anglo-Norman Pseudo-Turpin Chronicle *of William de Briane*, ed. Ian Short, ANTS 25 (1973).

'The Anglo-Norman "Hugo de Lincolnia": A Critical Edition and Translation from the Unique Text in Paris, Bibliothèque nationale de France MS fr. 902', ed. Roger Dahood, *Chaucer Review* 49:1 (2014), 1–38.

Anglo-Norman Letters and Petitions, ed. M. Dominica Legge, ANTS 3 (1941). http://www.anglo-norman.net/sources/

The Anglo-Norman Lyric: An Anthology, ed. David L. Jeffrey and Brian J. Levy (Toronto, 1990).

An Anglo-Norman Medical Compendium (Cambridge, Trinity College MS O.2.5 (1109)), ed. Tony Hunt, ANTS PTS 18 (2014).

'Anglo-Norman Medical Receipts', ed. Tony Hunt, in Short, ed., *Anglo-Norman Anniversary Essays* (q.v.), pp. 179–233.

[Antologia] *Storia di Haveloc e di altri eroi: Antologia del romanzo Anglo-Normanno (xii–xiii secolo)*, Margherita Lecco (Genoa, [2011]).

'*L'Apprise de Nurture* in Anglo-Norman Books of Courtesy and Nurture', ed. H. Rosamond Parsons, *PMLA* 44:2 (June 1929), 432–7, repr. from PMLA, pp. 383–455. http://www.jstor.org/stable/457474?seq=1#page_scan_tab_contents

Bede, *A History of the English Church and People*, tr. Leo Shirley-Price, R. E. Latham, and D. H. Farmer, revised edition (1955; repr. London, 1990).

Béroul, *The Romance of Tristan*, ed. Alfred Ewert (1939; repr. London, 1991).

The Birth of Romance: an Anthology, tr. Judith Weiss, FRETS 4, 2nd rev. edition (1992; repr. Tempe, AZ, 2009).

Bodel, Jehan, *La Chanson des Saisnes*, ed. Annette Brasseur (2 vols, Geneva, 1989).

A Book of Middle English, J. A. Burrow and Thorlac Turville-Petre, 2nd edition (1992; repr. Oxford, 1996).

The Book of the Knight of La Tour-Landry, Compiled for the Instruction of his Daughters, ed. Thomas Wright, EETS OS 33 (1868), translated from the original French into English.

The Book of the Knight of the Tower, ed. M. Y. Offord, tr. William Caxton, EETS SS 2 (1971).

[Bozon] *Les Contes Moralisés de Nicole Bozon, frère mineur*, ed. Lucy Toulmin Smith and Paul Meyer (Paris, 1889). http://gallica.bnf.fr/ark:/12148/bpt6k5101j

[Bozon] *Metaphors of Brother Bozon*, tr. J[ohn] R[ose] (London, 1913). https://openlibrary.org/works/OL6858872W/Metaphors_of_Brother_Bozon_a_friar_minor

Castleford's Chronicle or The Boke of Brut, ed. Caroline D. Eckhardt, EETS OS 305, 306 (2 vols, Oxford, 1996).

Chansons de Geste, extraits, ed. and tr. Robert Bossuat, nouvelle edition (Paris, [1935]).

Le Chant des Chanz, ed. Tony Hunt, ANTS 61–2 (2004).

Chardri, *La Vie des Set Dormanz*, ed. Brian S. Merrilees, ANTS 35 (1977).

Chardri, *The Works of Chardri: Three Poems in the French of Thirteenth-Century England. The Life of the Seven Sleepers, the Life of St. Josaphaz, and the Little Debate*, tr. Neil Cartlidge, FRETS 9 (Tempe, AZ, 2015).

Chaucer, Geoffrey, *The Riverside Chaucer*, ed. Larry D. Benson, 3rd edition (1987; repr. Oxford, 1988).

"Cher Alme": Texts of Anglo-Norman Piety, ed. Tony Hunt, tr. Jane Bliss, FRETS OPS 1 (Tempe, AZ, 2010), introduction by Henrietta Leyser.

'Christine de Pizan's *Epistre à la reine* (1405)', ed. Angus J. Kennedy, *Revue des Langues Romanes* 92 (1988), 253–64.

Chronicles of the Mayors and Sheriffs of London, with The French Chronicle of London, tr. Henry Thomas Riley (London, 1863).

Clemence of Barking, *The Life of St Catherine*, ed. William MacBain, ANTS 18 (1964).

Clemence of Barking, 'The Life of St Catherine', in *Virgin Lives and Holy Deaths*, tr. Jocelyn Wogan-Browne and Glyn S. Burgess (London, 1996), pp. 3–43.

Corset, Rober le Chapelain, ed. K. V. Sinclair, ANTS 52 (1995).

'*The Creation* of Herman de Valenciennes: An Unpublished Anglo-Norman Mystery Play of the 12th Century', ed. André de Mandach, in Short, ed., *Anglo-Norman Anniversary Essays* (q.v.), pp. 251–72.

Crow, Joan, ed., *Les Quinze Joyes de Mariage* (Oxford, 1969).

'*Des grantz geanz* — a new text fragment', ed. Diana B. Tyson, *Nottingham Medieval Studies* 50 (2006), 115–28.

Des Grantz Geanz, ed. Georgine E. Brereton (Oxford, 1937).

A Dictionary of Medieval Heroes, ed. Willem P. Gerritsen and Anthony G. van Melle, tr. Tanis Guest (1998; repr. Woodbridge, 2000).

Le Donei des Amanz, ed. Anthony J. Holden, ANTS PTS 17 (2013).

Durmart le Galois, ed. Edmund Stengel (1873; repr. Amsterdam, 1969).

Early Fiction in England: From Geoffrey of Monmouth to Chaucer, ed. Laura Ashe (London, 2015).

Early Middle English Verse and Prose, ed. J. A. W. Bennett and G. V. Smithers, 2nd edition (1966; repr. Oxford, 1985).

Edwards, G. B., *The Book of Ebenezer Le Page* (London, 1981), introduction by John Fowles.

Eighteen Anglo-Norman Fabliaux, ed. Ian Short and Roy Pearcy, ANTS PTS 14 (2000). http://www.anglo-norman.net/sources/

Euripides V: Three Tragedies (Electra, The Phoenician Women, The Bacchae), Euripides, ed. David Greene and Richard Lattimore, tr. Emily Townsend Vermeule, Elizabeth Wyckoff, and William Arrowsmith (Chicago, 1959).

Sir Ferumbras, ed. Sidney J. Herrtage, EETS ES 34 (1879), the English Charlemagne Romances, Part I.

Fouke le Fitz Waryn, ed. E. J. Hathaway, P. T. Ricketts, C. A. Robson, and A. D. Wilshere, ANTS 26–8 (1975).

The French Chronicle of London, ed. George James Aungier (London, 1844). https://www.cambridge.org/core/journals/camden-old-series/article/croniques-de-london-depuis-lan-44-hen-iii-jusqua-lan-17-edw-iii/869562AA4984646BD9B52CDE3F2A0586

Froissart, Jean, *Chronicles*, ed. and tr. Geoffrey Brereton (1968; repr. Harmondsworth, 1978).

From the Norman Conquest to the Black Death: An Anthology of Writings from England, ed. Douglas Gray (Oxford, 2011).

[Gawain] *Sir Gawain and The Green Knight, Pearl, and Sir Orfeo*, ed. Christopher Tolkien, tr. J. R. R. Tolkien (1975; repr. London, 1990).

Sir Gawain and the Green Knight, ed. J. A. Burrow (1972; repr. Harmondsworth, 1987).

Gesta Romanorum, ed. Hermann Oesterley (Berlin, 1872).

Gesta Romanorum, ed. Sidney J. H. Herrtage, EETS ES 33 (1879; repr. London, 1962).

Gesta Romanorum, or Entertaining Moral Stories, ed. and tr. Charles Swan and Wynnard Hooper (1876; repr. New York, 1959).

Gibbon's Decline and Fall of the Roman Empire, Edward Gibbon (6 vols, 1776–89; repr. London, 1969), vol. 4, introduction by Christopher Dawson.

Gilte Legende, ed. Richard Hamer and Vida Russell, EETS OS 315, 327, 328, 339 (4 vols, Oxford, 2000, 2006, 2007, 2012).

The Golden Legend: Readings on the Saints, Jacobus de Voragine, tr. William Granger Ryan (2 vols, 1993; repr. Princeton, 1995).

The Goodman of Paris (Le Ménagier de Paris), A Treatise on Moral and Domestic Economy by A Citizen of Paris c.1393, tr. Eileen Power (1928; repr. London, 1992).

Gower, John, *Confessio Amantis*, in *The English Works of John Gower*, ed. G. C. Macaulay, EETS ES 81, 82 (2 vols, 1900, 1901; repr. Oxford, 1979).

Grange, Huw, ed., 'A Paraphrase of the *Miserere* in Anglo-Norman Verse (Lambeth Palace, MS 431)', *Medium Ævum* 84:1 (2015), 40–59.

A Guide to Old English, Bruce Mitchell and Fred C. Robinson, 5th edition (1964; repr. Oxford, 1992).

[Harley 2253] *The Complete Harley 2253 Manuscript*, ed. and tr. Susanna Fein, David Raybin, and Jan Ziolkowski (3 vols, Kalamazoo, 2014–15), vol. 3.

[Harley 2253] *Facsimile of British Museum MS. Harley 2253*, ed. N. R. Ker, EETS OS 255 (London, 1965).

Historical French Reader, Medieval Period, ed. Paul Studer and E. G. R. Waters (Oxford, 1924).

The History of Reynard the Fox, ed. N. F. Blake, tr. William Caxton, EETS OS 263 (Oxford, 1970), from the Dutch Original.

The History of the Kings of Britain, Geoffrey of Monmouth, tr. Lewis Thorpe (Harmondsworth, 1966).

[Horn] *The Romance of Horn*, Mestre Thomas, ed. Mildred K. Pope, ANTS 9–10, 12–13 (2 vols, 1955, 1964).

Hue de Rotelande, *Protheselaus*, ed. A. J. Holden, ANTS 47–9 (3 vols, 1991–93). http://www.anglo-norman.net/sources/

The Idea of the Vernacular: An Anthology of Middle English Literary Theory 1280–1520, ed. Jocelyn Wogan-Browne, Nicholas Watson, Andrew Taylor, and Ruth Evans (Exeter, 1999).

Irving, Washington, *The Sketch Book of Geoffrey Crayon, Gent*, The People's Library 102 (1819; repr. London, 1909).

Le Jongleur par lui-même: Choix de dits et de fabliaux, tr. Willem Noomen (Louvain & Paris, 2003).

Kipling, Rudyard, 'The Enemies to Each Other', in *Debits and Credits* (London, 1926), pp. 3–20.

Kipling, Rudyard, 'Our Fathers of Old', in *Songs from Books* (London, 1920), pp. 127–9, reprinted from *Rewards and Fairies*.

Kipling, Rudyard, 'The Uses of Reading', in *A Book of Words* (London, 1928), pp. 77–96.

Kipling, Rudyard, *The Years Between* (London, 1919).

Lawrence, T. E., *Seven Pillars of Wisdom* (1926; repr. Harmondsworth, 1977).

Lectures françaises de la fin du moyen âge: petite anthologie commentée de succès littéraires, Frédéric Duval (Geneva, 2007).

Liber Eliensis: A History of the Isle of Ely, from the Seventh Century to the Twelfth, tr. Janet Fairweather (Woodbridge, 2005).

The Life of Saint Audrey: A Text by Marie de France, ed. and tr. June Hall McCash and Judith Clark Barban (Jefferson, NC, & London, 2006).

Lockhart, J. G., 'The King and the Minstrel, from the Norman French', in Frederic Mansel Reynolds, ed., *The Keepsake for 1829* (London, 1828), pp. 354–9.

Malory, Thomas, *Works*, ed. Eugène Vinaver, 2nd edition (1954; repr. Oxford, 1977).

Manières de Langage (1396, 1399, 1415), ed. Andres M. Kristol, ANTS 53 (1995). http://www.anglo-norman.net/sources/

Marie de France, *Lais*, ed. Alfred Ewert (1944; repr. London, 1995), introduction & bibliography by Glyn S. Burgess.

Master Richard's Bestiary of Love, and Response, Richard de Fournival, tr. Jeanette Beer (Berkeley & Los Angeles & London, 1986), engravings by Barry Moser.

Maurice of Sully and the Medieval Vernacular Homily, with the text of Maurice's French Homilies from a Sens Cathedral MS, ed. C. A. Robson (Oxford, 1952).

A Medieval French Reader, ed. C. W. Aspland (Oxford, 1979).

Merlin: Roman du XIIIe siècle, Robert de Boron, ed. Alexandre Micha (Geneva, 1979).

The Middle English Physiologus, ed. Hannah Wirtjes, EETS OS 299 (1991).

The Mirror of Justices, ed. William Joseph Whittaker (London, 1895), Introduction by Frederic William Maitland.

Mitchison, Naomi, *The Bull Calves* (1947; repr. London, 1997).

Montesquieu, *Lettres Persanes*, ed. Jacques Roger (1721; repr. Paris, 1964).

Nouveau recueil complet des fabliaux, ed. Willem Noomen and Nico van den Boogaard (10 vols, Assen, Netherlands, 1983–98).

An Old English Miscellany, ed. Richard Morris, EETS OS 49 (1872; repr. London, 1927).

The Origin of the Giants: The First Settlers of Albion, tr. J. S. Mackley (Northampton, 2014), bilingual edition.

The Oxford Dictionary of Saints, David Hugh Farmer, 3rd edition (Oxford, 1992).

Palgrave, Francis, ed., *Cy ensuyt une chanson moult pitoyable …* (London, 1818), with other texts from Harley 2253.

Les Paroles Salomun, ed. Tony Hunt, ANTS 70 (2012).

Parsons, Ben and Bas Jongenelen, '"The Sermon on Saint Nobody": A Verse Translation of a Middle Dutch Parodic Sermon', *Journal of American Folklore* 123 (2010), 92–107.

Le Petit Plet, Chardri, ed. Brian S. Merrilees, ANTS 20 (1970).

[Piers] *The Vision of Piers Plowman*, William Langland, ed. A. V. C. Schmidt (1978; repr. London, 1993).

Piers the Ploughman, William Langland, tr. J. F. Goodridge (1959; repr. Harmondsworth, 1975).

Piety and Persecution in the French Texts of England, ed. and tr. Maureen B. M. Boulton, FRETS 6 (Tempe, AZ, 2013).

Placita Corone, or La Corone Pledee devant Justices, ed. and tr. J. M. Kaye, Selden Society S. S. 4 (London, 1966).

Poems from BL MS Harley 913, 'The Kildare Manuscript', ed. Thorlac Turville-Petre, EETS OS 345 (2015).

Raymond, Royston, ed., *Fishermen's Tales* ([Alderney], [2015]).

Raymond, Royston, 'A Story my Grandmother told me, in Patois: "And then there were four"', *Alderney Society Bulletin* [50] (2015–2016), 88–92.

Recueil des lettres anglo-françaises 1265–1399, ed. F. J. Tanquerey (Paris, 1916). https://archive.org/details/recueildelettres00tanquoft

Revelacion, ed. Brent A. Pitts, ANTS 68 (2010).

La Riote du monde, ed. Francisque Michel (Paris, 1834), avec Le Roi d'Angleterre et le Jongleur d'Ely.

'La riote du monde', ed. Jakob Ulrich, *ZrP* 8 (1884), 275–89, includes edition of 'le jongleur de Ely et de mon seignour le roi de Engleterre'.

'Le Roi d'Angleterre et le Jongleur d'Ely', in *Recueil Général et complet des Fabliaux des XIIIᵉ et XIVᵉ siècles*, ed. Anatole de Montaiglon and Gaston Raynaud (6 vols, Paris, 1877), vol. II, pp. 242–56. http://gallica.bnf.fr/ark:/12148/bpt6k209380j

Le Roman de Renart, ed. and tr. Jean Dufournet and Andrée Méline (2 vols, Paris, 1985).

Le Roman de Thèbes, ed. Léopold Constans (2 vols, Paris, 1890). https://archive.org/details/leromandethbes01consuoft

Le Roman de Thèbes, ed. and tr. Francine Mora-Lebrun (Paris, 1995), f-p into Mn French.

Le Roman de Troie, Extraits, Benoît de Sainte-Maure, ed. and tr. Emmanuèle Baumgartner and Françoise Vielliard (Paris, 1998), f-p into Mn French.

'Le Roman des Franceis', André de Coutances, ed. Anthony J. Holden, in Félix Lecoy, ed., *Etudes de langue et de littérature du Moyen Age offertes à Félix Lecoy* (Paris, 1973), pp. 213–33.

'The *Roman des Franceis* of Andrew de Coutances: Significance, Text, and Translation', ed. and tr. David Crouch, in David Crouch and Kathleen Thompson, eds, *Normandy and its Neighbours: Essays for David Bates* (Turnhout, 2011), pp. 175–98.

The Romance of Fergus, Guillaume le Clerc, ed. Wilson Frescoln (Philadelphia, 1983).

'*The Romance of Fergus*', Guillaume le Clerc, tr. D. D. R. Owen, *Arthurian Literature* VIII (1989), 79–183.

The Romance of the Rose, Guillaume de Lorris and Jean de Meun, tr. Frances Horgan (1994; repr. Oxford, 2008).

The Romance of Yder, ed. and tr. Alison Adams, Arthurian Studies 8 (Cambridge, 1983).

Le Romanz du reis Yder, ed. and tr. Jacques Ch. Lemaire (Brussels/Fernelmont, 2010).

Rossignos, John of Howden, ed. Glynn Hesketh, ANTS 63 (2006).

Sanson de Nantuil, *Les Proverbes de Salemon*, ed. C. Claire Isoz, ANTS 44, 45, 50 (3 vols, 1988 (for 1986), 1988 for (1987), 1994 for (1992)). http://www.anglo-norman.net/sources/

Selected Fabliaux, ed. B. J. Levy and C. E. Pickford (1978; repr. Hull, 1988).

Sermons on Joshua, ed. Tony Hunt, ANTS PTS 12 & 13 (2 vols, 1998).

Shorter Treatises: Anglo-Norman medicine, ed. Tony Hunt (2 vols, Cambridge, 1994–97), vol. 2.

[Sibile] *Le Livre de Sibile*, Philippe de Thaon, ed. Hugh Shields, ANTS 37 (1979).

The Song of Roland, tr. Dorothy L. Sayers (1957; repr. Harmondsworth, 1965).

St. Erkenwald, ed. Ruth Morse (Cambridge, 1975).

Stevenson, Robert Louis, 'The Merry Men', in *Shorter Scottish Fiction* (Edinburgh, 1995), pp. 159–207.

Stubbs' Select Charters from the earliest times to the reign of Edward the First, ed. and tr. William Stubbs, 9th edition (1870; repr. Oxford, 1929), revised H. W. C. Davis. https://archive.org/details/selectchartersa01stubgoog

Swift, Jonathan, *Gulliver's Travels*, ed. Paul Turner (1971; repr. Oxford, 1986).

Thomas d'Angleterre, *Les Fragments du Roman de Tristan*, ed. Bartina H. Wind, 2nd edition (1950; repr. Geneva, 1960).

Thomas of Kent, *The Anglo-Norman* Alexander *(Le Roman de toute chevalerie)*, ed. Brian Foster and Ian Short, ANTS 29–31, 32–3 (2 vols, 1976, 1977).

Thompson, Stith, *Motif-Index of Folk Literature* (6 vols, Helsinki, 1932–36).

Three Receptaria from Medieval England: The languages of medicine in the fourteenth century, ed. Tony Hunt, Medium Ævum Monographs (Oxford, 2001), vol. N. S. XXI, with the collaboration of Michael Benskin.

Trinity Apocalypse, ed. Ian Short, ANTS 73 (2016).

[Tristan] *The Anglo-Norman* Folie Tristan *(d'Oxford)*, ed. Ian Short, ANTS PTS 10 (1993).

[Tristan] *La Folie Tristan de Berne*, ed. Ernest Hœpffner (Paris, 1934).

Tristan et Yseut: Les premières versions européennes, ed. Christiane Marchello-Nizia *et al.* (Paris, 1995).

Uncle Remus, or, Mr Fox, Mr Rabbit, and Mr Terrapin, Joel Chandler Harris (London, [n.d.]), with fifty illustrations by A. T. Elwes.

Valentine and Orson, ed. Arthur Dickson, tr. Henry Watson, EETS OS 204 (London, 1937).

Vernacular Literary Theory from the French of Medieval England: Texts and Translations, c. 1120–c. 1450, ed. Jocelyn Wogan-Browne, Thelma Fenster, and Delbert W. Russell (Woodbridge, 2016).

Verse Saints' Lives Written in the French of England, tr. Delbert Russell, FRETS 5 (Tempe, AZ, 2012).

La Vie de Seint Clement, ed. Daron Burrows, ANTS 64–5, 66, 67 (3 vols, 2007, 2008, 2009).

La Vie d'Edouard le Confesseur, ed. Östen Södergård (Uppsala, 1948), by a Nun of Barking.

La Vie d'Edouard le Confesseur *by a Nun of Barking Abbey*, Jane Bliss, Exeter Medieval Texts and Studies (Liverpool, 2014).

La Vie seint Edmund le Rei, Denis Piramus, ed. D. W. Russell, ANTS 71 (2014), with an art-historical excursus by Kathryn A. Smith.

La Vie Seinte Audree, ed. Östen Södergård (Uppsala, 1955), Poème anglo-normand du xiiie siècle.

'Vita S. Edwardi Regis et Confessoris', in Aelred of Rievaulx, *Patrologia Latina*, ed. J-P. Migne (Paris, 1844–64), vol. 195, cols 737B–790B.

[Wace] *The History of the Norman People: Wace's* Roman de Rou, tr. Glyn S. Burgess (Woodbridge, 2004), notes by GSB and Elisabeth van Houts.

Wace, *The Roman de Rou*, ed. Anthony J. Holden, tr. Glyn S. Burgess (St Helier, 2002), notes by GSB and Elisabeth van Houts.

Wace, *Le Roman de Rou de Wace*, ed. A. J. Holden (3 vols, Paris, 1970, 1971, 1973).

Wace, the hagiographical works: the Conception Nostre Dame and the Lives of St Margaret and St Nicholas, ed. Jean Blacker, Glyn S. Burgess, and Amy V. Ogden (Leiden, 2013).

Wace's *Roman de Brut — A History of the British*, ed. and tr. Judith Weiss (1999; repr. Exeter, 2002).

The Wars of Alexander, ed. Hoyt N. Duggan and Thorlac Turville-Petre, EETS SS 10 (1989).

White, T. H., *The Goshawk* (1951; repr. Harmondsworth, 1973).

Women and Writing in Medieval Europe: A sourcebook, Carolyne Larrington (London, 1995).

Secondary Texts

Anglo-français: philologie et linguistique, ed. Oreste Floquet and Gabriele Giannini, Civilisation médiévale 13 (Paris, 2015).

Archibald, Elizabeth, 'Variations on romance themes in the *Historia Meriadoci*', *Journal of the International Arthurian Society* 2:1 (2014), 3–19.

Arnould, E. J., 'Les Sources de *Femina Nova*', in *Studies for Mildred Pope* (q.v.), pp. 1–9.

Audiau, Jean, *Les Troubadours et l'Angleterre* (Paris, 1927), Contribution à l'Étude des Poètes Anglais de l'Amour au Moyen Age (XIIIe et XIVe siècles).

Bass, Ian, 'Miranda, Miracula, et Marchia Wallie: the *signa miranda* of Thomas de Cantilupe in Exeter College MS 158' (presented at Oxford Medieval Graduate Conference, April 2016).

Baswell, Christopher, Christopher Cannon, Jocelyn Wogan-Browne, and Kathryn Kirby-Fulton, 'Competing Archives, Competing Histories: French and Its Cultural Locations in Late-Medieval England', *Speculum* 90:3 (July 2015), 635–700.

Bernau, Anke, 'Beginning with Albina: Remembering the Nation', *Exemplaria* 21:3 (2009), 247–73.

Blacker, Jean and Jane H. M. Taylor, eds, *Court and Cloister: Studies in the Short Narrative in Honor of Glyn S. Burgess* (Tempe, AZ, [2017]).

The Blackwell Encyclopedia of Anglo-Saxon England, ed. Michael Lapidge *et al.* (Oxford, 1999).

Bliss, Jane, 'An Anglo-Norman Nun: An Old English *Gnome*', *Notes & Queries* 254:1 (March 2009), 16–18.

Bliss, Jane, 'Honour, Humour, and Women in the Romance of *Yder*', *Leeds Studies in English* (forthcoming).

Bliss, Jane, *Naming and Namelessness in Medieval Romance* (Cambridge, 2008).

Bliss, Jane, 'Vignalis, or Guénaël, of Alderney: A Legend and its Medieval Sources', *Reading Medieval Studies* 39 (2013), 49–64.

Bloch, R. Howard, *The Scandal of the Fabliaux* (Chicaco, 1986).

The Brewer Dictionary of Phrase and Fable, E. Cobham Brewer (1870; repr. Ware, Herts, 1986).

Bromwich, Rachel, 'Celtic Elements in Arthurian Romance: A General Survey', in Patricia B. Grout, R. A. Lodge, C. E. Pickford, and E. K. C. Varty, eds, *The Legend of King Arthur in the Middle Ages: Studies presented to A. H. Diverres by colleagues, pupils and friends* (Cambridge, 1983), pp. 41–55.

Brooke, Christopher, *From Alfred to Henry III, 871–1272* (1961; repr. New York & London, 1969).

Burgess, Glyn S. and Karen Pratt, eds, *The Arthur of the French: The Arthurian Legend in Medieval French and Occitan Literature* (Cardiff, 2006).

Burrows, Daron, 'Review: *Marie de France: A Critical Companion*, Sharon Kinoshita and Peggy McCracken', *ZrP* 131:2 (2015), 549–53.

Burrows, Daron, 'Review: *Storia della letteratura Anglo-Normanna (XII–XIV secolo)*, Margherita Lecco', *ZrP* 130:2 (2014), 550–57.

Burrows, Daron, 'Vers une nouvelle édition de l'Apocalypse en prose', in *Anglo-français: philologie et linguistique*, ed. Floquet and Giannini (q.v.), pp. 9–34.

Busby, Keith, '*Esprit gaulois* for the English: The Humour of the Anglo-Norman Fabliau', in Kristin L. Burr, John F. Moran, and Norris J. Lacy, eds, *The Old French Fabliaux: Essays on Comedy and Context* (Jefferson, NC, & London, [2008]), pp. 160–73.

Butterfield, Ardis, 'English, French and Anglo-French: Language and nation in the fabliau', in Mark Chinka, Timo Reuvekamp-Felber, and Christopher Young, eds, *Mittelalterliche Novellistik im europäischen Kontext: Kulturwissenschaftliche Perspektiven* (Berlin, 2006), pp. 238–59, Beiheft zur Zeitschrift für Deutsche Philologie 13.

Butterfield, Ardis, *The Familiar Enemy: Chaucer, Language and Nation in the Hundred Years War* (Oxford, 2009).

Carley, James P., 'A Glastonbury translator at work: *Quedam narracio de nobili rege Arthuro* and *De origine gigantum* in their earliest manuscript contexts', *Nottingham French Studies* 30:2 (Autumn 1991), 5–12.

Carley, James P. and Julia Crick, 'Constructing Albion's Past: An Annotated Edition of *De Origine Gigantum*', *Arthurian Literature* XIII (1995), 41–114.

Cavell, Emma, 'Intelligence and intrigue in the March of Wales: noblewomen and the fall of Llewelyn ap Gruffudd, 1274–82', *Historical Research* ([2014]), 1–19. http://dx.doi.org/10.1111/1468-2281.12068

Cerquiglini-Toulet, Jacqueline, *A New History of Medieval French Literature*, tr. Sara Preisig (2007; repr. Baltimore, 2011).

Chapman, Alister, John Coffey, and Brad S. Gregory, eds, *Seeing Things Their Way: Intellectual History and the Return of Religion* (Notre Dame, 2009).

Cheney, C. R., *A Handbook of Dates*, ed. Michael Jones, revised edition (1945; repr. Cambridge, 2000), for students of British History.

Christine de Pisan: A bibliography, Edith Yenal (Metuchen, NJ, & London, 1982).

Christine de Pizan: a bibliographical guide, Angus J. Kennedy (London, 1984).

Cobby, Anne Elizabeth, *The Old French Fabliaux, an analytical bibliography*, Research Bibliographies and Checklists n. s. 9 (Woodbridge, 2009).

Colegate, Isabel, *A Pelican in the Wilderness: Hermits, Solitaries and Recluses* (London, 2002).

Coleman, Joyce, 'Aurality', in Strohm, ed., *Middle English* (q.v.), pp. 68–85.

Corrie, Marilyn, 'Harley 2253, Digby 86, and the Circulation of Literature in Pre-Chaucerian England', in Fein, ed., *Studies in the Harley Manuscript* (q.v.), pp. 427–43.

Cox, D. C., 'The French Chronicle of London', *Medium Ævum* 45 (1976), 201–8.

Curley, Michael J., 'Conjuring History: Mother, Nun, and Incubus in Geoffrey of Monmouth's *Historia Regum Britanniae*', *JEGP* 114:2 (April 2015), 219–39.

Curtius, Ernst Robert, *European Literature and the Latin Middle Ages*, tr. Willard R. Trask (1953; repr. London, 1979).

Darmesteter, Arsène, *La Vie des Mots étudiée dans leur significations*, 4th edition (1886; repr. Paris, 1893).

Dean, Ruth and Maureen Boulton, *Anglo-Norman Literature: A Guide to Texts and Manuscripts*, ANTS OPS 3 (1999).

Dean, Ruth J., 'A Fair Field needing Folk: Anglo-Norman', *PMLA* 69 (1954), 965–78.

Dictionary of the Middle Ages, ed. Joseph R. Strayer (13 vols, New York, 1982, 1988).

Dictionnaire de l'ancien français, ed. Algirdas Julien Greimas (1979; repr. Paris, 1992).

Doherty, Paul, *Isabella and the Strange Death of Edward II* (2003; repr. London, 2004).

Dove, Mary, 'Evading Textual Intimacy: The French Secular Verse', in Fein, ed., *Studies in the Harley Manuscript* (q.v.), pp. 329–49.

Evans, Daffyd, 'The Taxonomy of Bird-Naming in Anglo-Norman and Channel Island Patois', in Short, ed., *Anglo-Norman Anniversary Essays* (q.v.), pp. 105–34.

Evans, Ruth, 'Gigantic Origins: An Annotated Translation of *De Origine Gigantum*', *Arthurian Literature* XVI (1998), 197–211.

Fein, Susanna, ed., *Studies in the Harley Manuscript: The Scribes, Contents, and Social Contexts of British Library MS Harley 2253* (Kalamazoo, 2000).

Fleury, Jean-François B., *Essai sur le patois normand de la Hague* (Paris, 1886).

Flora Britannica, Richard Mabey (London, 1996).

Foot, Sarah, 'Has Ecclesiastical History Lost the Plot?', in Peter D. Clarke and Charlotte Methuen, eds, *The Church on its Past*, Studies in Church History 49 (Woodbridge, 2013), pp. 1–25, Presidential Address.

Gaunt, Simon, *Retelling the Tale: An Introduction to Medieval French Literature* (London, 2001).

Gautier, Alban and Jean-Pascal Pouzet, eds, *Langues d'Angleterre: au-delà du bilinguisme*, Médiévales (Paris, 2015), vol. 68.

Gowans, Linda, 'Sir Uallabh O Còrn: A Hebridean Tale of Sir Gawain', *Scottish Gaelic Studies* 18 (1998), 23–55.

Grange, Huw, 'Review: Rewriting Saints and Ancestors: Memory and Forgetting in France, 500–1200, by Constance Brittain Bouchard (Philadelphia, 2015)', *French Studies* 70:1 (January 2016), 98.

Gray, Douglas, *Simple Forms: Essays on Medieval English Popular Literature* (Oxford, 2015).

Griffin, Miranda, 'Gender and Authority in the Medieval French Lai', *Forum for Modern Language Studies* 35:1 (1999), 42–56.

Gutt, Blake, 'Review: Barbara Newman, Medieval Crossover: Reading the Secular against the Sacred', *Medium Ævum* 84:2 (2015), 327–8.

Hogg, Richard M., ed., *The Cambridge History of the English Language* (6 vols, Cambridge, 1992–2001), vol. 1.

Howlett, D. R., *The English Origins of Old French Literature* (Dublin, 1996).

Hsy, Jonathan, *Trading Tongues, Merchants, Multi-lingualism, and Medieval Literature* (Columbus, 2013).

Hunt, Tony, 'Review: *Anglo-Norman Literature*, Ruth Dean and Maureen Boulton', *Medium Ævum* 70:2 (2001), 340–3.

Hunt, Tony, 'Review: *The Romance of Yder*, Alison Adams', *Modern Language Review* 80 (1985), 932–3.

Hunt, Tony, *Teaching and Learning Latin in Thirteenth-Century England* (3 vols, Cambridge, 1991), vol. 1.

Hyams, Paul, 'The legal revolution and the discourse of dispute in the twelfth century', in Andrew Galloway, ed., *The Cambridge Companion to Medieval English Culture* (Cambridge, 2011), pp. 43–65.

Hyams, Paul, 'Serfdom Without Strings: Amartya Sen, Poverty and Entitlement in the Middle Ages', in Maureen Miller and Edward Wheatley, eds, *Emotions, Communities, and Differences in Medieval Europe: Essays in Honor of Barbara H. Rosenwein* (London, 2017), chapter 12.

Hyams, Paul R., 'Thinking English Law in French: The Angevins and the Common Law', in Belle S. Tuten and Tracy L. Billado, eds, *Feud, Violence and Practice: Essays in Medieval Studies in Honor of Stephen D. White* (Farnham, 2010), pp. 175–96.

Ingham, Richard, ed., *The Anglo-Norman Language and its Contexts* (Woodbridge, 2010).

Ingham, Richard, *The Transmission of Anglo-Norman: Language history and language acquisition* (Amsterdam & Philadelphia, 2012).

Ivanov, Sergey and Svetlana Kleyner, 'The English Versions of the Friday Legend: Three and Twelve', *Medium Ævum* 84:2 (2015), 189–212.

Jefferson, Judith A. and Ad Putter, eds, *Multilingualism in Medieval Britain (c. 1066–1520): Sources and Analysis* (Turnhout, 2013).

Jeffrey, David L., 'Authors, Anthologies, and Franciscan Spirituality', in Fein, ed., *Studies in the Harley Manuscript* (q.v.), pp. 261–8.

Jersey Folklore & Superstitions: A Comparative Study with the Traditions of the Gulf of St. Malo (the Channel Islands, Normandy & Brittany) with reference to World Mythologies, G. J. C. Bois (2 vols, Milton Keynes, 2010), vol. 1.

Johnson, Lesley, 'The Anglo-Norman *Description of England*: An Introduction', in Short, ed., *Anglo-Norman Anniversary Essays* (q.v.), pp. 11–30.

Johnson, Lesley, 'Return to Albion', *Arthurian Literature* XIII (1995), 19–40.

Kelly, Douglas, *Medieval French Romance* (New York, 1993).

King, Andrew, The Faerie Queene *and Middle English Romance: The Matter of Just Memory* (Oxford, 2000).

Lecoy, Félix, 'Un épisode du *Protheselaus* et le conte du mari trompé', *Romania* 76 (1955), 477–518.

Legge, M. Dominica, *Anglo-Norman in the Cloisters* (Edinburgh, 1950).

Legge, M. Dominica, *Anglo-Norman Literature and its Background* (Oxford, 1963).

Lewis, C. S., 'Is Theology Poetry?', in *They Asked for a Paper: Papers and Addresses* (London, 1962), pp. 150–65.

Leyser, Henrietta, *Beda: A Journey through the Seven Kingdoms in the age of Bede* (London, 2015).

Lusignan, Serge, *La langue des rois au Moyen Âge: Le français en France et en Angleterre* (Paris, 2004).

Marvin, Julia, 'John and Henry III in the Anglo-Norman Prose *Brut*', *Thirteenth Century England* XIV (2013), 169–82.

Masters, Bernadette M., 'Anglo-Norman in Context: The Case for the Scribes', *Exemplaria* 6:1 (1994), 167–203.

Mayrhofer, Sonja Nicole, 'From Ekphrasis and the Fantastic to Commodity Fetishism in the *Roman de Thèbes* and Chrétien de Troyes' *Erec et Enide*' (MA thesis, University of Iowa, Iowa, May 2010). http://ir.uiowa.edu/etd/2940/

McCash, June Hall, '*La Vie seinte Audree*: A Fourth Text by Marie de France?', *Speculum* 77 (2002), 744–77.

McEvoy, James, *Robert Grosseteste* (Oxford, 2000).

Medieval France, An Encyclopedia, ed. William W. Kibler and Grover A. Zinn (New York & London, 1995).

Meyer, Paul, 'Les manuscrits français de Cambridge (pt. ii)', *Romania* 15 (1886), 236–357, for pt. i see *Romania* 8.

Mills, Kristen, 'Grief, Gender, and Genre: Male Weeping in Snorri's account of Baldr's Death, Kings' Sagas, and *Gesta Danorum*', *JEGP* 113:4 (Oct 2014), 472–96.

Minnis, A. J., *Medieval Theory of Authorship: Scholastic literary attitudes in the later Middle Ages*, 2nd rev. edition (1984; repr. Philadelphia, 1988).

Morrissey, Jake Walsh, '"To al indifferent": The Virtues of Lydgate's "Dietary"', *Medium Ævum* 84:2 (2015), 258–78.

Newhauser, Richard G. and Susan J. Ridyard, eds, *Sin in Medieval and Early Modern Culture: The tradition of the Seven Deadly Sins* (York, 2012).

Nolan, Barbara, 'Anthologizing Ribaldry: Five Anglo-Norman Fabliaux', in Fein, ed., *Studies in the Harley Manuscript* (q.v.), pp. 289–327.

O'Donnell, Thomas, 'Anglo-Norman Multiculturalism and Continental Standards in Guernes de Pont-Sainte-Maxence's *Vie de Saint Thomas*', in Tyler, ed., *Conceptualizing Multilingualism in England, c. 800–c. 1250* (q.v.), pp. 337–56.

Owen, D. D. R., 'The Craft of Guillaume Le Clerc's *Fergus*', in Leigh A. Arrathoon, ed., *The Craft of Fiction: Essays in Medieval Poetics* (Rochester, MI, 1984), pp. 47–81.

Owst, G. R., *Literature and Pulpit in Medieval England*, 2nd rev. edition (1933; repr. Oxford, 1961).

The Oxford Concise Companion to Classical Literature, ed. M. C. Howatson and Ian Chivers (1993; repr. Oxford, 1996).

Pagan, Heather, 'Review: Tony Hunt, ed., *An Anglo-Norman Medical Compendium*', *French Studies* 70:1 (January 2016), 93.

Paradisi, Gioia, 'Les *Folies*, les premiers romans tristaniens et l'Angleterre: Remarques sur la transmission des textes', in *Anglo-français: philologie et linguistique*, ed. Floquet and Giannini (q.v.), pp. 119–34.

Petit, Aimé, *Aux origines du roman:* Le Roman de Thèbes (Paris, 2010).

Poems Without Names: The English Lyric, 1200–1500, Raymond Oliver (Berkeley, 1970).

Prestwich, Michael, *Plantagenet England 1225–1360* (Oxford, 2005).

Ramey, Peter, 'The Poetics of Caxton's "Publique": The Construction of Audience in the Prologues of William Caxton', *English Studies* 96:7–8 (November–December 2015), 731–46.

Reeves, Andrew, *Religious Education in Thirteenth-Century England: The Creed and Articles of Faith* (Leiden, 2015).

Reichl, Karl, 'Debate Verse', in Fein, ed., *Studies in the Harley Manuscript* (q.v.), pp. 219–39.

Revard, Carter, 'From French Fabliau manuscripts and Harley 2253 to the *Decameron* and the *Canterbury Tales*', *Medium Ævum* 69 (2000), 261–78.

Rigg, A. G., *A History of Anglo-Latin Literature 1066–1422* (Cambridge, 1992).

Robert Grosseteste, Bishop of Lincoln 1235–1253, J. H. Srawley ([n.d.]; repr. The Friends of Lincoln Cathedral, 1966), Lincoln Minster Pamphlets no. 7.

Rossi, Carla, 'A Reflection on the withheld Name of Marie in the Epilogue of Guernes' *Vie Saint Thomas*, accompanied by a brief sociolinguistic Observation on the Use of the Expression 'de France' in the Epilogue of the *Fables* by Marie de France', in *Il Nome Dell'Autore: Studi in Onore di Giuseppe Tavani* (Rome, 2015), pp. 1–20.

Schoepperle, Gertrude, *Tristan and Isolt: a study of the sources of the romance* (2 vols, London, 1913). http://dbooks.bodleian.ox.ac.uk/books/PDFs/N13081788.pdf

Short, Ian, ed., *Anglo-Norman Anniversary Essays*, ANTS OPS 2 (1993).

Short, Ian, *Manual of Anglo-Norman*, ANTS OPS 8, 2nd edition (2007; repr. Oxford, 2013).

Short, Ian, 'Review: Mari C. Jones, Variation and Change in Mainland and Insular Norman. A Study of Superstrate Influence (Leiden/Boston, Brill 2014)', *ZrP* 132:1 (2016), 310–14.

Simpson, Jacqueline, *British Dragons*, 2nd edition (1980; repr. Ware, Herts, 2001).

Southern, R. W., *Robert Grosseteste. The Growth of an English Mind in Medieval Europe* (Oxford, 1986).

Spearing, A. C., *Medieval Autographies: The I of the Text* (Notre Dame, 2012).

Stanley, Eric, 'Beowulf's *Wundordeað*', *Notes & Queries* 63:3 (September 2016), 343–5.

Storia della letteratura anglo-normanna (xii–xiv secolo), Margherita Lecco (Milan, 2011).

Strohm, Paul, ed., *Middle English* (Oxford, 2007), *Oxford Twenty-First Century Approaches to Literature*.

Studies in French Language and Mediaeval Literature presented to Professor Mildred K. Pope (Manchester, 1939).

Sutherland, D. R., 'On the Use of Tenses in Old and Middle French', in *Studies for Mildred Pope* (q.v.), pp. 329–37.

Thomson, S. Harrison, *The Writings of Robert Grosseteste, Bishop of Lincoln 1235–1253* (Cambridge, 1940).

Trachsler, Richard, 'Review: Logan E. Whalen, ed., *A Companion to Marie de France*', *Encomia* 34–35 (2015), 34–9.

Trotter, David, 'Review: *Donei des Amanz*, ed. Holden', *Romania* 133:3–4 (2015), 512–15.

Tyler, Elizabeth. M., ed., *Conceptualizing Multilingualism in England, c. 800– c. 1250* (Turnhout, 2011).

Tyson, Diana B., 'Two Prophecies and a Talking Head — An Anglo-Norman Text in the Lanercost Chronicle', *Nottingham Medieval Studies* 53 (2009), 39–52.

The Universal Chronicle *of Ranulf Higden*, John Taylor (Oxford, 1966).

van Loon, Hendrik, *The Story of Mankind* (1921; repr. [USA], 1922).

Wace: A Critical Biography, Jean Blacker (Jersey, 2008).

Walters, Lori J., 'Wace and the Genesis of Vernacular Authority', in Catherine M. Jones and Logan E. Whalen, eds, *"Li premerains vers": Essays in Honor of Keith Busby* (Amsterdam & New York, 2011), pp. 507–16.

Weir, Alison, *Eleanor of Aquitaine: By the Wrath of God Queen of England* (1999; repr. London, 2000).

Weiss, Judith, 'Emperors and Antichrists: Reflections of Empire in Insular Narrative, 1130–1250', in Phillipa Hardman, ed., *The Matter of Identity in Medieval Romance* (Cambridge, 2002), pp. 87–102.

Weiss, Judith, 'Modern and Medieval Views on Swooning: the Literary and Medical Contexts of Fainting in Romance', in Rhiannon Purdie and Michael Cichon, eds, *Medieval Romance Medieval Contexts* (Cambridge, 2011), pp. 121–34.

Weiss, Judith, 'A reappraisal of Hue de Rotelande's *Protheselaus*', *Medium Ævum* 52 (1983), 104–11.

Whelan, Fiona E., 'Urbanus Magnus: A Twelfth-Century "Courtesy Text" and three Oxford Manuscripts', *The Bodleian Library Record* 27:1 (2014), 12–35.

Wogan-Browne, Jocelyn, 'Wreaths of Thyme: The Female Translator in Anglo-Norman Hagiography', in Roger Ellis and Ruth Evans, eds, *The Medieval Translator IV* (Binghamton, 1994), pp. 46–65.

Wogan-Browne, Jocelyn *et al.*, eds, *Language and Culture in Medieval Britain: The French of England c. 1100–c. 1500* (York, 2009).

Woledge, Julia, 'The Use of *Tu* and *Vous* in Medieval French Verse Romances from 1160 to 1230' (PhD thesis, University of London, London, 1976).

Indexes

Manuscripts

Bible References

General Index

www.ingramcontent.com/pod-product-compliance
Lightning Source LLC
Chambersburg PA
CBHW070802030726
47504CB00003B/667